Beyond Casablanca

Beyond Casablanca

M. A. Tazi and the
Adventure of Moroccan Cinema

KEVIN DWYER

INDIANA UNIVERSITY PRESS
Bloomington and Indianapolis

This book is a publication of

Indiana University Press
601 North Morton Street
Bloomington, IN 47404-3797 USA

http://iupress.indiana.edu

Telephone orders   800-842-6796
Fax orders   812-855-7931
Orders by e-mail   iuporder@indiana.edu

*The paper used in this publication meets the
minimum requirements of American National
Standard for Information Sciences—Permanence of
Paper for Printed Library Materials, ANSI Z39.48-1984.*

MANUFACTURED IN THE UNITED STATES OF AMERICA

Cataloging information is available from the
Library of Congress.
ISBN 0-253-34462-X (alk. paper)
ISBN 0-253-21719-9 (pbk. : alk. paper)

1   2   3   4   5   09   08   07   06   05   04

For Lilia

Contents

Acknowledgments

Among the many debts I incurred while carrying out this project over the period 1998–2003, I would like to acknowledge:

—the National Endowment for the Humanities' financial support (Grant #FB-35259-98) for the first year of research and the American University in Cairo for financial aid to attend Morocco's national film festival in 2003 and to finish preparing the manuscript;

—the staff of the Centre cinématographique marocain (CCM) and, especially, Messrs Stitou, Bghezli, Zaakour, and Araib;

—Noureddin Sail for help at the start, before the project found its focus, and Roy Armes for his encouragement throughout;

—the many members of Morocco's film and cultural worlds who were generous with their time, particularly (and alphabetically) Samia Akkariou, Nabil Ayouch, Khalil Benkirane, Najib Benkirane, Farida Benlyazid, Ahmed Bouanani, Muhammad Dahan, Abdou Filali-Ansari, Muhammad Guessous, Moulay Driss Jaidi, Abdelkader Lagtaa, Nabil Lahlou, Fatima Mernissi, Hakim Noury, Daoud Oulad-Syad, Abdelwahad Ouzri, and Muhammad Rzin;

—Muhammad Abderrahman Tazi and his family for their sincerity, their easy and sustained hospitality, and their patience in putting up with many intrusions;

—everyone at Indiana University Press involved in this book's publication and, especially, Michael Lundell for his sympathy, judgment, and understanding.

Finally, I owe my having initiated and completed this project to the intellectual stimulation, infectious energy, and caring support of my wife, Lilia Labidi. Also, her comments on the manuscript and her active assistance at two Moroccan national film festivals helped me immeasurably.

Beyond Casablanca

Introduction

Third World, Many Worlds

Filmmaker in the (Third) World

A Third World filmmaker may smile wryly upon hearing the stock phrases "cinema is both an art and an industry" and "a film is both a creative product and a commodity." He (or in rare cases she) might retort, "How can our cinema be considered an industry, our films commodities, when production financing usually comes from state and international aid; when the film has little chance of reaching the marketplace and, even if it does, theaters are so few and audiences so limited and impoverished that costs cannot be recovered let alone profit be made; when, however successful your film may be, you have no assurance that you'll ever again have the means to make another?" Perhaps the only ways in which Third World cinema resembles an industry are that making a film requires substantial capital outlay and that the filmmaking sector is inevitably inserted, as it has been from its beginnings, into the many-tiered, multi-faceted global complex of creation, communication, and consumption.[1]

Whatever its particular difficulties, Third World filmmaking over the past few decades has given birth to a significant number of important artists and individual works that have gained national and international recognition.[2] Yet, flanking these filmmakers there are many others deserving recognition beyond their national borders (and greater recognition within them) but who, for reasons having little or nothing to do with the quality of the work, have not received it.

Making a film anywhere in the world illustrates the tension between creative élan and economic constraints, and this is worked out
in particular political and cultural contexts, filtered through the lens
of individual filmmakers and expressed in their unique films. In this
book we are going to try to follow this process on three different but
interrelated levels by exploring, more or less simultaneously, the birth
and development of one Third World national cinema (Morocco's),
the unfolding of a particularly rich career within it (Muhammad Abderrahman Tazi's), and the first four feature films Tazi has made. My
aims, among many others, are not only to improve our capacity to
assess Tazi's achievements and those of the national cinema of which
he is a part but also to furnish some insight into the situation of Third
World creative artists—in this case filmmakers—working in the context of a global culture industry. Perhaps too, this book will help us
appreciate the many different worlds—social, cultural, psychological,
domestic, regional, international (one could go on)—that seemingly
local developments carry within them.

Glimpsing Tazi's World:
A Hit in Morocco, a Trace in New York

Muhammad Abderrahman Tazi's third film, *Looking
for My Wife's Husband,* had its premiere in Rabat, Morocco, in late 1993.
As the show ended and with the audience's laughter still ringing in
his ears, Tazi was hailed by the head of the Moroccan Film Center,
who came over to him and said, "This film is going to be a really big
hit."[3] No one, however, could have had any idea just how big a hit it
would be, because no Moroccan film before it, nor any since, has
approached this success. In the months following its release, *Looking
for My Wife's Husband* reached close to one million spectators, almost
twice as many as its closest rival to this day. In addition, a vast number
of pirated videotapes were produced and sold at rock-bottom prices
throughout the country.

At about the time Tazi's *Looking for My Wife's Husband* was breaking
records in Morocco I was visiting New York City, where I had been
born and raised. As a social anthropologist working on the Middle East
and North Africa and specializing in Morocco (where I had done several years of fieldwork), I was intrigued to find a Moroccan film being
shown at a festival at the Museum of Modern Art—an extremely rare

occurrence in any New York venue. I had no professional interest in films but I looked forward to seeing this one, called *Badis*, directed by a certain Muhammad Abderrahman Tazi. As the film unfolded, tensions grew taut and the plot seemed to be moving inexorably to a climax. I was riveted and thought to myself, "What a pleasure to be in the grip of a real filmmaker." To my great frustration, I had to leave before the film's end because of a conflicting appointment. Months later, as engrossing as the film had been, I realized that, when I tried to recall it, I had already forgotten its title and director and that only a faint trace of the story remained with me.

About five years later I developed a professional interest in film or, more precisely, an anthropological interest in Moroccan cinema. I soon learned that Tazi was one of Moroccan cinema's central figures and that his career had followed a complex itinerary. Issuing from the bourgeoisie of Fez, having spent most of his career in Morocco and its film world, yet also having had his feet firmly planted at various times in Europe and the United States, Tazi played a key role in building the Moroccan national cinema, from its early days after the country regained independence from France in 1956 up to the present. Trained in the early 1960s in Paris as a cinematographer, returning to Morocco to work within the state film institution (the CCM), he then co-founded a filmmaking cooperative that produced what is recognized as the first truly Moroccan feature film (*Weshma*, Hamid Bennani, 1970), on which he served as cinematographer. Under his own name he had made four feature films (with his fifth completed just as I was finishing this book, he is among Morocco's most prolific film directors): his second film (*Badis*) was highly acclaimed critically, both nationally and internationally, and won a number of festival prizes; his third, we saw, became the most successful feature in Moroccan film history; his fourth made him the first Moroccan director to try to film a feature in northern Europe. In addition, over the course of his career he had worked with a number of well-known international directors—among them John Huston, Robert Wise, Francis Ford Coppola, and Martin Scorsese—on films they made in Morocco.

In this book, in the context of the development of Moroccan cinema, we will be spending considerable time on Tazi's career and the issues raised by his first four feature films—each of which presents an interesting mix of stylistic and topical concerns. His first, *The Big Trip* (1981), is a road movie that follows a novice truck driver's ordeal as he winds his way from southern to northern Morocco and is progressively dispossessed of his belongings, ending his journey stranded in a small boat in the Mediterranean, off the shores of Tangiers. *Badis* (1989), in the style of a Greek tragedy, is the story of a schoolteacher who, to punish his wife for her real or imagined infidelity, moves with her to a remote fishing village, cutting her off from the animation and stimulation of Casablanca. The wife befriends a young village woman and the two join forces in a struggle against the men who rule over them. *Looking for My Wife's Husband* (1993)—a domestic comedy and the most popular Moroccan film ever—had audiences laughing throughout as they watched Hajj Ben Moussa rashly divorce the youngest of his three wives. Immediately regretting this, he learns he can regain her, according to Islamic law, only if she first marries another man and then divorces. The Hajj embarks on the humiliating search for a new husband for his (ex-)wife, eventually succeeds, but before the couple can divorce, the husband flees Morocco and the film ends as the Hajj, desperate, sets off after him. Tazi's fourth film, *Lalla Hobby* (1997), follows the Hajj into Europe as he pursues the husband and suffers new indignities, of the sort that would ring true to the many Moroccans with immigrant experience in Europe.

Moroccan, World, Third World, and Arab Cinemas

MOROCCAN CINEMA: PERILS AND PARADOXES

Over the course of several years, as I watched Tazi juggle many different projects in order to earn a living even while he was trying to advance his next film's screenplay, and as I talked to many other Moroccan filmmakers, I came to understand more fully the financial, practical, and artistic difficulties these filmmakers face. I often wondered how, in such circumstances, a Moroccan film gets to be made at all.

Moroccan filmmakers, like most of their Third World counterparts, see overall movie attendance decreasing and theaters closing or, if remaining open, showing mostly foreign imports. They work in a sector that suffers from lagging technical capabilities and where training is rudimentary and, in some specialties, absent. Their own relatively small and poor national markets have limited consumer capacity and extremely scarce investment capital, and the national languages in which they film are thought of as "local" by international distributors who refuse to carry the films to markets abroad. And in some countries—Morocco is one of them—foreign films being shot locally often push aside the nation's own filmmakers, distorting the demand for actors and technicians and encouraging higher fees than local producers can pay. Any one of these factors would make the goal of profit for a Moroccan film recede into the distance; taken together they turn even the more modest aim of recouping investment into a mirage.[4]

Yet, a striking paradox distinguishes the Moroccan situation: under such perilous conditions and with so many fundamental problems affecting filmmaking, a healthy number of Moroccan films have been produced in the past few years and the Moroccan public, after decades of showing little interest in Moroccan films, is now welcoming these films with great enthusiasm and supporting them at the box office.[5]

The screening of a new Moroccan film has now become a significant moment in the country's cultural life. However, with no more than ten films produced each year and a significant number of them never shown in the theaters, several months might elapse between the premieres of new Moroccan films, and this makes it difficult for the national cinema to have sustained impact on citizens' daily lives. A more intense experience does occur every few years, when a National Film Festival is held. Here filmmakers, critics, and film buffs have the opportunity to see all the Moroccan films made since the previous festival and to watch the films vie for the various prizes. The festivals arouse wide interest, leading to numerous press articles and television and radio programs and providing the occasion for everyone from taxi drivers to diplomats to comment on the state of Moroccan cinema. On the day following a film's showing, its director and other contributors to the film face questions from the public and emotions often run high, with the head-to-head encounter between filmmakers and public often very intense and sometimes even quite harsh, fueled by the feeling filmmakers often have of being caught in a double bind—being asked, simultaneously, to both stimulate mass appeal and produce a work of depth, to be both public entertainer and public intellectual.[6]

The film sector in Morocco, then, is in very precarious and somewhat perplexing circumstances. On the one hand, film production and attendance at Moroccan films are at record levels and, as we will soon see, political and cultural trends are rather encouraging. On the other, many fundamental problems remain: infrastructural, financial, the size of the market, the lack of specialized training, and problems of poverty, illiteracy, and unemployment, to name a few. All things considered, although there are many promising signs, there are no conclusive reasons for believing that they foreshadow a rosy future. To understand these circumstances better, to see how Moroccan cinema and Tazi's filmmaking fit into the global film industry, let us make a quick tour of the major film zones within which Moroccan filmmaking takes place.

WORLD CINEMA

Only five countries in the world—the United States, India, China (including Hong Kong), the Philippines, and Japan—produce more than two hundred films in an average year. As this list suggests, quantity is not related directly either to population or to national wealth. While highly populated China and India each produce many films, some countries with large populations produce relatively few (for example, Indonesia, fourteen annually, population over two hundred million). Some relatively poor countries with much smaller populations produce many films (the Philippines and also Thailand, 194 films annually, population of 70 million). Yet, with a few notable exceptions, most countries outside the "big five" fortunate enough to have film production have film sectors that are laboring and some are threatened with extinction.[7]

What does it take to build a productive national cinema? Or, phrased somewhat differently, what are the reasons for this "bipolar" pattern, for there being a handful of major producing countries and scores of struggling national cinemas? The answers to these questions are to be sought in the history of cinema as a worldwide industry. The example of Hollywood's success in dominating both its national and overseas markets can provide us with a quick summary of this story. Benefiting from both a large domestic market from the earliest decades of film history and the active support of U.S. government policy that restricted imports and promoted exports, Hollywood was able to build on its control of the domestic market to gain leadership in external markets by virtue of practices amounting to commodity "dumping": able to recoup costs in the U.S. market alone, distributors set U.S. film prices abroad low enough to undercut competition and win market share.[8]

Consequently, film producers in smaller countries, not having sufficient resources to secure international distribution and needing significant payments from local distributors to recoup their production costs, found themselves in direct competition in their national markets with films from abroad available at rock-bottom prices. Local distributors inevitably avoided the national films and the greater risks their higher fees entailed, knowing that in all likelihood these fees would not be offset by higher box-office receipts. As a result, locally produced films were not screened, had no chance of recouping costs, and thus could not attract future private financing.

This "bipolar" pattern of international film production means that smaller countries wishing to continue film production must find financing outside of the private capital market, leading to what has been called the "dual structure" of today's smaller national cinemas, which are "marked by a distribution/exhibition sector that is under the control of private commercial entrepreneurial interests . . . very much tied to the Hollywood majors for much of the programmes that they screen [and a] second sector of . . . film production within the national territory [that] is characterized by the active support of government and other elements of the state. . . . This dual structure is present across the globe—from Ireland to India and from Britain to Brazil" and includes, as we will see in greater detail, Morocco.[9]

A few exceptions stand out against this predominantly bleak portrait of cinemas outside the "big five." As we have seen, the examples of the Philippines and Thailand show that it has been possible for some smaller countries to sustain healthy film production. France provides a particularly instructive instance of how state policy can aid national production. With a population of just under sixty million, France produced an average of 183 films annually over the period 1988–1999, putting it near the top of the league in per capita film production. France's major European partners—countries comparable to France in size and wealth but with less supportive policies—have not done nearly as well: the UK, with roughly the same population, produced not even half as many (seventy-eight films annually, population just under sixty million); Germany has been even less productive—with one-third greater population it produced only one-third France's number of films (sixty-three films annually, population over eighty million).[10]

While financing for production is key, just as key for the health of the film sector is access to the distribution networks and the theaters, at a first stage on the national level but on the international level as well. Without this access tickets are not bought, films are not seen, costs are not offset. Yet the international distribution network seems to have no room for productions other than those from the major countries and does not even have room for all of them. "Hollywood studios have a worldwide share of 85%, with peaks above 90% in some European and Latin American countries, while India, Philippines and Hong-Kong SAR output reaches 95% market shares in their own continent, South America, and Africa."[11] European countries, in spite of their wealth, and France, in spite of its healthy production level, have found no answer to Hollywood's domination of international distribution: "Only around one in five European films was ever seen in a cinema outside the country in which it was made, and even then it was difficult to find an audience; even in France, where cinemagoers had always been sympathetic to European art-house films, only 4% of the annual box office was accounted for by films from other European countries."[12]

Here we see stark evidence of the straits even wealthy, relatively populous countries find themselves in regarding national film production and distribution: unable to recoup costs in their domestic markets, they require a series of state and international support mechanisms if they are to continue film production. What then can we expect of Third World cinemas and the regional cinemas of Morocco's neighbors?

THIRD WORLD AND ARAB CINEMAS

While Moroccan cinema has its own particular history and characteristics, in many essential respects it is typical of other Third World cinemas facing declines in numbers of theaters and attendance, inundation by foreign imports, and great difficulties in production and distribution.[13] Looked at from the perspective of the filmmaker him- or herself, the following description of African national cinemas could just as easily have been written of Morocco's (and, for that matter, of Tazi's):

> Many filmmakers . . . can make films only as a second-string activity, or must have a second job in order to make a living . . . or make videos and films on commission . . . the films are often made with mixed crews [and] the presence of European technicians can pose specific problems. . . . The low level of budgets involved very often forces directors to operate in "one-man band" fashion. . . . Filmmakers dream of technical autonomy so that they do not have to pay high prices for post-production in Western countries, and can therefore establish their independence. . . . Unexpected problems tend to mount up; non-professional actors take longer

than would normally be the case; there are insufficient resources for time to be managed efficiently. . . . Many a filmmaker has got into debt in an effort to finish a film. . . . Some [African filmmakers] had their fingers burnt with unfortunate experiences in which certain [European] produc- ers turned out to be charlatans . . . it took [one filmmaker] an eighteen- month trial to reacquire the rights [to his film] . . . [for another] it took a six-year court case against her [French] producer to get [her film] re- leased. . . . With no real market, the African producer is . . . like a "trapeze artist without a safety net."

As the author summarizes, "An account of the hurdles to be got over in making a film would merit a book in itself."[14]

While sharing these aspects with many of the other national cin- emas on the African continent, Moroccan cinema is different in several crucial respects. On the one hand Morocco shares with its Maghreb neighbors Algeria and Tunisia a (more-or-less) common spoken lan- guage and a significant cultural heritage; on the other it belongs po- litically, ideologically, religiously, and, on the complicated dimension of "identity," to an even larger regional unit, "the Arab world" (al- though on both levels we must remain sensitive to differences and variation). These are sharp contrasts with sub-Saharan African cine- mas, marked as most national contexts there are by great ethnic, re- ligious, and linguistic diversity. One overwhelming similarity common to all these situations, however, is a negative one: the almost total absence of cross-border film distribution.

Within the Maghreb, the three main national cinemas developed very differently despite the broad regional resemblance. Algerian film- making, after two productive decades following independence in 1962, entered a crisis in the late 1980s from which it has not yet emerged—a crisis resulting both from a reorganization of the film sec- tor in a privatizing direction and the outbreak of civil strife in the early 1990s.[15] Symptoms of this crisis abound: whereas there were some four hundred theaters in 1986, only around ten continue to show films today and, over the same period, attendance fell from forty mil- lion annually to approximately fifty thousand. With decreasing atten- dance and revenues, many theaters have been converted to video and game arcades and other remunerative activities. With so few specta- tors, the state funds collected as a portion of the ticket price and used to support filmmaking amounted to only some $13,000 for all of 1999, not enough to make even one film short in 2000. Overall, only a handful of films were made over the second half of the 1990s.[16]

In Tunisia the role of cinema as a critical form of societal expression was quickly appreciated, partly as a product of pressure from film clubs (the first *"Fédération des ciné-clubs"* in Africa was created in Tunisia in 1949) and other grassroots structures. In 1957 a state-owned company was founded to manage production, import, distribution, and exhibition, but this effort eventually failed, in large measure because the majors began a distribution boycott of Tunisia in the early 1960s, leading the Tunisian government to relax its control over the sector. In addition, film production was slow to start because of the small internal market (today's Tunisian population is approximately ten million).

Although confronting these barriers, Tunisian film activists continued to see cinema as having a purposeful role to play in society. The Carthage Arab and African Film Festival, widely recognized as one of the most important showcases for Third World films, was inaugurated in 1966 and has been held with unfailing regularity every two years. This activism was also expressed in films with strong social and political themes, and a number of powerful films were made during the 1970s and 1980s.[17] By the mid-1980s several independent, specialized producers began to emerge, thanks to a 1981 law that introduced a system of aid for film producers based on a levy at the box office. This resulted both in increased cooperation with foreign productions made partly in Tunisia (*Star Wars* and *The English Patient* are perhaps the two best-known examples) and in a financial boost for Tunisian films in the form of international co-productions, one of which (*Halfaouine,* Férid Boughedir, 1990) became the highest-grossing film in Tunisian film history.

While enabling the production of several important films this internationalization, coupled with the continued weakening of state institutional support (the state-owned company was eventually absorbed by the French-based pay-TV channel Canal Plus Horizons in 1994), had some negative effects. The very existence of "co-production" with Europe opens the director to the accusation of being "inauthentic," of having "compromised," "given in," and made films to please the West.[18] Also, after the great triumph of *Halfaouine* and, on a lesser scale, *Silences of the Palaces* (Moufida Tlatli, 1994)—two co-productions that did very well both nationally and internationally—and after several modest successes into the mid-1990s, Tunisian films have fared poorly both domestically and abroad. Since 1996 Tunisian audiences have turned away from all Tunisian films and, in the year 1998–1999—to take one telling example—the two Tunisian films released had a total attendance barely one-tenth that achieved by the vehicle of the Egyptian star Muhammad Heneidi.[19]

Which brings us to the only national cinema in the Arab world that has its films systematically distributed throughout the region and that can properly be called "industrial"—that of the region's most populous country, Egypt.[20] Egypt, which began film production in the 1920s, was already producing more than fifty films annually by the 1940s, reached a record annual total of ninety-six films in 1986, and today has amassed a corpus of some three thousand films. While it still produces by far the most films of any Arab country, Egypt (like many other Third World countries) has seen its production level fall in recent years, from numbers often exceeding fifty films per year during the 1980s to an average in the late 1990s of fewer than twenty. Even at the higher level Egyptian cinema was not strong nor was it immune to threats. True, its films were distributed regionally and its film sector had the advantage of a "general industrial infrastructure, an urban mass audience with money to spend on entertainment, an organized system of film distribution, and access to capital for investment in facilities as well as in production itself" but, even so, as two experienced critics argued, "self-sufficiency cannot be assured, since the profitable operation of the system needs several hundred films a year. . . . Thus Egypt's output of some fifty films a year ranks it fairly high in the list of film-producing nations . . . but leaves it vulnerable to imported films."[21]

With most wealthy, populous countries having great difficulty sustaining production, to say nothing of increasing it, and with the same being true for a poorer, middle-level producer like Egypt despite its demographic and infrastructural advantages and the fact that it is the only Arab cinema enjoying regional distribution, how much more vulnerable are smaller Third World producers, such as Morocco, which do not enjoy these advantages? Yet, vulnerable as these smaller, poorer producers are, we have also seen that the situation is not hopeless and that it is possible for them to build and maintain viable film production, through financial investment from outside the private capital markets, buttressed by some sort of ensured access to the theaters.

How does a Third World cinema like Morocco's, developing in a context where world film production, distribution, and exhibition dwarf and threaten to submerge it, poised in unstable equilibrium where the slightest misfortune or change in public policy might topple it, attain its undeniable achievements and substantial, albeit frail, national success? How does one individual within Morocco's film world maintain the optimism, commitment, and creativity that enable him to confront the obstacles and the several years of effort it will take to make another feature film? Muhammad Abderrahman Tazi's films and career are going to provide us with the lens through which to explore these and related issues.

Turning toward Morocco

AN ANTHROPOLOGIST IN MOROCCO

At the start of my career, after doing fieldwork in Morocco, I taught anthropology in New York City universities for several years; then, in the late 1970s, I moved to London to direct human rights research on the Middle East for Amnesty International. In 1990 I remarried and moved to Tunisia where my wife was a university professor and where I continued my anthropological research and writing. As an anthropologist, I was interested in the broad question of how culture shapes human behavior and how people create and shape culture; during my work in the human rights field I developed a growing interest in a similar issue that was of great urgency—how new ideas and visions, such as those related to human rights, are elaborated and communicated, how they enter the public sphere and become part of a people's shared culture. In exploring these kinds of questions, I began to look closely at how cultural products in general, among them feature films, were created in the Arab world and the kinds of visions they conveyed. In the spring of 1998 I obtained research funding from the National Endowment for the Humanities and, focusing on cinema, I began to concentrate on the early stages of this process: what is the situation of the creative artist and how are creative works produced. In the fall of 1998 I began the research with a visit to Morocco.

Situated in the northwest corner of Africa, less than 20 km distant from Spain across the Straits of Gibraltar, Morocco is a moderately large country, significantly larger than France, as large as Texas, but less than one-third as large as its neighbor Algeria.[22] Its geographical complexity, marked by four mountain chains and a climate that varies from Mediterranean to arid desert, is paralleled by a heterogeneous population speaking two main languages, Arabic and Berber (of which there are several dialects), and numbering more than thirty million (roughly equal to Algeria's), slightly more than half of which is urban. Islam is the state religion and Arabic the national language.

Morocco regained its independence in 1956 after some four decades as a French Protectorate and was ruled for most of the next four decades by King Hassan II, under a monarchical system where the king's power was paramount and was wielded at times coercively, at times more permissively. From the mid-1980s on, the Palace began to show more tolerance and "civil society" activities expanded noticeably, with increasing freedom of speech and expression providing a fertile terrain for the birth and growth of many new associations concerned with social issues. In March 1998, after elections in which opposition parties gained the lion's share of the vote, King Hassan and the parties negotiated the installation of a *"gouvernement de l'alternance"* led by a coalition of opposition parties but in which the king retained most of his key royal prerogatives and powers.[23] These developments on the level of both government and civil society contributed to the strong feeling in Morocco that substantial and perhaps even irreversible steps toward a more democratic and open system were being taken.[24]

In July 1999 the death of King Hassan and the smooth succession to the throne of his son, King Muhammad VI, gave further support to this hopeful mood. The new king quickly established a strong royal presence, making a series of visits to some of the country's poorest regions and lending his name and prestige to a number of social initiatives. One of the sharpest signals he gave of his intention to break with the past was his dismissal, four months into his reign, of the minister of the interior closely associated with the harsher side of King Hassan's rule.

Throughout the several years of my research, the king continued to rule and the *"gouvernement de l'alternance"* continued to administer but, by mid-2001, the "honeymoon" that both enjoyed was beginning to fade, for neither alone nor in tandem were they moving effectively to solve the country's serious problems of poverty, illiteracy, high unemployment, and poor health care, among others.[25] Challenges to the government were growing more severe, both from within and without, social unrest was never far beneath the surface and at times erupted above it, and the occasionally heavy-handed response of the security forces to popular demonstrations led many to suspect that the oppressive practices of the past had not been left definitively behind. Yet, all the while, civil society activities retained their dynamism and freedom of expression—although still a terrain of struggle—was as strong as it had ever been. The general movement of society over the past decade in the direction of greater openness, increased tolerance, and growing dynamism seemed undeniable.[26]

ENCOUNTERING TAZI

Such was the general atmosphere when I went to Morocco in September 1998 to start my research. Muhammad Abderrahman Tazi was one of the many people I wanted to meet and we were soon introduced by a mutual friend, the well-known writer and sociologist Fatima Mernissi. Tazi, born in 1942, was roughly my age and had a beard that journalists repeatedly described as "salt and pepper." At our first meeting he was understandably reserved: although I had knowledge and experience of the region as a whole and of Morocco in particular, and my command of Moroccan Arabic usually eased communication and helped build what anthropologists like to believe is "positive rapport," in Tazi's own field I was a novice—I was just beginning to study Arab cinema and knew about filmmaking only what a regular, somewhat attentive moviegoer might know.

Tazi and I met twice during the month I was in Morocco and he was very helpful in providing names and addresses of Moroccan filmmakers and critics and sharing with me his assessment of the best films Morocco had produced. Most crucially, he provided what I asked of most of the filmmakers I was meeting—copies of his feature films—which at that time numbered four. I made no attempt at this point to discuss "substantive" issues—it seemed presumptuous to do so before seeing his films.

I returned to Morocco two months later, in November, to attend the Fifth National Film Festival being held in Casablanca. I had now seen Tazi's four films and wanted to do an extended set of interviews with him, but he and I were unable to meet to discuss this, in part because he was "boycotting" the festival and didn't want to be seen near it, in part because I had to shorten my visit and return to Tunis suddenly.[27] I did, however, suggest the project to him over the telephone, saying, "Each of your feature films is very interesting in its own way. *Looking for My Wife's Husband* has a special significance because it was enormously successful in Morocco. Your second film, *Badis,* has been haunting me for a long time because some years ago, in New York, I found it gripping, even though I had to miss the ending.

Do you think it would be possible to discuss your films and your career at some length the next time I come to Morocco?" His response to my comment on *Badis* was gracious and restrained, along the lines of, "Thank you, I'm glad you liked it." I sensed that his reaction to the larger question was positive, but I couldn't gauge it accurately over the telephone.

Another two months passed and, in January 1999, I returned to Morocco. Tazi invited me to his home for lunch and I suggested the project again, proposing, somewhat imprecisely, that we go through his entire career—his start in filmmaking, then each of his films in turn, and then some of the themes the films conveyed. Perhaps having already thought the matter over, he answered, "I have a different idea. I'll tell you stories about my experiences on my own films, on foreign films, and so on, sort of a 'behind-the-scenes' approach. This will be much more interesting than simply going through my career and the themes of my films. The best way to do this is just to have a free-wheeling conversation. Of course, after that you'll have to do a re-structuring, a reworking."

At that point I had no intention of writing a book that focused on Tazi. However, after the first few meetings and taking into account what I was learning elsewhere about Moroccan cinema, I began to consider such a project. What eventually emerged followed neither his early plan nor mine but took on aspects of both, as well as reflecting ideas we developed subsequently. We ended up, some two years later, having accomplished sixteen taped interviews in all, each lasting about two hours and each taking place in his home, either early in the morning or in the evening.[28] For the first group of interviews I followed a simple chronological framework; later, we talked about a number of overriding themes in his work, as well as particular issues in his films and his career that interested me. These interviews left ample room for changes of direction and subject, shifts of attention, and interjections, and for the many anecdotes that came to Tazi's mind. They were not immune to interruptions (mostly from the telephone, which, when it rang too insistently, Tazi switched off; sometimes from his wife or his infant daughter). By the end of our time together I had developed a better acquaintance with Moroccan films and with his films in particular, I knew more about filmmaking in general, we had a deeper fund of common knowledge, and we knew one another better and were more relaxed. Our discussions, although still following a question-answer format, took on a more conversational, give-and-take flavor.

Throughout this period I was, among other research-related tasks, transcribing and translating the interviews and doing the "restructuring and reworking" that Tazi had referred to at the outset. I was also filling in details, adding background material, and ordering the sections so that they fit together into what seemed to me a continuous narrative. I gave these "rough cuts" to Tazi to read at various stages, and he usually made a few small changes of fact, sometimes striking out a name that, I agreed, was better left unmentioned, but never challenging a line of questioning or any substantive matter. In a visit in January and February of 2001, at the time of the Sixth National Film Festival held in Marrakesh, he and I went over many detailed points. I did a final update in June 2003, when the Seventh National Film Festival took place.

Points of View, Partiality, and Mixed Purposes

As I carried out this research and then tried to put it in book form, I found a number of issues to be particularly difficult ones. Among these were problems of genre (for example, how to fit writing and film together?), of audience (to what extent do I aim for a Moroccan and/or Western audience?), of translation (the interviews were in French, with some Moroccan Arabic, the book would be in English), of context (how much historic, cultural, political, and/or economic context needs to be presented?), and of orientation (is this to be a biography, a filmography, is it to look at the creative process or the product? is it to look at a film as an aesthetic unity, as a window to society, as a form of social practice?).

Similarly, to what extent can we hope to be faithful to the specific creative product and/or to the entire life's work—in their uniqueness, but also in their intensity and duration? How, in a book of several hundred pages, can we convey without too much distortion some sense of the many months, even years, of collective effort that go into making a film? How, too, can the reader gain some insight into the research process itself—how the study was conceived, carried out, and then put into the form that is now in his or her hands?

This book reflects an attempt to respond, in varying degrees, to all these concerns, and therefore betrays mixed purposes: not a history of the Moroccan cinema, yet it conveys much of that history; not a systematic examination of the relationship between Third World film production and the global film industry, yet this is a key theme throughout; not an attempt to interpret a particular director's films utilizing a film critic's repertoire, yet all of Tazi's films will be discussed in some detail. Finally, I am not trying here to provide a study of Morocco at the societal or cultural level or to construct Morocco through the window of film but, inevitably, I move in these directions much of the time.

My approach is, admittedly, partial; partial insofar as I am not attempting to treat any single aspect comprehensively and I am privileging the vision and perspective of one particular Moroccan filmmaker. Partial, too, in a third sense: Tazi formulates his vision in response to an anthropologist with particular interests, whose questioning informs each interview's content, and who is solely responsible for the book's final form. This third kind of partiality—how one anthropologist constructs and represents other individuals and specific domains of human activity—is part of the basic problematic of anthropology and those interested in this level of interpretation may find some provocative material presented here.[29]

The partiality and mixed purposes are deliberate and I hope they help this book reflect both the orientations of the two people most directly involved in it as well as the societal contexts (both national and international) within which they move, all of which are full of partiality and mixed purposes. I also hope the book's structure, responding to these varied aims, will help readers focus on what may be of primary interest to them—be it the content of the films, the experience of producing them, or the economic and institutional development of the Moroccan national cinema.

Each chapter explores a particular stage in Tazi's career and introduces relevant aspects of Moroccan cinema's political, economic, institutional, and/or cultural environment, with Tazi presenting his views in interview format. Four chapters are followed by a complementary section, an "interlude" (also in interview form), that addresses either a specific issue raised by film or Tazi's experience in producing and directing a particular film.

Chapter 1 concentrates on *Looking for My Wife's Husband*—that most successful of Moroccan films. Its success is set in the context of changes in Moroccan film distribution that opened the way for Moroccan films to be screened commercially. We then discuss the film in detail, highlighting seven motifs that I found particularly interesting. In the following interlude Tazi discusses his general ideas concerning film's power and function.

Tazi's childhood provided much of the inspiration for *Looking for*

My Wife's Husband, which is his most autobiographical film and which leads us, naturally, to chapter 2, where Tazi discusses his childhood, then how he decided to become a filmmaker, how he trained for it, and the first two decades of his career. This period, taking us from pre-independence Morocco to the early 1980s, is marked by the reconstruction of the Moroccan nation after a long period of French colonization and by the first, tentative steps in the building of Morocco's national cinema. For Tazi, this period culminates in his first feature film, *Ibn as-Sabil* (*The Big Trip,* 1981), which we discuss in the interlude.

In chapter 3 we follow Tazi's experience working on foreign films made in Morocco and hear not only of the personalities and professional practices of several world-class filmmakers but also of the complex relationship between "local" and "global," between what Tazi likes to call "Moroccan filmmaking" and "filmmaking in Morocco."

Badis (1989), Tazi's critically acclaimed second film, is the subject of chapter 4. Co-produced with Spanish television and made at a time when Moroccan state aid to film production was being restructured, this film steers us toward an examination of how films are financed in Morocco. Tazi and I then discuss several motifs in *Badis* concerning questions of content (the situation of women, mixed marriages, the legacy of colonialism) and style, and I also raise an "anthropological" issue—how does this filmmaker approach a village and its inhabitants and how might this approach compare to an anthropologist's? *Badis* was frequently praised for the strength of its story and in the subsequent interlude Tazi discusses narrative and his use of symbols.

In chapter 5, using as a focus Tazi's fourth feature, *Lalla Hobby* (1997), much of which he filmed in Europe, we look at Tazi's filmmaking experiences abroad and examine how he negotiates the local, national, regional, and global. For Tazi, the filming of *Lalla Hobby* repeatedly borders on the catastrophic and almost ends in tragedy; in the interlude we look more closely at certain aspects of *Lalla Hobby* and at Tazi's experience shooting it as a "foreign filmmaker abroad."

In chapter 6, in a first movement, Tazi looks back over his career and assesses some of the major changes in Moroccan filmmaking, first on the organizational and technical levels, then with regard to the audience's shifting tastes and changing reception of Moroccan films; then, he looks forward and speculates on both the future of Moroccan filmmaking and his own future within it.

In the conclusion, in my own voice, I address a number of themes that run throughout this book, first reflecting on this encounter between filmmaker and anthropologist and suggesting what an anthropologist's contribution to the study of cinema might be. This will lead us to assess Tazi's work and career in relation to Moroccan, Third World, and World cinemas, and to speculate about the future prospects of Moroccan and Third World filmmaking in a world marked by tensions and controversy over "free trade," "the cultural exception," and "cultural diversity."[30]

Chapter One

The Most Successful
Moroccan Film Ever

Introduction: "A Societal Phenomenon"

Unprecedented acclaim greeted the release of *Look-ing for My Wife's Husband* in 1993: "The first entirely Moroccan film that makes us laugh . . . [with] much talent and subtlety," "without doubt the best Moroccan film I've ever seen . . . the public, more than a thousand people . . . were all bursting with laughter," "we rediscovered the pleasures of a fertile and supple narration of the kind that constituted the millennial charm of Arab stories," "this new film of M. A. Tazi keeps the director among the best, and perhaps even the best, of Moroccan filmmakers," "M. A. Tazi shows . . . that the Moroccan cinema can give pleasure to a broad public without making thematic, artistic, or technical compromises with regard to the essentials of our own experience, or falling into the sarcasm of light melodramas of the Egyptian sort." This critical praise, voiced both at home and abroad, was echoed by the Moroccan public, which came out to see the film in record numbers, turning it into what was often called "a societal phenomenon."[1]

What made this success even more surprising was that it emerged against a historical background in which, for decades prior to the early 1990s, the distribution circuit was dominated by films from abroad and Moroccan films had great difficulty finding theaters for screening. In the early 1990s one Moroccan distributor decided to begin dealing

The poster for *Looking for My Wife's Husband*

in Moroccan films and *Looking* was his second success in a row.[2] Today, with this distributor frequently handling Moroccan films and other distributors doing so occasionally, and with the public often responding positively, a new Moroccan film's prospects, while not rosy, are certainly more promising than they were a mere decade earlier. Why were distributors and theater owners refusing Moroccan films into the early 1990s and what led this one Moroccan distributor to break the pattern?[3]

Distributing and Screening Films in Morocco

Patterns of film distribution and exhibition have their roots in the colonial period, when foreign-owned, vertically integrated companies were established in Morocco to perform these activities. These companies distributed imported films and owned theater networks but, operating as subsidiaries of the major, Western-based distribution companies, they had little choice in the films they were offered—these were determined overseas by the major foreign distributors and offered in the form of "block booking." Even with independence in 1956 and the later "Moroccanization" of such enterprises in the early 1970s, this basic structure continued to dominate the sector.[4]

The state never showed much interest in influencing the economics of distribution and exhibition, and these have remained fully privatized throughout Moroccan history. Both distributors and exhibitors seek to generate profit by keeping the amounts they pay for films as low as possible. Imported films are systematically available more cheaply than Moroccan films, since the latter need to recoup their costs in the small national market, whereas imported films have already paid off their investment in their runs abroad and can be priced as low as is necessary to ensure market share. Consequently, from the distributor-exhibitor perspective, renting the national film constitutes an unwarranted financial risk.

Nor has the state sought to weaken the preponderant influence of foreign interests by introducing measures such as quotas on imports or by imposing quotas on exhibitors.[5] Nor is any special benefit provided to either distributor or exhibitor that might encourage them to take on a Moroccan film. As a result, the local distribution and exhibition firms "play an important role in the integration of the local market into the global market, answering to the needs of the latter," leading to a distribution-exhibition sector that is highly concentrated in nature and dependent on the supply of films from abroad.[6] A further consequence is that, in these circumstances, there was no room for the spectators themselves to express whatever preferences they might have had for Moroccan films, because these films had practically no chance of being seen on the screens.[7]

However, in the early 1990s, although the sector's basic economic structure remained the same, the availability of Moroccan films for the public was about to increase. This resulted from the happy coincidence of a Moroccan distributor viewing a number of recently made Moroccan films in which, until then, he had had no interest, and his sensing the commercial possibilities of at least one of these films. Here is how he tells the story:[8]

> I come from a family of distributors, with my father and three uncles all in the distribution business. For years after I entered the business in 1983 I never gave a thought to Moroccan films and knew nothing about them. In any event, everything you would read about them in the press or hear from the critics was unfailingly negative—they were poorly made, incomprehensible to the public, and so on. Our company had no interest in them because we imported mostly series B films—action films, adventures, westerns, war films, Italian films with elaborate mise-en-scène of the *Gladiator* sort but of course with nothing like the same budget. In those days, everything did well in the theaters because there was little competition—not many TVs, no video clubs, no satellite dishes, nothing like that. I really knew nothing about Moroccan films—I didn't know directors, producers, actors, technicians—nothing. A little contradictory, you might say, for someone who's a Moroccan!
>
> Then, I was put on the jury of the 1991 National Film Festival in Meknès and I saw a number of films, some of which I found very interesting.[9] On the whole, I thought, "Well, these films are quite attractive esthetically, there's a real search going on in many of them for something beyond the ordinary."
>
> One film in particular struck me, Abdelkader Lagtaa's *A Love Affair in Casablanca*. I thought that this was the most commercial film of the group—its story of an unnatural love affair wouldn't leave people indifferent and it left the beaten path followed by so many of our films that deal with poverty and the negative aspects of daily life. Although it was rather controversial I thought that, on the whole, people would go to see it. So I distributed it and the public proved me right.[10]
>
> After that, I was on the committee that reviewed films seeking state aid and I saw Tazi's *Looking for My Wife's Husband*. I remember, at the time, people were saying, "Oh, it's a nice little film, it will do well in one or two theaters." But I thought, "No, this film will go through the roof." And that's what happened.

Since then I've become *the* specialist in distributing Moroccan films, and it probably accounts for 70 percent of my business. On the one hand, distributing these films is a delicate enterprise—you're accountable to the film's director-producer, to the press, to the public. And then you have the problem of the theaters—this is very difficult because there are only about 20 theaters in all of Morocco that produce money and you have to keep your relationship to the owners of those theaters on an even keel or you won't get access to their screens. You can't take the chance of convincing the owner to take a film that turns into a flop, because the next time you ask him for a few weeks of screen time he won't give them to you. And without those theaters, you can't make a penny, no one is happy, and everyone thinks it's all your fault. On the other hand, when you succeed, when the film does well, it's exalting, you can say to yourself, "At least I've gotten the public out to see a Moroccan film. They're happy, the director-producer's happy, I'm happy and so on." And if a Moroccan film does well, its receipts might go five or six times as high as a reasonably successful American film. So there's a double satisfaction, both material and personal.

The enthusiasm for Moroccan films generated by *A Love Affair in Casablanca* and by Tazi's *Looking* signaled new circumstances in Moroccan filmmaking and established a new mood—what was often referred to as "the reconciliation between filmmaker and public." From that moment on, Moroccan films had at least one distributor willing to promote them—providing the film met his commercial criteria—and the distributor found exhibitors willing to show them. Also, Moroccan filmmakers, now having well-founded hopes that their films might reach an audience, began to take this audience into account, straying significantly off what the distributor had called "the beaten path" and making films with subjects and settings different from those made previously. The public responded with a growing eagerness to see Moroccan films. Since Tazi's film, it has become quite common for upwards of a hundred thousand spectators to view a Moroccan film and some films have done considerably better.[11]

Looking for My Wife's Husband (1993)
SUCCESS: "WE HAD NEVER SEEN ANYTHING LIKE THAT"

Before we turn to examine *Looking* in detail, let us hear Tazi talk of the atmosphere surrounding the film's release and success.

K. Did you have any idea that the film was going to be such a success, that it would have close to one million viewers in Morocco, making it by far the most widely seen Moroccan film in history?

M. Basically, we never imagined it would be such a success and I was very surprised. I can tell you for certain that the film had at least eight hundred thousand spectators. We do have standard ticketing in Morocco, so there is a systematic record of receipts, but these are not 100 percent reliable.

The first hint I had of success was when we held the premiere at the Zahwa Cinema in Rabat. We did this in a rather special way, with some financial support from the ministry of immigration and the ministry for Moroccans abroad, inviting perhaps a thousand people and treating them to something like a traditional Fez wedding. While the film was being shown, we set up the lobby in just that kind of style, with waiters serving pastries, and trays full of delicacies, and with the smell of incense. We even brought in an Andalusian-style orchestra and all that goes with it. When the audience started to come out at the end of the film, they were surprised to find an ambiance that prolonged the feeling of the film. A lot of people came up to congratulate me but Souheil Ben Barka was the first to say, "This film is going to be a really big hit."[12]

That's how it started. Souheil felt it and so did some of the journalists. I had planned to introduce the actors on stage after the showing, but as soon as the film was over people immediately went up to them without waiting for them to go on stage. It was really impressive. That's when I started to say to myself, "Hey, maybe, it's just possible that . . ." And right away, in the first weeks, it became a kind of craze, something I never expected.

We'd never seen anything like that for a Moroccan film, with the theaters full for weeks and weeks. We started pretty modestly with two or three copies of the film on distribution, but we soon reached five or six throughout Morocco. For us that was unheard of, there had never been more than one or two copies of a film out at one time. But five or six, all developed in France, all with subtitles—that was quite an expense, it was a considerable investment. But there was a public, an enormous public.[13]

One of the really gratifying things about this was that there were a lot of young people in the audiences. They knew nothing about traditional life beyond what their parents had told them, and now their parents were encouraging them to go see the film.

"... AND PIRATED VIDEOCASSETTES"

M. Of course there was another side to this that angered me tremendously: a few people with a good nose for business began to make pirate copies of the film. There were an unimaginable, incalculable number of pirated videocassettes sold.

K. Were you able to do anything about these pirated copies?

M. After the film had been out for three or four weeks, I heard there were cassettes being sold in Derb Ghallef, in Casablanca. I went there and found people selling the cassettes for up to 300 dirhams [DH] a copy, and selling them from big baskets or sacks that could hold several hundred at a time. I bought myself a copy—I still have it—and from it you could figure out in which theater the cassette had been taped. At that point I made a complaint to the CCM and then to the police. The police went and seized the cassettes in the marketplace and the guys selling them, and from the evidence they collected you could conclude that one person was behind the whole operation and that there were about forty thousand cassettes on the market, all of *Looking*. That's what I call an industry! And it was so badly filmed that you can see the edges of the screen. A simple investigation could have gotten to the root of the problem. But the authorities just arrested some of the sellers, who of course were only middlemen. They never got to the source. It makes you think that there was complicity somewhere.

Eventually, the CCM proposed a law that was finally adopted by the government, to protect authors in the creative domain. But the repressive side is weak—you can't actually take someone to prison for stealing your property, so the punishment is likely to involve destroying the cassettes or closing the video club.

So, on a lot of levels, the film had a significant effect. Not only did it bring the public into the theaters, which was something rather new, but even on a legal level there were some important consequences.

K. How long would you say enthusiasm for the film lasted within Morocco?

M. About four or five months. For example, at the Zahwa Cinema in Rabat, where a film never lasted longer than two or three weeks, it played for twelve weeks. In Fez too. And in Casablanca, it played between eight and twelve weeks. It was amazing.[14]

Muhammad Abderrahman Tazi during the filming of *Looking for My Wife's Husband*

THE FILM AND SOME MOTIFS

In the history of Moroccan filmmaking, *Looking for My Wife's Husband* innovated in at least two major ways: it was one of the first Moroccan films, if not the first, to be set in the milieu of the traditional bourgeois family and it heightened this by placing the family in Morocco's most "traditional" city, Fez; second, it was a film that had people laughing from beginning right up to the end. *Looking* is also one of many films to take women's lives as a primary subject, a main theme in Moroccan films from their earliest days into the present. These three areas—the bourgeois setting, humor, and the depiction of women—were the focus of most of my questions. In addition, the ending is in a different register from the rest of the film and this contrast raises the issue of Tazi's views on film's function and power, a subject we will discuss in the interlude following this chapter.

ACT ONE: SETTING UP THE BREAKUP

Houda, the youngest of Hajj Ben Moussa's three wives, is hanging clothes on a roof terrace overlooking the city of Fez and glancing flirtatiously at a man on a neighboring roof. Singing to herself, she goes down the stairs into a large bourgeois residence, walking through its hallways, picking up and talking to various children. The Hajj himself, a stocky, well-to-do 60-year-old, owns a jewelry store in the heart of Fez. He is a man of grimaces and pouts and a roving eye that leers brazenly at his women clients. Self-indulgent, not quite as clever as he thinks he is, the Hajj appears fundamentally good natured. Houda has yet to bear him a child, but she fully participates in a household where each wife has a special role: the eldest, Lalla Hobby (a term of endearment, meaning "My lady love"), has adult children and runs the household efficiently and sympathetically—she is now the Hajj's pal and confidante and often "mothers" him; the second wife, Lalla Rabiʿa, has been busy producing children—she has had four, all young and still at home; and coquettish Houda, who excites the Hajj sexually and whom he first met when she and her mother, of very modest circumstances, came to sell their jewelry in his store.

One day, Houda opens the door to a man delivering sheep the Hajj has just bought at the livestock market for an upcoming religious feast. Houda lets the man in, cues him with a playful look, and begins to banter. The Hajj unexpectedly returns home and bursts into anger at Houda's presence in front of this outsider. The other two wives

Hajj Ben Moussa's three wives

Houda and the Hajj in the bedroom

attempt to cool things down, but the Hajj's temper flares; Houda responds feistily, dishing out as much invective as she receives. Losing his self-control (not for the last time), the Hajj repudiates his marriage to Houda—this is the third repudiation and, in Islamic law, constitutes divorce. Houda leaves the Hajj's home and returns to live with her parents.

First Motif: The Bourgeois Milieu of Fez
"I'M THE MAIN AUDIENCE"

K. What made you decide to set the film in the bourgeois milieu of Fez?

M. After my second film, *Badis,* I was quite frustrated, because that was a film I had aimed at the Moroccan audience and it just didn't find that audience. Of course, you can point to the film distribution problem, to the decrease in the number of theaters, and so on. But still—not only did *Badis* win something like fourteen or fifteen prizes at international festivals, but the critics here in Morocco were absolutely unanimous in praising the film. The film was released in a theater in downtown Casablanca, and you would have thought that word of mouth would bring out the

Tazi filming the livestock market

Houda returning to live with her parents

public. But no—after a week we had barely more than three hundred viewers. I was really disappointed.

So I said to myself, "All right, now let's *really* try to make something for our own audience." By this I didn't mean pandering to the public taste for Egyptian or Indian films. Not at all. I meant that I was going to aim for our own audience but stay close to our own heritage—I was going to aim for a "proximate" cinema [Fr. *un cinéma de proximité*], showing things that were embedded in our own society.

I thought, "I'll make a film where *I'm* the main audience—a film that I'll get a lot of satisfaction making and that I'll also enjoy as a spectator." For this there is nothing better than going back to one's own childhood and, in my case, to my childhood among all the women of our household—what's commonly known as the "harem"—because both my grandfather and father had more than one wife. I thought I'd join to this something that's fairly common in our old traditional cities: the third repudiation of a wife. In all the neighborhoods of Fez, you'd hear that so-and-so, a wealthy bourgeois, had just repudiated his wife for the third time and that, according to Islamic law, he could only remarry her if she first married another man, had at least one fully consummated night with him, and then he agreed to divorce her.[15] And this bourgeois would have to hunt all over for a husband for his ex-wife, a kind of "straw man," someone who would marry and then divorce her. Everyone had heard these stories; this kind of news quickly spread far and wide.

That was my first reason. Also, I had the impression that most of Moroccan cinema was a kind of sociological cinema—and not only sociological, but located in the countryside or in the urban slums and shantytowns. I had the feeling that people had had enough of going to the cinema to see the same kind of poverty and misfortune that marked their lives—and to pay good money for this as well!

Not that I wanted to deny these things or paint a rosy picture, but I said to myself that Moroccan society isn't composed only of suffering classes. There's also a bourgeoisie, a kind of aristocracy, people who live very well. We should show them too. In my home city of Fez—the spiritual and religious capital of the country and for a long time its political capital as well—these social groups exist, they have marked Moroccan history very deeply, yet they had never been seen in films. I was sure I could find inspiration in that setting.

"ATEMPORALITY"

K. In *Looking* you take a bourgeois setting but you situate it temporally in a complex way. We're struck by the contrast between the Hajj's somewhat timeless bourgeois residence, which is within the city walls of Fez, and the character of the city outside the walls, where we see cars and other signs of today's Morocco. You said in one of your interviews, "Within the walls of Fez, we're in the 1950s; . . . once we're outside those walls, we're in the modern 'ville nouvelle' of the early 1990s. I wanted to play with these two different worlds."[16]

M. Absolutely. I situate the film toward the end of the 1950s, and we can see a photograph of Muhammad V that places the film chronologically.[17] I also talk about what I call the "atemporality" of the medina of Fez. When I go into the Fez medina I'm taken out of the present, out of the period in which I normally live. I have that feeling when I go into the medina even today—except, of course, when I go up on the roof and see all the satellite dishes. [Laughs.]

But along the passageways of the medina, with the donkeys and mules hauling clay, oil, construction materials, and all the rest of it, I can feel myself in the 1950s without any difficulty. And when you see the leather craftsmen, the tanners, the tailors working with parchment, the little kids working with the weavers, you could be in the Middle Ages, or even beyond time! In the film, when we are within the walls of the city, we are in another time, a kind of indeterminate era. That's what I'm evoking, the sort of internal beauty of Fez.

We shouldn't forget, by the way, that this atemporality inside the Fez medina reflects the particular history of Fez and is one of the effects of French colonization. When the French arrived, they said, "All right, we'll leave the natives, the indigenous people, in their own city, within the walls. For ourselves we'll build a new city." That's what we call that section today, "the new city" [Fr. *la ville nouvelle*].

For example, toward the beginning of the film, when the Hajj's grown daughter—a doctor—encounters the Hajj as she's getting into her car, she has just exited the medina through the city walls. Inside the medina there aren't any cars. That's the key: when you go from one side of the wall to the other, you go from one world to another. Later, when you see Houda and her friend go on a shopping spree or go to the hairdresser, they're in *"la ville nouvelle,"* that is, in the "modernity" of 1993 when the film was shot.

Let me just say that as far as filming this internal beauty of Fez goes, with its narrow passageways, you can't even begin to think of installing tracks for tracking shots. So, in order to follow the Hajj through Fez, I had to rent a Steadicam, which is enormously expensive.[18] But I really felt a strong need to show the city in this way, because foreign productions focus on all the exotic elements but miss the city's true internal beauty.

Second Motif: Why Make a Humorous Film?
"COMEDY OF SITUATION . . . ON THREE LEVELS"

K. The films you made before *Looking* were not humorous films. Quite to the contrary. One of the most important reasons for the success of *Looking* was that it was a very funny film, it really got audiences laughing. Was the desire to make the audience laugh part of the original idea for the film?

M. Not really, no. I didn't say to myself, "I'm going to make a comic film, I'm going to get people to laugh." No. I said, "I'm going to tell a story that really touches me." I started with the rather ordinary occurrence in Fez of a third repudiation. For the couple involved this may be rather tragic, something the concerned family tries to conceal, but for the rest of us in the neighborhood it's laughable.

There's really a comedy of situation on three levels. First, the man and his three wives: he's tossed back and forth from one wife to another and this is not a situation any Moroccan would wish for himself. Second, there's the comedy of someone who divorces a wife he loves. Third, we have someone who, in order to get his divorced wife back, has to take some fairly bizarre measures and suffer a painful comeuppance as a sort of mandated punishment for his lack of self-control. All this gave me the pretext I wanted, to show my native soil, my native city of Fez, in a way different from the way it is shown in foreign productions.

"THE OTHER SIDE, THE WOMAN'S IMAGINATION"

K. I know that the basic idea behind *Looking* was your idea. How did you go about developing it?

M. At the outset, it was going to be a short film. When I first thought of it, I believed in a kind of horizontal production structure, between Moroccans, Algerians, and Tunisians. At the Third National Film Festival in Meknès in 1991, I talked to some other filmmakers from the Maghreb, like Mahmoud Zemmouri and Merzak Allouache from Algeria, and Taieb Louhichi and Brahim Babai from Tunisia. The idea was that we would make a Maghreb film with sketches on the theme of marriage. We even had a framework agreement and Zemmouri and Louhichi wrote their scenarios. But the idea fell through, for a number of reasons. Afterward, when I mentioned my idea for a screenplay to Noureddin Sail he said to me, "This looks like it could be a feature film. Let's phone Farida and talk to her about it."[19]

I gave Farida a finished synopsis—the story of a Fassi bourgeois and his three wives, up through the divorce. Farida's contribution amounted to something like putting the intervening images in animated stories: you have the basic framework images and then you fill in the links between them. It was this intervening work that Farida did with, of course, the qualitative addition of a woman's imagination—something I have great appreciation for. You know, we men always need to have the other side, the woman's imagination. Farida took two months to work up a screenplay for a full-length feature, and her screenplay contained pretty much the entire flow of the film—everything except the ending, which I kept to myself. I knew what this ending would be, but I didn't want to tell anyone about it, not even the crew.

ACT TWO: THE HAJJ SUFFERS AND MOANS

Houda has gone to live with her parents, taking with her much of the household's liveliness, and the family she has left behind is morose. The Hajj, always short on self-control, grows increasingly irascible, venting his anger on his other wives and children and punishing one of his boys by introducing him to Koranic school, "to make a man of him." Increasingly despondent, the Hajj spends one evening drinking alcohol and, growing maudlin, tries to get into bed with his wives, each of whom spurns him: Lalla Hobby, the eldest, chides him for allowing the drink to "loosen his tongue" and notes how much time has elapsed since his previous "visit"; Lalla Rabi'a, with her teething infant beside her in bed, pushes the Hajj away to prevent his crushing the child. He whines to both wives that he needs someone to take care of him, but they quickly grasp that he is angling for a new third wife. Both scold him roundly, with Lalla Rabi'a warning that she'll leave him and make him care for all the children himself, should he take another wife.

The Hajj and his fellow jeweler

During the day, while tending his jewelry store, the Hajj confides his troubles to a fellow jeweler who teases and taunts him. Finally repenting, the Hajj decides he wants Houda back but realizes that under Islamic law he must undergo the punishment due a man who has lost control of himself in this way: Houda must first marry another man, consummate that marriage, and be divorced. Only then will the Hajj be able to remarry her.

Third Motif: Portraying Women
WOMEN'S STRENGTH, "TENDERNESS . . . [AND] SO MUCH KNOWLEDGE"

K. Another striking element in the film is the strength of the women characters, particularly Lalla Hobby and Houda, and the tenderness with which women's lives are treated. Where does this attitude come from?

M. The tenderness really has an autobiographical source. In my own childhood I was always among the women, whether it was my mother, my aunts, or the maids around the house. They were the ears that listened to me and the mouths that explained things to me. On the other hand, upon reaching adolescence—we start "adolescence" from the time you are no longer allowed to go to the Turkish baths [Ar. *ḥammam*, Fr. *bain-maure*] with your mother—you pass from the women to your father.[20]

This passage can be very frustrating, because when you're with your father and begin to ask questions, the answer always is, "When you're older, you'll understand." You never get to imbibe knowledge from men the way you do among the women, where things were just wonderful. Among the women I found not only tenderness but also so much knowledge, all those experiences they had of life. And they told us stories about it all—especially my grandmother. What a joy to listen to all this—lucky for us there was no television then! [Laughs.] We used to have our daily story sessions, with tales of ogres and ogresses, all kinds of stories. It was really very enriching and it was the kind of experience you never had among the men, among your uncles, older brothers, and so on. With them it was always, "Oh, you'll understand." As though they just didn't have the time. The women were always available, and they seemed to take such pleasure in you and in giving you knowledge and awareness.

K. In the film, an early scene shows that kind of pleasure among the women: shortly after we first encounter Lalla Hobby, who has carelessly let a standing closet fall on top of her, luckily to no ill effect, we watch the women partying, with music and dancing, celebrating Lalla Hobby's full and rapid recovery.

M. That kind of thing was very common: the women would get together in the afternoon and have small parties for themselves, with pastries, tea, music, dancing, and so on. It was kind of a release, it existed among almost all social classes in Fez. Even if there was no real occasion for it, the women created the occasion.

K. You also see Lalla Hobby's strength of character in these early scenes. Once, when Lalla Rabiʿa goes to Lalla Hobby to complain that Houda goes out all the time and that the Hajj could get angry at that—in fact this is one of the first hints that the kind of explosion that leads to the divorce might occur—Lalla Hobby takes Houda's side, saying "Look, times have changed."

M. Yes, she's philosophical about it.

"MOTHER, BREEDER, LOVER"

K. With respect to the relationship between the Hajj and his three wives, each of whom you've described as having a different function—the eldest as his "mother," the middle one as "breeder," and the youngest as "lover" [Fr. *la mère, la pondeuse, l'amante*][21]—how grounded in reality is that? How normal is it to have a young wife and then older ones with whom sexual relations have seemingly ceased, bearing in mind that according to Islamic law the husband must treat all the women equally, sexually as well as in other ways?

M. It's true more often than not. It depends somewhat on the structure of the harem. In this particular case, the difference of age between the women isn't just a few years. Early in the film you come to understand that the first wife, Lalla Hobby, has clearly become a companion, a friend, that there are no longer sexual relations between them, and that long ago they produced children who are now adults. The second wife: well, Lalla Hobby says about her that she thinks of nothing other than giving birth and the Hajj himself calls her "the breeder," meaning that every time he goes to bed with her she produces a child. In fact, once she hatches the child she then smothers it with care. For this second wife, nothing else exists.

It's as though the Hajj had a good car for many years but then needed a new one. The old one served very well so he keeps her, but he needs a new one to revive his sexuality and to have more children. So he takes a second wife and she fulfills those purposes. Then, some years and quite a few children later, he wants a third wife. For him, the new wife is a kind of legal mistress.

K. He also tries to push Houda, the new wife, to have children. When she asks for some nice jewelry, he gives her something cheap and says she'll get the more expensive pieces when she gives him a child.

M. Yes. The idea is, as the traditional saying puts it, "A woman without children is like a tent with only the central mat." Which means there's no place for her, she must have children to have a place in the household. But Houda has other ideas—she doesn't want to have children because to have them with a man as old as the Hajj means they'll quickly become orphans. Also, she's from a poor family herself, she's an only child, so there are many things that contribute to her attitude.

MOTHER AND SISTER

K. I noticed that *Looking* is dedicated to your mother.

M. Yes, it is, and very much for the reasons I've been explaining: how much I learned from the women, and how difficult and even traumatic it was among the men, with their constant, "You'll understand later." And I also dedicated the film to my mother because there are scenes in it that reflect almost exactly scenes from my own childhood.

K. Is your mother still alive, was she able to see the film?

M. No. She died well before the film was made, a long time before, in 1971. She died of cirrhosis of the liver although she'd never touched a drop of alcohol! [Smiles slightly.] But I have a sister who went to the premiere; when she saw the dedication she was so affected that she burst into tears and left the theater. It was only later, when she finally brought herself to see the film, that she understood why I dedicated it to my mother.

ACT THREE: THE HAJJ CONFRONTS RIDICULE, HOUDA TASTES FREEDOM

The Hajj now begins the "search for his wife's husband." His first efforts immediately turn him into a butt of laughter and ridicule. Both the butcher and the baker poke fun at his predicament and the mother

Houda and her friend at the café

of the local "idiot" mocks the Hajj's request, deeming Houda unworthy of her son because she's now a frivolous divorcée.

Meanwhile, Houda is experiencing the freedoms, constraints, and risks of the single life. Now living with her mother and hemiplegic father in simple surroundings, she is at first enthusiastic and points with pride to her newly decorated room. She enjoys a shopping spree with her young widowed friend Khadija and shares a meal with Khadija and her young daughter, ending it by asking that they all sing a song of liberty. With Khadija she goes to enjoy a drink at a fashionable outdoor café. Here, they are eyed by two men their own age. Khadija warns Houda to be more reticent, to stop returning their glances. The two men join them at the table and, with Houda eager and Khadija wary, the two women agree to a short drive to a hotel café on the outskirts of Fez. This ends badly: the men, taking the women's agreement for granted, rent a hotel room. Khadija, deeply offended, angrily rejects the overture while Houda looks on, somewhat bewildered and out of her depth at the turn of events. The men retaliate by telling the women to fend for themselves, and Houda and Khadija end up walking back to Fez, as Khadija lectures Houda on her naïveté.

Abandoned, the girls walk home on their own

Fourth Motif: Humor—Proximity, Criticism, Transgression

Humor has been the dominant tone throughout the film, and here, as the Hajj begins the search for Houda's husband, it reaches a higher pitch. Although not the first humorous Moroccan film, it was certainly the first to gain wide distribution and public success and, therefore, the first to get an audience to laugh from beginning to end (or almost).[22] I wondered why a humorous film emerged when it did and how Tazi and his collaborators developed the humor. But I was also perplexed as to why some scenes, clearly meant to be humorous, didn't have that effect on me—what was I missing here?

"A THERMOMETER OF DEMOCRACY"

K. Why did a humorous film like *Looking* come at the particular time it did? Was there something about the changing social, political, cultural atmosphere in Morocco that encouraged making such a film?

M. At that time there was a lot of movement in what we call "civil society," with the formation of many organizations, associations, and so on. In fact, during the shooting of *Looking*, there was a big public discussion going on over reforming the Mudawwana, and a lot of this revolved around questions concerning divorce and repudiation.[23] The society was really opening up. You could even see it in our newspaper cartoons, which are a good measure of the degree of democracy in a society, especially in the Arab world—it's kind of a thermometer of democracy. Being able to have cartoons in the newspapers that made fun of ministers of state was a sign that we'd reached a certain level of progress and freedom.

For me, making this film a humorous one was in part a means of criticizing certain aspects of society, but without falling too deeply into caricature. I take a person and use him to criticize our own society, but I still try to do this with a certain amount of dignity and respect.

K. So the idea of putting humor into a film was "in the air," so to speak.[24] I noticed in an interview you gave in 1990, well before *Looking,* that you spoke then of wanting to do a comedy, saying, "I would like to do a comic film . . . we're losing our sense of humor. I think it's indispensable to bring the public to laughter through an approach and themes that are self-critical towards our society, our behavior, our daily lives."[25] Does that mean that you felt this then as a personal need?

M. I did have that concern, partly because it seemed to me that people were losing their sense of humor. Obviously, a number of socioeconomic factors—poverty, unemployment, and so on—contribute to this and these factors are still relevant. But when I go to the grocer or tobacconist, or when I buy my newspaper, I like to kid around with the guy I'm talking to. However, in those days I was starting to feel that people were getting more and more thin skinned. I'd be joking and they'd interpret it as an attack, and this was getting really disagreeable. I said to myself, "Well, our television, theater, and cinema ought to be encouraging a sense of humor." So, yes, it was a concern.

EGYPTIAN HUMOR, MOROCCAN HUMOR

K. I'm struck by the contrast with Egypt. To generalize for a moment: one has the feeling that Egyptians conceive of themselves, in part, as people who create laughter—"we make people laugh, we make everyone laugh." Whereas Moroccans don't seem to think of themselves in that way at all.

M. Yes, I think that's absolutely true. Moroccans have a good sense of humor but it has to correspond to our society. For example, the French film *Les Visiteurs* was an enormous hit in France—it had some fifteen million viewers there—but here, in Morocco, it had no impact at all. It was a kind of laughter that had no appeal to us, that didn't refer to our lives, our history, or whatever.

As far as Egypt is concerned I'd say the same thing. Adel Imam is perhaps someone who's very exceptional, whose comedies have had great success in the Arab world, but there are a lot of people here who are totally insensitive to that kind of comedy, even though the publicity for Egyptian comedy is always being hammered at you. We do have a large number of humorous television programs originating in Egypt and Moroccans laugh along with these easily enough. But it's a kind of humor somewhat distant from our own local humor and there are things that make Egyptians laugh that don't make me laugh, that leave me cold. I know people say that laughter is what's special about being human, but you need keys to appreciate the humor; and what I call "keys" are matters of local knowledge and taste.

How much happier Moroccans would be to have the humor growing out of a situation much closer to them. For example, over the last couple of years we've seen a number of Moroccan theatrical productions that have toured the country with enormous success. This is humor, Moroccan humor. It's true that often it's very burlesque. But still—and I've said this again and again—people here are so stuffed full of images from abroad, even Arab images from abroad, that they'd love to see images that are closer to home, that come from their own country. That's what I put in this film, or at least tried to: humorous situations, Moroccan situations.

COMEDY: SCREENPLAY, ACTING, REAL LIFE

K. How did you develop the comedy in the film? Was it more on the level of the screenplay, or the acting, or the cinematography?

M. Well, not from the cinematography. In the screenplay, it's already clear and obvious that there are situations that are fully comic ones. For example, take the scene after the repudiation when the Hajj scolds his son at dinner—that scene is very faithful to the screenplay.

By the way, the sequence after that, where the Hajj takes his son to the Koranic school [Ar. *Msid*] and the son comes back sick with fever, almost exactly reflects an incident from my own life. One day my father, in an angry reaction to something I did, decided to take me to the *Msid* for the first time. And he left me there, just as it was done in the film.

K. You mean where Hajj Ben Moussa says to the religious teacher [Ar. *fqih*], "My son is now yours. If you kill him, I'll bury him."

M. Yes, exactly. So I spent that whole morning in the *Msid*. All around the room, there were little cupboards with doors where the writing materials and other things were stored. When my father left, the *fqih* asked me, "Do you know what's in those cupboards?" "No." "Well, they are full of rats. And if a kid doesn't do his work properly, I put oil all over his head and I shut him in there." And we all knew that rats love oil! That's exactly what he told me. When I heard that I was traumatized, and I came back home with a fever of 40 degrees [104 degrees Fahrenheit]. My mother told my father, "That's it! If you take him to the *Msid* once more, I'm going back to my parents."[26]

There's another part of this sequence that didn't happen to me, but has its source in something my father told me. You know, the *Msid* was usually a room situated a little above street level, about one or one and a half meters above, walled with *mashrabiya* [a screen of turned wood that allows light to pass through]. In the film, when the Hajj takes his son to the *Msid*, he tells his boy that in the old days the children who went to the *Msid* wore ponytails—their heads were completely shaven except for a braid, a

At the Koranic school

little like what you used to see in Japan. And then the Hajj tells
his son the story of a teacher who got so angry that he grabbed a
kid by this braid and threw him over the balcony, and "the braid
remained in his hand, and the kid lay on the street" [Ar. *el-qern
ibqa f-yiddu, wa derri msha l-il-zilka*].

So, the sequence where the father takes his son to the *Msid*
and the son returns feverish has its roots in my own life. I eliminated the part about the rats in the cupboard, but I put in the
story of "the braid in the hand, the kid on the street." In any case,
there's enough there to traumatize any kid!

The screenplay has lots of other humorous scenes: for example, where the Hajj repudiates Houda, or where he tries to coax
his second wife to secretly help him find a new third wife and she
begins to shout it out so loudly to Lalla Hobby that all the neighbors might hear.

The humor wasn't only in the screenplay, because the actors
contributed a lot too. Don't forget that Bashir Skiredj, who plays
the role of Hajj Ben Moussa, is an actor who, at the very beginnings of Moroccan television in 1963, 1964, played the fool, the
clown, and made everyone laugh, the young and the not so
young. Afterward he sort of disappeared. He's someone who's very
funny by nature, and he filled out the character with a number
of his own tricks. He's an actor with a lot of talent.

But his training as a clown—clown in the noble meaning of
the word—created some difficulties in the filming. Skiredj has a
way of reacting to the camera as though he were addressing the
audience. In other words, we'd shoot a scene and just before it
ended he'd sort of turn to the camera to say, "So, how did you
like me?" It was really difficult. For him the camera was the audience, he was always conscious of the camera, and it was like he
had to turn to it to get the audience response. [Laughs.] I finally
had to start calculating the scenes so that I could say "cut" just
before he turned toward the camera. [Both laugh.]

DRINKING ALCOHOL

K. Much of the humor is also based on transgression of normal,
proper behavior. In one scene the Hajj, suffering from Houda's
departure, picks up a bottle of what looks like whisky and, drinking freely and becoming quite drunk, tries to get into bed with
each of his two remaining wives. In a bourgeois Fassi context, how
true to life is this drinking?

M. You know, I lived in Fez and I've seen the relationship that existed
between a certain kind of Fassi bourgeois and the Jews of the
Jewish quarter [Ar. *mellah*]—it was the Jews who provided this
kind of eau de vie [Ar. *mhayya*]. It was used in a very discreet
manner inside the homes, but the drink was indeed alcoholic!

K. I know the same thing was practiced in the south, in Taroudannt.

M. Absolutely. Obviously, you had to be very discreet—your kids
shouldn't know about it and so on—but your wife would be fully
aware of it, so would the servants. I once showed *Looking* at
Khouribga[27] and a Moroccan dignitary came up to me and said,
"Aren't you ashamed to falsify reality in this way, to show things
that don't happen!" I told him that the only thing I falsified as far
as that character was concerned was that I had him drinking alcohol out of the bottle whereas, in fact, people in those days drank
the eau de vie from a bowl usually used in Fez for water. This
disguised the drink and gave the eau de vie a wooden, tarry taste.
I'd seen it with my own eyes and it doesn't make any sense to
conceal things that actually happened.

"RAW" HUMOR

K. Other transgressing scenes occur during the Hajj's search for a
husband for Houda. For example, when the Hajj suggests to the
butcher that perhaps he might like to do the good deed for just
one night, the butcher wants to know the quality of the flesh and
says that you can't just plant something, you also have to help it
fructify. A little later, the baker jokes with the Hajj's maid, saying
that he's able to tell what a woman is like just from the kind of
dough she sends to the oven and that he'd be happy to taste that
dough for one night if his own wife wasn't such a devil.

M. Yes, the humor there is certainly a bit raw. [Both laugh.] The
approaches to the butcher and the baker involve merchants whom
you see every day and who are likely to know what the score is
with a lot of people.

K. How did you work out these somewhat "raw" scenes with Farida
Benlyazid as the screenwriter and with Ahmed Tayyeb el-Alj
working on the dialogue?[28]

M. El-Alj, in particular, gave these scenes a lot more bite and weight.
He was able to spice it up quite a bit—he's very good on those
kinds of things. And then there were also some visual gestures
that were a bit vulgar that added to the humor.

THE "IDIOT" AND FAMILY ARROGANCE

K. One sequence, clearly meant to be funny but that I found less successful, revolves around the plan to get the mother of the neighborhood "idiot" [she is played by the well-known sociologist and feminist Fatima Mernissi, who is also of Fassi origin] to agree to marry her son to Houda for one night. Is this idea of the "idiot" just a bit of comic "business"?

M. No, it's part of our tradition. The aim, most of the time, is to find someone who's poor, who really needs the money—perhaps the baker at the oven, for example, or someone who's marginal, who can't in any case satisfy the material needs of a bourgeois woman.

The idiot, this retarded young man, would be an ideal candidate for the Hajj. First of all, he's not really going to know what to do with the woman and he's certainly not going to be able to keep her. That was always a danger, that the new husband might decide to keep his new wife! How many stories we heard in Fez of people who got married in these circumstances and then refused to divorce, or others who took advantage of the situation to extort money, perhaps a lot of money, before agreeing to divorce the woman! And then, of course, there were also cases where the new bride and groom found themselves very well matched indeed and decided to remain together. For the Hajj, the idiot is ideal.

K. Why does the mother refuse this marriage? Is she protecting her son's morality?

M. Yes she is, but there's more to it than that. First of all, to her mind Houda isn't good enough for her son because Houda supposedly hops around from roof to roof, so to speak. But also—and this brings out something that is characteristic of our city of Fez— there's a lot of family arrogance, a kind of superiority complex. Some Fassi families are so endogamous as a result of their superiority complex that they are passing on hereditary defects, but they refuse to take this into account. For this mother her son, be he an idiot or whatever, is the finest man on earth and she's very proud of him. What—have him marry, even provisionally, this shameless tart? "No way! This will stain the honor of my family," she says, "It's impossible!"

A quick word about shooting this scene: you know, Fatima is certainly used to audiovisual presentations, interviews and all that, but she's not used to rehearsing and having to repeat things three or four times. To relax her, we shot this scene in the house

Fatima Mernissi playing the "idiot's" mother

of her childhood, where she lived into adolescence. It was the house of her parents, and she may even have been born there.

HEMIPLEGIC HUMOR?

K. If the humor around the "idiot" left me a little uncomfortable, I was much more uncomfortable at the humor around Houda's hemiplegic father. Here, I wasn't even smiling, although I felt the film was calling upon me to laugh. What were you trying to do in these scenes?

M. All right. I understand your point of view—you don't think that the diminished physical state of a person calls for laughter. I fully agree with you. In these scenes I wasn't trying to generate laughter at the father's condition—he's in a pitiful state, has to ask for help when he urinates. He's something of a vegetable. So it's not funny at all.

K. But it was just that kind of transgression—when the father says he has to pee—that pulls laughter from the audience. This is what signaled to me that we were being called to laughter here.

M. Well, we're kind of trapped by the situation, because we're in a film that has been making us laugh. So we laugh when he says, "pee," and when he makes those somewhat grotesque motions, and at his manner of eating. But right after that, we realize that the situation's more serious, that he's hemiplegic. Then, we hold back our laughter, or at least that was my aim.

K. Did people laugh at these scenes?

M. Oh yes, they did. I don't know whether they laughed without ambivalence or whether, afterward, they realized they weren't supposed to continue laughing. But certainly, when you hear the word "pee," you laugh spontaneously, unconsciously.

K. You seem to be somewhat ambivalent yourself about these scenes.

M. Yes. Yes . . . yes. These are scenes that are meant to call forth laughter and pity at the same time.

But I should also say that there is a certain lack of feeling, or even nastiness, toward such things that sometimes comes out in our society. For example, take the case of Mongoloids. We no doubt have as many Mongoloids here as there are in Europe, but here you don't see them, they're kept out of sight. In Europe, you can see them in the streets, in the cafés, and so on. I've even seen some kids here throw stones at a Mongoloid—there is that kind of unprovoked nastiness that sometimes surfaces and that must have come to us from something in our childhood. It's true too with regard to the "village idiot," and almost every village has one: sometimes kids start throwing stones and otherwise mistreating him. In these scenes I was also referring to that phenomenon, even if I did it in a way that was drawing laughter within a rather tragic situation.[29]

In any case, these scenes are built on a kind of bi-emotionality: there's the comic dimension because we've been laughing throughout at a funny film, and then there's the affection I wanted us to have for this poor man. One of the illustrations of this is the moment when Houda says, "We have to get him a doctor," and her mother answers, "The only doctor who can help him is God," meaning that death is really the only release for this kind of suffering.

K. Yes, you feel their tenderness toward him. For example, when Houda comes home in the miniskirt and her mother says accusingly, "What's that you're wearing?"

M. And Houda answers, softly, "My father likes me like this."

K. And then they all embrace one another. There was a lot of tenderness that came out toward the end of this scene.

Fifth Motif: The Mixed Blessings of a Woman's Freedom
RACISM?

K. At first Houda seems to be enjoying her newfound freedom, but later her feelings become ambivalent. Shortly after leaving the Hajj, she and her friend Khadija had quite a good time ogling the men from the window, "this one has beautiful hair" or "that one is very handsome," and so on.

M. I'm glad you brought up this scene because I once showed the film in the United States or Canada—I'm not sure which—and the first question raised after the projection was from a woman who referred to this scene and said, "There's some racism in your film." I asked her where she saw this and she said, "When the girls are commenting on the men from the window, one says, 'How nice and tall and white and handsome that one is.' And the other answers, 'Look how brown and beautiful that other one is.' And the first responds, 'That one is the son of a slave.' " This is what the woman questioner objected to.

But this is a very plausible bit of dialogue in Morocco and doesn't have anything like the same connotation it might have for Americans, because the institution of slavery was very different in the two places. Here, a slave's children were fully integrated into the household whereas in the United States they lived apart, weren't recognized, remained slaves. Here, the son of a woman slave and the master was recognized as the master's son.

K. We could get into a very long discussion about this! You're not saying that Moroccan society is without racism, are you?

M. No, not at all. But it is of a very different nature here from what it is in the United States. Just as with humor, you need keys to understand racism—it's not the same from country to country.

HOUDA'S EXCURSION, SCREENWRITER'S AVERSION

K. Coming to the negative aspects of Houda's experience of "freedom," I'd like to ask you a little about her excursion with her friend Khadija to the café and their encounter with the young men. You told me that Farida Benlyazid, the screenwriter, was reluctant to write this scene.

M. You know, writing a screenplay is done in stages. I work in the following way: the screenwriter goes to work on a certain number of scenes and we meet once or twice a week to discuss them and move forward.

When we came to writing this scene at the café, I wanted the young men to show a certain kind of violence—not getting what they want from the women, they abandon them. But Farida said, "No, I'm not for this kind of violence, it has to happen differently." She wanted the guys to drive the women back to Fez.

This kind of thing happens every so often with a screenwriter, where he or she says, "No, no, I don't feel the scene like this." Usually, I say, "OK, just leave it for now," or "Write it the way you feel it." And then, later, I can still do it my way. The most important thing is not to get hung up on a scene. If the screenwriter doesn't feel the scene, that's perfectly normal. I can't say, "You *have* to feel the scene!" I say, "Write it as you feel it," or "Just go on to something else."

K. But taking this scene, where Farida says, "No, I don't feel it this way," what happened?

M. Farida already didn't like the idea of the guys taking the girls to the hotel café, intending to get them into bed. For her, that's just not proper, it's not the way things happen. But I really wanted this to be the place where Houda realizes what it's like to go out with men her age, many of whom are only thinking of that one thing. To my mind, we needed a strong scene to show this, to show that the guys will go so far as to punish the women by abandoning them.

As an aside, do you know that this scene has just cost me the sum of 3,000 DH [about $300], an amount I had to pay to a lawyer? The hotel brought suit against me, claiming that I had given the hotel a bad name by showing it this way in the film. The case didn't get settled until 1999, but I won it. I might have lost it if I hadn't hired the lawyer. [Laughs.]

K. Houda's attitude in this sequence is rather credulous. As the girls are leaving the hotel, she says she thought the guys had worthy intentions.

M. Yes, that's when Houda says to Khadija, "You see the kind of situation you got us into." Khadija answers, "But *you're* the one, it was *you* who wanted us to come here with them." And then Houda explains, "But I thought they had worthy intentions." Khadija looks at her in disbelief, "What, do you think guys like that are looking to get married? They're just looking to take advantage of you, that's all."

K. So, at the end of this sequence, Houda has understood.

M. Yes, she has. And this has helped change her attitude. These are the scenes that, for me, help justify her wanting to go back to the Hajj. Now she's seen what the external world is like, that it's full of people—and especially men her own age—who are thinking only of sex.

ACT FOUR: HOUDA'S ONE-NIGHT MARRIAGE, BUT THEN?

At long last, the Hajj finds a suitable candidate to marry Houda, a man home on vacation from his job in Belgium. The marriage is agreed and the entire celebration is held at the Hajj's expense. Attending the ceremony, the Hajj is laughed at from all quarters. No longer able to stand it, in another lapse of self-control he dismisses all the celebrants and then must himself be coaxed to leave while, in the neighboring bridal chamber, Houda prepares herself, smiling, for her new husband. The husband enters, he and Houda exchange some pleasantries, and he brings her to bed.

Meanwhile, the Hajj, at home, is again suffering, now like a spoiled child in a tantrum. His wives try to comfort him while pointing out that he is getting his just desserts, since he made them suffer something similar each time he brought a new wife home. Able to bear his pain no longer, the Hajj makes an early morning visit to the groom's home, hoping to wake the couple and retrieve Houda on the spot. But it is too early; he is chased away by the neighbors and returns to wait petulantly at home.

Back in the bridal chamber, husband and wife are sleeping contentedly side by side. Suddenly, a visitor enters the home, the husband wakes, leaves Houda, and the two men speak together in hushed tones. The husband has to flee Morocco for Belgium in great haste because an illegal scheme of his has been discovered and there is no time or thought for divorce. Before leaving, the new husband forbids his mother to open the door to anyone.

With the door to Houda's new home closed to all outsiders, the Hajj only learns a few days later of the husband's flight. Resourceful and determined to bring back the husband for a divorce and then to remarry Houda, the Hajj goes to the Belgian consulate for a visa, but his application is rejected. There now seems to be no hope. But, as the film ends, the Hajj, stubborn to the point of risking self-destruction, embarks on a small boat, in the crowded company of other men desperate to emigrate to Europe. As the journey begins, he gazes at the sea around him with a terrible fear in his eyes.

The Hajj is refused a visa for Belgium

Sixth Motif: Houda's Behavior—A New Morality?

THE IMMIGRANT GROOM'S ATTRACTION

K. I want to continue discussing Houda's behavior, but first, why is the Hajj so attracted to having the prospective husband be an immigrant worker?

M. Well, we live a lot here on gossip, on word of mouth, and it could be pretty awkward for the Hajj to have someone living in Fez and talking about this experience over and over again. This way, with the immigrant abroad and out of the way, the Hajj wouldn't have to worry about having someone saying, "Ah, I slept with so-and-so's wife and here's how it happened," and so on. For the Hajj the big advantage is that this guy will be with Houda merely for one night and then be out of the picture and won't be heard from again.

HOUDA'S "ONE-NIGHT STAND"

K. Coming back to Houda: here we see her marry a man for a night, give herself fully to it, and take some pleasure in it. How do you evaluate her behavior?

M. For her, this is something of a game. Also, it's like having an affair that, in addition to everything else, is fully approved. [Laughs.] There is even a sweet dialogue between the two of them. She lends herself to it, it's an adventure for her. And, she's allowed to do this by her true husband who is going to be taking her back.

K. Was one of the ideas behind these scenes to show the emergence of a new morality in a society that might now be taking sexual relations more lightly?

M. No, not at all. As I said to you, the Hajj has only one way to get Houda back—the knife is really at his throat, he has no other way to do it.

K. The knife may be at the Hajj's throat. But looking at Houda, at her way of participating in this process, of having sexual intercourse with a man she doesn't know, a one-night stand—she doesn't seem embarrassed or discomforted at all. She's quite pleased with the jewelry she's wearing, too.

M. But, as you well know, in a traditional marriage the woman has never met the man she marries, the man she will have children with. Houda's situation isn't all that different. The man takes the woman, it's often as simple as that, and that is what I was criticizing somewhat here. She has sexual intercourse the first time she encounters her new husband, in the same manner as many women do. That's just the way it's done. There was no engagement period, no time to get to know one another, no flirting or whatever. It was just straight ahead to the "Japanese flag," as we say.[30]

K. But the fact that it's only going to be for one night makes this somewhat different, doesn't it?

M. Well, this is what the Hajj has to go through, and it's what Houda has to go through too. She's had some experience now of the outside world, she's seen the aims young men have, and she's disappointed in all that. So she wants to return to the Hajj.

It's true that this may seem to be a reactionary idea: How can this young woman who has been singing of freedom now submit to this process and then return to the Hajj? This is a question I'm often asked. I explain her attitude, first of all, by her negative experience of the outside world. But I think it's also important to see this in relation to the poverty and misfortune in her own family and the illness of her father, all of which is very painful for her. This justifies her having married an old man when she herself was quite young. These are poor people—as the Hajj tells his colleague, "I met Houda when her mother came to sell her jewelry"—and she obviously went into this marriage to help her family survive.

With the Hajj she lives very well and is continually getting gifts from him, an idea that is reinforced when she returns home to her mother one evening to find that the Hajj has sent a thoughtful present for the family on the occasion of a religious holiday.

K. Yes, she seems quite affected by that.

M. Of course she is. She's seen the outside world, she's seen what the young men her age are like, and she's disenchanted, she's upset by the aggression she's witnessed and by this view of the woman as sexual object.

Seventh Motif: The Ending—From Dream to Reality

Houda's wish to return to the Hajj was clearly one of the reasons why this film has been called "conservative," and Tazi himself was among the first to call it that. I would come back to this question later, but first wanted to discuss the film's ending because the contrast between it and the rest of the film raises a number of questions about Tazi's views of the function of film and its source of power. Before approaching these more general questions it was necessary to look at the ending more closely.

THE TRAGEDY OF CLANDESTINE EMIGRATION

K. The ending is one of the few moments in the film where there is no comedy at all. Here, all of a sudden, we grow apprehensive at the fate of this man about to cross the Mediterranean in a small boat. He and the others in the boat are in great jeopardy and might perish. Why didn't you want this ending known to your crew and other collaborators until the completion of the shooting?

M. It's true that the ending is a sad one. It's also true that it is anachronistic and conflicts with the *entire* development of the film. I decided not to disclose this ending because I was afraid that the crew would start to discuss it and then perhaps challenge it. In fact, in the screenplay, the film ends with a freeze shot of the Hajj in front of the counter trying to get his visa for Belgium.

But when the shooting seemed over I said to everyone, "OK, now let's go and take a little trip north, to the Mediterranean." And that's where I took them to shoot the final scene, which no one had any inkling of. In fact, when I told the main actor, Bashir

Skiredj, that we had one more day of shooting, he wasn't enthusiastic and said, "All right, but what for?" When I explained the idea to him he was all for it and said, "Absolutely, let's do it."

In this ending I wanted to point to the problem of clandestine immigration, which is an almost daily occurrence and is absolutely horrible and tragic.[31] I'm sure Skiredj responded positively in part because we all share this problem of clandestine immigration, we all know that deaths occur almost every day as people try to cross the Mediterranean in these makeshift boats. We all knew about this even though it was a problem our press and television were keeping quiet—we knew because we could see it on Spanish television and read about it in the Spanish and French press. But here in Morocco total silence reigned on this issue. For me, this ending was a way of raising a problem that continues to haunt me even today. I have an enormous amount of documentation on this issue but when I went to the Moroccan television to see what they had in the archives, they had absolutely nothing, not one image. It was incredible, as though you could make the problem disappear by not dealing with it.

As I said to you, this was a film where I wanted to put in exactly what I wished. Another reason was that I didn't want to end my film without using the sea as signature.[32] This is one of the advantages of being my own producer, of not having someone else looking over my shoulder, saying, "Watch out, the sun's going down, watch out or we're going to have to pay overtime to people." This is one of the few problems that I haven't had to deal with, up until now at least!

This film was going to be *exactly* as I wanted it. No one was going to say, "Careful, this scene isn't going to please a lot of people. . . ." Actually, every so often some of the crew acted as censors, saying things like, "Watch out, people aren't going to like seeing the whiskey or wine bottle, or whatever." But I said, "That's OK, I'll assume the risk." And I'm glad I did. Because once you start with self-censorship you don't know where you're going.

COMIC VERSUS TRAGIC

K. This ending takes a film that has been rather atemporal in style—the entire story of Hajj Ben Moussa and his three wives could have taken place at almost any time—and resituates it fully in the present.

M. Exactly. We created the atemporality at the outset with the photo of Muhammad V but at the end of the film, when we raise the problem of clandestine immigration, we're right in the present. Public awareness of this problem really had to be sharpened.

K. I suppose it might have been difficult for a public that had been laughing in delight throughout the film to switch gears when the film's tone changed at the very end.

M. Yes, that was a problem. If we had ended on that fixed image, the audience would have been thinking, "So, now he's going to get a visa to try and track down his wife's husband? This guy is really nuts!" That would have been much truer to the spirit of comedy—in that spirit, the film could well have ended there.

There were even quite a few people laughing as the Hajj and the rest of them pushed the boat out to sea. The idea behind all this is indeed laughable—that after going to so much trouble to find a husband for Houda, that husband slips through the Hajj's fingers at the last moment. But at the very end, as the Hajj sets off in the boat, you quickly realize that this could become a voyage to death.

A SEQUEL IN MIND?

K. With the film ending as the Hajj embarks on a very dangerous voyage, the spectator can't help but wonder, "What is going to happen now—is he going to survive the passage? And if so, what then?" This certainly makes a very convenient starting point for the sequel that you would eventually make.

M. Yes, but as I've told you and said in many interviews, when making *Looking* I had absolutely no thought of a sequel nor of giving the audience the desire for a sequel.

K. How could you? After all, you couldn't know while making the film that it would be such an overwhelming success.

Interlude

Film's Power and Function

Looking's success would indeed lead to a sequel and to a host of problems we will be exploring in chapter 5. For now, the strong contrast in *Looking* between its overall comic tone and the specter of potential tragedy at the end made me wonder exactly what kinds of experiences Tazi wanted to give spectators and what were his more general notions about the power and function of film.

The "Magical," the "Real," and the Critical
POWERFUL MAGIC, REAL CONCERNS

"TO DREAM . . . IN DARKNESS"

K. What gives the cinema such power over us, why does the public spend a considerable amount of money, time, and energy, to go see a film? And why do you, the filmmakers, in view of all the difficulties you face, continue to try and make films?

M. First of all, I think there is a magical element in film: in the space of an hour and a half or two hours, a person can shed his or her daily concerns and plunge into a magical world. And we Orientals [Fr. *nous, les orientaux*]—even if this term isn't an exact one—really need that. When you look at India, which produces some five hundred to six hundred films a year, all consumed in the most natural way, like a habit, like our going to a café to have a morning cup of coffee with friends, you see how important it is to have this rupture from daily concerns. We all need to dream, in poor societies as well as in rich ones. The cinema brings you that: for a couple hours you disconnect from reality and you experience a love story, or a story in Roman times, or a Western, or whatever.

There is also the societal level. In some places perhaps the written word dominates and literature has a great impact on people—for example, when I'm in the Metro in Paris or New York, everyone is reading something. But here in Morocco the audiovisual dominates. If I get into a bus or train hardly anyone is reading. Even if someone is holding a newspaper he or she tends to be doing the crossword puzzle. But if you're in a café or a tea room with a TV, absolutely everyone will be watching the TV—no one will be in conversation or playing a board game, or anything like that. With television, images have become part of our daily lives, and even in countries where the written word is important the audiovisual is playing a larger and larger role.

But, of course, there is a significant difference between TV and the movies. It's not the contrast between nonfiction and fiction, because even on TV somewhere between 70 percent and 80 percent of programs are fiction. The difference lies in the actual nature of the experience. In the early days of TV, the family gathered around, the light was dimmed, and you were very attentive. Now everyone does his or her own thing while the TV is on and perhaps, at a certain moment, it might attract your attention. In the theater you see a film in isolation, in darkness, projected in two dimensions, with all your attention focused on the screen, an experience that plays out in the individual's unconscious. That's what makes film magic so powerful and that's the big distinction between cinema and TV.

"YOU CAN RAISE ALL THESE QUESTIONS WITHOUT MAKING IT EXPLICITLY POLITICAL"

K. When you make a film, what kind of feeling are you trying to arouse in the spectator?

M. I want to put every spectator in the same magical mood I was in as a child when my aunt or grandmother told us stories. These stories always dealt with our lives, our history—they carried a certain Moroccan essence. Some of the stories were very troubling, like when our Dada—our governess—told us how she had been a slave, how she had been kidnapped and sold to a bourgeois family in Fez. We listened very closely and felt a lot of compassion for the storyteller. We also began to understand something of the problems of slavery, racism, and so forth. When I think back to all the stories and tales these women told, how they conveyed their lives to us, I think the stories could all be turned into screenplays, they could all become films! So, I'd like every spectator to be simultaneously in a magical and in a real world, to find him- or herself in front of a Moroccan film that has a Moroccan story that he or she can identify with.

K. I see the "magical" part very well, but what kind of "real" do you want in your films?

M. First of all I want to recount, through images and sounds, stories that are part of my society—even the most banal stories, stories that everyone knows and is familiar with. This is a way to preserve them and this is what our identity, our heritage, is composed of. Identity and heritage—these are the ideas that most preoccupy me now. With globalization and standardization, we're in the process of losing everything related to our identity. Perhaps, thanks to image and sound, we'll be able to preserve the memory of these things so that we can return to them, even if only as nostalgia.

Second, I want to put into my films the issues that deeply concern me. In my fourth film, the sequel to *Looking,* I took on a problem that really disturbs me, the problem of "boat people," of illegal immigration. Some of the extras I used had actually tried to emigrate once or even several times, and they all assured me that the next time they had the opportunity they would try to do so again. When you hear their experiences, you have to ask, "Why do all these people want to leave? What's the nature of their malaise—is it political, social, religious, economic? Is there repression? Is it because there's no democracy?" Then you start to appreciate that it isn't with a magic wand labeled *"l'Alternance,"* in quotes, that things will change. The problems go much too deep for that.[1]

In a film you can raise all these questions without making it explicitly political, and you can help people become aware of reasons for not leaving our country, of the need to do something here. This can all become a film's theme but in a film, obviously, you have to dress the theme with a plot, a love story, and things like that.

FILM AS SOCIAL CRITICISM

"SOCIOLOGICAL" OR "SOCIALLY CRITICAL" CINEMA?

K. In *Looking for My Wife's Husband* there is a very strong tension between the "magical" aspect and the realism of the very end. During the entire film we have been charmed into a dreamlike state but, at the end, with the Hajj Ben Moussa risking his life in a boat, we are rudely awakened, the real takes over from the dream.

Which leads me to ask you: What kind of films are you trying to make? Your other three films have a very strong critical vision and address what we might call "societal problems." Should we see *Looking for My Wife's Husband* as a small detour, a film that mostly satisfies our dreams, in a career marked by films that have largely tried to demystify dreams?

M. I suppose it is possible to look at it that way. You know, you can make a film that is situated within the limits of a certain daily social reality but then you fall into the difficulties of a sociological cinema, one of them being that, even while you're making the film, reality may leave you behind because it changes so quickly.

K. To what extent, then, do you want your films to work as a critique of society?

M. Of course, one often has the aim of criticizing aspects of society and I'm an activist in support of certain general principles—democracy, human rights, things like that. But, at the same time, I don't think an artist, a creator, ought to have, so to speak, a political party card. Militancy within a political party limits one's field of vision, it means putting on blinkers and seeing only what one's ideology or political concepts allow. Becoming a political militant, or a militant for one ideology or another, always involves a rather limited selection from the vast variety of visions that an individual has available and makes it difficult to form a somewhat objective view of reality. In this way, it limits your freedom to criticize things, which is something you have to keep.

"ATEMPORALITY" AND SOCIAL CRITICISM

K. Isn't there a tension and perhaps even a contradiction between a "magical" cinema and a socially critical cinema? Doesn't a magical cinema tend to infantilize the spectator, whereas a socially critical cinema tries to raise the spectator's consciousness?

M. This is where a technique like "atemporality" comes in, as I used it in *Looking*. "Atemporality" means taking something that is happening today and situating it in a rather timeless period, allowing you to be critical but not in too obvious a way. In fact, that's one of the best ways to be socially critical—to adopt some historical distance with regard to the present.

For example, I'm now working on the screenplay of a story that takes place in the fourteenth and fifteenth centuries, and the author put the events at this remove in order to have more freedom of expression. Of course this technique isn't at all new: there are La Fontaine's fables, the works of Ibn al-Muqaffa', and so on.[2] There, already, you had the techniques of substituting an animal for a person or of placing things in the past so you could adopt a more critical stance.

K. Was there any other way in which this "atemporality" enabled a critical approach?

M. Well, it also allowed me to highlight the fact that Morocco lives at two different speeds. There are those who, like the weavers, the tanners, and so on, live at the speed of traditional Morocco; then there are those who live the rhythm of modern life—like the guys who pick up Houda and her friend in their car and take them to the hotel. You can also see this contrast in the difference between the lives of the women in the Hajj's house and the lives of the grown daughter and her husband: the daughter is a doctor who's always rushing to see patients and her husband's always running off to meet clients. This is an observation, not a critique.

But there is a critical aspect in that "atemporality" helped me to present an intermediate phase, exemplified in the very modest home of Houda's parents, with its television set—something, by the way, that you don't find in the Hajj's wealthy residence within the city walls. I wanted to use these scenes in Houda's parents' home to criticize our national media. On one level, the state channel isn't good enough even for the hemiplegic—he's trying to capture a foreign station. On a second level, in juxtaposing watching TV and being hemiplegic, I'm suggesting that we may all become hemiplegic from watching too much television with its distorted and impoverished images from either here or abroad.

K. The hemiplegic metaphor, here, sounds similar perhaps to our American term "couch potato."

M. That's right. There are quite a few notes like that in the film, but they haven't always been detected by viewers or critics.

K. What about using humor as a critical weapon? The humor around the hemiplegic father had a critical function. Did the humor in the film have a broader critical purpose—for example, ridiculing the polygamist as a way to criticize patriarchal society?

M. No, I don't think so. After all, the film only talked about the ridiculous situation of that particular man, it didn't attack the foundations of patriarchal society. In fact, men haven't seen my use of Hajj Ben Moussa's ridiculous situation as a challenge to the role and power of men. Also, I think many men recognize that, although we live in a patriarchal society, in a household where there are a number of women it's often more like a matriarchy. [Laughs.]

Dignity, Identity, and Heritage

DIGNITY AND "CONSTRUCTIVE NOSTALGIA"

CONSERVATISM AND DIGNITY

K. On occasion you have described *Looking* as "fundamentally conservative," saying that the film's success was due, in part, to its not calling things into question, to its showing people what they wanted to see.

M. Yes, that's true. First of all, the Moroccan is conservative. But there are different types of conservatism. For example, one can be a nostalgic conservative, hearkening back to the great Islamic civilization in Andalusia. In general, the Moroccan is the sort of conservative who can tolerate criticism in many areas, but be careful, because there are limits beyond which one must not go; one must not be *too* critical of society. We are still a pretty sensitive community. People have a sense of humor, you can make fun of someone—mock his frugality, for example—and as long as this stays relatively dignified and under control, there will be no reaction. But just go one step further—attack his dignity, offend his pride—and he'll react, and very nastily too.

That was sort of my thermometer. You have to know at what moment to stop making fun of someone. Let me take an example from the film. When Hajj Ben Moussa comes back from the livestock market and finds his wife Houda behaving like Dulcinea in front of the deliveryman, he throws a fit. But, at the same time, we stay within the limits of humor—he begins to count the sheep and counts himself among them because he too has horns, he's a cuckold. Then, referring to Houda, he yells out, "Look at her, look how naked she is," whereas she's dressed in an absolutely appropriate manner. So we're still within the limits of the ridiculous. If we went past that, it's true that the film might have been taken as a direct attack on the patriarchal system.

This is why the notion of dignity is so important. First of all, if you lose that dignity, you run the risk of offending people's sensibilities too deeply. For example, if I wasn't concerned about dignity, I might have focused on another solution to the problem of the third repudiation, one that is not very widely known and that I think has never been practiced, although it is found in our traditions. In this solution, the husband who wants his divorced wife back but doesn't want her to go through marriage to another man must himself come to the mosque on a Friday, completely naked, and walk from one end of it to the other, so that everyone will see him. To humiliate yourself in this way means that your word no longer has any value. For the rest of your life you would be called *safih*, someone who's shameless and of no account.[3]

K. I guess we can see why this isn't practiced. And also why you wouldn't want to film it. [Both laugh.]

EMIGRATION, THE LURE OF TELEVISION,
AND "CONSTRUCTIVE NOSTALGIA"

M. There's another reason why I'm insisting on the notion of dignity, a reason related to the problem of emigration. There are a lot of people in Morocco who see nothing of value here, who accuse the country of all sorts of ills. Some of the surveys that have been done are astonishing, showing an overwhelming majority of people between the ages of 18 and 25 wanting to emigrate.[4]

Obviously, one of the big reasons for this feeling of rejection is that people succumb to the inviting lure of television [Fr. *la télévision, ce miroir aux alouettes*] and completely lose their bearings. After all, the West that you see on the TV is not the real West at all, but the TV presents it in such a way that it is natural for people here to think of leaving. That's the tragedy of it. And for me this rejection constitutes a dramatic problem.

Now, this rejection goes along with a lack of knowledge of the country and its heritage. How, then, to get people to love their own country again? For me, the way to do this is to enter into what I call a "constructive and positive nostalgia." This involves showing what we were like. What were our daily lives like? What was it like to live in an Arab-style house? What kinds of furniture did we have? What sorts of relationships existed between people? This is different from the nostalgic dreaming I mentioned earlier, a dreaming that brings us nothing.

K. Can we see your attempt to get people laughing in *Looking*, to put them in a mood of "constructive, positive nostalgia," as a way of making people aware that there are already many things in their lives, in their milieu, that they are very attached to? Leaving the country would mean leaving these things behind.

M. That's right. When I made *Looking*, I took a lot of pleasure not only in telling stories from my own past but also in looking for a house that reflected the home of my memory. It took me a long time to find an appropriate house. Then, because the house that we did find was unoccupied and empty, I had to put a lot of effort into finding the right furniture, item by item, objects like those of that era. And we also had to find items that I had known in my childhood—the phonograph, for example.

Just a few days ago I was speaking with some young people and I mentioned the ember brazier [Ar. *el-kebrata*]. They had absolutely no knowledge of it. We used the ember brazier before we had all these electrical appliances—when you had an infant at home whose diapers had to be washed very frequently, we'd build a kind of reed dome over the brazier during the bad weather and spread out the wet diapers on it. It worked wonderfully. Now this object has completely disappeared, and not because it would no longer be useful.

That's why the notion of heritage is coming to play a larger and larger role in my convictions. Every day I see more and more of our heritage disappearing, completely eclipsed in this wave of standardization and universalization. And it's a standardization that originates exclusively in the rich countries with the simple aim of finding consumers. This means that plastic destroys the person who makes the special bowls and spoons we use for Ramadan, destroys the guy who makes the beautiful inlaid wooden buckets [Ar. *qraqeb*] in our *ḥammam*s. These wooden buckets, and also the bath shoes that had a strip of leather so we wouldn't slip on the wet floors, are objects that date from the Roman period;

I've seen them in collections of Roman objects. These were things
we used every day, for us they were nothing special at all.

There are very many items that you can't find at all anymore.
Some of this, I should add, has to do with tourism, because Moroccans sometimes sell their own decorated windows and doors
to tourists, to say nothing of silk tissue and so on. Well, if we can't
keep our own objects on hand any longer, at least we can keep a
memory of them in a film!

K. Did you find hunting for all those objects you used in *Looking* an
enjoyable part of the project?

M. Well, on the whole I had a lot of fun with that film. But I also
suffered a lot. Shooting in the winter wasn't easy—it was cold
enough to freeze a duck in that house in Fez, so cold that we
didn't call it the "set" or the "house," we'd say, "Let's go over to
the icebox." [Both laugh.] And then I had a lot of conflict with
the main actor, as you know. And we had a terrible problem with
some defective film.[5]

All in all, making *Looking for My Wife's Husband* was a tremen-
dous amount of work, but I was fully convinced of the need for
it, because we have to impress these things on our memory.

IDENTITY, HERITAGE, AND
THE MOROCCAN MOSAIC

IDENTITY AND HERITAGE

K. One of the ways individuals as well as peoples respond to what is
called "globalization" is by looking for points of attachment in
their own particular environments, their own immediate daily experiences, their own, shall we say, "identity." This issue is clearly
one of your central concerns. How do you conceive of notions like
identity and heritage?

M. First of all, there is a general context: here in Morocco, today's
consumer of films or other audiovisual forms is so sick of all that
comes from abroad, of this surfeit of images of the other, that
there's a real rejection of these and a very strong desire, on the
part of all generations, to look at what belongs to us, to our own
region. In this situation, it's not at all surprising to see the Moroccan spectator's growing interest in Moroccan films and to ob-
serve the audience turning back to our national channels in spite

of their rather mediocre content. This desire to return to one's own identity isn't peculiar to Morocco but is an international phenomenon—you find it in central Europe, in the Basque country, and many other places. I would say it's a necessary desire, given that we're all moving toward a certain standardization with great speed.

When I speak of heritage, then, I'm thinking of the objects, expressions, words, that are disappearing daily and that constitute our particularity.

NOT STEREOTYPES, NOT FETISHES, BUT "PARTICULARITIES"

K. You say you want to emphasize heritage, but you've also said you want to avoid stereotypical scenes. For example, in *Looking* there is talk about a circumcision but the circumcision ceremony isn't shown in the film. Wouldn't that be part of the heritage you're talking about? Did you intend to film such a scene?

M. No, never! Those are the kinds of scenes that I won't show because they've been so fetishized and shown to death in films—the scenes where a chicken or ram is slaughtered, or where henna is put on, or where a child is circumcised, or a funeral cortege passing—I'm really fed up with scenes of that sort.

K. So, for you, that's not "heritage"?

M. Heritage, for me, has to do with our daily lives, but it must not become a kind of fetish for the West. We've had enough of that!

K. When you name the objects that are part of the heritage, you're usually referring to well-defined entities such as words, expressions, objects, and so on. I've heard some people speak of a sort of "Moroccan-ness" of spirit, of mentality. Does your notion of heritage encompass that?

M. Hold on—I was speaking of *particularities*. A word like "Moroccan-ness" is rather overblown and implies a "specificity," a general "uniqueness" that all Moroccans share. I wouldn't go that far. Remember that Morocco is a mosaic, a mosaic of Berbers, Africans, and Arabs, and fortunately all these elements have contributed to our language, to our society, and so on. That mosaic, that mixing, has brought us enormous richness. If you want to talk of "Moroccan-ness" then it's this ensemble: we start from Berber society; we then mix in Arabs, who were almost all men and who came largely as horsemen; then add the returning populations from Andalusia; and augment this with people coming north from south of the Sahara, from Senegal for example.

There are so many different strata of society in Morocco and many different civilizations. This mosaic and this history is a great treasure and leads to certain particularities. I can see such particularities, for example, when I'm in the High Atlas Mountains and I encounter a way of living, a way of viewing things very different from what we find in the Gharb.[6] That ensemble of particularities constitutes our heritage but it doesn't make up what you might call a Moroccan "specificity." In any case, it's very difficult to speak of a "specificity" now that we're all part of what some people like to call the "global village."

FILMING HERITAGE, CONVEYING WORTH

K. How do you express this heritage in films—do you have any guiding principles here?

M. In the first place, it means that when I tell a story, even of a minor event, I'm not going to tell it like Agatha Christie would, I'm going to tell it in another way because all my narration will take into account the context in which we find ourselves.[7]

There are two other things to keep in mind here. On the one hand, people pay their money to go to the movies because they want to see a film that's close to them, that has images that are familiar to them, and they also want to dream and enter into a story that transports them. On the other hand, many people now won't pay money to look in the mirror and see still more of the misery they see around them every day—for decades our films were more sociological than anything else and were set in poor, rural, wretched contexts.

As a result, it seems certain, today, that the Moroccan public is very keen to see images that concern them *and* give them worth. "Worth" is the key word. The public wants images that give them worth—they may be images that criticize society, but this criticism should only go so far. That's why I talk of "positive nostalgia" and that's why we have to hammer away at the notion of heritage. This is the concern that haunts me—how to express, every time I have the chance, the worth of our heritage, and how to do this in a context where many people are devaluing it.

You know, we have our own celebrations, extraordinary ones, that are equivalent to Christmas, to Easter, but people don't know about them. It's all disappearing quickly and being replaced by things that have their roots in the West.[8] Here we are in a society undergoing transformation, a transformation that is speeding up with this emphasis on a new world order and globalization. But to be part of the globalizing trend you have to bring something to it, and we won't be able to bring anything to it if we've lost all knowledge of our own heritage. In that case, we'll be confined to the role of pure consumers of what others bring to it.

Chapter Two

Building the National Cinema, Building a Career

Introduction: Revisiting the Past

Tazi was in secondary school and not yet 14 years old when Morocco regained its independence in 1956 after forty-four years of French (and in some areas Spanish) colonial rule.[1] Twenty-five years later, in 1981, as he was approaching the age of 40 and had just finished his first feature film, the Moroccan political system was centered on a strong monarchy, albeit one that had weathered several serious, almost fatal threats to its existence just a decade earlier. These decades saw the training abroad of a number of Moroccans in several basic film specialties and established a foundation, precarious though it was, for the institutionalization of film production. It took until the late 1960s—more than ten years after independence—for Morocco to produce its first feature film, and it was not until the 1980s began that film production gained the systematic, if limited, state financial support necessary to ensure continuity. It is with an overview of these early decades of Moroccan independence and Moroccan filmmaking that we will open this chapter, before we turn to Tazi's experiences during this period.

We have seen how autobiographical Tazi's *Looking for My Wife's Husband* was, how his attachment to memory and his emphasis on the importance of heritage and on bringing into adulthood traces of childhood were prime creative sources. One might even argue that this autobiographical perspective, encouraging what Tazi called "constructive and positive nostalgia," was just as central to the film's great success as setting it in the bourgeois milieu in Fez and giving it the very strong dose of humor. We will begin tracing Tazi's own career by taking this autobiographical lead and going back with him into his childhood, in search of some of the memories that, at least as he sees them retrospectively, may have influenced his decision to learn film-making and his approach to it. We will then follow him as he studies in Paris, works for a number of years at the CCM (part of the time as director of the weekly news review shown at theaters throughout the country), and plays a key role in making *Weshma* (*Traces*, 1970), con-ventionally taken to be the first authentically Moroccan full-length fiction film. Finally we will place Tazi's first feature film, made in 1981 as state financial support for production was instituted, in the context of Moroccan filmmaking of that time, preparing us for the interlude in which we discuss the film in some detail.

Morocco and Moroccan Cinema: The First Decades of Independence

MOROCCO: REBUILDING THE NATION

At independence in 1956, Morocco emerged from a period of more than four decades of colonial rule, during which resistance had been violently repressed, the best agricultural land had been appropriated by the colonizers, key Moroccans were objects of assassination attempts, French (or Spanish) administrative practices were imposed throughout the country, and ethnic and class differ-ences were deliberately sharpened by colonial policy (with the ironic result that these groups then often came together in their struggle against the common oppressor). To recover from what France liked to call its "civilizing mission" was, for the newly independent nation, no simple task. The country then had a population of approximately ten million, of which about one-quarter was urban, and which suffered from a glaring lack of education, an absence of vocational training, poor health care, and widespread poverty.[2]

In rebuilding the nation-state it was not only important to provide basic social services and infrastructure—schools, hospitals, roads, training for administrators and other specialties—but on the political level the institutions of power and administration had to be installed and routinized. King Muhammad V, a man who had been widely revered and had served as an effective personification of the independence struggle, ruled over independent Morocco for half a decade and upon his death in 1961 was succeeded by his son, King Hassan II, who was to reign for almost four decades, in a system where the palace retained almost all political power. Just as his father had (and as his son who followed him would), Hassan II claimed both a religious and political legitimacy: on the one hand, he was a descendant of the Prophet Muhammad and recognized as "commander of the faithful"; on the other, he continued the political rule that the Alawite line had exercised in Morocco continuously since the seventeenth century.

Over the first twenty-five years of independence, the Moroccan political system successfully weathered a number of storms, the most threatening of which occurred in the early 1970s when Hassan II barely survived two assassination attempts. Throughout these first decades there were periodic outbursts of popular unrest, and political repression into the early 1980s was very severe. The main external threat involved recurring tensions between Morocco and its immediate neighbor to the east, Algeria. A few months after Algerian independence in 1962, a six-month border war between the two countries broke out and tensions continue today over the Western Sahara, an area that Morocco recovered from Spain in 1976 but where an independence movement headed by the Polisario Front has received consistent Algerian support.[3]

By 1981, King Hassan's rule and government institutions were solid. The social fabric often showed strain as when, in June 1981, discontent with living standards and trade union demonstrations triggered mass protests and a violent reaction by the police and army led to more than six hundred demonstrators being killed in Casablanca. Similar unrest occurred in 1984, with many fewer killings. Around the same time, religious movements were gaining force. However serious these challenges have been over the following decades, they have not called into question the stability of the regime nor have they constituted serious threats to the fabric of society.

MOROCCAN CINEMA FROM INDEPENDENCE UNTIL 1980

Some of the events just described had a direct impact on the film sector in Morocco: when Egypt took Algeria's side in

its border war with Morocco, Morocco boycotted Egyptian film imports and these never recovered their earlier importance on theater
programs; in the assassination attempt on King Hassan at his palace
in Skhirat in July 1971, the director of the CCM was among the more
than fifty people killed.

On a more general level, where did cinema fit into national development policy? We saw in chapter 1 that, for the state, the feature
film sector did not figure in its plans at all and importing, distribution,
and screening were left completely in private hands, resulting in a
continuation of the pattern established in the colonial period—feature
films showing in the theaters were foreign-made films. With the film
sector having no role to play in the development program, Moroccan
feature film production was not on the agenda.

The state may not have been interested in the feature film over
most of the first twenty-five years of independence, but it was very
interested in various specialized film genres and continued to support
the CCM, a state institution founded by the French in 1944 to administer and control film production. The CCM produced educational
and informational films for the general population (promoting, for
example, health and agricultural programs), documentaries presenting
the achievements of the country or of certain ministries, tourist promotion shorts, and, very importantly, the news reviews that were distributed to theaters throughout the country on a weekly basis and
that constituted, for many spectators, the most popular part of a film
program. Many of the shorter films of an educational sort were shown
not only in theaters but were distributed via film buses (Fr. *ciné-bus,
ciné-caravanes*) into the most remote corners of the country and shown
on screens set up in open air, as had been done during the Protectorate
years. On the margins of these productions there was some limited
room for filmmakers to make short fiction films. At independence the
CCM was the main pole of employment for those trained in film and
it continued in this role for several decades, with Moroccan television
providing another pole starting in the early 1960s.[4]

Meanwhile, the profit-oriented components of the film sector expanded considerably, with film distribution, numbers of theaters, and
attendance increasing almost without interruption up until the early
1980s. In 1956 Morocco had 156 theaters, attended by more than
eighteen million spectators; by 1981, with a population that had doubled to twenty million, 40 percent of which was urban, the number
of spectators exceeded forty-five million and a year later the number
of theaters reached 251. These last figures have turned out to be the

highest ever attained in Morocco, despite the fact that both the total population and its urban portion have continued to grow.[5]

Although the numbers of theaters and filmgoers were increasing, Moroccan feature film production was very slow to start. In 1956, Morocco had only three formally trained film directors, all of whom were working at the CCM, and it was not to produce a commercial feature film until 1968.[6] Over a period of more than two decades, from independence in 1956 through 1979, Morocco produced fewer than twenty feature films, whereas Tunisia—a country with one-third Morocco's population—produced about twenty-five and Algeria, with a population comparable to Morocco's but independent only since 1962, produced more than forty.

When Moroccan feature film production finally did begin in the late 1960s, the first three productions were a response to two basic needs, neither of which had much to do with the creative impulse of the filmmakers themselves.[7] The three films, all clear imitations of Egyptian melodrama, were, on the one hand, an attempt to satisfy a demand for Egyptian films that had been unmet since the stopping of Egyptian film imports in the early 1960s. Second, and perhaps more importantly, these three films (for which the CCM was producer or co-producer) were all planned and made to give Morocco something to show at two film festivals the country organized, the first in Tangiers in 1968 and the second in Rabat in 1969.[8]

What can we say about broader Moroccan film culture during this period, above and beyond the fact that it was strongly, perhaps indelibly marked by the predominance of imported films? It is clear that by the late 1960s the general attitude toward Moroccan filmmaking was changing, on the part of both filmmakers themselves and the film-oriented public. The feature film *Weshma* (*Traces*, Hamid Bennani, 1970) was hailed as a breakthrough in Moroccan filmmaking, for reasons we will come to shortly, and was the cooperative effort of a short-lived production group, Sigma 3, which Tazi co-founded with several classmates from IDHEC. After *Weshma*, the 1970s saw a good number of films (in a rather small corpus overall) attempting to root expression in Moroccan culture rather than in imitations.[9]

Starting in the late 1960s and into the 1970s some portions of the Moroccan public began to show a serious interest in Moroccan films, with membership in film clubs expanding and publications giving greater space to Moroccan cinema. Film clubs had started during the 1940s, within the community of colonizers. At independence, these clubs continued to be dominated by the French colonial community, reinforced by a new group of French residents in Morocco ("*les coop-érants*") who appeared on the scene with a number of French technical and cultural assistance programs. However, by the late 1960s Moroccan membership and leadership was coming to the fore. The year 1973 marked a turning point, with the film clubs gaining the dynamic leadership of film critic and activist Noureddin Sail, who held the presidency until 1982.[10] The film clubs constituted a space where discussion of cultural matters could be tied to the political situation and the film clubs participated in the heightened political militancy of the late 1960s and the 1970s.

Meanwhile, publications began to devote more attention to film. Already in 1966, the review *Souffles* had published a roundtable discussion on Moroccan cinema in which ten of the most important figures in the Moroccan film system took part and addressed many of the basic problems that were still relevant twenty years later, and that, in some areas, are still relevant today.[11] Nineteen seventy saw the birth of the first periodical devoted entirely to cinema, *Cinéma 3*, under the direction of Noureddin Sail and situating itself, in its own words, "as part of the process of demystification and theoretical and practical reinvention of film language."[12] Although short lived (only four issues were produced, between January and December 1970), it was an important sign of the public's growing interest in cinema and it was one of a number of cultural reviews that appeared (and disappeared) over the decade. As well, Noureddin Sail had for some years a regular television program that discussed films.

These positive developments notwithstanding, as the 1970s ended the very idea of Moroccan feature film production was problematic— only one feature was produced in the final year of the 1970s, only five over the decade's final three years. There was still no training available in Morocco for filmmakers and, by the end of the 1970s, fellowships to support study abroad had practically ceased, with the result that "self-training or training in the form of internships during the shooting of films became the only possibility for training."[13]

By the end of the 1970s, with feature film production almost at a standstill, the situation was critical. Professional groups of filmmakers, although occasionally coming together to meet and make recommendations, were not able to act with sufficient force to get their resolutions implemented.[14] A number of filmmakers were now engaged primarily in other activities—making advertising spots, documentaries, television shows, working on foreign productions. Nor had Moroccan film distribution problems been solved. Of the eight films produced from 1970 to 1976, only one received a commercial release and was counted a great commercial success for a Moroccan film, although only an estimated thirty-four thousand people saw it.[15] The distribution situation had not improved by the late 1970s. As the director of one of the most lauded films of the period remarked, referring to two other filmmakers, "Will we be condemned forever to do as Farida Benlyazid and Jilali Ferhati did: rent the theater ourselves, go from street to street in Tangiers in a car with a loudspeaker, and then see 9,000 spectators desperate to see a Moroccan film fill the theater for a full week, watching a film that makes no compromise to commercial tastes?"[16]

Yet, during this critical period, Bouanani notes that "public awareness was becoming more and more acute, press articles more frequent, questioning the existence and the legal foundations of the national cinema; impassioned debates, often unruly, within the various associations and professional groups, were demonstrating that the film sector was no longer a matter of indifference."[17]

In these volatile circumstances—volatile at least for the small world of people passionately concerned with Moroccan film—state financial aid for Moroccan productions was finally introduced in 1980. It was at the very outset of this period of state aid that Tazi directed his first feature film—a film whose screenplay and production were assured by none other than Noureddin Sail. From that time on, Morocco's rate of production increased significantly, although with great inconsistency in number and quality.[18]

From Hope through Disillusion to a First Feature: The First Decades of a Career

Once Tazi decided to study filmmaking and managed to succeed in the various preliminary examinations, he went to Paris to learn his craft, for there was no training available then for filmmakers in Morocco (nor is there today). In 1964 he finished his studies and returned to Morocco to begin his career working at the CCM. Two key experiences in these first decades mark both Tazi's career and the development of Moroccan cinema. The first was his participation in the founding of the filmmaking cooperative that produced *Weshma,* which many take as the film that marks the birth of the Moroccan national cinema; the second, some ten years later, involved directing his own first feature, *The Big Trip*, the timing of which coincided with the beginning of state aid for film production. Our first step in following these years more or less chronologically will take us into the deeper past, as we explore Tazi's childhood and family life and the experiences that led him toward cinema.

FAMILY: "THE NEED TO COMMUNICATE"

FIRST SON; "WONDERFUL MEMORIES"; "ALL KINDS OF GAMES"

K. Could you describe for me the kind of family you grew up in?

M. I have an older sister who never went to school; then, twelve years later, I was born; and I have two younger sisters and a brother, all of whom went to school and then to university. I was sort of the bridge between the older and younger.

In this family unit I was the eldest son, and what made this even more true was the long period between my elder sister's birth and mine, during which my mother had great difficulties and numerous miscarriages. She must have believed she would never have another child. And then I came along, twelve years after my sister. My father also had another son—my half-brother—who is much older than I am, probably about 80 by now. He didn't live with us for very long because he was very close in age to my mother, whom my father had married when she was 15 years old.

To really understand my family you have to know a little more about the context. My family—an extended family—had its main residence in Fez. My grandfather was the one who had amassed our family's large property holdings. At the beginning of the century and during the First World War, he had made a great deal of money as a meat wholesaler, exporting meat to Europe. With this money he began to buy land in the Gharb, which has the richest land in all of Morocco and which, of course, was the land most desired by the French in those first years of colonial rule. For the French my grandfather constituted just the kind of competition they wanted to eliminate, and they tried to eliminate him, to physically eliminate him. They didn't succeed, but they did assassinate his brother who was his business associate and resembled him physically—one night, while he was asleep, they shot him dead.

As children we knew little of this history. But we knew we had a very large family and we all have some wonderful memories from this. For example, every year at the beginning of July, at the time of the grain harvest, we would leave Fez to go spend the summer with my grandfather on his large estate in Sidi Slimane, about 100 km from Fez. The entire family went—we made up a caravan of about ten automobiles, and we'd stop every couple of hours to rest and picnic, so it would take us a full day to make the trip. With all the cousins, male and female, we were very numerous and there were always enough of us to make up two football teams—we played all kinds of games. Although I should say that some of our games, as I mentioned when talking about *Looking,* manifested a kind of infantile cruelty.

K. Could you give me an example?

M. One that I remember very well—even though it's a bit gruesome to talk about—had to do with sparrows. Sparrows were a terrible nuisance, they'd eat the grain in the fields, and our parents encouraged us to destroy them. So, while our parents would take their afternoon nap, we would climb up the eucalyptus trees and we'd gather the little infant sparrows—they were no more than little balls of feathers and couldn't move or fly or anything. We'd gather them, and lay them out in a line on the road, waiting for a car to come. We called this "the machine gun game," after the sound made as the car crushed them. For us, these sparrows had to be destroyed and it was best to destroy them at the very beginning, while they were still in the nest when we could catch them. Now, when I think of it, it's a horrendous sort of cruelty.[19]

SON AND FATHER

K. What sort of relationship did you have with your father?

M. Well, as I said, I felt like his first son. But my relationship with him was a very distant one, which is a pity, because I never benefited from all his knowledge. For example, I used to see him with an astrolabe, calculating what seemed to me something about an eclipse, or something else, but I never was able to benefit from this.

K. This sort of distant relationship between father and son is rather normal in Morocco, isn't it?

M. Yes, absolutely. It was a very distant relationship. But in our social class, with our high standard of living, with all sorts of material benefits, you could imagine that this might be otherwise. After all, he wasn't the kind of father who works in the fields all day and then comes home so beat all he can do is sleep. But, just the same, the relationship was a very distant one.

My father's life was full of all kinds of rituals. He used to listen to the news on the radio—of course, this was before independence—and he listened to it as a ritual. And then there was the ritual of cleaning his rifle; there was the ritual of cleaning, greasing, and setting the clock; the ritual of working on the generator to give us electricity; the ritual of hunting; the ritual of going to the weekly market—the *suq*—every Wednesday. And the ritual of going to school: because we lived quite a distance from the village, we went to school in a horse-drawn carriage, a true English style carriage, with driver, bells, and all that. [Laughs.] My father hated automobiles! Colonization was in full flow at this time, our lands were in one of the richest regions of Morocco, and we had the colonizers all around us. Living in the middle of this community, we had access to all the comforts you could imagine, like electricity and so on.

ASPIRIN FIXES CINEMA

K. By the time you reached secondary school, did you feel any particular interest in film?

M. The visual had already made a strong impression on me when I was even younger than that. In fact, I've often said that I went into filmmaking thanks to aspirins! While we were living in Sidi Slimane, I would go with my father to the weekly market every Wednesday—one of those rituals that I was just talking about—to buy food for the house, to walk around, to meet people. One day my father refused to buy me something I wanted—I don't remember what it was, I was no more than 10 years old at the time—and I walked away from him in anger. Sure enough, I got lost, and my father told me afterward that he had looked all over for me. The marketplace was rather far from the village where we lived and I couldn't get home on my own. The market finished at about 3 in the afternoon; at 5 P.M., I was still walking around. The sun was beginning to set. All of a sudden, on what was otherwise a vacant lot, I saw a big picture projected on a giant white screen rising up in front of me. This was the first time I had ever seen a film and it was a revelation, seeing three dimensions on a screen that had only two. People were gathered on both sides of the screen and it was really impressive. And what was being projected? An advertisement for aspirin!

From that point on, cinema was fixed in my brain.

A YOUTH'S FILM CULTURE

K. How old were you when you started to think that you could perhaps become involved in filmmaking?

M. I guess I must have been about 16, about two or three years after independence.

K. What was the cinema like in Morocco at that time?

M. In the mid-1950s, when I was an adolescent, cinema had a very strong presence. There were already a lot of theaters given the relatively small population—more than 150 for a population of less than ten million; today, with more than three times that population, we have only a few more theaters than we had then.

K. What kind of films were being shown in those theaters?

M. There were a lot of Egyptian films—Arab nationalism was very much in vogue—and there were also Indian films and films from the West, mostly American films and especially Westerns.

But before the main film was shown there was also the preliminary program, consisting of a news review and a short. The news film was a synthesis of national and international news, along with sports, features, and other things, and this gave us a glance at what was going on in the world. This part of the program was very popular and greatly appreciated by the audience, and the news review was often the most interesting element in the entire evening's presentation.

K. Would you say that these news reviews were perhaps a more significant influence on you than the feature films themselves?

M. Absolutely. Especially what were called the "National Snapshots," where of course you saw the activities of ministers and other official events. But within this section there were three to four minutes on social, cultural, artistic events going on in the country. This was a real pleasure and I'm sure, at that time, people felt this need to see our own images. Everything on the screen then tended to come from abroad so even the official pictures with the flag, the marching guard, and so on, really responded to a deep need.

This all contributed to making communication my main aim; this was my major concern from about the age of 15 or 16. I wanted to communicate, and to communicate with the greatest possible number of people. Obviously, at that time we didn't yet have television, but there was the radio and the press. Radio seemed to me the more effective, insofar as the illiteracy rate was very high, over 70 percent at that time. But a little later I realized that the most effective way to communicate was by joining image and sound, because in this area no one is illiterate. And that's what launched me into the study of filmmaking.

I wasn't thinking of "creating" at that point, my orientation was much more toward "reporting," conveying what was happening. You know, I wanted to participate in the awakening of our society so that it not remain on the margins of what was going on in the world and, especially, that it not be limited to the role of consumer. That's why I wanted to act as a crafter, a producer of images.

STUDY FILMMAKING? AN "ADVENTUROUS" CHOICE

K. So, how did you go about this?

M. Right after independence, all the departments in the different ministries were looking to train personnel. Every week their representatives would come to the lycée, especially as we were coming to the end of secondary school and were preparing to take the baccalaureate examination. The country needed to train people and had to start this process from square one. Filmmaking was obviously not a high priority and, in fact, everything artistic was seen as minor. In any event, the offers from the ministries were often tempting, and to some extent we also wanted to test ourselves, if only to say, "OK, there's a competition for admission to the School for Administration—well, I'll try out for it." Sometimes, however, we did this without real conviction.

K. At the time you started to think seriously of studying filmmaking, toward the end of the 1950s, this must have been a rather unorthodox, even somewhat rebellious choice.

M. It's true that toward the end of the 1950s and into the beginning of the 1960s, to set out to study filmmaking was rather adventurous with regard to my society, my family, and even those in my own social group.

K. What kind of future did your parents want for you?

M. My father's deepest wish was that I go into law and he greatly encouraged me to go in that direction. I went into the competition for admission to the National School of Administration and for the Statistics Institute, and I succeeded in both places. But really, I was just testing myself and wasn't at all interested in these fields, just as I wasn't interested in scientific ones like medicine or pharmacy. I had a need to communicate but I didn't know how to work this out concretely.

One day, I saw a notice that the CCM wanted to train technicians. The CCM was both a production and distribution body, producing the news review, among other things. It was a very important body during this period, producing between twenty and thirty short films each year. They needed technicians in the fields of directing, editing, cinematography, and sound. This was the period, the late 1950s and early 1960s, when Morocco trained most of its film technicians—every year, four or five people were sent to Paris for training.

So I answered the advertisement. There was a competition to select seven or eight of us, with scholarships offered by the French technical assistance program. I remember how my test went—I took it with the film director Muhammad Afifi.[20] First he showed me a film—Orson Welles's *Touch of Evil* [1958], in which Welles also acts—and then I had to discuss it: what had I seen that was interesting, what had I noticed about it, and so on. And then I was asked what my plans were once my studies were completed. Those of us who were selected went to Paris, where we first took a foundation course and then another exam in order to be admitted into IDHEC.

FAMILY REACTION

K. How did your family react to your intention to go abroad and study filmmaking?

M. I had already decided to study abroad and had figured out how to do it before telling them anything! I was afraid that if I told them earlier they'd stop me from going. I finally told them about it only two or three days before I was to leave! It was like BOM— like that—BOM—"I'm going abroad." You know, I was just afraid of their protective attitude and that they might waylay my plans. In fact, this was the first time I was going abroad, although most of my friends had been abroad already, some of them often. But the first time I went abroad was for my filmmaking training. They reacted strongly but they were already faced with a fait accompli and they didn't have enough time to counteract my plans. So I left. It was rather painful for all of us.

You know, during all my time in Paris my father wrote me

every two days or so—it's a very lengthy correspondence and I've saved every letter. He needed to have this contact and this was his way of keeping us together. I was very surprised because when I was with my father we didn't really talk to one another, out of respect. If I wanted to go to the barber or to the movies, I wouldn't talk to him about it but would go through my mother so she'd get the money from him. Even when we went hunting—my father was a serious hunter and we had land with a lot of game on it—I'd always be at his side, trying to learn from him, but there was no dialogue. There was so much respect that dialogue between us just didn't exist.

But suddenly, as soon as I was far from him, he had the need to communicate. I don't know whether this was some kind of compensation or what. And the things he told me were all of a trivial sort: that someone had come to the house, that he had met someone else, that he had read something in the newspaper—that kind of thing. He needed a dialogue with me, perhaps because during my entire adolescence our communication amounted to nothing more than, "Did you do well in class today? Did you get a good grade?" Things like that.

PARIS AND THE START OF A CAREER

PARIS: THE POLITICAL ATMOSPHERE

K. You were in Paris from 1961 to 1964. During that time, what was the political atmosphere like for you, as Moroccans?

M. There was a very special atmosphere. You know, students in France were very politicized during that period, with a strong influence from the trade union movement and from the French Communist Party, and both these influences were very strong among the IDHEC students. For us, Moroccans, politics wasn't sectarian, at least not yet. We had gained our independence just a few years earlier and we were still full of nationalistic feelings. Also, many formerly colonial states were just gaining theirs. In this context, we were elbow to elbow with a lot of very militant students who were in the Communist Party or in the Communist Youth Organization, and so on. This all contributed to the atmosphere.

K. This was the time when the war for Algerian independence was coming to an end.

M. Yes, that was the main political activity as far as we Moroccan students were concerned—demonstrating for Algerian independence.

K. What kind of relationship did you have with the other Moroccan students at IDHEC?

M. There were five of us and we were a very tightly knit group. My strongest tie was with Ahmed Bouanani, who is a wonderful editor and filmmaker and whose only full-length film, *as-Sarab* [*The Mirage,* 1980], is a very fine film. I was also close to another filmmaker in the group, Majid Rechiche.

CINEMATOGRAPHY—DIRECT ACCESS, "FREE SPIRIT"

K. How were your studies at IDHEC structured?

M. There were five different specializations—directing-producing, editing-script, cinematography, set construction-design, and sound engineering. There were also core courses that everyone took, such as "the history of cinema," "aesthetics," "criticism and analysis," "shooting a film." These included everything about cinematic language—learning how to express things cinematically, the entire study of basics and form in the classical world cinema, going through the American, Swedish, German cinemas, expressionism, and so on.

But every section also had its own courses where we went more deeply into the study of a particular aspect. For the directing section, there were practical courses that would take you into studios to see how actors were directed, or into theaters. Meanwhile, those of us specializing in cinematography might be working in the lab, to understand sensitometry or something similar.[21] I chose to specialize in cinematography, because I liked to maneuver the camera and I wanted to express directly what was happening around me.

K. Did you ever think of specializing in something else, like directing or editing?

M. No. I thought directing would mean having a cameraman intervene between me and the event, making me lose half of the event. As for editing, although it obviously has great importance and was part of our program, it's not a specialization that interested me, particularly because it means being shut inside an office. I felt I was more of a free spirit, someone who always wanted to be outside. Sitting at the console in front of a filmed reflection, shut up in the dark, didn't tempt me at all. I thought that shooting with

the camera—the risks, shooting from the air or from the sea—
was more my style.

K. When you talk of learning to use a camera, I'm reminded of something Orson Welles said, that he had learned all he needed to
know about cinematography in just a couple of weekends with
Greg Toland.[22] How much of an exaggeration is that?

M. Well, when you're talking about Orson Welles, you're talking of
a very special case—he was such a genius I suppose anything is
possible. The fact that he made *Citizen Kane* at the age of 26, introduced the ceiling, which you'd never seen in films before that,
found out how to use the wide-angle lens and depth of field so
that you can see the glass in the foreground and then the girl on
the bed in the background all in clear focus from a distance of 50
cm up to . . . well, infinity—this was very acrobatic. So, he's a very
special case, and if he was able to assimilate all this in a few weeks,
it's extraordinary. But, that was Orson Welles and he's one of a
kind.

I can see how you could assimilate what you need to know
about directing in a few weeks. To direct you need to orchestrate
many different elements to transform a work into images. Before
you even start you have to have a particular sensibility, some
training, a strong interest, a wide culture. If you can marshal those
qualities you might be able to learn to direct in a few weeks. But
cinematography, and editing too, need more time than that.

With cinematography you have to learn a lot of technical
things. You have to learn the capabilities of each lens; you have
to learn how to use lighting, especially when you're working inside; how to use backlighting, how to work "day for night," how
to work the shadows. To really evaluate a cinematographer, you
have to see how he works with black and white, which requires
you to be something of a sculptor: you work on a view and then
you use the shadows to express the actor's tensions, or the atmosphere, or whether it's fantasy or comedy, and so on. And I
haven't even mentioned other kinds of problems, like chemical
ones. You have to study how film reacts, you have to know about
color curves, color charts, the color grid, how the colors you shoot
will appear when it's black and white, and so on. You need to
know sensitometry, photometry,[23] and chemistry in order to master working on the image through all its phases, to know what

you're going to get and how to get what you want. You can't learn all this in a few weeks. You really need a lot of work.

K. Of course, I didn't really expect you to agree! [Both laugh.]

Now, returning to Paris . . .

PARIS: THE CINEMATHEQUE, MITRY, SADOUL

M. Yes. In addition to the formal instruction we all wanted to see as many films as we could. So, after class we'd go almost every day to the cinematheque. It was certainly enlightening to have all the theoretical discussion about German expressionism, for example, but it was another level of learning entirely to go and see Fritz Lang's films, especially for those of us specializing in cinematography. Really, the courses continued at the cinematheque. We also had the opportunity to have a once-a-week course with Raymond Rouleau—a wonderful theater director who also made some films—and we went to his theater on rue de la Huchette. This was voluntary, not obligatory, and it was fascinating.

K. You had some very well-known teachers at IDHEC, didn't you?

M. Yes, two were particularly prestigious—Jean Mitry, who taught us film aesthetics, and Georges Sadoul, who taught film history.[24]

I'll never forget the first course Mitry gave, even though it's almost forty years ago now. He based it on a film short he had made to the music of Honegger[25] and he used this to show us how a film's rhythm was constructed through its editing. He could give you a session that lasted two or three hours, discussing the message and the medium [Fr. *le contenu et le contenant*], discussing a chair and its signifier—it was extraordinary, really very important for us. He could take any subject at all and hold forth on it for hours and hours.

At the time, perhaps we found Mitry a little too . . . academic. But now, when you think back on it, he was very profound. And also, he had a very visible passion, a great mastery, and deep convictions. But for me the most interesting parts were the concrete examples, and that's why I remember *Pacific 231*, Honegger, and the discussion of montage and aesthetics.

K. And Sadoul?

M. Sadoul was different because he was truly an encyclopedia of world cinema—he had seen so many films from all over the world and knew all about the various trends and movements. Obviously, he had a preference for the Soviet cinema and the cinema from the communist world. But he had impeccable knowledge of every cinema—the Asian; the American, which he knew perfectly; the European; and so on. He was particularly good on what happens behind the scenes in a film and knew by heart the biographies of directors, actors, and so on. It was really amazing and very interesting, and his course was always very crowded because you really learned a lot.

VERTOV, "FILM TRUTH," MOROCCAN REALITY

K. Overall, while you were in Paris, what would you say were the most important influences as far as your orientation toward filmmaking is concerned?

M. During my training I was very interested in documentary filmmaking. So there was first of all the influence of Dziga Vertov, who made films in a style called *"cinéma vérité," "cinéma-oeil,"* where you record things from day to day. There was the influence of early films like *Nanook of the North,* and of Western filmmakers like Chris Marker or Joris Ivens, all more oriented toward documentary than fiction. These were the influences that marked me the most strongly and this reflected my personal interests—for the *"cinéma caméra," "cinéma oeil,"* for a cinema based in reality, in people's daily lives, without having fiction intervene, without what I call "reconstitution."[26]

You have to bear in mind what our own reality as Moroccans was. I wasn't thinking that the training would allow me to express things as you would see them in the world's great film classics. I knew that our country wasn't yet ready to produce feature films, so there was no sense dreaming about that. Documentary and educational films to inform the population would be our reality and this was what we expected with, of course, the dream of an occasional escape for the length of a film short.

So, for me, the aim of film training was to acquire all the knowledge that would allow me to master a vocation. In fact, the IDHEC training turned out to be like an apprenticeship in cinematic expression—in a film school you can learn how to express things in images and in sound but they can't teach you talent, or imagination, or ideas.

RETURNING TO MOROCCO, THE CCM, "LEARNING OUR CRAFT"

K. When you returned to Morocco in 1964, what professional jobs were open to you as an IDHEC graduate?

M. First of all, I have to say that we came back from Paris with a lot of theory but little practical experience. It was really after my return to Morocco, during my work at the CCM both as a reporter on the news review and then as its director from 1969 to 1974, and then also in my work on documentaries and other short films, that I learned the craft—all this was a really fine school.

When we all came back from IDHEC, you could say that there was no film activity outside the CCM, because television was only in its second year at that point. The CCM was very productive, producing up to thirty shorts a year. In addition to their documentaries the CCM also produced some short fictions that were proposed by the directors themselves. And the CCM had equipment and film, and its film lab in Souissi had one of the best black-and-white film labs—I would even say one of the best in the world—producing an extraordinary quality of black and white. The CCM was really where you learned the craft, where you could really exercise your profession. We had thought of going to work for television and we offered ourselves—the five IDHEC graduates—to the TV as a team. The TV people hardly even gave us a hearing, they sent us off without a second look. So we went to work at the CCM—after all, it was thanks to the CCM that we had had our IDHEC scholarships and that we first began to learn our craft.

For two or three years we all worked at the CCM and we did a lot of projects as a team—this was the period when we made the shorts *6–12, Tarfaya,* and about forty or so short features, four to five minutes long, dealing with social problems, artistic questions, all sorts of different topics. For example, we'd take an iron craftsman and do a feature on the art of wrought iron, with interviews and so on. When there were floods we'd go and talk to the peasants, to show what they were going through and how they felt. It was very interesting work and through it we learned how to use various techniques to express ourselves. All this was within the framework of the CCM. At the same time we began to work with an interdisciplinary group that had been formed a few years earlier, in 1962–1963, to make informational and mobilizing films for the ministry of agriculture, working in tandem with many different kinds of technicians.[27]

DOCUMENTARY, INFORMATIONAL, EDUCATIONAL, ETHNOGRAPHIC—MOROCCO "INCH BY INCH"

M. Over this entire period there was an enormous amount of audiovisual work to be done for Moroccan society. New crops were being introduced—sugar beet and sugar cane, for example—and

Tazi at the CCM, filming the news review

films were commissioned to convince the peasant to switch part of grain or corn production into these crops. Filmmaking was very exciting—making these films with the participation of the peasants was really an extraordinary experience. Then we'd go and show the films in the open air—with film buses—we'd discuss them with the peasants, and sometimes we'd even redo part of the film to take into account their comments, which were usually right on the mark.

K. This seems like a kind of ethnographic filmmaking.

M. It *was* ethnographic filmmaking! Absolutely. At the same time it was also didactic, popularizing, and informative. Sometimes, too, we made these in a fictional form, recounting the story of a peasant family's life, in order to show that we needed to cultivate sugar beet or sugar cane.

For example, there was one film I made collaborating with Latif Lahlou, called *Sin Agafaye*, meaning "the two water sources." This was truly an *ethnographic* film—we traveled high into the mountains, a journey on mule that took three hours, and then actually lived with the population in order to make the film.

K. I suppose this was also a chance for you to get to know Morocco much more deeply.

M. Absolutely. This is one of the reasons I said this was a very fine school, because filming the news reviews and making these kinds of features enabled me to crisscross all of Morocco inch by inch, to get to know the full mosaic of the country: the mountains, the countryside, the coast, the south—pretty much everywhere; and to get to know Moroccan society with all its constituent parts, to talk with all kinds of people, listen to their stories—it was very enriching. We would do traveling shots from the back of a mule, and with a CinemaScope camera no less! Or traveling shots from a wheelbarrow. And with all this we'd still manage to get good shots! It was really exhilarating—it was as though we were sort of inventing writing. For me, this period was the best school of all.

THE NEWS REVIEW AND PLACING THE CAMERA

M. And all the time I spent as a reporter for the news review was a wonderful school as far as learning where to place the camera goes. When you're on that kind of job, you're more or less on your own, there's no one to tell you how do to it. At an important event—officials are coming together for a handshake, or to embrace one another, or an important document is going to be signed—where you're trying to film with some thirty or forty people milling around, you have to find that one best place to put the camera and not miss anything that's essential.

K. Going back to Orson Welles for a minute, he also said that he never had a problem deciding where to place the camera, that this was something he felt more or less instinctively.[28]

M. That's more evidence of his genius. I do know directors who have no sense of camera angle, no idea of the possibilities of a given lens, no idea of what is commonly called "the field" of a camera. You see a lot of people muddling through this, first putting the camera here and then there. In fact, I think it *is* rather difficult to know exactly where to place the camera. But there are instruments like viewfinders [Fr. *viseur*] through which a director can look to get an idea how the action will appear, helping him decide where to place the camera. I hate that instrument, I've never used one and never had to, because I had that training as a reporter, learning what angle will best capture the moment.

MOROCCO'S FILM NEEDS

K. Looking back on the experience of making informational and training documentaries for the state, what do you think of the idea of using cinema in this way?

M. You know, Morocco is basically an agricultural country, and this was the path we took from the outset—even the king's directives went along these lines, promoting the building of dams and so on. This was especially true at independence when probably 70 percent of the population lived in the countryside, in agricultural occupations. There was a real need to change people's mentality and to modernize our agriculture. I was all for working to change people's mentality in that direction.

In areas like health, where vaccination campaigns were essential, and in agriculture, nothing could be as effective as the audiovisual. How I would have liked to see more films made to promote education and encourage civic spirit—and this is still a big need today. We hear a lot of talking about human rights and such things, but these notions can be conveyed much more effectively by audiovisual means than by talking.

WESHMA: THE GREAT DISILLUSION WITH COLLECTIVE EFFORT

By 1970 only three professional Moroccan feature films had been made, each of them an attempt to reproduce the appeal of the still-prohibited Egyptian films.[29] In the late 1960s Tazi and several of his fellow graduates from IDHEC formed a cooperative, Sigma 3, which led, in 1970, to the making of *Weshma* (*Traces,* Hamid Bennani), a pathbreaking effort both in its cooperative production structure and, to more lasting effect, in its staying close to Moroccan social and cultural reality, giving it pride of place as the first feature film that was genuinely Moroccan in character.

Weshma is divided into two roughly equal parts, the first dealing with the childhood of an adopted boy, Messaoud, and the second taking him into his late adolescence. Hamid Bennani, the director, described the film's title as "underlining the weight of tradition and the fate against which, in fact, the film rebels."[30] In the brochure Sigma 3 produced to accompany the film, Bennani evoked its haunting and somewhat mythic tone:

> Weshma, the Trace—how can we define it? For it is manifold: physical, social, psychoanalytic, ontological . . .
> The first trace is of a lack: Messaoud, the foundling, has no origin. Adopted by a well-to-do landowner, Messaoud finds in him a generous,

authoritarian father whom he admires but with whom he is destined to clash, because the strict father cannot break into the solitude of the false child . . .

For society, evil dwells in Messaoud. . . . As a young man, he cannot fit into the world of work, nor even into a gang of adolescent delinquents. Messaoud's search continues, through his dream of his adoptive mother's tenderness . . . until he finds his only truth in annihilation.

The story of a failure . . . even while calling the spectator to reflection.

The plan was for each of the founders to direct, in turn, his own film as part of the cooperative enterprise but, just as the plot in *Weshma* was "the story of a failure," so too was the story of this filmmakers' cooperative, despite the promise this first film carried.

A FILMMAKING COOPERATIVE

K. Could you tell me the story of *Weshma* and of Sigma 3, which you formed with two other filmmakers, Ahmed Bouanani and Muhammad Seqqat?

M. Of all the IDHEC graduating classes during the early years, I think ours was the only one that really worked together. But our attempt to build a cooperative was a bit utopian in that each of us, while wanting to make fiction feature films, also had to earn a living—Bouanani continued to work in an office at the CCM, I was always on the lookout for a documentary project, and Seqqat was starting to make advertising films. But we had a very strong desire to make a feature film, we were militant about it, and it had really become an idée fixe for all of us. So three of us who had been together at IDHEC—myself, Bouanani, and Muhammad Seqqat—formed Sigma 3, trying to figure out how to work together in a more creative way. Then Bennani came back from IDHEC and had a subject that was ready to go and that excited us all. His idea had the strongest effect on Bouanani who, as a poet and writer, was the most literary among us. He read some pages and spoke to us about it, and we were all enthusiastic.

"WE HAD SUCH MOTIVATION, SUCH PASSION"

K. How did you work on *Weshma*?

M. We divided up the tasks: Bouanani worked on the continuity and was editor and assistant director, I was the cinematographer, Muhammad Seqqat was director of production, and Hamid Bennani was the director. We applied what we'd learned at IDHEC, where each of us had a specialty but had also been trained for versatility and could perform other functions. We all worked so long on the screenplay that we knew it by heart!

I even had the chance to put in a scene referring to my own father, the scene where the father greases the gun. This was one of his rituals that I mentioned to you. When we filmed it I had the actor make exactly the same gestures my father used to make—like the way he manipulated the rifle—as I remembered them in my mind. We even used my father's gun!

And everyone contributed what he could materially—car, gasoline, and so on. I had a trailer at the time and that's where we all slept. This was really militancy: we all had the will to achieve our goal and to prove that one could make films, without all kinds of pretentious talk, without bringing in foreigners for the images and the sound—we could express ourselves without CinemaScope and even without color. And certainly without equipment like cranes. And without a sound camera—we did all the postsynchronization in a studio in Casablanca, even to the point where we ourselves dubbed in the neighing of the horses. [Laughs.]

It was really exciting. I talk of it now with a lot of nostalgia, but I also have a lot of regrets that we weren't able to continue in that manner. We had such motivation, such passion—the passion of our craft, the passion for cinema as a whole—and we didn't put any limits on our effort, on our commitment. Anything we owned—"hey, this table here, will that work for such-and-such a scene?"—if it would work in the film we'd say, "OK, load it in the truck," even if this was the only table in our house! We all lived in the trailer in the countryside and shot out there, and nothing stopped us from shooting—not problems with the decor nor with a star nor with equipment. We just all went about our work with a kind of basic simplicity.

THE IMPACT OF *WESHMA* AND
"CREATING A NATIONAL CINEMA"

K. What was the relationship between *Weshma* and those first three Moroccan films?

M. There was no relationship whatsoever! First of all, there wasn't the slightest hint of commercial spirit in the making of *Weshma*. In those three earlier films, the main idea of the producers was to take a kind of cinema that had had good success—in this case Egyptian films—and to substitute a Moroccan film, saying, in effect, "if we can replace ten Egyptian films with one Moroccan film, we can count that a great success." They copied the musical aspect and took a well-known star, the singer Abdelwahab Doukkali, brought together some actors and foreign technicians, filmed in CinemaScope, and dealt with subjects that had no particular relationship to Morocco. Basically the aims of those films had nothing to do with our aim with Sigma 3, which was that of contributing to creating a national cinema.

K. Were those three films successful?

M. Not at all, not at all. For the public these were indeed the first Moroccan films, but they had no impact at all. Of course, neither did *Weshma* have any impact on the public!

You have to understand: we had absolutely no way to get a film on the commercial screens! *Weshma* was certainly talked about in the film clubs and the press and it won some prizes in foreign film festivals, but you can't say it reached the public—that would be false. However, this was the case for all Moroccan films—there was no distribution and no commercial screening.

K. Although the wider public never had a chance to see the film and give its opinion, the film was highly praised in the press, in the film clubs, and so on. Why do you think this was?

M. First of all, this wasn't a film you liked because of the star, or the actor, or anything on that level. It was a film that addressed a subject central to Moroccan society, central to its identity—the problem of adoption, which is still a big problem today. The film didn't gloss over things—we wanted to show this problem not only during childhood but also all the damage this leads to when the child becomes an adult. We wanted to treat it simply, directly, cinematically.

Also, from a technical and artistic standpoint, I still think this film is a very valid one, and in these ways it marked the cinema of that time. Afterward, starting in 1973–1974, there were a number of fine films—from Moumen Smihi and Souheil Ben Barka, for example—made with the same basic objective we had with Sigma 3, that of expressing and building a national cinema rather than plagiarizing the Egyptians, expressing ourselves as a group with a film from our own . . . terrain. That's it, it was as simple as that.

"OUR WINGS WERE . . . CLIPPED"

K. Given this relatively successful outcome, why was Sigma 3 unable to produce another film?

M. After *Weshma* was completed and shown, what had been a collective effort began to be seen as basically the work of "Monsieur" Hamid Bennani. [Tazi used the title "Monsieur" disdainfully.] The rest of us grew increasingly frustrated with this; we felt our wings were being clipped.

K. Why did this happen? Do you think it had something to do with the notion of *"cinéma d'auteur"* that was so strong in France—the idea that it was the director who took full responsibility and credit for the film, even when it was a collective effort?

M. I think this Western idea definitely had something to do with it. But you have to say that Bennani bears his share of the blame. No doubt he didn't want to pull the covers to his side at the outset, but when the press and the media put him on the spot he didn't explain how things were. So the rest of us were very discouraged and lost the enthusiasm needed to continue in this manner. We were all upset to find ourselves in this position, all the more so because for each of us this was just the first step on a long march. Bouanani had his film all ready to go and this had to wait another ten years before being produced. Then I was going to direct a film, and there would be another by Seqqat.[31]

K. What was the film you planned to make?

M. We were discussing a number of stories, but I can't say that at that moment I had a clear subject that I was ready to put on the table. I still wasn't really thinking about fiction. I was part of this group, participating in my specialty and using my versatility, but I wasn't yet ready to make my own fiction film.

COLLECTIVE EFFORT, *CINÉMA D'AUTEUR,*
AND SOCIETAL CONTEXT

K. What finally happened with the Sigma 3 cooperative?

M. It broke up after *Weshma*, completely dissolved. Some of us kept up contact on an individual basis, but there was no structure. It was a great disappointment, especially because we all gained from the symbiosis of ideas, effort, beliefs, motivation, and so on.

It wasn't just the disappointment. The effect was societal, in fact, because the unhappy end to this experience had the effect of completely eliminating the collective spirit in filmmaking. When you think of this notion of *"cinéma d'auteur,"* where you try to eliminate everything that happens "in the wings" of a production, where you try to put everything on the shoulders of one person, the director—obviously, all kinds of misunderstandings can arise. I remember arguing at some length that this notion of "author" can't really exist in our cinema, not yet at least. To have an "author," a *"cinéma d'auteur,"* you have to already have an existing filmmaking tradition. But here we don't have that—you might talk of a cinema of artisans, or some such term, but you can't talk of a *"cinéma d'auteur."*

It really was a pity that we couldn't go forward with Sigma 3 because I think that the cooperative structure—producing as a non-profit-making entity—was the most suitable one for the situation of Moroccan filmmaking at that time. In any case we would not be making profit, because a Moroccan film can never recoup its costs simply from spectators—we're nowhere near making a profit! We can only make films thanks to subsidies, to financial support, whether from Moroccan or foreign institutions. So, whether we like it or not we are necessarily in the non-profit-making sector.

K. I recently read an interview with the Cuban filmmaker Tomàs Gutierrez Alea, in which he talked about spending half of his time training people to make films cooperatively. He said that this cooperative effort was one of his greatest joys. Making films under his own name, like *Memories of Underdevelopment* [1968], obviously gave him pleasure, but it was the cooperative work that he felt gave meaning to his labor. In Cuba structures were created to support that kind of cooperative activity; here, obviously, that was not the case.[32]

M. That's right. In fact, things moved in the opposite direction. Starting in 1977, if you wanted to make a film you became legally required to form a production company. From that moment on, if you hadn't created a company you couldn't get authorization to shoot, or be on the business register, or work on a project, or apply for a contract from a ministry. You could no longer exist simply as an individual in this profession. But creating a production company only is meaningful if the profession becomes profitable, which it isn't by any stretch of the imagination. The proof of this is that now there are some 270 production companies in Morocco, because every time a project is on offer production companies are created just to apply for the project and then they disappear right afterward. Given all this, I think that a cooperative structure might have been the most appropriate for us as film-makers, but it's only now, with this distance from the past, that we can see this.

CAREER CHOICES AND THE MOVE TOWARD FICTION

"A KEY PERIOD . . . PEOPLE WERE TALKING ABOUT NATIONAL FICTION FILM PRODUCTION"

K. After the disappointment of *Weshma,* what was your attitude to-ward filmmaking and toward your career?

M. To start, let me explain a little about the context of filmmaking in Morocco during the 1970s because this was a key period. It was key on the career level because many of us at the CCM were growing restless and we wanted to move on to something else. Some remained at the CCM as administrators; others wanted to go into the private sector, feeling that there you could perhaps make films, or at least certain kinds of films, like advertising; still others wanted to continue making documentaries, which contin-ued to be the province of the CCM. There was also the possibility of television, and some filmmakers went there with a view to making television films.

It was also a key period because people were talking more and more about national fiction film production. After *Weshma,* films like Souheil Ben Barka's *A Thousand and One Hands* [1972], Moumen Smihi's *Chergui* [*The Wind from the East,* 1975], Ahmed Maanouni's *Al-Yam al-Yam* [*The Days, the Days,* 1978] had all been financed entirely with private funds. The CCM had given some support in the form of equipment, technicians, and sometimes the lab work; also there were some private patrons, some contributors. But it was a very risky business and we were beginning to think that state aid might be forthcoming.

This was also the period when Noureddin Sail had a TV pro-gram, a kind of nightclub, that focused on the classical world cin-ema, with guests from all over to talk about the cinema. So this was a key period also as far as the public's film education was concerned.

"DURING THE 1970s . . . A GOOD DEAL OF UNITY AMONG FILMMAKERS"

K. And what was the filmmaking community like during that period?

M. During the late 1960s, into the early 1970s, and up to the end of the 1970s, the training of filmmakers and technicians abroad continued in a rather consistent manner; also, some of us had had university training and had enough background and baggage to think seriously about cinema. But toward the end of the 1970s or a little later, formal training stopped to all intents and purposes, leading to the kind of situation we have now, where all you have is on-the-job training, without any serious reflection going on concerning the problems of cinema.

During the 1970s, there was a good deal of unity among filmmakers, because we all had common interests. We hadn't yet begun to provide services in a major way for foreign productions nor were we racing one another for advertising contracts. To the contrary; among all of our filmmakers trained in different foreign institutes and universities there was one common concern: how to help the birth of a national cinema, how to encourage *our* cinema, to provide it with the necessary foundation, financial and otherwise, that could lead to viable and continuous production.[33] We published all this in a manifesto, arguing for the creation of a national cinema and looking for ways to encourage private capital to invest in Moroccan films. We were all militants for these goals.

"REORIENT[ING] MYSELF TOWARD FICTION"

K. As far as your own career is concerned, what were your main activities during this period?

M. Up until 1974 I was at the CCM, responsible for directing the news review. But I was really feeling a need to retrain, so I set out on a new path and went to the United States, to the School of Mass Communications at Syracuse University, to study communication and the mass media for two semesters. Here, again, I was motivated by the desire to communicate and I wanted to learn new methods in order to communicate more effectively.

When I got back to Morocco in 1975 I started a production company, with the aim of working in advertising and in documentaries, not with the aim of making fiction films. I started with documentaries on a contractual basis for various ministries—public works, agriculture, health, communication—documentaries for training purposes or of an educational nature, on many different subjects. But after a couple of years of this I began to see that this was going to absorb all my time. It was very, very remunerative, that's true, but it looked like it would take all my time, at the expense of other things that I really wanted to do. At this time I guess I was beginning to reorient myself toward fiction.

Situating *The Big Trip* (1981): "Bumblebees fly . . . and we make films!"

At the time Tazi made his first feature film, state funding for Moroccan film production was just beginning and, as we have seen, this was to have an immediate positive effect on quantity: after having produced only seventeen feature films in the twenty-four years from independence through 1979, Morocco was to produce thirty films in the following five years.[34] However, the problems of distributing and screening Moroccan films had not been addressed and Tazi's first film, despite positive discussion in the press and some festival screenings, never reached the Moroccan public.

Before we look at this film in some detail in the interlude, let us situate it in its broader context, explore Tazi's views of its potential public, and discuss how this film influenced his attitude toward film-making and his career within it.

PRODUCTION CONTEXT

CINEMATIC AND FINANCIAL

THE BIG TRIP AND OTHER FILMS OF THE PERIOD

K. When you made *The Big Trip*, there had already been a number of important Moroccan films produced, such as those of Ben Barka, Maanouni, and Bouanani, that we've already mentioned.

M. Yes, and a few others as well. These were all done in the same spirit, often in 16 mm, always without live sound, with a very small team, with very reduced means. Obviously, this had its effect on technical aspects, because there was no way to have the traveling shots you wanted, or the cranes, or a helicopter, things like that. But all these films carry a real author's sensibility and the credibility that comes from the author's sincerity. They were all made in that spirit, and that's very important.

K. How would you situate *The Big Trip* with respect to the other films we've just mentioned?

M. Each of us, as filmmakers, has different concerns, both in style and what we want to express. But the main difference, as I see it, is that *The Big Trip* opens up somewhat our usual notions of story, of fiction, normally a bit enclosed within certain settings and certain characters. *The Big Trip* was a kind of adventure, in the sense of embarking on a road without knowing what you will run up against.

With *The Big Trip* we start from a town in the south, in the Souss region, and we go along the coast from one end of Morocco to the other, as far north as possible, ending up in cosmopolitan Tangiers. In Morocco we have serious communication problems so one of our main concerns was, in each part of the country, to treat the characters in relation to their particular manner of speaking, being sensitive to differences in dialogue, in language, in dialect. In the course of the trip, we encounter a full mosaic of dialects, people, mentalities, behavior, even age, and this enabled us to express a kind of sociological vision of the full Moroccan mosaic. This distinguishes the film from most of the others of that period, which were situated in a specific region and spoke of a specific group of people—at times rural, at times urban. So I think the special character of this film is to have dealt with such a broad variety of Morocco's population.

FINANCING—"A LOT OF HELP FROM FRIENDS"

K. How did the financing go?

M. The state's Support Fund was just starting but they didn't give you the funds in advance. This led to what was called "the bounty hunt" [Fr. *la chasse à la prime*], with people shooting films on a shoestring budget and then making do with the minimum amounts the Support Fund awarded, and sometimes even making money out of it! People started shooting thousands of meters of film without really satisfying the basic cinematic criteria.

The Big Trip was awarded a derisory sum, something in the neighborhood of 200,000–250,000 DH, but this was to be paid only when the film was finished. As a result, we had to start borrowing money everywhere. But the technicians and the actors all waited for their pay until we got the money from the Support Fund. Neither Noureddin nor I were paid at all! Souheil Ben Barka really helped me to get the film going, lending me 100,000 DH. Of course, he was the first to be reimbursed, but I'll never forget that loan, for which I could offer no guarantee.[35]

K. Obviously, a film like *The Big Trip* was never going to make money but did it at least manage to reimburse the debts and to pay the salaries?

M. The film only cost about 400,000 DH to make, partly because some important items were not charged, like the screenplay. It helped enormously that we had the participation of many friends and a lot of encouragement: one friend lent us the truck, another gave us reduced prices at hotels—these were crucial because we had to drive the truck and stay in hotels from one end of the country to the other. We also had assistance from technicians, actors, from everyone, to keep the costs down. All we really had to pay out of pocket were the production expenses.

Also, I had lots of friends who came up to me at various moments, saying, "Can I help you out on the film?" Sometimes we found acting roles or even created characters for them—I used a Moroccan filmmaker and friend of mine in one role and another played the beggar in the café. I even used Souheil Ben Barka as an extra—he was keeping an eye on the film's production and he came to El-Jadida while we were shooting, so I sat him down in the café and shot him as an extra.

We also had a lot of help from friends during postproduction. You know, this film was not shot with live sound but only with a guide sound track, so we had to dub the texts during postproduction. As it turned out, about 80 percent of the spoken material recorded in the studio was performed by people who hadn't played the role but were simply friends helping us out.

As far as the financing went, all in all about two-thirds of the cost came from the Support Fund. Income from distribution to the theaters was practically nil: it amounted to about 20,000 DH for the film's entire career. In fact, it's hard to see why a distributor would even pay that much for the film, because it's like throwing the money away. Afterward, there were some sales to TV stations, and any money that went into our pockets came from that.

You could say it was a film that had much more of a personal investment than a monetary one.

K. At least you didn't lose money.

M. No. It was an experience. We didn't gain any money but we didn't lose any either. But that was because of all the support we were given. When I spoke earlier of motivation, this is what I meant: people wanted to participate in Moroccan national creation—although "national" is a notion that would require some more discussion. But people came willingly, without even asking to be paid. They just wanted to participate, that was all.

And of course all of this helped me get through what was really a very important experience—getting my feet wet as a director—while at the same time limiting the damage that might ensue.

AUDIENCE

At home: no distribution, no public, "we just wanted to prove . . . we could reach harbor"

K. When you were making *The Big Trip*, what sort of public did you have in mind?

M. Absolutely none at all! That's one of the "naïve" aspects of that film. We were still at a stage in Moroccan filmmaking where, simply, we had to prove that we could make fiction films with the very few means at our disposal. Never, absolutely never, did we think about the public—neither how the public might evaluate the film, nor whether the public would like it, nor whether we should do it this way or that in order to please the public. In fact, I think that for my first three films—I'm not counting *Weshma* because that wasn't my film—this notion of a public never concerned me and I never gave it a thought. After all, our films weren't even distributed! We just wanted to prove that we could tell a story in film and we could reach harbor with very few means. That was far and away the main concern. We wanted to build a different kind of cinema, our own cinema. That was our aim.

K. Along the lines of what was called "Third cinema," influenced by Brazilian filmmakers?

M. Yes, by that and by Italian neorealism. They were important influences.

Abroad: "the film speaks for itself," the "romantic" view of the artist

K. How about *The Big Trip*'s reception at festivals—did you go and present the film to audiences?

M. I treated this film the same way I treated a short film or a documentary: "It's done, it's on the road, it's not my concern any more." Of course I knew there were film festivals, there were cultural events and things of that sort, but I was still rather shy about publicizing my work in that way. The very thought of confronting the public and answering questions had me trembling, partly because I'd already seen how films could get criticized in the film clubs. You know, you might have two hundred or three hundred people in the audience, hanging on your every word—I was incapable of holding a microphone in that kind of context without trembling.

K. Well, you're certainly not trembling now. [Both laugh.]

M. I remember once going to Algiers, to the Algerian cinematheque, to present *Weshma*. It must have been 1972 or 1973. This was a real ordeal for me. In that kind of environment there are always film buffs and habitués of the cinematheque who really love to split hairs. I suppose for them their questions were absolutely normal and I wasn't actually attacked, but it really stressed me. That experience was enough to make me hate all contact with the public and afterward I came up with the excuse "the film speaks for itself." Some time later I realized that you need to go around with the film and that this just requires a little practice.

In fact my second wife, who was Spanish and whom I married in 1978, really helped me to deal with the public. I had been married once before, much younger, while I was studying in France but I got divorced in 1972. My second wife was an architect and a real film fan. Also, she was an extremely good communicator, something that is basic to Spanish society—I think that 90 percent of Spaniards are good communicators. They learn this very young—you see children in the restaurants and bars with their parents at midnight or even at two or three o'clock in the early morning. They're so used to communicating with one another that they have no shyness at all, and this leads to people who have a great talent for communication. With my second wife I spent a considerable amount of time in Spain during what was a very turbulent and lively period there—this was shortly after the death of Franco. People in Spain weren't shy at all! I think that time was crucial in curing me of my shyness with the public. And I'm also very happy for my children, because they've inherited that capacity to communicate.[36]

But, at the time of *The Big Trip*'s release, I still thought that the film should speak for itself, that it wasn't my function to explain it, that if it couldn't speak for itself then it was a failure. I refused a lot of invitations at that time and Noureddin was the person who usually went to present the film in public. Sometimes my wife did. Of course, I was very pleased when it was selected for a festival—and it was in quite a few festivals, like Berlin and Valencia—but I saw no need to accompany it.

K. So, at the time of *The Big Trip*, you had something of the "romantic" notion of the artist, working alone, not taking steps in the direction of the public.

M. Absolutely. It was only later that my behavior changed. [Laughs.]

Remember, at the end of the 1970s and the beginning of the 1980s, we hadn't yet had the explosion of festivals that we have now. This phenomenon came somewhat later. But you can create all kinds of needs and now the need to see images from the South has been created. Today you can see our films in many different kinds of festivals: Mediterranean, Arab, Maghrebin, African, and so on—we can be mixed into almost any sauce. For a number of organizations this is now their breadwinner, they live off films from "elsewhere."

"WE MADE THIS FILM . . . WE EXISTED"

"A FEELING OF PRIDE"

K. After finishing *The Big Trip* and seeing that it had reached no public at all in Morocco, did you experience something of a depression?

M. No, not at all, it wasn't frustrating at all. First of all, there was a feeling of pride in having managed to make the film, in spite of all the difficulties. You know, once I started to accompany my films and discuss them, I began to use the following anecdote: a bumblebee weighs 40 grams, the surface of its wings is 2.2 square centimeters, the wings are inclined at an angle of 30 degrees— well, according to the laws of aeronautics, it's impossible for that insect to fly. [Laughs.] But bumblebees fly just the same! That's just the way it is for our cinema: there's no infrastructure, minimal financial aid, no public, no encouragement—there's nothing! So we can't make films but, just the same, we make films![37]

This film now existed. *We* made this film. And from time to time there was some pleasure, "Look, it's being shown in Valencia; it won a prize; it was referred to in a publication—in *Le Monde*, or *Positif*, or *Cahiers de Cinéma*." There was some satisfaction that our cinema, modest and humble as it was, had nonetheless attracted the attention of a "universal" public, of critics, and so on. It allowed us to say that *we* existed, that there was an interest in a cinema that was, so to speak, outside the usual cinematic canon.

WHO ARE "WE"?

K. You emphasize "*we* existed."

M. As far as filmmaking goes, I always have kept and still keep the collective aspect of the work at the forefront. When I would speak about films, I never said "I," it was always "we." And when I say "we," I mean all the people involved, from the screenwriter to the extras. It's a collective effort, requiring everyone to contribute. When we were making *The Big Trip*, everyone believed in this kind of effort. After all, nobody was going to work with me day and night, in cold and terrible weather, just for the money I was going to pay. That money amounted to very little and the person would have to wait quite some time to collect it! So there had to be a very strong motivation. I can't say "I"—to say "I" would be like exploiting all of the people I worked with.

K. Did the "we" in "we existed" also refer to Morocco?

M. No, not really. There wasn't that "patriotic" aspect, if you will, to Moroccan cinema. Even today, I find it difficult to speak in those terms.

K. When you spoke earlier of the effort to create a national cinema, I had the impression that you weren't using "national" to mean, "the Moroccan nation."

M. That's right, I didn't mean it that way at all.

K. Was it more in the sense of, "that it is possible for Moroccans to make films in Morocco"?

M. Exactly.

"I THOUGHT IT WOULD BE POSSIBLE TO MAKE
ONE FILM A YEAR"

K. How did you see your career once you had finished *The Big Trip*?

M. I believed it would be possible to make more films. Without being pretentious, I even thought it would be possible to make one film a year or at least one film every two years. But I also knew that I wasn't going to be able to survive just on making feature films. To the contrary—*The Big Trip* ate up some of the money I had managed to save from working on a foreign film or making a documentary. Making feature films wasn't viable from a financial point of view, but it was viable in that it allowed you to pursue the desire to express things through film and to tell stories. I used to cite the Senegalese filmmaker Ousmane Sembène very often for saying that we can count a filmmaker successful when he will have taken the place of the storytellers who are disappearing so quickly. And how many people used to come to listen to those storytellers! But now all that is disappearing because new story-tellers have come along—the TV and so on. If the filmmaker can captivate people and bring them together into the theater to listen to his story, that will be an enormous victory.

Interlude

A First Feature—*The Big Trip* (1981)

The Big Trip's Arabic title, *Ibn as-Sabil* (literally, son of the road) means "traveler" or "wayfarer." Tazi noted that the term was used often in the Qur'an—some dozen times, he said—that it was frequently applied to orphans, and that, more generally, it connoted someone who needed protection. This is certainly true of *The Big Trip*'s main character.

At one point, Tazi summarized the film for me, saying: "The basic idea was to treat the relationship between the north and the south of Morocco. The main character, who comes from the south, is increasingly beaten down the farther he moves north, in part by the northerners' facility with language. By the time he reaches Tangiers, at the end of the film, he's practically mute: when he's with the girl he can hardly speak because the others are more skillful with words than he is. He is completely bamboozled because their tongues are quicker than his."

The Big Trip—Summary

ACT ONE: OMAR SETS OUT

Omar, a man about 30, gets a truck-driving job: setting out from a town near the southern Moroccan city of Agadir, he must deliver a cargo of dates the following day to Tangiers, at Morocco's northernmost extremity, a trip of more than 900 km that will take him through most of the country's major coastal cities.

Early in the trip Omar helps a woman driver fix her flat tire, and she gives him some pastry in thanks; soon after, he picks up a pair of young Western hitchhikers. He drops them off at his first stop, the city of Essaouira, generously giving away his *jellaba* (a body-length outer garment) to the young woman for warmth. Someone in Essaouira asks Omar to deliver an envelope to the next city, Asfi. In Asfi, the recipient asks Omar to take a religious teacher (Ar. *fqih*) to Omar's next stop. The *fqih* is silent during the trip, but greedily eats the last of Omar's pastry.

ACT TWO: OMAR'S PROBLEMS BEGIN, THEN WORSEN

Reaching Casablanca, Omar stops for a bite to eat. As he leaves the café he suddenly realizes he's left his jacket behind with all his money in it. He rushes back, too late—his jacket is gone and the people in the café offer him no sympathy. Desperately needing cash, he sells a few cases of the dates he's transporting and heads toward Rabat.

In Rabat Omar sells more dates and the buyer asks him to deliver a package at his next stop. In the city of La'reich, in a bar, Omar hands over the package, goes to wash up, and returns to find the entire café brawling—no doubt over the package—and police sirens blaring. Omar manages to reach his truck but, just as he's driving off, the badly wounded recipient of the package pulls opens the passenger door and begs for a ride. They drive off, with Omar very fearful. The man falls unconscious and Omar pulls over and drags the man from the car, leaving him motionless, possibly dead, by the side of the road.

Night has fallen, and Omar has difficulty keeping awake at the wheel. He pulls off the road and sleeps. He wakes up as morning breaks and goes to stretch his legs. Reaching the back of the truck, Omar sees boxes strewn about and realizes that his cargo has been stolen and that the dates were only a decoy—the boxes show he was transporting electronic goods, certainly smuggled. In desperation he flags down a passing truck driver. As Omar is explaining his plight, a car screeches to a halt and dumps a badly beaten young woman on the side of the road. Both drivers rush over to help, Omar gives her his sweater, and she decides to go with him toward Tangiers.

ACT THREE: A WAY OUT?

On the road Omar and the girl rarely speak but Omar, noticing her shivering, stops in the next town and buys her a *jellaba*. When he briefly recounts his ordeal, she suggests, "Why don't you just sell the truck and use the money to go abroad?" Omar answers, "You're crazy," but immediately afterward he is in a vehicle junk shop in Tangiers, selling the truck for the paltry sum of 3,000 DH. The girl knows a broker in Tangiers who can arrange Omar's sea passage to Europe. She negotiates on Omar's behalf and the broker's fee is 3,000 DH, just what Omar received for the truck. The voyage is planned for that very night.

Omar and the girl spend the day walking through Tangiers. She suggests a movie—James Bond is on the screen, interrupted several times by projection failures. She falls asleep and Omar shyly puts his arm around her shoulders.

That night, the broker picks up Omar and the girl in a van and takes Omar down to a rowboat off the quay, settling him in it, taking his 3,000 DH, and giving him a sandwich. He tells Omar to just sit tight, that overnight he will be towed to Spain where he will be given 5,000 pesetas. With a show of concern, he covers Omar with the blanket, from head to toe, and leaves.

Omar recounting his ordeal

Omar and girl at the movies

Omar preparing to embark

Against the background of dock sounds, a boat's motor, ships' horns, and waves lapping, Omar falls asleep retracing his trip in flashback. The following morning he wakes to find the sea surrounding him and his rowboat adrift. Omar looks around frantically, awkwardly trying to row. Standing up, he takes off his hat and begins to wave it in distress. Over a still shot of Omar with his left hand raised seeking help, the credits roll up the screen.

Directing a First Feature Film
SCREENPLAY AND SHOOTING

"LIMITING THINGS SOMEWHAT"

K. How did you come to make this first feature film?

M. As the 1980s began, the start of state aid really encouraged us to make feature films—finally, we could get some financing. At that time I was working with Noureddin Sail on his TV program, *The Big Screen*, and we used to talk a lot about what kinds of projects we might do together. At some point, he gave me the screenplay for *The Big Trip* to read. I had already directed actors in short films where I was the cinematographer; and I had often watched directors, some well known, some hardly known at all, directing actors; but I had never myself directed a full-length film.

To cross over into that activity, it seemed best to start by limiting things somewhat—limiting the number of characters, limiting the number of situations. That was one of the aspects that tempted me in Noureddin's screenplay, which, to some extent, was indeed written with this in mind. Also, I was tempted by the genre—the road film, with a series of encounters all tied together by one main character; a film with movement; a film that traveled, that would free me from the restrictions of unity of place, that would allow me to use images to express the countryside, with traveling shots, the truck, and so on. These are some of the elements that tempted me and the entire project suited a first feature film effort.

K. So, practical considerations were key?

M. Absolutely, absolutely. But I also liked the fact that many elements in the film aren't very clear, the meaning isn't fully transparent. A third aspect that attracted me was the notion of communication—the radio, the roads, exchanges between people—and just as often the lack of communication.

"A SCREENPLAY IS LIKE THE FLOWER BEFORE THE FRUIT"

K. How faithful was the film to the screenplay?

M. Noureddin always says, "A screenplay is like the flower before the fruit." Once you have the fruit, no one thinks anymore about the flower that gave the fruit. Naturally, every film has to adapt the imaginary of a screenplay to the reality of shooting, to the circumstances, to the terrain. This often enriches the screenplay, which, coming as it does from the domain of the imaginary, is necessarily circumscribed and enclosed.

On the whole, the film is very faithful to the screenplay, except in a few of the details; also, there were some things I felt were too clear in the screenplay and there I tried to introduce a degree of ambiguity. You have to realize that Noureddin knew my concerns, my capacities, my potential, my orientation, and he wrote the screenplay keeping in mind that this was my first effort to make a fiction film. In my later films, where I took a much more active role in creating the screenplay, the changes I introduce are much more significant.

"A VERY SMALL CREW"

K. How did the shooting of the film go?

M. We completed the shooting in four weeks in spite of the weather, which was really terrible at times, particularly in Tangiers where, during February and March, it was still very cold.

Noureddin was with us the whole time, both because he had to redo the dialogue and rewrite scenes as we went along and also because he was in charge of production. All in all we had a very small crew, just six or eight people: an electrician, a gaffer, the sound recorder; I also had someone taking care of production tasks and an assistant director. That was all.[1]

CHARACTERS AND ACTORS

THE "STAR COMPLEX"

K. Let's talk for a moment about Omar's character, a difficult one on which to base a film: he hardly speaks, his face is rather expressionless—in fact I wonder whether he smiles even once during the entire film. In addition, he is fundamentally a good and generous person: he refuses money from the woman whose flat tire he changes, he offers food and even his *jellaba* to the hitchhikers, he gives his sweater to the girl and buys her a *jellaba* when he sees her shivering. He seems to take everyone at their word although we, as spectators, can readily see their hypocrisy. How did you find the actor? He plays the role very well and seems to use little more than his eyes to express his disappointment and even despair.

M. It's funny you should ask, because there's something of a story here. We first had an actor from Casablanca whom I had chosen myself. We had been shooting for three or four days and were all staying in a hotel among foreign tourists. Straight away this actor started cavorting around with all the tourists as though he was a big film star. That was the first problem, the "star complex."

Also, before I hired him I had asked him if he knew how to drive a truck and if he had a truck-driver's license, and he answered, "Yes." But it turned out that he had no license and couldn't drive a truck. So, for the first few days of shooting we had to rent another car to tow the truck, always keeping the truck at a distance. This was terribly expensive, in addition to all the shooting problems.

After four or five days of this—of his behaving like a star, becoming very difficult to deal with, working only when he wanted to, and so on—Noureddin, the location manager, and I put our heads together and decided that we had to get rid of the actor. So we gave him his pay, bought him his return ticket, and sent him on his way. But we didn't know whom to replace him with, especially because we'd already been shooting for about a week!

We had a trainee sound technician who was working more or less for nothing—his job was to record the guide sound track. He said, sort of jokingly, "You know, I'm not an actor but I do have my truck-driver's license." So we said, "OK, you're going to do a test, and we'll see how you look driving the truck." [Laughing.] Well, the test was decisive and he ended up playing Omar *and* driving the truck. So the sound recorder played the main role. [Laughing.]

K. So, starting as a sound recorder and finishing as the main actor, he really did make *"The Big Trip!"* [Both laugh.]

M. Absolutely. And the whole episode also served to demystify the "star complex."

OMAR AS CANDIDE, "THE AMBIGUITY OF CONNECTIONS
BETWEEN PEOPLE"

K. Omar appears to be a Candide-like character, with his basic good-ness brought into relief in opposition to the indifference, hypoc-risy, and manipulation that goes on all around him.[2]

M. Yes—he is so good that he wants to share all he has, which isn't very much. But the goodness goes in one direction only—neither the hitchhikers, for example, nor anyone else gives him anything.

K. The hitchhikers don't even provide any conversation, which is the very least a hitchhiker can do for a driver.

M. That's right—and they even change the radio station so they can listen to Western pop music. In effect he is annihilated by all those around him.

But in some ways things are even worse than that for Omar, because you sense there might be a connection, even a conspiracy, among the people who manipulate and dispossess him. When he loses his jacket and money in the bar, someone says to him, "But look, you shouldn't have left your jacket in the men's room." It's as though people were marking him, just waiting for the right moment to steal his things, like an organization that tries to take advantage of any outsider. There's a kind of complicity against him and he has no recourse, because you know that even if you man-age to get someone to investigate, the complicity is likely to extend to the investigators as well.

This kind of complicity continues up to the end of the film. It's even possible that the girl was deliberately thrown on the side of the road to entrap him—perhaps even by the same group that stole his cargo. Perhaps Omar, naïve and good as he is, was already noticed in Casablanca and taken for a mark, for someone who could be dispossessed of everything he had.

But this isn't spelled out in the film—I wanted to keep the ambiguity of this and the ambiguity of the connections between people.

THEMES AND SCENES

MOROCCAN "MOSAIC"; TURTLES AND O'TOOLE

K. You talked earlier of *The Big Trip* giving you the occasion to show something of Morocco's variety—you called it the "mosaic." Could you give me an example?

M. Sure. One way to show Morocco's mosaic was to convey something of the particularity of each city that Omar stopped at. Take the example of Essaouira, Omar's first stop: the particularity we chose was that its strong sea wind is said to drive people mad. So, when Omar goes into a bar there, we find a guy telling the same story—about turtles—over and over again, as well as repeating himself in the middle of the story. Perhaps at one time he'd been some kind of intellectual, but now he's completely flipped.

There's actually a story behind this story. The turtle story originally comes from the English actor Peter O'Toole. We got it from Larbi Yacoubi, who plays the flipped-out storyteller and who often works with me as a costume designer and usually has a small role in each of my films. Larbi Yacoubi spent a lot of time in the artistic and actors' milieu in Tangiers, during its golden years. He was in contact with all sorts of people, both Moroccans and foreigners, people like Muhammad Choukri, Tennessee Williams, Paul Bowles, and so on. One of those was Peter O'Toole and he told Larbi the turtle story. It seems O'Toole told it in something like the following way, saying, "You know why I can't stand Moroccans? It's because of these poor turtles." And he would go on to describe how difficult it is for turtles to mate, how they struggle to mount one another but keep falling off, again and again. Finally, after all that trouble, they might be successful and eventually produce an offspring. But, in Morocco, what happens to that little offspring when it grows up? After all the trouble its parents took to produce it, Moroccans take that turtle and turn its shell into the base of a mandolin, which you can buy in almost any market, just to make some music. For O'Toole, this was too much to take! [Laughs.] And that's the story we used in the film.

A BARROOM BRAWL

K. When Omar delivers the package in La'reich—a package that may or may not contain drugs—a brawl breaks out in the bar. This is quite a melee and I wonder how you went about filming it.

M. I don't think there is much difficulty at all organizing this kind of

O'Toole's turtles and mandolins

violence in Moroccan films. My theory is that this kind of violence acts as a safety valve. We find this sort of behavior in *moussems*, which are festivities to celebrate a saint's anniversary or mark the coming together of a brotherhood or sect. Here people really let loose and everyone who carries latent violence inside him has the opportunity to express it. In these *moussems*—particularly those of the Aissawa and the Hamadsha—people really let themselves go, both physically and morally.[3] We all have this internal violence inside us—stoked of course by what we see on TV and in the cinema—and it all comes to the surface very quickly once the occasion arises. There is nothing simpler than filming a melee—I had absolutely no difficulty filming that scene. [Laughs.]

K. Did you tell the actors where to go, what to do?

M. There's no need to direct—no need to tell the actors anything specific. You just say, "You have to start a big melee" and before you know it they're unleashed. [Laughs.]

FLASHBACKS AND A DIRECTOR'S "MANEUVER"

K. Almost at the end of the film, Omar is in the boat and we assume he's asleep. The film goes into a series of flashbacks. Other than two brief flashbacks earlier in the film, the film proceeds in strict chronological order as Omar travels northward. But now, in this series of flashbacks, key scenes are shown in reverse order until, in the last scene in this sequence, we see a scene we haven't witnessed in the film—a home interior, children sleeping, a man washes with his wife's help, then walks out of the house leaving his wife with the children.

M. That flashback scene, where the man prepares to leave home, was originally meant to be at the beginning of the film.

K. But in the film, the first time we see Omar he is closing the door behind him as he goes into the street.

M. Yes. But when we had the original actor playing Omar, this sequence in the flashback was meant to be the opening sequence of the film, with Omar preparing to leave home. However, once our sound recorder became Omar, that original actor had no role in the film and this scene no longer fit. The problem was, I was really attached to that scene. It was a scene I had prepared, I had suffered for, because it's an extended sequence shot lasting almost a minute: we follow the man shaving, the children sleeping, the mother preparing his suitcase; then he starts to leave, going down the staircase. This was a sequence shot I had prepared and filmed myself and I was very pleased with it. I wanted to figure out a way to put it in the film, and I came up with that maneuver. I think, actually, that the series of flashbacks was put in there so that I could put in that particular scene. [Laughs.]

K. I thought it worked very well and was easily understood as a scene from Omar's childhood—even though it was the only sequence in the series that we hadn't already seen in the film.

M. Yes. Instead of it being Omar leaving home as originally planned, it becomes Omar seeing his life in flashback, ending with him as a child, sleeping, as his father leaves the house.

THE ENDING

"Last minute" ending

K. Coming to the ending itself: Omar is standing in the boat, distraught, with the sea all around—naturally, we ask ourselves, "What's going to happen to him?"

M. This ending wasn't in the screenplay, just as with the ending of *Looking for My Wife's Husband*. Here it was because we were uncertain about how to end the film. Should Omar try to go abroad or shouldn't he? It was only very near the end of the shooting that I came up with the idea that the middleman would put him into a rowboat—what fishermen call the "lifeboat" [Fr. *barque de secours*], which they tow behind them in case of a problem. I must say that I like to change the endings somewhat at the last minute, letting everyone think it's going to end as it does in the screenplay but then surprising them. And also, I love the sea, and I like to have a film either begin or end in the sea.[4]

You can't imagine how much I wanted to have a helicopter for that scene. I would have been able to zoom away from the boat and show it as just a point in the vast sea—that's how the film would have ended. But I couldn't afford a helicopter. So we filmed it in the Tangiers port, from the quay. Ali Hassan—the sound man who suddenly became an actor—didn't know how to swim and was terrified.

K. He didn't seem to know how to row either.

M. He didn't! He asked me how to row and I told him, "You're doing just fine, because I want you to row like someone who has never rowed a boat in his life." We didn't rehearse it, just shot it, that was the first take and it was the best. Sometimes you have to do things just as you feel them, at the very moment.

Suspended endings? Sequels?

K. The film ends with Omar in a still—one can't help but think of the ending of Truffaut's film *The 400 Blows* [*Les 400 Coups*, 1959].

M. That's true. But I think you could say that there is a suspended ending in all my films, the ending is never conclusive. In fact, I hate things that end. The saddest moment of the day for me is when the sun sets, because something is dying. Luckily we know that the sun will come back the next day. But endings with finality I find very painful. In all my films, without exception, the ending is without finality; there is always a potential opening, both in interpretation and in the story's continuation.[5]

K. In one of your interviews on *The Big Trip*, you said that the ending "left open the possibility of making a sequel." This is rather ironic given all the problems you had making the sequel to *Looking for My Wife's Husband*.

M. In fact, I did think seriously of making a sequel to *The Big Trip* and we even had the outline of a screenplay. I had some talks with Ali Hassan about it and we thought that Omar, after indeed going abroad, would return to Morocco six or ten years later as a very successful businessman. His business would have been something rather unique, a service for transporting back home the corpses of Muslims who had died in non-Muslim lands. We would see him going to the airport in some European city in the hope that each arriving airplane might have some business for him, might have someone who had died and could be sent back in a coffin. You know, this is an actual activity in real life.

K. The motif appears in *Lalla Hobby*, I remember.

M. Right. So Omar comes back to Morocco, rich, and he retraces his earlier trip, this time from north to south, and he tries to take revenge on each person who had outwitted him years earlier. The ending to *The Big Trip* was an open one that could have easily led to a sequel, but we didn't have the time or the occasion to do it. In any case, I'm now 99 percent convinced that it's a delusion to make a film in the belief that you are continuing in a vein that the public liked, because you can never predict that you'll be on the same wavelength as the public.

The Big Trip in the Rearview Mirror

"A FIRST DRAFT," LIMITS TO EXPRESSION, "A JOINT EFFORT"

K. When you look back at *The Big Trip* now, what do you think of it?

M. For me, *The Big Trip* was an important experience, a debut. It has its good qualities but, all things considered, it remains a kind of first draft [Fr. *une première copie*]. The basic ideas hold true—about problems of communication between people, about language—but the images used to convey them might have been different.

Now, about twenty years later, I have a different vision of things—not for all my films, but for this one. I think there was a certain naïveté—first of all in the subject, then in the characters—and I would portray these differently today. Of course, the purity and naïveté of the main character were desired, it was done on purpose.

I think I would have been more explicit regarding certain aspects that were kept somewhat veiled. I don't know if this had to do with self-censorship, or if these elements weren't made clear in the screenplay, or whether there were other reasons. For example, we know that Omar is a victim and we know that this truck isn't carrying dates, it's carrying black-market goods of some sort. I could have emphasized this more. Another example: the whole question of the crisis in Moroccan films is only touched upon.

K. You're referring to the scene where Omar and the girl go to see a James Bond film in Tangiers and the projector breaks down?

M. Yes, I could have done more with that.

Also—and this is common knowledge—any truck traveling on our roads will be stopped thirty-six thousand times by the police for no reason whatsoever, leading to all kinds of corrupt practices. But at the time of the film it was very difficult to approach such a subject, just as it was difficult to approach smuggling. I remember how, six or seven years later when I wanted to use the uniform of a policeman or someone from the road patrols, I had to go from one government office to another for a year, and after all that I still couldn't get to use the uniform. Whereas today you can use the uniform of a policeman, a soldier, and even use their weapons. Earlier this was unimaginable. So just try to imagine the problems we would have had trying to show motorcycle cops stopping the truck, asking Omar for his papers, his offering them money, and so on. Keeping these things off the screen was required by the times. Today my approach would be different.

K. I could imagine some wonderful scenes of this sort.

M. Absolutely. And it would have fit in nicely with the deadpan, camouflaged humor of the film.

But, looking back and taking everything into account, I have to say that this film reflects a particular period in my life, it represents a beginning, it responds to some of my deep concerns, and it is the product of a joint effort with a friend with whom I have shared many things.

Chapter Three

Huston, Wise, Coppola, Camus . . . and Pasolini, Scorsese . . . and Some Others

Introduction: Making a Living

When Tazi returned from the United States in 1975, he knew it was impossible to earn a living making Moroccan feature films. He opened a production company in Rabat and began to make various kinds of films on contract—documentaries for government ministries, advertising clips for private enterprises, short films on social subjects, and so on. Also, with the help of people he had met during visits to Los Angeles and Hollywood, for much of the next fifteen years he worked on foreign films being made in Morocco, coming into contact with John Huston, Robert Wise, Francis Ford Coppola, Robert Dalva, and Martin Scorsese, among others. This activity tapered off after the mid-1980s and ceased altogether by 1990, for reasons we will soon be coming to.

Tazi views his advertising work and his participation in "civil society" in the following way:

M. The advertising work was sometimes very interesting, especially when you had some freedom of expression—and freedom of expression is a very interesting issue in this area. But more often it was just a question of simply translating what was little more than an advertising blurb, where the client would come with a French product and its French advertisement and would simply say, "Do exactly the same thing here."

Even worse: often the client would require us to bring in a

French director to supervise the entire process. In fact, this practice still continues today when French and English directors make advertising spots here—they have no confidence in Moroccan technicians, they don't think that people here have the ability to express themselves in advertising. When I've been given the freedom to make the spots I wanted, I've made spots that have won prizes. But as things stand, it's very difficult to convince a client to allow us to make a spot reflecting our own society, the client usually wants a simple remake of the foreign spot. Continuing in advertising work in such conditions had no interest for me other than as a money spinner.

So I pulled out of this kind of work, but I kept the production company going. At that point, in the early to mid-1980s, although I had a clear desire and will to make more fiction films, I still had to make a living, ensure that there was food on the table. I tried to do this while retaining a certain dignity, intellectually speaking—not making advertising spots for some kind of dishwashing product or other—and working within the framework of my own social and intellectual concerns.

I still had my deep interest in communicating, so I began to turn toward television. I was also participating, as the 1980s progressed, in what we now call "civil society" activities, although at that time we weren't yet using this term. Here I came into contact with a number of people who were interested in using audiovisual means to encourage greater social mobilization. We began to make what were called "socio-clips"—short films, usually no more than two or three minutes long, meant to encourage people to question the social system—and we completed a number of these during the second half of the 1980s. These were collaborative products involving sociologists, anthropologists, artists, and intellectuals—all of us trying to figure out how to raise peoples' consciousness of the conditions around them—with the real force behind this project being Fatima Mernissi.

We made some of these socio-clips with the United Nations University, working together with Algerians and Tunisians. We dealt with a lot of different subjects—the situation of women, of rural women, of young girls, the problem of education and training in the countryside, and so on. Some of the clips were distributed rather widely and reached television screens in Germany and France as well as in Tunisia and Morocco.[1]

My production company is still a going concern—I use it for

documentaries, multimedia projects, sometimes to do a spot when it's for something useful, like a humanitarian issue—and I've continued these kinds of activities for the past twenty years or more. But no longer for dishwashing products and the like.[2]

Foreign Productions in Morocco

Working on foreign feature film productions was Tazi's core professional activity from the mid-1970s through the mid-1980s and one that engaged him very intensely. Foreign film production has a long history in Morocco, with its origins intimately tied to the country's colonial past. Over time, its character has changed considerably, as has, consequently, its relationship to Moroccan filmmaking.[3]

The story begins, as many of these stories do, with the Lumière brothers, who shot at least one of their early scenes in Morocco, toward the end of the 1890s and before the establishment of the French Protectorate. Soon after there was a private film showing at the Royal Palace in Fez.[4] Several years later, in the summer of 1907, the Lumière brothers' Algerian-born cameraman, Félix Mesguich, filmed French military action in Casablanca.[5] Mesguich reported his first hours there in the following terms, "When we arrived the city was smoking under the shelling. A navy troop escorted us to the French consulate where we entrenched ourselves. I filmed the passing of some troops in the devastated streets filled with corpses that attracted clouds of flies and from which arose a stinking odor. I then filmed groups of Algerian riflemen and the foreign legion."[6] By late September Mesguich was back in Paris and scenes from his filming were appearing on Paris screens. The French troops, meanwhile, having earlier established control over a number of Moroccan cities, now secured a foothold in regions outside Casablanca, all as preludes to their systematic colonization of the country, consecrated in 1912 by the Treaty of Fez, which formally established the French Protectorate. Also in Fez and also in 1912, the first public film showing was held, in the open air, with a giant screen placed against the walls of the city.[7]

The screening of films was very slow to advance but, as early as the 1920s, foreign filmmakers were showing great interest in the country and some fifteen films were made during the decade.[8] This affinity continued throughout the Protectorate period, during which some eighty films in all were shot in the country, with both French and Spanish directors usually working in their respective colonial zones.[9] Many of these films were made with "Orientalist" themes, aiming to satisfy European tastes for the "exotic"; on occasion, utilizing recipes already well established in Egypt, these films attempted to wean Moroccans away from the Egyptian films that had great appeal.

During the Protectorate period, some of the world's top directors made films in Morocco, including André Zwobada (*La septième porte,* 1947, and *Noces de sable,* 1948), Jacques Becker (*Ali Baba et les 40 voleurs,* 1955), and Alfred Hitchcock (*The Man Who Knew Too Much,* 1955). Perhaps the best known is Orson Welles's film *Othello*—shooting began in 1949 and the film was presented at the Cannes Film Festival in 1952 under Moroccan colors, where it shared the grand prize. There is an obvious irony here, in that the film most associated with Morocco—*Casablanca* (Michael Curtiz, 1943)—had not one foot of film shot there (it was shot in Utah and California). Yet, as we will see later in this chapter, this film still calls up the image of Morocco for many, including at least one foreign filmmaker.[10]

Although Welles's film was nominally Moroccan and although all films made and produced by the CCM during the colonial period were technically Moroccan in nationality (even though the people running the institution were French), none of the films made in Morocco were made by Moroccans. At most, some low-level Moroccan technicians were involved as were some Moroccan extras who, occasionally, received secondary billing.[11] In fact, it was not until the final years of colonial rule that the French Protectorate authorities, who established filmmaking capacity in Morocco largely to serve and publicize the needs of French administration, made some effort to train Moroccan filmmakers.[12]

With the arrival of independence, foreign films continued to be made on Moroccan soil, although the pace was very uneven: from 1956 to 1980, approximately 30 foreign productions were shot in Morocco (or a little more than one per year), and then approximately 160 foreign films were made between 1981 and 1998 (averaging almost 10 per year).[13] These included features by some of the world's best-known filmmakers, including David Lean (*Lawrence of Arabia,* 1962), Henri Verneuil (*100,000 Dollars in the Sun,* 1963), Jean-Luc Godard (*Le Grand Escroc,* 1963), Pier Paolo Pasolini (*Oedipus the King,* 1967), Franklin Schaffner (*Patton,* 1970), John Huston (*The Man Who Would Be King,* 1976), Mustapha Akkad (*The Message,* 1976), Franco Zeffirelli (*Jesus of Nazareth,* 1977), Claude Lelouch (*Edith and Marcel,*

1982), Raul Ruiz (*Treasure Island,* 1986), Martin Scorsese (*The Last Temptation of Christ,* 1987), Bernardo Bertolucci (*The Sheltering Sky,* 1989), and many others. Over the past several years we continue to find major productions such as Scorsese's *Kundun* and Spielberg's *Young Indiana Jones* in 1996; William Friedkin's *Rules of Engagement* and Ridley Scott's Oscar-winning *Gladiator* in 1999; Tony Scott's *Black Hawk Down* in 2001; and Oliver Stone's *Alexander the Great,* which began production in 2003.

Although the number of foreign productions per year has remained relatively constant recently, the amounts these productions invest in Morocco vary greatly. One big-budget film can make all the difference: in 1996, Scorsese's *Kundun* accounted for more than half the investment of all foreign features combined and in 2001 *Black Hawk Down* accounted for almost two-thirds.[14] With the stakes this high, it is not surprising that Moroccan state institutions seek to make Morocco an attractive investment by offering great advantages to foreign producers.[15] However, it is also not surprising that the large sums invested by foreign productions have significant negative effects on Moroccan films, not least of these being that foreign productions dwarf the investments by Moroccan features and accentuate the scarcity for Moroccan filmmakers of technicians, actors, and other collaborators, making it even more difficult for Moroccan productions to pay their way.[16]

Today Ouarzazate, formerly a remote town in the High Atlas Mountains but lately the main location for films such as *Kundun* and *Gladiator,* has become an enormous production center for foreign films.[17] Hundreds of extras may be tested on almost any day. Their wages, while healthy by the standards of rural Moroccans among whom, in any event, unemployment is high, are dramatically lower than those obtaining in western Europe or the United States.[18]

Huston, Wise, Coppola, Camus . . . and the Others
OVERVIEW

TAZI'S CREDITS ON FOREIGN PRODUCTIONS[19]

1963. Trainee. *Cent mille dollars au soleil.* Henri Verneuil.
1972. Cameraman, second crew. *Impossible Object.* John Frankenheimer.

1973. Cameraman, first crew. *Two People.* Robert Wise.

1975. Location manager. *The Man Who Would Be King.* John Huston.

1976. Production manager. *Silver Bears.* Ivan Passer.

1976. Production manager. *March or Die.* Dick Richards.

1983. Production manager. *The Black Stallion Returns.* Robert Dalva. Zoetrope Productions (F. F. Coppola).

1983. Production manager. *Bolero.* John Derek.

1983–1984. Location scouting, costume production. *The Last Temptation of Christ* (1987). Martin Scorsese.

1984. General location manager. *King David.* Bruce Beresford. [This was not filmed because of resistance on official levels in Morocco to filming a "prophet."]

1985. Associate producer and coordinator. *Luna de Agosto.* Juan-Miñon Echevarria (Spain).

1985. Production manager. *Jewel of the Nile.* Lewis Teague. Produced by Michael Douglas.

1989. Associate producer and artistic and technical adviser. *La forja de un rebelde.* Mario Camus. Produced by TVE (Spain).

1990. Executive producer. *Requiem para Granada.* Roberto Bodegas (Spain). Produced by TVE.

FROM CINEMATOGRAPHER
TO PRODUCTION TASKS

K. How did you first start working on foreign productions in Morocco?

M. While I was in the United States, studying at Syracuse University, I had gone to Los Angeles, to Hollywood, and when I returned to Morocco I was in touch with some producers and others who were working on these foreign productions.

At that time—the early 1970s—very few foreign films were being shot in Morocco. There had already been *Lawrence of Arabia* and *Cent mille dollars au soleil*—a French film I had worked on as a trainee—and a few others. But Moroccan participation on these films was very limited as far as technicians were concerned. The foreigners just came to shoot here and hired a few assistants. The whole field wasn't yet institutionalized the way it is today, when a lot of money comes in and benefits just a few individuals.

K. You were trained as a cinematographer—was it in this capacity that you did most of your work on foreign productions?

M. I started out that way, but after a few films I got more into the production side, which involved many different tasks, from constituting a technical crew, to renting trucks and transportation, to bringing together groups of extras for walk-on roles, and everything that had to do with casting, set construction, choice of locations, relationships with the technicians, dealing with the authorities, and so on.

JOHN HUSTON AND *THE MAN WHO WOULD BE KING* (1975): LOCATIONS, ENGLISH METHOD, HUSTON'S CURIOSITY

"HOW MANY HOURS BY TRUCK . . . MULE . . . DONKEY?"

K. Could we take a few of these as examples and explore how your work proceeded?

M. Let me first take the case of John Huston's *The Man Who Would Be King,* which for me is a true classic of world cinema. Here, I went around with him helping look for locations, showing him areas of the country that might fit his needs, and choosing actors. He decided to film in three different locations: in Marrakesh where the Afghani village was built, in Ouarzazate, and at Tinghir in the High Atlas Mountains, which stood in for the Khyber Pass. Three Moroccan filmmakers worked with him, each of us working on one of the locations. I was in charge of organizing the work at Tinghir.

As far as my work went, at the outset we had to look over all the possible locations in order to decide where to shoot. Then we had to find people—this was in Morocco's southern regions—who were of a type that corresponded to Afghani people. Already there was a significant geographical
similarity between Afghanistan and Morocco but Huston, in addition, was looking for facial resemblance between the people, physical resemblance. That's why we went all over, among the Ait Hadidou tribe and into the area of Imilchil, to find the kind of people he was looking for.

Some of the Khyber Pass sequences involved between five hundred and eight hundred extras. Although there was an English production director and an English location manager, you still needed to have a Moroccan to actually organize things on the ground. And the Moroccan and English organizational styles were actually quite distinct. Imagine, for example, English production managers trying to solve the problem of getting two hundred to three hundred people from different villages to show up at the same time at the shooting location—they would go about it by taking compasses and rulers, tracing lines on a map, thinking about means of transportation. We Moroccans merely had to think of how our local and regional festivals occur—our *moussems*—and everything turned out to be much simpler.[20] We would just tell people, "We'll all come together at such-and-such a place on such-and-such a date," and then we wouldn't have to worry whether they were coming in a truck or on a donkey or on foot. But the English tried to foresee everything—and they had technical assistants to do that: "How many hours will this trip take by truck, how many by mule, how many by donkey . . . ?" They were much too methodical and it didn't fit at all with Moroccan methods—we know how to respect timing and planning, but we do so without being slaves to what you might call a "Cartesian" system.

Not an "Orientalist vision"

K. What kind of relationship did you have with Huston, from a human point of view—was it like that of student to teacher, or of pals, or what?

M. Neither, really. Huston was interested in you because you knew your craft and because you could help him deepen his knowledge of the subject, of the setting, so that he wouldn't miss out on things. He had an enormous curiosity to get to know the various regions of Morocco, its different groups of people, their customs, and so on. He had nothing of that bias that many Western filmmakers have—that Orientalist vision. Of course, he was saved from that in part because the film *The Man Who Would Be King* had nothing to do with Morocco, it was about something happening in a part of the world very distant from Morocco and it was just a question of finding locations and people representing that other part of the world.

Wherever we went he was curious and wanted to deepen his knowledge, often on small details, such as why the clothing of the Ait Hadidou tribe was in black and white. At one point in the shooting he asked for long explanations of the meaning of specific elements in Berber jewelry—why there was a spiral here, a triangle there, and what the other signs might mean. There is a village between Ouarzazate and Zagora known for having the largest market for silver jewelry of this sort, and when his wife

arrived in Ouarzazate he came looking for me and had me escort
her to this village. I had a lot of work to do on the film, but he
said, "No, you go with her." So I was sort of transformed into a
guide, but this was done very respectfully. He knew that I had
good knowledge of this kind of jewelry and he knew she wanted
to buy the real thing, objects of real value, and that I was the
person to help her out so she wouldn't be gypped. His wife really
loved the jewelry and she bought a lot of it—especially pieces
made of amber and silver—and she spent an enormous sum of
money. She was a charming woman—in fact, she was a screenwriter and had written the screenplay for the film.

TWO PEOPLE (ROBERT WISE, 1973); *MARCH OR DIE* (DICK RICHARDS, 1976); *THE BLACK STALLION RETURNS* (ROBERT DALVA, 1983)

K. What were the other films that you worked on during this period?
M. I had worked on several films before going to the United States.
There was *Silver Bears,* directed by Ivan Passer, who had been a
screenwriter for Polanski. This was a big production but a failure
as a film. The major films I worked on, in addition to Huston's,
were *Two People* by Robert Wise of *West Side Story* fame, which I
did before going to the United States; then, just after working with
Huston, there was another important film—to my mind at least—
an American film called *March or Die,* directed by Dick Richards,
starring Gene Hackman and Catherine Deneuve. This too was a
film with a big budget. And then, a few years later, there was *The
Black Stallion Returns,* directed by Robert Dalva and produced by
Francis Coppola.

TWO PEOPLE: FROM PRODUCTION ASSISTANT TO CAMERAMAN

HIDDEN CAMERA, FALSE BEARD
M. On *Two People* I was hired as a production assistant. The film
starred Peter Fonda and was the story of a GI who deserts the
army in Vietnam, meets a girl—a model—who is on her way to
Morocco, and he goes with her. One day we were supposed to

film a scene in Jemaa el-Fna. Wise, thinking of this in the American way, as a large studio, wanted to pay everyone there as though they were extras. Not only would that have meant sinking an enormous part of the budget into this, but once you do that you change everything and you no longer can film it like it really is.

So I suggested filming Jemaa el-Fna with a hidden camera. You know, at that time, the theaters would advertise what was showing by taking a large poster, mounting it on a small carriage, and hiring someone to push this through the streets and passageways of the town. I told Wise you could add a camera to such a carriage and you could film in this way.

And that's how it was done. After that, I became a full-fledged cameraman on the first crew. I also suggested something else: for traveling shots inside the medina and also for filming in Jemaa el-Fna, you could dress as a porter in a *jellaba*, carry a suitcase on your shoulder, and inside the suitcase put a camera and film scenes that way. And that's how I shot those scenes, and those scenes are there in the film. I became sort of indispensable in finding solutions to these kinds of problems, in finding ways to shoot without bringing in big equipment like cranes and so on, and in setting up what are called "cutaway shots," which are absolutely essential but can't be set up through trial and error.[21]

I'll tell you something amusing that happened while we were making that film. Wise wanted to find someone for a walk-on role who looked like a drug dealer. He saw a guy in town with the kind of look he wanted, a guy with a big beard and so on, so we hired him and we shot film with him on Wednesday, Thursday, and Friday. We were going to begin shooting again on Monday, so we told all the actors to come back then. Monday arrives, we look around for the dealer and we can't find him anywhere. We call him on the megaphone and finally he shows up, but he had completely shaved off his beard. No one had thought to tell him, "Careful, don't shave your beard," because, for us, this was completely self-evident. But now we were saying to him, "You're crazy, you're absolutely crazy to have gone and shaved your beard." "But I only had the beard because I didn't have enough money to get shaved. When you paid me for last week's work, the first thing I did was use the money to get shaved!" [Both laugh.]

K. So, what did you do?

M. Well, we'd taken Polaroids of the guy with his beard and with the help of the make-up person we were able to reconstitute the look. But at what a cost! And, above all, we had to do this without the director finding out anything about it!

MARCH OR DIE: "BIG STARS . . . IN FRANCE IT DID RATHER WELL"

DENEUVE, DOCTORS IN THE CANDY STORE, SAND TO NEVADA

K. What about *March or Die*?

M. We filmed this mostly in locations south of Agadir, and there was a crew composed largely of Americans and Britons, with a few French. It was the story of Abd el-Krim and the struggle he led against the Spanish occupation of north Morocco during the 1920s. But, as you'd expect, it was very much a romance, there was a strong romantic element. The film had some big stars— Gene Hackman, Max von Sydow, with Catherine Deneuve supplying the romantic interest. The film may not have been very widely distributed in the United States but in France it did rather well, under the title *Il était une fois la légion.*

At times there was some tension with the director. I remember witnessing a rather ridiculous incident where Catherine Deneuve—a very big French star, of course—arrived on the set a little late. The director, Dick Richards, began to harangue her, saying things like, "You know, to make films you have to have discipline, you have to follow the schedule," and so on. Catherine Deneuve, very coolly, answered simply, "Listen, I didn't realize I was going to be making a picture with a director of advertising clips."

On this film I was production manager and in that capacity I had to take care of the local casting, make sure there were provisions for their health care, make sure the training of the extras was going well, and so on. There were a lot of extras on this film— perhaps three hundred fifty to four hundred, whom we hired from around Agadir—and every morning, between 7 A.M. and noon, there were training sessions for these people, training in sword fighting, rifle use, and so on.

After four or five days of work, I noticed something funny: right after we served the extras their breakfast, very long lines began to form at the medical tent—we had an English doctor and several nurses there. Everyone was complaining either about a headache, or a stomach ache, or that their son had one or that their mother had one. The lines seemed without end, and the doctor and nurses were very patient about it all. And then, one day, I was driving from Agadir to the set and I noticed the doctor's car stopped outside a small grocer's store. I thought perhaps he had some problem with his car, and because I had to keep an eye on everything that might affect production I pulled over to see what was the matter. There was the doctor, buying boxes and boxes of *smarties,* you know, that small candy with different colors [the French equivalent of M&M's]. "Why are you buying all that—to give to children in the villages?" "No," he answered, "it's a secret." Actually, he had used up all the medicines he had, and now he was giving the *smarties* to the nurses to put in different bottles according to color, and then to give out one color for headaches, another for stomach aches, and so on. [Laughs.]

I should tell you one more story about this film. Every day we had to travel about 20 km from Agadir to the location, and the last 10 km or so of this was on pretty rough unpaved roads. The main character was played by Gene Hackman and one day, just before we reached this part of the trip, "Mister" Gene Hackman, if you please, began to have bad pains in his back.[22] Right away, the insurance company was contacted and they agreed to allow Hackman to continue filming provided that he be transported from hotel to location by helicopter. We managed to rent a helicopter from Gibraltar, which came all the way down to Agadir so that Gene Hackman could go the 20 km from Agadir to the location. That routine continued for five or six days, but Mister Gene Hackman still had back pains. At this point, the insurance company refused to have the shooting continue, because a permanent injury to Hackman could cost them a lot of money.

But they couldn't stop the shooting completely because of all the contract obligations, so they suggested shooting the film somewhere in the deserts of the United States, in Nevada I think. However, it just so happens that the color of the sand dunes in Agadir is not the same as the color of the sand in Nevada. So they sent over some big American transport planes—C-130s—to transport tons and tons of sand from the Agadir dunes to camouflage the sand of Nevada.

K. Unbelievable! You couldn't match the colors by using filters or something like that, could you?

M. No, the filter will change not only the color of the sand but the color of people's skin and so on.

Well, for me, a Moroccan, to imagine that—sending these big transport planes to move tons of sand—it's really unimaginable, you had to have been there.

K. Bringing sand to Nevada—that's a wonderful update to the old English saying about "bringing coals to Newcastle."

M. And, of course, the insurance paid for everything.

THE BLACK STALLION RETURNS: "THAT'S WHAT I CALL BEING METHODICAL, THINKING OF THE CONSEQUENCES"

COPPOLA AND COMPUTERS

K. How about your work on *The Black Stallion Returns* and with Francis Ford Coppola?

M. Coppola—Zoetrope Productions—was the producer of this film, rather than the director, but he was on the set very often—it was his "stable," so to speak. The film was a sequel to a very successful film called *The Black Stallion.* This second film, which was shot entirely in Morocco, had less success than the first, but it was a very nice story of the love between an American boy and a horse. His Arab stallion is stolen and the boy comes to an Arab country to try to find it. It was a good film for young people as well as for the not so young. We filmed in some very beautiful locations around Agadir, Taroudannt, Ouarzazate, Zagora, all over in fact.

Coppola came from time to time to see how things were going. I was amazed then, and it's amazing even now, to think that already in 1980 Coppola went around with a computer that was hooked into satellite transmission. On his portable computer he was able to view sequences from another film he was in the process of shooting. It was really extraordinary.

K. Coppola was always known for his fascination with the latest technology.

M. To such an extent that his son seemed to have the same bent. Once, his son stayed with us while we were filming—we were staying in the Europa-Maroc Hotel. I remember the hotel manager came running up to me, completely beside himself. "Coppola's son is destroying his hotel room! Come with me, right away!" And there was Coppola's son, sitting on the carpet, with the room's TV and radio completely taken apart and laid out in front of him. I told the manager not to worry, this wasn't a big problem. I went to Coppola to tell him about it and he reacted with great pleasure, saying, "I'm really happy that my son is interested and capable of doing this kind of thing. Go tell the manager that we'll pay for everything." [Laughs.]

K. Everything was taken apart?

M. Yes, completely disassembled. And I guess his son was about 14 or 15 years old. Later, the manager said to me, "You know, those are high-tension wires, thank god the kid didn't electrocute himself!"

K. I suppose insurance wouldn't have been much help with that!

INSURANCE, AGAIN

M. Speaking of insurance, that reminds me of something else that happened on this film. For *The Black Stallion Returns* we had to find a valley where we could have something like three hundred horses in a wild state, Arab stallions and so on, roaming freely. We looked all over and finally settled on a valley that's about 15 km from Tafraout, a really beautiful valley. And we also had to build the set, and these constructions are always made out of earth and straw. At the very outset, the American production director said to me, "We'll have to get in touch with the meteorological services—I want to know what the rainfall records are over the last ten years, how much it has rained, how often it has rained, and so on." I didn't know why they wanted this, but I went ahead and it must have taken me a week to accomplish—meeting people from the meteorological services in Casablanca, obtaining as much detail as we could concerning rainfall in the area. As far as we could tell, over the previous ten years it had never rained in this valley at this time of the year—it was November. So we went ahead and constructed the sets, and the production people insured the set for a very high value to protect against the risk of destruction, however that might occur.

We had just about finished the construction when, sure enough, we had torrential rains in Tafraout, destroying absolutely everything that we had built. You know, the Qasbah that we had constructed out of earth and straw, well, it just became mud. [Laughs.]

A few days later, the insurance people arrived from the United States. And that's when I understood why we had gotten the meteorological data over the past ten years. Because that's what the production people gave the insurers—"Look, we made sure that over the last ten years it hadn't rained here, that was the guarantee. If it hasn't rained for ten years, there's no reason for it to rain now." [Laughs.] So the insurers had to pay a lot for this, given the high stated value. With the insurance money the entire set was reconstructed, and they probably made four or five times the cost of that in addition! That's what I call being methodical, thinking of the consequences.

THE GROTTO

M. There's another amusing anecdote related to this film. At one point in the film, the American boy meets a shepherd who takes him to a cave where they find cave paintings on the walls. We found an appropriate cave near the village of Qel'at Mguna, near the town of Boumalne, not too far from Tinghir.[23] But we needed the paintings. So we brought a set designer from Italy to draw the paintings inside the caves. We shot the scenes, they were successful, you can see them in the film. This took place in 1980 or so.

About five years later, in 1985 or thereabouts, I was in that area looking for locations for another film—a film that never got made, by the way—and I got to the spot where that cave was. Actually, there's a descent by the side of the road, with a river down below, and then you ford the river to get to the cave. Coming up to that point in the road, I saw some tourist buses, a bunch of tents, kiosks selling postcards and handicrafts, some makeshift stalls where you could eat a *tajine* or something simple like that. I was very surprised because this was an area I'd been to many times over the years and I'd never seen such a thing.

Sure enough, five years after the Italian had done the cave paintings, the tourist guides had promoted this into a tourist destination, claiming these were true rock paintings. An entire agglomeration had been constructed, a lot of trade was going on, on the basis of paintings that had been done only five years earlier! And you could even hear the guides telling the tourists that these paintings were more than ten thousand years old.

K. The decorator wasn't aware of this, I suppose.

M. No, not at all.

K. Too bad. Most artists try to create something that lives on after them, but this set designer managed to create something that lived before him! [Both laugh.]

M. Absolutely. The sheikh[24] of the area came up to me and said, "I know this is phony, but look how many people it is supporting." I then realized I couldn't go ahead and expose it for what it was, there were too many people from the area earning their living from it.

K.   Have you been back there since?

M.   No—that was in 1985–1986—so that's quite a few years ago. Really, it was a beautiful area, just off the road from Mguna toward Imilchil. I have to go back there soon, to see if it hasn't become something of a city! [Laughs.][25]

COMPARING DIRECTORS

Huston's "humanism," Coppola's "modest[y]," Wise's "studio mentality"

Huston: "it was really very, very joyful"

K.   Looking back at your work on these films and with these well-known directors and producers—Huston, Wise, Coppola—are there any interesting similarities or differences?

M.   Oh yes, of course, there were great differences in approach. John Huston, for example, whom I consider one of the world's truly great filmmakers, with his unique character and particular psychological contours, was enormously different from others I've worked with; he had very much his own approach. Huston was full of humanism, a kind of sociologist even, a very human person. With Robert Wise, you have the classic filmmaker, the traditional studio director. The Coppola I saw on *The Black Stallion Returns* was very modest and measured, but of course I can't speak of the Coppola of *Apocalypse Now,* with all the stories we've heard about how that shooting went.

K.   In what ways was Huston a "humanist," a "sociologist"?

M.   First of all, he always listened very carefully to what you were saying, he was learning all the time, like an anthropologist, like a sociologist. All this learning enabled him, with great success, to use the Moroccan people and Moroccan locations to represent a completely different population and location and to create a monumental portrait against the background of Morocco's mountains. He treated Moroccans with respect and he had great respect for the customs and traditions of the people, even though he was a complete outsider to the country. Even where he had little direct contact with some of these people, he was still able to cast them very intelligently.

It was a great opportunity for me to learn from the way he

worked—he was someone who could get in the Range Rover and sleep in a tent for five or six days, in the middle of nowhere, and in any conditions.

K. When you say he treated Moroccans with respect, what do you mean, exactly?

M. When I say "respect," I mean that when we gathered four hundred or five hundred people in one place in order to create a sort of agglomeration, he didn't pack them into tents as I've seen done elsewhere. He would ask the people to come a week early, ask them to set themselves up as though they were going to a *moussem,* so that they'd be at their ease, relaxed, not on top of one another. They'd keep their normal habits, their usual ways of expressing themselves. He respected their practices and people were able to continue their lives almost as normal.

As you know, when these people are at a *moussem* they're always putting on big shows. So we'd have displays and performances every night—it was really very, very joyful. Everyone there, men and women, would prepare and eat their own meals. So we weren't bringing these people to live in military barracks or tents. We let them live as they usually did, and that's why I'm sure everyone was in such good spirits.[26]

Now, Robert Wise had a different mentality, a studio mentality, where everything had to be organized, everything had to be calculated beforehand: the bus had to leave from exactly this point, to within a millimeter; it had to stop at exactly that spot over there. Things were so carefully calculated that they could never be carried out exactly, especially in exterior locations and with a population that was somewhat spontaneous. But he would try anyway. However, when people were told, "You go through here, then the bus will stop exactly there, you go toward the door of the bus to watch the person coming out . . ."—well, it would never work out exactly like that.

MARIO CAMUS'S CULTURAL ENTHUSIASM FOR "A NEW WAY OF LIFE"

"HE WAS ALWAYS READING SOME MOROCCAN LITERATURE"

M. In addition to these directors there's another type entirely, best exemplified by the Spanish director Mario Camus, whom I had seen quite often while I was living in Spain. Years after the films we've been discussing I worked with him on a wonderful film called *La forja de un rebelde* [*The Forging of a Rebel,* 1990], about the rise of Franco during the years he was stationed in northern Morocco. Camus was the kind of person who comes to a country for the first time, discovers a new way of life, and wants to learn about it far beyond what the film requires.

He had started with a little knowledge of Franco's early days and the Spanish conquest of northern Morocco, but he knew nothing of Morocco itself, as it was on the ground. But he was always on the lookout for some Moroccan literature, something he could read about Morocco. He was a director who at 5 P.M., after an eight-hour workday, would stop thinking about the shooting, wouldn't worry about what was going to be shot tomorrow, or what the casting would be, and so on. He wasn't like some other directors who are obsessed by the organization of what they are filming. He'd stop work at 5 P.M. and then plunge into a book on Morocco. He was always reading some Moroccan literature. During this period he read *By Bread Alone*,[27] three or four other novels—anything in Spanish he could get his hands on. In fact there wasn't much available then—other than Choukri's novel there were also perhaps two books by Tahar Ben Jelloun, but not much more than that.

For example, while he was shooting the film the Nobel Prize was awarded to the Egyptian writer Naguib Mahfouz. All of a sudden Mario came up to me saying, "I've just finished reading *Stories of Neighborhood*.[28] This book is wonderful, I'd love to adapt it for the cinema. Do you have any contacts in Egypt?" I told him I had very good contacts in Egypt and he answered, "During our shooting of this film, we have to get started on this next one, and you have to get busy with this." He was a man of such wide experience—his current film was being shot, but he was already enthusiastic about what might be his next one.

He got in touch with a friend of his, a production manager who was also a lawyer, and said to me, "Look, you and I can't go to Egypt, but give me all the coordinates of your contacts, and we'll send someone there to begin the process." I contacted my friend Tawfiq Saleh in Cairo and then I asked Noureddin Sail if he would go to Egypt to get the rights to adapt the novel for the screen.[29]

K. Tawfiq Saleh had already worked on films with Naguib Mahfouz.

M. Right. He's a great friend of Mahfouz and that's why I thought of him right away. Camus's lawyer friend and Noureddin went together to Egypt, they met Tawfiq Saleh, and they obtained an option on rights to the novel. Unfortunately, the film was never actually made.

But it shows you Mario Camus's spirit: he discovered Naguib Mahfouz and immediately this became the book he *had* to adapt. Afterward he did a lot of work on it and the preparation was moving ahead rather well. Then I think there were some problems, the producer lost interest, and the project stalled.

PASOLINI, SCORSESE . . .

PASOLINI (1972–1973)

"SOMETHING OF AN ENCYCLOPEDIA"

K. I know you had dealings with some other well-known directors on projects that didn't actually pan out. Could you tell me about some of these?

M. One of the first was Pasolini—I think this was in 1972 or 1973. He was preparing a film of *A Thousand and One Nights* and wanted to shoot in Morocco. But he had some problems here and eventually shot it partly in Tunisia and partly in Jordan.

At that time I was working at the CCM and Muhammad Ziani, then its director, gave me the job of going with Pasolini to Marrakesh to look over the sets he was preparing and help him scout locations. One evening, Ziani came to Marrakesh to have dinner with us, at the Moroccan restaurant in the al-Mamounia Hotel where we were staying, which was the top of the line in Marrakesh at that time. Before dinner, we were all sitting around, talking, and Pasolini got up, asking, "What time is dinner?" We said, "At 9 P.M.," and Pasolini went back to his room. It was perhaps a little after 8 P.M. and the rest of us—Ziani, myself, and two others—stayed there, talking.

We continued talking until about 9:05 or 9:10. Then we went to the restaurant, but Pasolini was nowhere in sight. Finally, ten or fifteen minutes later, he came in, dressed in the strangest way, with a shoelace hanging from his neck. Now Pasolini, you know, always dressed in a flamboyant way, very chic but flamboyant. But even for him this was strange. So we asked him, "What's going on?" "Well, I came here at exactly 9, as we agreed, and went into the restaurant. But the maître d'hôtel refused to allow me in, saying, 'A tie is required.' And here I was, with a beautiful silk shirt, a jacket, and very chic trousers. So I said, 'I'm very sorry, sir' and I went upstairs to change."

He had gone back upstairs, put on a pair of completely washed-out jeans, a grimy cardigan, a tattered shirt, and he'd taken a lace from his shoes and put it on as a tie. And that's exactly how he was dressed! [Both laugh.]

Of course, this story has less to do with his films than with his personality, with what you might call his philosophy of life. As far as this philosophy was concerned, Pasolini was something of an encyclopedia.

He was quite unique as a personality, quite introverted. We didn't communicate with one another a lot. He observed things, he was watching all the time, but he wasn't very open in his talking. We used to talk a bit in English, a bit in French. But his French was weak and I don't speak Italian—still, we always managed to understand one another. I suppose, too, that he saw me as part of the administration, part of the "official" world, so that may have contributed to his reticence. But he liked going into the working-class neighborhoods where there was a lot of life and action, a lot of people milling around, and to mix with the local population.

K. He did that in Italy, and it seems elsewhere too.

M. It was a product of his curiosity; also, perhaps, of his homosexuality.

K. Was he open about his homosexuality?

M. He was very discreet, his homosexuality wasn't flagrant at all. He certainly acknowledged the fact that he was homosexual but he wasn't provocative or anything like that. He was introverted, always in the process of watching, observing, or, as I said, going out on his own. Obviously, there is always the hint of homosexuality when you think of him moving around in these neighborhoods, when you think he's doing this because he's looking for some kind of relationship of that sort. But I think, beyond this, he had a great curiosity and desire to learn more about the society. And because he was preparing *A Thousand and One Nights,* he wanted to know Arab-Muslim society better, have a closer relationship with it— even though *A Thousand and One Nights* is Persian, not Arab. But, of course, *A Thousand and One Nights* still inevitably calls Arab society to mind.

CONTRASTS WITH BUNUEL AND FELLINI

K. I suppose Pasolini's films are not the kinds of films you have great affection for.

M. That's true; there's a scatological element that I find difficult to take—for example, when you see people eating their own excrement. But a film like *Satyricon,* a film with a historical theme, can be very interesting. But, yes, the scatological aspect disturbs me.

K. Do you have any ideas regarding where this mixture came from— the scatological element on the one hand, and the richness in decor on the other—or do you have any thoughts on the style of his films in general?

M. Well, there is certainly a settling of accounts with the bourgeoisie, and there is a kind of maliciousness in this, the aim of destroying a certain social system. This comes back again and again—hatred for the bourgeoisie—even though he himself lived in the most bourgeois style imaginable, even to the point of having his own castle! [Laughs.]

K. Whom do you think he's similar to—Bunuel perhaps?

M. No, not Bunuel at all. Fellini, too, is something else entirely. I think Pasolini made very much his own kind of film, resembling no one else's.

   I have enormous admiration for Fellini's films—the beauty of his subjects, the sense of humor, the irony, the ridicule. Pasolini's is a militant cinema—also a cinema with ridicule, but different from Fellini's. In Pasolini's, there's an attitude of destruction and ridicule toward so many things—love, sexuality, friendship. It's not a cinema that I am drawn to.

K. Fellini, you think, is much warmer?

M. Yes, much warmer, more human.

K. When I mentioned Bunuel, I was thinking of his distaste for the bourgeoisie, as in *The Discreet Charm of the Bourgeoisie,* for example.

M. In *Viridiana* too. But Bunuel does things differently and I am very partial to his films, for a number of reasons. First of all, his subjects are often very close to what you can see here in Morocco, subjects that I might even treat. When you think of *Pity for Them* or *Los Olvidados*—there are very many elements in them that you could find here. When he deals with Spain right after World War Two, you can see a lot of similarity between that society and ours. And his relationship to the blind, to the deaf and dumb, and so on— these are people I could run across in my own Moroccan society.

This isn't the case with Pasolini. Also, with Bunuel there is no scatology.

K. What about the scene in *The Discreet Charm of the Bourgeoisie* where each person goes into an individual cubicle, like a toilet, to dine, and then they come together to sit around the table to defecate?

M. Yes, yes. But that's different.

K. More like a gag, a display of wit?

M. Yes, that's it. But showing people eating their own excrement, that's a bit hard to take.

K. Yes, that is hard to digest. [Puns unintended.]

SCORSESE AND *THE LAST TEMPTATION*

"COMPASSION . . . CURIOSITY"

K. I know you worked for a time with Martin Scorsese. How did that go?

M. Yes, that was in 1983–1984, when he was scouting locations for *The Last Temptation of Christ.* I took him south and then I went to Marrakesh to set up a workshop to make the costumes. In fact, most of the costumes you saw in films shot four or five years later were costumes we had made in that Marrakesh workshop.

During this period he and I spent only about two weeks together, starting from his arrival in Casablanca. From there we went to my office in Rabat where I showed him some slides and videotapes so I could get an idea of exactly what kind of locations and sets he wanted in order to recreate the biblical atmosphere in the film. I had already seen the screenplay, which I thought was wonderful by the way, taken from a Greek novel.

K. Yes, by Kazantzakis.

M. Right. From Rabat we went to Marrakesh, then to Zagora, Er-Rachidiyya, Rissani [these last three are all in southeastern Morocco] and so on—we covered an enormous area.

In only two weeks you can't really get to know a person, you have to be with them over a longer period as I had the chance to do with John Huston, when we had quite a few weeks together. And it also depends on the individual—because some people communicate and others don't. Scorsese was one of those who didn't. Often, his mind seemed elsewhere. When the day's traveling was over, he'd go to his room, he didn't really hang out with us. You only saw him when you were actually doing the work—on the road, looking for locations, and so on. But he asked a lot of questions about the area, the people—why women did this, why the boys behaved like that, all sorts of things about society and the social system. And he was very touched by the poverty he saw, that really shocked him, he really showed compassion toward these people.

I was also very struck by his simplicity, as well as by his very focused curiosity. We went over large sections of the country by car; it was spring but it can get very hot, especially in the south. This didn't seem to bother him at all. And he was so happy when someone would invite us into a home, a very simple dwelling, to offer us tea, enabling him to spend some time with people and learn what their concerns in life were.

K. When you see him from a distance, without knowing him, you get the impression that he's extremely nervous, very tense.

M. He's . . . preoccupied. He's always thinking about something and can even be quite absentminded.

One of the strongest memories I have of him is how terrified he was of airplanes and helicopters. He was blue with fear at the idea of traveling by air, and that's why he covered the country completely by car. I also remember how one of the production people was already using a minicamera, a really small film camera to shoot the locations. With our equipment we really attracted a lot of attention in the villages. Once, not far from Rissani, on the way to Merzuga, we took out our gear—say, the Steadicam with the paraphernalia that keeps it stable—and people looked at us like we had landed from Mars.

Controversy and a lost project

K. I was in Fez, sometime in 1986 or 1987, and I saw Scorsese with his entourage at the Palais Jamai [the "top-of-the-line" hotel in Fez]. I think he was scouting for locations then too.

M. This must have been after the first project fell through. After we had scouted the locations, he was planning to shoot the film at the end of 1984 or the beginning of 1985. We set up the workshop for costumes and accessories and we hired a number of technicians to construct the sets in the Marrakesh region. But when Scorsese got back to the United States, religious demonstrations against the film started up. The film's producers lost courage and withdrew their support and the project was abandoned until Scorsese was able to put life into it again a few years later. So he shot it in Morocco in 1987.

When he came back to Morocco in 1987, I was in Spain. Some time later I learned about the shooting and I phoned him in New York. He told me he had tried to contact me—I'm sure that's true because we had had a very good relationship. He said everyone in Morocco whom he'd asked had answered that they had no idea where I was nor what I was doing.

K. But some people must have known.

M. Of course they knew, everyone knew how to contact me! But for whatever reason—probably thinking only of their own interests— no one would tell him where I was. Bad faith, that's what it was.[30]

"THE RELATIONSHIP BECOMES MECHANICAL"

K. I know he now often uses the setup in Ouarzazate for his films.

M. I think the first film he made in Morocco he made with special feeling. After that, he often came to shoot in Ouarzazate. You knew Ouarzazate thirty years ago—well, if you can believe it, Ouarzazate has now become a gigantic outside studio, with big cranes and all that stuff. [Laughs.] I once went through Ouarzazate and there was Scorsese, making commercial movies just like anyone else, no longer making movies like those of the Scorsese we knew. Someone told me that when the scene is all ready to be shot, Scorsese turns up at the last minute, sits down in his chair, says "Action" and "Cut" [snaps his fingers in imitation], and that's it. The relationship becomes mechanical. It's now part of the system, it's no longer the Scorsese of *Taxi Driver.*

K. Or *Mean Streets.*

M. Or *After Hours.* There's no longer the intimacy of the earlier films. Now, it has become industrial.

THE END OF THIS ROAD

"TENTS, CAMELS . . . THAT ORIENTALIST VISION"

K. You said that by the mid-1980s you'd really had enough of working on foreign productions. Why was that?

M. Up to a certain point this was a very enriching experience for me. But it couldn't continue unless you wanted to spend the rest of your life in that kind of mercenary activity. Also, it started to get monotonous: when people think "shooting in Morocco" they think of the south, tents, camels, folklore—again, it's that Orientalist vision. I would be organizing the same things over and over and over again. After seven or eight films you've done just about everything and you start to get pretty fed up. So, starting in 1985, I dropped this kind of work almost completely—in addition to having become repetitive and routine, the field wasn't well regulated and attracted a lot of people who in fact knew nothing about filmmaking.

Also, there were a few experiences around the mid-1980s that made this even more clear to me. One involved a film John Derek was making and another concerned *Jewel of the Nile*, produced by Michael Douglas.

BOLERO (JOHN DEREK, 1983)

"MY PRIDE, MY COUNTRY, AND MY COMPETENCE HAD BEEN INSULTED"

M. Sometime in the early 1980s I was contacted by the director John Derek—he died not very long ago, by the way—who was at that time married to the American actress Bo Derek, well known for her semi-erotic films. They were filming in Spain and wanted to come to Morocco afterward, to film for two or three weeks. They asked me to come to Madrid, so we could prepare everything they wanted to shoot in Morocco—this was to involve the usual accent on the "exotic": camels, tents, encampments, oases, and the like.

Working from the screenplay, I provided a breakdown of the Moroccan scenes and we signed a contract for the preparation and the shooting. When they all reached Morocco, everything was ready—the encampment in the dunes with some two hundred to two hundred fifty horsemen, the tents, and so on. Also, we had prepared restaurant scenes, because Derek wanted to recreate the idea of the café from the film *Casablanca*, a motif that is called up even today when many people think of Morocco and of filming in Morocco.

The first few days everything went normally. Then we came to the scenes with the horsemen, the tents, the oasis, and so on. The idea was to place the camera at the base of a sand dune and the horsemen would charge toward the camera. Well, I knew these horsemen because I'd worked with them before on other films, and I knew their capabilities. These are horsemen who are practiced in the Fantasia, so they know how to charge at full speed and then pull up short just a couple of meters from the tents—

it's like with ABS brakes—they can do this with no problem at all.

I advised Derek that we ought to run through the action once or twice to make sure exactly where to put the camera so it didn't risk being trampled or anything else. He answered, "No, I like to shoot the first take, it's more spontaneous and more interesting." This gives you an idea of the difference between someone like Derek who knows nothing about the society, who just comes to film a scene and then takes off, and people like Huston or the early Scorsese, who want to learn about the mentality of the people, how to approach them, how to deal with them, how to direct them. For me this is a very serious difference and Huston and Scorsese are obviously much more interesting to work with.

So, Derek was behind the camera, at the base of the dune, and the horsemen came charging toward him. He must have gotten terribly frightened—as they approached he jumped away from the camera, even though the horses did in fact pull up without any problem, without touching the camera at all. Frightened, distressed, Derek started yelling at me—"What the hell am I doing here in this country? Why didn't I go to Israel, where people are more civilized, where people are less like savages?" At this point I said to him, "Well, if that's the way you feel, that's no doubt the best thing for you to do—stop shooting your film here, go shoot it in Israel or wherever you want. And the sooner the better because who knows, if you stay here too long perhaps all these savages will eat you up or something!"

I left the set, letting everyone know that my pride, my country, and my competence had been insulted. I told them I was quitting but that those who had been hired to work with Derek should continue working without me. But they absolutely refused to go on working even when, as is usual in the American system, money was thrown at them to solve the problem. In this case they didn't accept the money, and the remaining scenes couldn't be filmed. So Derek had to leave and finish the film elsewhere. One of the surprising things is that when I went to see the film—he had finished the film in Spain—there was that scene with the horsemen charging the camera. And it was very well filmed!

Derek just had no idea what was going on. And that's why it's so important for a filmmaker to know what it's all about—if he wants to film a Fantasia, he has to feel it, he has to know what's going to happen. He can't just film it in one take without ever having seen it before. This is true for horses, but it's also true for the entire system. The problem is that so many people in the West have an Orientalist vision—they come here with a Western lens and through it they see what they've already read or what they want to see, rather than what is.

K. I suppose it's as though the country outside your own prior view of it doesn't really exist, it just serves as decoration.

M. Just decoration. And it costs less to do it here, and the administration gives you a lot of help. So why not? After all, for these people the country is just a movie set and nothing more.

JEWEL OF THE NILE (LEWIS TEAGUE, 1985)

THE "MERCENARY" ATTITUDE

M. The other disheartening incident occurred while I was working on *Jewel of the Nile*. After scouting locations, we were preparing the sets—we were about two weeks from the start of shooting, after preparations that had already taken two to three months. Our base was in Fez, we had other locations in Er-Rachidiyya and Ouarzazate, and we also often had to go to Casablanca and Rabat for all kinds of permits, permissions, and so on. I was production manager, making sure that everything was ready to be carried out according to the work plan, so I was often traveling from place to place with Michael Douglas's brother, in a small one-motor plane that we'd rented from England and that was piloted by a retired English war pilot who had started his own little company.

One morning four of us were to board the plane and fly from Fez to Er-Rachidiyya, planning to return that evening. When I got to the Fez airport I realized that I wasn't really needed on this trip, my assistant in Er-Rachidiyya was capable of handling everything, and that, in any case, I had plenty of work to do in Fez. So I waved good-bye and they left without me—the pilot, the set designer, and the English production director Brian Coates, who, by the way, was a great friend of mine; we had worked together on *The Man Who Would Be King* and on another film too, I think it was *Silver Bears*. I went back to Fez and worked through the day.

At 5 P.M. I went to the airport to meet them. Six o'clock passed and then, by seven o'clock, we began to fear the worst. In fact the plane had nose-dived into a mountain, although we didn't actually find this out until a week later. It eventually took a week of searching to find the plane—there was terrible weather, snow and everything.

I was supposed to be on that plane. Inevitably that gets you thinking. But what was even worse was the attitude of some people while the search went on—the lack of human feeling—that's something that really revolted me about foreign productions. You know, work on the film stops and some people are saying, "Well, when are they going to find these bodies so we can send them back to their own people and get on with the work on this film!" When you get to that point, where there's no human feeling, where there's only the dollar, only money, only business—it's just revolting.

I was starting then to see the end of the road of what you might call this "mercenary" activity. It was becoming less and less possible to be emotionally involved in a production and, also, you could see that this wasn't providing much any more in terms of building my own career. Of course today, for people doing this for their entire working lives—working as assistants, as associate producers, as location managers—this is a real job within the foreign production industry in Morocco. But when you have other concerns and other interests, you can't stay in this forever.

Taking Stock

THE FRENCH; YOUSSEF CHAHINE AND OTHER ARAB OR NON-WESTERN FILMMAKERS

TREATING MOROCCANS "AS MERE SUBALTERNS"

K. I notice that you've worked with the English, with Americans, with the Spanish, but you haven't mentioned working on any French films. Why is that?

M. I've hardly ever worked with the French. I almost worked on a French film when I was just starting to do this kind of work, but I withdrew.

First of all, there's the question of the French relationship to Morocco. Fundamentally, when the French come to Morocco they think they are coming to a conquered country, because it's a former colony. And they think they are always more professionally skilled than we are. For them, the idea of putting a Moroccan in a position of responsibility is, to all intents and purposes, excluded. The French would come with a complete crew, treating the few Moroccans they took on as mere subalterns, as the assistant of an assistant's assistant, so to speak. With the English or the Americans you could get a position of responsibility. With the French this was out of the question and that's why I've never worked with them, with the exception of my first foreign film, *Cent mille dollars au soleil,* where I was just a trainee.

And, no doubt, this also has something to do with my own feelings toward the former colonizer.

K. It's hard to escape history, on both sides.

M. Exactly—on both sides.

YOUSSEF CHAHINE—NO SPECIAL TREATMENT

K. You also haven't mentioned any non-Western films. I know that Mustapha Akkad, the Syrian filmmaker, made *The Message* [1976] here—were there any films made here by directors from other Arab countries, particularly Egypt?

M. Well, Youssef Chahine, the celebrated Egyptian director whom I've known for years, tried. In 1995 we met at a festival in Montpelier where a number of us were forming an Association of Mediterranean Filmmakers. At that time, he talked to me about his intention to make a film on Ibn Rushd, to be called *Destiny* [*al-Masir,* 1997].[31] In fact, he gave me the screenplay and said, "I would like very much for you to be a partner in this project, because I would like to shoot it in Morocco."

I returned to Morocco, read the screenplay, which I thought was very interesting, and gave it to a historian I knew who found many errors of historical fact. In the meantime, Youssef Chahine had sent a letter to the ministry of communication requesting Morocco's participation in the project, mentioning that I was his Moroccan partner and that the ministry should contact me for further details. After I read the screenplay, broke it down and saw what the requirements were, I got in touch with the ministry in my capacity as Chahine's representative, so we could begin to get the shooting organized.

I think mistakes were made on both sides, both on the Moroccan government's side and on Youssef Chahine's. Chahine asked for a special subsidy for the shooting, because he was used to this kind of treatment from France's Minister of Culture Jack

Lang. Here, the ministry's view was, "You have a Moroccan partner who has a production company. Your project will be proposed to the Aid Fund just like any other project, and it will be given the support that is appropriate." But Youssef Chahine wanted special treatment and at one point even wanted to present his case directly to His Majesty. He couldn't understand why he couldn't get the kind of direct aid he got in France, Egypt, or Syria, nor why he had to go through all the normal procedures like everyone else. However, we have rules and procedures in this country and you have to respect them.

I worked a lot on this project—for nothing as it turned out, because the film was never shot in Morocco. I was caught between the hammer and the anvil. I really loved the subject—in spite of the historical errors—and it could have been shot in a magnificent way here in Morocco. As it turned out, Morocco was replaced by Syria and there were a lot of false notes. When you want to show Andalusia, when you want to show its architecture and so on, Morocco is much more appropriate than Syria.

MOROCCO'S COMPARATIVE LACK OF FILMMAKING INFRASTRUCTURE

K. Do you know any other Egyptian filmmakers who tried to film in Morocco?

M. None that I know of. There may be some who have filmed for TV, or spots, perhaps, but I don't think there were any as far as the cinema is concerned. Much earlier, Chahine had shot some sequences here with the Moroccan singer Abdelwahab Doukkali but, other than that, I don't think there have been any Egyptian filmmakers who worked here.[32]

In fact, it's not surprising. It's as though you were to ask me to go film in Mauritania where they have much less infrastructure, much less of everything you need to shoot a film. Egypt has all the infrastructure, the technicians are always working, they have a filmmaking tradition, a history, an industry. Of course, you could imagine co-productions, but then you have to think of the market, of exchanging personnel, of all sorts of things.[33]

K. Any Indians, by the way, given how popular Indian films have been here?

M. That's even less likely! With all the infrastructure and other facilities the Indian film industry has, that's very hard to imagine.

FOREIGN PRODUCTIONS
OVER THE YEARS

FROM "REAL TECHNICIANS" TO "PROVIDERS OF SERVICES,"
FROM "READY-MADE STUDIO" TO "FILMING CHEAPLY"

K. As we look back over the entire experience, I have two questions: First, how has the practice of making foreign productions in Morocco changed over the years? Then, how do you think your experience in this area influenced your own filmmaking?

M. Looking back from today's vantage point, we can see some big changes. In our work on foreign productions in the 1970s and into the 1980s, we had real responsibilities. The kinds of roles I had—or that Larbi Ben Chekroun, or Muhammad Abbazi, or some other Moroccan technicians had—were much more those of *real* technicians.[34] Now things have changed. Now, the responsibilities Moroccans have are purely financial—they provide services, they receive money. This kind of mercenary orientation creates a lot of problems for our own national filmmaking. Many Moroccan actors and technicians simply won't work for us on national films because they would rather sit and wait for a foreign production to come along that will pay them much better. But just because they're better paid doesn't mean they have real responsibilities.

There's another distinction: foreign films now being shot in Morocco aren't filmed here because of the director's enthusiasm for or interest in the country or the society. They're shot here because of the economics of it, or because of some production facilities being offered. During the earlier period, many of these films were made in Morocco because Morocco was actually the setting of the film—like *March or Die* and *The Black Stallion Returns*—or because, as in Huston's film, Morocco had a great resemblance to the actual setting of the film. These earlier films were made with the idea that Morocco was a ready-made studio with certain kinds of natural scenery. There was a real desire for Morocco, rather than simply the advantages of filming cheaply.

Unfortunately, foreign films are usually made here now because it's inexpensive to do so. Also, for the foreign producers it's like open season here—they can do pretty much what they want and, in addition, the state provides all kinds of assistance without the filmmakers being accountable to anyone for anything. Obviously, when you think of the costs in Morocco—the

cost of casting extras, the cost of leasing and renting, and so on—
it's absurdly cheap here compared to the West. That's why
there's such a rush of foreign productions here. But that's not
why John Huston made *The Man Who Would Be King* here, that's
not why *The Black Stallion Returns* was made here. In those cases
it was because Morocco as a setting, as an environment, suited
the story or, sometimes, the story had actually been written
with Morocco in mind.

What is also interesting is that in some instances, although the
director may have come here initially for economic or historical
or other reasons, he actually became very taken with the country
and wanted to come back again. This was the case with Scorsese,
who loves the country and likes to come back to film here—and
God only knows what he might see in Ouarzazate that reminds
him of Nepal![35]

The same was true of Mario Camus. His film, of course, had
to be filmed in Morocco—this was a film about Franco, who had
launched his attack on Spain from Morocco, and we spent a lot
of time looking around northern Morocco to find the old Spanish
barracks. But he immediately got very interested in the country
and, in fact, in everything that concerned Arab culture.

LESSONS POSITIVE
AND NEGATIVE

LEARNING FROM THE "MASTERS"

M. As far as the influence on my own filmmaking is concerned, I
think the experience was positive in giving me the opportunity to
learn from some of the great masters—their vision of filmmaking,
directing actors, organizing scenes, and so on. I learned an enormous amount.

I learned some very important things about production, too.
For example, I learned to take out insurance—this is crucial—and
I always do that now. I think a number of Moroccan filmmakers
also do this, but I only really know for certain that Souheil Ben
Barka and I do it. And it has helped me, particularly when I was
shooting *Looking for My Wife's Husband,* where we had a tremen-
dous problem. It was never exactly clear what happened but
something like 1,200 meters of film that we had shot—which is
an enormous amount—were returned to us completely unusable.

We never found out whether the original film sold to us by Kodak had been defective or whether the lab had ruined it, but this meant that we had to reshoot two weeks' worth of film, two weeks' worth of work. We had to set up a number of scenes again, and all that was very difficult. What's more, it was the beginning of Ramadan and we had to keep the actors on past their contract date, which costs money too. But the insurance paid. If I hadn't had that insurance, I doubt that I ever would have been able to finish the film; I would have been totally blocked. These kinds of things happen and you have to do what you can to reduce the risks.[36]

As I've said, each film is an adventure; also, each film recedes into the past like in a rearview mirror—which means, whatever you've learned on a particular film won't necessarily help you on the next one, because each film has its own particular story and becomes its own special adventure. Each film is really its own thing.

But I think the most important thing I learned had to do with the human relationship between the director and the entire artistic and technical staff. This is extremely important because it's the harmony between all these elements that contributes so much to making a good film. During the shooting, the director at times becomes the confidant, or the father, the adviser, the boss, even sometimes the torturer, for all these people. And you have to manage it all in order to create level-headed relationships with everyone.

You know, when you're very busy setting up a scene and the electrician comes up to you and tells you that his son has a bad toothache, you have to listen to him. Or the actor who's an insomniac or had a bad dream; or the technician who needs school supplies for his kid, or maybe his wife slipped and sprained her leg—these are very simple things but, at the same time, they are very important for these people. After all, we're all together, like a family, for a couple of months, so you sort of become everyone's father, you feel responsible for them. This kind of human rapport—I think I learned it from those directors who have a certain inner serenity, a kind of philosophical outlook on the world. You need that in order to be sensitive to everyone's problems.

When you have a master of filmmaking in front of you, you want to see how he treats people—is he haughty and dismissive, approachable, or what? I think I learned the lesson best with John

Huston. When he was finished with the work he'd welcome any or all his collaborators to his room, they'd sit around talking about the newspapers that had come in from London, or discuss politics, or things like that. Also, well before that, I saw something similar with Henri Verneuil. Verneuil would even organize performances or sketches with the actors and crew, so that everyone would feel part of the film, would be motivated, wouldn't feel like just a spare part.

LEARNING "WHAT YOU CAN'T POSSIBLY
DO IN YOUR OWN FILMMAKING"

M. Not the least of the things I learned was what would *not* work as far as my own Moroccan filmmaking was concerned. These foreign filmmakers had colossal budgets, vast means at their disposal, something that can only be a dream, a utopia, for those of us here.

A simple example: in the Robert Wise film *Two People,* we rented the railroad between Ben Guérir, Casa, and Marrakesh. This meant stopping all the trains, renting the train and tracks for an entire week, during which the train and the tracks in effect belonged to the production. For me, this is utopian. Or taking shots from the air, that's also utopian. If you could see how a film like Michael Douglas's was prepared—it's unbelievable how they can throw money at a problem. Watching that, you learn all there is to know about *what you can't possibly do* in your own filmmaking, and what you'd never want to do even if you could, especially if you really want to make films close to your own situation, if you want to make what I call "a cinema of proximity."

Chapter Four

Badis (1989)

Introduction: Producing and Co-producing

After finishing *The Big Trip* in 1981, Tazi had hoped to make a feature-length fiction film every one or two years. However, eight years passed before his next film, *Badis*, appeared. Tazi was certainly disappointed with the delay but in one respect, at least, this second film was well worth the wait: it had great critical success, both locally and internationally, winning prizes or special mentions at festivals in Amiens, Montreal, Locarno, Milan, Carthage, and Meknès, among others. Tazi also had a number of stimulating experiences showing the film abroad.[1]

In addition, perhaps no single sequence in the history of Moroccan cinema has been more discussed or more controversial than the final scenes in *Badis*. Yet, notwithstanding the overwhelmingly positive critical reception and the discussion and controversy the final scenes generated, when *Badis* was released in Morocco it closed after one week, drawing a total of barely three hundred spectators.

While elaborating the *Badis* project, Tazi was able to propose to Spanish television (TVE) that it "co-produce" the film. This is a form of production where a foreign backer helps finance the film, usually gaining certain distribution rights in return. In addition, whereas *The Big Trip* had been made when financial aid from the state first became available, *Badis* was made just as this aid was undergoing substantial revision. Before launching into a detailed discussion of *Badis*, let us see how Moroccan film financing has developed over the past two decades, a period during which the modalities of state aid changed significantly and co-production grew in importance, but where film financing remained, on the whole, problematic. We will look first at state funding, which is the core of each film's budget, and then turn to other sources.

Adversity in Diversity: Film Financing from the 1980s to the Present

STATE AID: FROM BOUNTY HUNT TO AID FUND

Perhaps the defining condition of Moroccan film financing is the fact that, given the high cost of making a film on the one hand and the limited buying power of the Moroccan public on the other, Moroccan filmmaking can only continue by injecting funds that do not require repayment. Were Moroccan filmmaking to be left wholly dependent on the marketplace it would no doubt perish. In fact, it did almost perish—twice—in the late 1970s and then a decade later.

The period from the late 1960s through the end of the 1970s was one in which, with no clear sources of funding and no commercial distribution, most Moroccan filmmakers made what were often heroic efforts simply to finish their films, cobbling together, by hook or crook, funds, equipment, and technicians, with no eye to the approval of anyone but themselves and their immediate collaborators. Under these conditions, it is not surprising that by the end of the 1970s production had come almost to a standstill—only seven films were made in the decade's final four years—and it was unclear whether it would ever regain momentum.

However, in 1980 film finance was given a foundation, although not a very firm one, with the introduction of state aid to production (the so-called "Support Fund"), restructured in 1987–1988 as the "Aid Fund." The Support Fund led to an immediate explosion in production, with thirty films produced in the five-year period from 1980 to 1984. This explosion, due no doubt in part to pent-up creative energies unable to find expression previously, kept the Support Fund's basic deficiencies hidden for some time. Among the fund's defects were the small sums offered and the fact that these sums were awarded only after the film's completion.[2] As a result, film producers continued to inject their own funds, call upon the generosity of friends and crew members, and incur onerous loans that were often impossible to acquit because the film was usually not distributed and earned little or no money.

In addition, Support Fund awards were automatic, requiring only that the producer-director and technical crew be Moroccan, that most of the film be shot in Morocco and use the country's technical infrastructure, and that the film satisfy certain basic criteria, such as being of a certain minimum length and having acceptable image and sound.[3] This led, on occasion, to what was called a "bounty hunt" psychology, where some filmmakers made the quick calculation that, if they neglected quality and filmed very cheaply, they might even be able to make money on the automatic award. To make matters even worse, in 1985 changes in the tax law significantly reduced the total amount available to the Support Fund for distribution to filmmakers.

Production went into precipitous decline in the mid-1980s (the final five years of the decade were particularly fallow, with only eight films made), by which time it was clear to almost everyone in the Moroccan film world that the funding system had to be changed if filmmaking was to continue. When it was restructured in 1988 as the Aid Fund some of the defects were remedied, some new ones were introduced, and, with some subsequent slight modifications, this is substantially the system of state aid that exists today.

Under the Aid Fund the award is no longer automatic but selective; also, larger sums are awarded, although these are still insufficient to complete most films.[4] Two subcommittees examine each proposal, the first reading and ranking the screenplays, the second deciding on the feasibility of the project and amount to be awarded. Time limits were also introduced between the granting of the award, the start of shooting, and handing in the print—deadlines that must not be breached or the aid is automatically withdrawn. In addition, rather than awarding the money after the film's completion as the Support Fund had, the Aid Fund awards it at four separate moments in equal 25 percent portions, with all or part of the final portion subject to cancellation at the committee's discretion and upon written and reasoned notification to the producer.[5]

Although a considerable improvement over the Support Fund, the Aid Fund still has some serious shortcomings: amounts offered are small compared to a film's total budget and therefore do not in themselves ensure a film's production; the stipulation requiring that the amount awarded not exceed two-thirds of the film's estimated budget encourages the submission of inflated budgets; the committee system allows personal relations, patron-client ties, and other such considerations to overrule cinematic merit, making decisions highly unpredictable (or, in some cases, only too predictable); the Aid Fund Commission's right to withhold the final portion is seen by many filmmakers as a form of implicit or threatened censorship and as pushing them to censor themselves; and, until recently, the total amount of money available was determined by overall box-office receipts, leading funding to fall significantly with falling film attendance.[6]

THE MIXED BENEFITS
OF CO-PRODUCTION

With state aid insufficient, over these past two decades director-producers continued to seek funds from other sources, in the form of bank loans, sponsoring, producers' own contributions, and so on. One measure that had been tried earlier, that of forming a filmmakers' cooperative, has been seriously attempted only once since state aid was introduced (the cooperative later disbanded), perhaps an effect of filmmakers having had to form their own production companies.[7]

A primary source of additional funds for Moroccan (and other Third World) filmmakers, particularly since the mid-1980s, consists of organizations and agencies abroad, primarily in Europe, Canada, and the United States, where money might be available within development aid programs. The aid might come from ministries, bilateral cultural programs, or international aid programs (the most frequent sources, in Morocco's case, appear to be the French cultural programs Fonds Sud and ACCT).[8] Even where the foreign co-producer is a private company, the ultimate funder is likely to be a state or international funding agency, because a purely commercial producer would not choose to invest money in a Moroccan film that had little or no likelihood of making a profit. A very significant private source of financing consists of foreign-based TV channels (Channel Four in the UK, Canal Plus Horizons in France, ARTE in France/Germany), with their contribution usually coming in the form of participation in production costs and/or advances in return for rights to show the film.

The director-producer frequently combines funding from these different sources to meet the total budget and, as it has turned out, filmmakers sufficiently well connected to get funding from one of these sources are also likely to be able to get support from the others. However, the very diversity of sources may increase rather than decrease risks, because the failure of any one of them can put the finishing of the film in jeopardy.[9]

There have been two main criticisms of these foreign funding sources: first, that co-producers on occasion have sought to influence the final product in ways that run counter to the producer-director's conception, particularly where these influences tend to push the film toward satisfying rather predictable Western "Orientalist" tastes for the "exotic"; second, that the foreign location of the co-producer makes it difficult to enforce the co-producer's contractual obligations.[10]

TODAY: INCREASED PRODUCTION, SQUANDERED ENERGY

Notwithstanding the defects of the various forms of state aid, the drawbacks of each different funding source, and the broader problems of film financing, the period during which the Aid Fund has been in operation has seen a significant increase in production levels, starting in the second half of the 1990s and continuing into the next decade.[11]

Several recent developments indicate that this trend may continue. The ministry of communication and culture has taken some steps to ensure that the level of funding will not fall below a certain minimum, independent of box-office receipts; and, as we have seen from chapter 1, some distributors-exhibitors are entering the field of production. This may be the first sign of a trend toward the greater integration of production, distribution, and exhibition, an integration that characterizes most of the "mature" cinemas of the West. In addition, financial support from Moroccan television has been increasing in recent years, both in the form of free advertising and in direct aid to film production.[12]

In the circumstances just described, it is inevitable that much of the time and energy a Moroccan director might devote to filmmaking is, in fact, squandered in the search for funds—an activity for which he or she has no training and, usually, little inclination. But how can this situation, harmful to both the quantity and quality of filmmaking, be otherwise, when films cannot make a profit and when, as long as they cannot, specialized producers who would take charge of these tasks are unlikely to emerge? Nonetheless, this situation, burdensome as it may be, has not prevented Moroccan filmmakers from making some very powerful films, of which *Badis* is a prime example.

Badis—The Film

Badis was the film I had liked so much when I had seen the first part of it in New York sometime in the early 1990s. Among the aspects I had remembered and that have been reinforced now after repeated viewing are the beauty of the setting, the general seamlessness with which the film followed its half-dozen main characters, the simple and evocative music, and the slow but deliberate forward movement that heightened tension, contributing to the spectator's sense that a striking climax was in store.

Before we discuss this film in detail, let us quickly explore how Tazi decided to make this film, how it came to be made as a co-production, and then how he situates *Badis,* his second film, with regard to *The Big Trip,* his first.

BACKGROUND

IDEA, CO-PRODUCER, SCREENPLAY

"I FELL IN LOVE WITH THE PLACE"

K. Where did you get the idea for *Badis*?

M. During the early 1980s I was doing a lot of underwater fishing all over the Moroccan coast, particularly the Mediterranean coast. Once, I came across a tiny island called "Peñon de velez de la Gomera," which held a Spanish fort and was attached by a thin strip of land to the Moroccan mainland, where the village of Badis was located. For me this was a revelation—I fell in love with the place and I knew immediately that this had to be the setting for my next film. Of course I didn't have the faintest idea what kind of story would be in this film!

Something else was going on in my life at this time. In 1978 I had remarried, and my second wife was Spanish. We were living in Morocco but she was still studying architecture and, when she had to spend two or three months in Spain, I would go with her.

The Spanish fort, attached to the Moroccan mainland

In 1986, after she finished her exams, we decided to move to Spain, where I was based for the next four years. This was a very exciting period in Spain: Franco's legacy was disintegrating and there was enormous cultural dynamism—what was called "*la movida.*" New television channels were springing up almost every day and while I was there I participated as technician and collaborator in the birth of two new TV stations—the public channel Tele-Madrid and a private channel.

During this period—the 1980s—I was growing more interested in opportunities for co-production. I preferred becoming a partner, a stakeholder, rather than remaining a "mercenary" on foreign productions. Also, I was sick and tired of the rut we were in regarding French-Moroccan co-production. Unfortunately, the move toward Maghrebin co-productions, involving Algerians and Tunisians, didn't give any long-term results—there was too much deception and everyone had to watch what everyone else was doing. This was a shame, and it was another big disappointment.[13]

As my relationship with Spain grew deeper, I developed many good contacts there and I made a number of documentaries and shorts with the Spanish, as well as some co-productions with Morocco and Tunisia—documentaries on al-Murabitun, al-

Muwahhidun, on the Arab legacy in Spain, on *al-mudejar*.[14] It was a very, very rich experience, a kind of retooling with regard to my relations with the public, my experience in television, and my international experience. In fact, the whole experience completely transformed me. It was thanks to this Spanish period and my experiences there that I was able to make *Badis* as a co-production with Spanish television.

THE SPANISH CONNECTION

K. How did you actually enlist Spanish television in this project?

M. Badis—the village and its setting—has such an interesting history, not the least of which is the Spanish occupation of the fort over five centuries, that I thought it wouldn't be too difficult to find a co-producer. One day I was invited to a reception given by the Spanish ambassador in Morocco, and I met Pilar Miro, the woman who was then directing TVE. I mentioned the idea to her, as a story that involved both our countries. She was a very progressive woman, also a film director, and a very important woman on the Spanish scene—unhappily, she died not long ago—and she said, "Absolutely. When you come to Spain, give me a proposal."

Two or three weeks later, that's exactly what I did. They accepted it, and it turned out to be really a perfect case of collaboration and partnership, perhaps the only such case. And this was true from the screenplay through to the end.

"I WASN'T GOING TO CHANGE EVEN A COMMA"

K. Did you have any problems about the screenplay after you submitted it?

M. When I submitted it I added the following proviso: "I don't want anything added to or subtracted from this screenplay. If somebody wants to change it, you can count me out." What I meant was, I wasn't going to change even a comma. And they accepted it exactly as it was submitted.

K. Why were you so insistent about not making any changes?

M. There had been a number of co-productions around this time in which, whatever the original intention of the filmmaker from the South had been, as soon as it became a co-production, belly dancing and all sorts of other "exotic" elements were suddenly introduced. When co-producers push you in this direction and you start to think about appealing to different publics, you often end up with elements in a screenplay that are very artificial.

In the case of *Badis*, I wanted to avoid a situation where the co-producer might say something like, "Listen, for the Spanish public, we have to put in a little flamenco." I didn't want to fall into that trap, just for the sake of the money. I suppose it was my idealistic side.

K. But there *is* a little flamenco in *Badis*. [Laughs.]

M. Yes, but that was already there in the original screenplay! [Both laugh.]

COLLABORATORS AND CREW

"AN IDEAL ARRANGEMENT"

K. What was the structure of the co-production, and how did you select the crew—actors, technical staff, and so on?

M. First of all we agreed that, in addition to the Spanish side having no say regarding the screenplay, it would have no one monitoring the shooting. Second, the Spanish side would shoulder the costs of the cinematographer, his equipment, the film, the lab costs in developing, and so on. This made things much easier for me and, in fact, it was an ideal arrangement.

I needed two Spanish actors, one to play the soldier and another to play the girl, and the TVE gave me some suggestions. For the role of the soldier I hesitated between Miguel Molina and Antonio Banderas—the very same Banderas who has now become a big star and a director himself. I talked to both of them and Miguel Molina seemed a better fit. For the actress, my selection of Maribel Verdu was rapid and without hesitation.[15]

I had already worked with the cinematographer Federico Ribès on a number of documentaries we made in Spain and we had a wonderful harmony, so I insisted that he be the cinematographer. In addition, he played the role of intermediary between the crew and Maribel Verdu, who only spoke Spanish—at that time she was only about 18 years old and, in fact, her mother accompanied her during the shooting. So, all I had to worry about was the organization, the shooting, the rest of the crew, and the Moroccan actors.

All in all, as far as this particular co-production went, I have to say that I was very pleased with the collaboration with the Spanish. It was really carried out according to the rules, with full mutual respect. The contract was clear: I had responsibility for such and such a market, they had responsibility for their market—Latin America and so on. They carried out their side of the con-

Maribel Verdu as Moira in a scene from *Badis*

tract and I carried out mine, and none of us looked over the other's shoulder wondering, "How much did you make on this . . . did you do what you were supposed to?" And just as important: they have the original copy of the film in their lab and we both have rights to it. Whenever I request a new copy of the film, they provide it without any problems.

BADIS AND *THE BIG TRIP*

CHALLENGES; MAKING EACH ACTOR "CENTRAL"

K. From a director's point of view, what kinds of challenges did *Badis* present to you when compared to *The Big Trip*?

M. Well, having the setting as point of departure challenged me in several ways. The unifying element in *The Big Trip* was the itinerary—the character was constantly on the road and there was no unity of place. *Badis*, on the other hand, took place in one village. So we don't have thirty-six sets, we have just one; one single village. Second, there was the challenge of bringing together and directing a significant number of actors—some half-dozen— as an ensemble, where none of them is the single key, where all are central. I guess I wanted to get past the kinds of complexes

one can have about directing actors. Those were the main challenges I set myself.

K. How did it work out with the actors on the whole?

M. During the shooting, which lasted five weeks, I put the entire crew
together in one hotel in al-Hoceima—all the artistic and technical
people—so we wouldn't be dispersed all over the place. We then
traveled back and forth to the set each day. Every evening I went
from one actor to another—the young girl, the father, the teacher,
his wife, and so on—so that each would feel his or her role to be
very important, paramount. And each came to believe that he or
she was *the* principal character. It all worked out very, very well;
it allowed everyone to remain focused during the entire period.

THE FILM AND SOME MOTIFS

BADIS'S THEMES, THE ANTHROPOLOGIST'S INTERESTS; BADIS'S MAIN CHARACTERS

Badis had a number of different themes, among them the continuing
legacy of colonialism, the patriarchal context of women's oppression,
the problems of mixed marriage, the nature of relations between
Muslims and non-Muslims—some of which I wanted to explore with
Tazi.

But there was another story too, of particular interest to the anthropologist in me: that of a filmmaker's relationship to a village community. Having "fallen in love" with a beautiful setting and its complex history, Tazi had made repeated visits to the village and then
constructed a story he believed reflected the setting and the life of its
people. This raised two issues, at the very least. Filming in these conditions—in natural locations, with many nonprofessional actors, operating with budgetary constraints that limit or make impossible the
use of sophisticated equipment—is common to many filmmakers in
the Third World where cinema is not an industry, where "professional"
filmmaking is an extremely marginal activity, and where the aims of
most of the local community are not directed toward making the film
at hand. Such circumstances, less a matter of choice than necessity,
require the filmmaker to have great qualities of improvisation and
adaptation.

Secondly, constructing a story designed to reflect the life of a particular community was a task central to my own professional field,
anthropology, and often posed certain kinds of ethical as well as rep-

resentational dilemmas. I naturally wondered how Tazi's effort as a filmmaker might compare to an anthropologist's.

In the course of our discussions, I would try to follow these three strands—the themes in the film, the relationships behind the camera between filmmaker and community, and how that community was represented.

List of Main Characters
Ba Abdallah: a fisherman
Moira: his half-Spanish daughter; she lives alone with her father, her
    Spanish mother having left them when Moira was still young
A schoolteacher: just transferred from Casablanca
Touria: the schoolteacher's wife, herself a schoolteacher but without
    an assignment in the village
Woman café owner: something of a busybody, she has a husband who
    works abroad and periodically sends her money so she can expand
    the café into a small hotel for tourists
Si Mokhtar: the local postman, a full-time meddler; stationed in this
    village for some time and seeking a transfer, he has developed a
    more-than-casual relationship with the café owner
A Spanish soldier: his task is to fetch water, daily, from the village well
    and transport it back to the Spanish fort

ACT ONE: CONFLICTS BREWING IN AN IDYLLIC SETTING

A minivan winds its way across mountain roads, a fort appears in long shot displaying a Spanish flag, reveille sounds. A seaside Moroccan village is waking up in the fort's shadow. A young woman (Moira) returns home from the well, humming while going about her household tasks. Her father, back from fishing, appears abruptly and tells her to stop singing. A young Spanish soldier crosses the village guiding a donkey and cistern, and some lines of explanation roll up the screen: "It is now 1974. The island's fort holds Franco's political prisoners and . . . water is drawn from a well in the village . . . [which is] the task of a Spanish soldier . . . every morning at sunrise . . ."

Meanwhile, under the watchful eyes of the café owner and the postman, the minivan pulls up in front of the café and a couple in city clothes get off. He is the new schoolteacher. Shortly afterward, the couple explores their lodgings, which the wife (Touria) finds dreadful. Her husband answers angrily, "Here, you won't be able to

Filming, with fort in the background

Filming the café

do what you did in Casa." She responds, "But it's all in your imagination." He grabs her violently, she twists away, throwing herself on the bed.

First Motif: Filmmaker and Village, Part One—
Arrival, Adjustments, Limitations

The schoolteacher and his wife, outsiders to the village, arrive and settle themselves in, an intrusion that will affect the community in unforeseen ways. In outline, this might be seen as a metaphor for the arrival of Tazi and his crew and for the beginning of an anthropologist's research. I inquired first about the historical background; then, I wanted to explore how Tazi went about introducing himself to the village, examine some of the practical aspects of his and his crew's relationship to this community, and hear how villagers responded to this "intrusion."

"A TINY VILLAGE . . . FULL OF HISTORY"

K. When you first went to the village, was the fort still occupied by the Spanish?

M. It was then and it still is today! The Spanish have occupied this little island since the sixteenth century—in fact, it is one of several Mediterranean islands still occupied by Spain. This one isn't even an island but is attached to the mainland by a strip of land that you can only traverse at low tide—at high tide it disappears. Up until 1976 it was a prison for opponents of Franco; after that it became a training station for those involved in the struggle against ETA.[16]

But Badis has much more history than those five centuries or so of occupation. Badis is a very old name; it was the port the Romans chose when they colonized Morocco—the closest port to Volubilis, at the time the largest Roman city in Morocco—and it served as their main trading station. So Badis has a relationship to the Romans, to the Mediterranean, to pirates, to the Spanish—it's full of history, even into the present and the role the fort played during the Franco period. There's even a famous Moroccan saint, al-Badisi, whose origin was in Badis.[17]

On the other hand, today it is just a small fishing port, one of the calmest in Morocco, with a tiny village of just some fifteen to twenty families—perhaps one hundred to one hundred fifty inhabitants—living from traditional agriculture, fishing, and some livestock.

DEVELOPING VILLAGE RELATIONSHIPS

K. How did your relationship with the village develop, how did you approach people, how did you explain your intentions to them?

M. First of all, although I'd had the "revelation" that this was the setting in which I wanted to make a film, for quite some time I had no idea what this film was going to be about. [Laughs.] At a first stage, I went to the area two or three times. It's not such an easy trip: the town of al-Hoceima is quite a distance from Rabat[18] and the village itself is about 30 km from al-Hoceima, 20 on dirt roads with some very difficult sections that are unusable when it rains. And of course there are no hotels, so I'd spend the day in the village and then return to al-Hoceima at night. The entire trip, traveling and staying there, would take five to six days.

I began to talk a bit to people in the village and to learn a little more about relations between the military in the fort and this small village. I learned that it was a very conservative area, that women weren't allowed to appear in public, that the men were very mistrustful of everything that came from outside the village. That's when I discovered that water had been the tie between fort and village—the initial idea, then, was that of the Spanish soldier who comes to the village to fetch water. All this time I went about things very slowly, going to have a tea in the café, discussing the weather, the harvest, and so on. I still wasn't taking any photos—I didn't want to ruffle people. That's how I became something less than a total stranger.

After this I made about four visits there, more serious visits. At this point I was taking photos, talking to the people much more. They started to tell me all sorts of legends and stories and I spent hours listening to them, making a lot of audio recordings. One day, I decided to tell them why I was there—in fact, I was already looking for locations. So I said, "I'm planning to make a film here, and this is what it's about." They were very curious about my plan to make a film. Of course, for some that curiosity quickly turned to self-interest, because shooting in their area for four to five weeks would give a number of people a substantial amount of work. Also, the fishermen would be selling us their fish and we were going to rent a few of their homes. Remember, this is a very poor village. On the one hand, the film would serve their interests; on the other, they also had a kind of pride, even an arrogance, about their principles and way of life.

All this preparatory work took quite a long period. I think it took some six or seven years from the time I first saw this area while doing underwater fishing until we actually started filming. It took that much time for the project to ripen.

"We never had any real conflict"

K. Who were your main collaborators in the village? Did these tend to be people who'd already had experiences outside the village?

M. Not necessarily. In fact it was rather the opposite: the people who'd never seen a film camera, who didn't know what it was to shoot a film, who'd perhaps never even seen television, were the people who seemed more interested in learning about and understanding what we were doing. The others—those who had experienced what some call, in quotes, "civilization"—were perhaps quicker to think of profiting from what we were doing. Of this second sort, there were some flagrant cases.

On the whole, our relationship with the villagers wasn't strained at all, although sometimes we had to set some limits on the prices. But we never had any real conflict, we never had to call upon the authorities to help settle things. And this is rather unusual, because when you're shooting a film you generally need some assistance from the authorities to persuade people to cooperate—sometimes this is done gently, sometimes they use the boot. But here we had no problems of that sort.

Explaining the film to Badis

K. How did you explain to them that a film was going to be shot in their midst?

M. I tried to help them understand why I wanted to make the film, what the subject of the film would be, what making a film consisted in, and what it might mean to them. I'd get together with the fishermen to explain to them what a story was, trying to explain to them that the idea was to treat the chronic problem of colonization. Here was a village with the island and fort in plain view, yet the village gained absolutely nothing from the presence of the fort. The helicopter flew in every two or three days to deliver supplies, to deliver even water to the fort. There was absolutely no exchange between the two communities. That's what interested me the most.

It also helped that we were able to give them assistance in some ways. When I spoke to them about a scene I wanted to film in the mosque, they said, "Fine, but first come and see our mosque." It was in terrible shape, completely dilapidated. So I told them, "All right, the film will contribute to the construction and refurbishing of the mosque, because that will help us in shooting the film. And then, that mosque will continue to be yours after we leave." And the café I mentioned visiting when I first went to the village was nothing more than an area on the ground set aside for serving tea, coffee, and so forth, like those you see in rural marketplaces. The café you see in the film was actually built *for* the film.

There were a number of things like that, that facilitated our acceptance. Also, the two Spanish actors and the Spanish cinematographer helped to contribute to a kind of nostalgic feeling, a memory of the time when the area was occupied by the Spanish. In addition, we didn't descend on them the way a film crew from the West does. We integrated ourselves into the village: we rented one villager's home to store our equipment, another to prepare our food, another to serve as our canteen. There were five or six villagers who volunteered to help us out and were our closest collaborators; they were the ones who hosted us, who aided us in many ways, and who found solutions to many of our problems. All in all, there was a very harmonious atmosphere between the crew and the villagers.

"NATURAL LIGHT AND THE STRONG . . . COLORS"

K. This village obviously wasn't designed for shooting films, to say the least. What were some of the difficulties you had, some of the adjustments you made, and how did these affect the look of the film?

M. As far as the shooting is concerned there were a number of what I call "limitations," such as the fact that there was no electricity and bringing our own generators was a difficult enterprise. This meant that we were more or less forced to shoot most of the film during the day. Luckily, much of village life takes place outdoors— not only fishing, agriculture, and pasturing, but all the houses have courtyards and patios. So there is always natural light and the strong colors—ochre and blue. All this is even more striking because for every religious occasion the women completely repaint the house in white and an acetylene blue. In addition, one of the particularities of the Rif region in the north of Morocco is that people go to great effort to keep the house interiors in top shape—so even the floors are whitewashed. In these respects it was really an ideal setting.

Another problem was the difficulty of finding all the locations you need in one single village. This meant that a number of scenes had to be filmed elsewhere, particularly many of the interiors, as well as a few other scenes where we needed electricity. We filmed these in another village or near al-Hoceima.

ACT TWO: BOUNDARIES BREACHED

It is morning and children are setting off for school. The woman café owner calls on Touria, the teacher's wife, and remarks to her that in this village women are like goats: when they see someone they hide behind rocks. Touria says she'll never get used to this kind of life. The café owner invites the new arrivals for lunch but later, when the teacher returns home, he rejects the idea and tells his wife to put away her makeup bag.

Moira, singing happily at home, pulls a suitcase from underneath her bed and slowly takes out some "Spanish" things—a photo of her mother, a fan, a dress. She puts on lipstick, a beauty spot, the dress, and begins to dance.

A Friday: as the men leave the mosque, Ba Abdallah invites the teacher, with his wife, for lunch that day. When the couple enters the fisherman's home Moira and Touria exchange a sympathetic first look, while the teacher eyes Moira with desire. That evening, as Touria is in bed reading a book, *Birds Hide to Die,* the teacher suggests that she give Moira Arabic lessons.

A few mornings later, Moira goes to the well to fetch water. The young Spanish soldier approaches, startling her. He tells her not to be afraid and she answers somewhat boldly, "I'm not afraid, but if anyone sees us my father will kill you." And she hastens away.

In the café, the teacher is holding forth, arguing that the situation in Palestine is a disgrace, that other nations don't want the Arabs to unite. The postman cynically comments that he himself doesn't understand politics, "it's beyond me" [in French in the film, "*Ça me dé-passe,*" signaling, among other things, his intellectual distance from such concerns and his social distance from the villagers]. The teacher mentions to Ba Abdallah that his wife would like to give Moira Arabic lessons, something that would "bring her closer to Islam." The postman's face shows his disdain and distrust of the teacher's posturing.

Teacher and postman in the café

Second Motif: Religion and the Notion of Decency

Whereas the first act established the general context, presented the main characters, and gave us a hint or more of conflicts simmering on the personal level (between Moira and her father, between the schoolteacher and his wife) and on the social level (between men and women, between the locals and the Spanish), the second act sets up two potentially explosive alliances: between Moira and the Spanish soldier, which breaches the boundary between local and foreign, and between Moira and Touria, which will unite the two women in their struggle against oppressive men. The plot hasn't really been launched yet, and we will be discussing these themes later when it has.

For the moment I had several questions about the depiction of religion and this led to a discussion of Tazi's notions of decency and his preference for an "objective" camera. Notwithstanding the "objectivity" of his camera, we will see immediately afterward how "subjective" his relationship to the story in fact was.

"ANTI-VOYEUR," "OBJECTIVE CAMERA"

K. You've said that the film helped rebuild the mosque; however, the mosque only appears in one brief scene—Ba Abdallah's lunch invitation to the teacher—and then only from the outside. Did you originally plan to use the mosque more extensively and perhaps to film it from the inside?

M. No, not at all. The idea behind this scene is that after the Friday midday prayer—the weekly prayer that brings the community together—people feel more free and available. As the men leave the mosque, this is the natural moment for Ba Abdallah to extend the invitation. The scene was planned for the exit of the mosque.

I wasn't planning to film inside the mosque because I approach religious belief exactly the way I approach the erotic—that is, there is the problem of intimacy. I don't have to show a woman's nude breasts in order to express the erotic; you can express the erotic across a veil—you can see how this is done in Iranian cinema, even with all the difficulties it has in showing just a naked face. Similarly, when you are at prayer, you are in some sense isolated from the world around you, you are in a direct relationship with the Creator. I don't see any reason to show people actually praying; this would be pure voyeurism. With the mosque in the background, beautiful in its simplicity, the idea of people praying is conveyed when we see their sandals and shoes collected outside the entrance. When they come out and exit the exterior gate, they are back in the everyday world with the fort and colonialism right there in front of their eyes, and this is roughly when the camera picks them up. In my fourth film, *Lalla Hobby,* I do something similar, introducing the camera into the mosque only after the prayer has ended, when people start to talk about the problems of the society they live in.

So, in general, I don't see why the camera should be a "voyeur" in either one case or in the other. Showing moments of intimacy is just voyeurism. With regard to certain activities, therefore, I like to keep this kind of discretion and distance—what we call "*al-ḥeshma,*" which you might translate as "decency." My desire for this kind of decency and respect for the other means avoiding a strong voyeur appeal, and that's what I mean when I say I'm anti-voyeur in my films.

K. When you talk of a certain distancing of the camera, is this because you want an objective rather than a subjective camera, a camera that observes rather than participates?

M. Yes, and perhaps that results from a kind of occupational distortion [Fr. *une déformation professionnelle*], coming from my many years of news reporting. There the camera occupies the position of observer looking at a performance, not a subjective presence but a third party. Automatically, once a third party is present, what might have been intimacy takes on a certain reserve. So the camera, which is this third person present in a situation, is there as an observer rather than as a party to the interaction.

For example, in *Badis* I tried to make clear the contrast between the camera as observer and the voyeur: when the postman observes another person's intimacy, when he spies on Moira and the Spanish soldier, he uses binoculars. In this way, the voyeur function is distinguished from the camera's.

Third Motif: Creating from "the Guts"
A RELIEF, NOT A CURE

Tazi's preference for an "objective" camera did not mean that he himself was not deeply implicated in the *Badis* story. Once, while he and I were discussing *Badis*, his wife was sitting in the same room, working on the computer. I left the room for a few minutes and when I returned he continued.

M. My wife was just saying that she thinks you express things best when it comes from your guts [Fr. *les tripes*], when it's something that affects you deeply, some experience you've gone through. And she thinks I've put a lot of myself and my experiences into this film. After all, I'm a Moroccan and I was married to a Spanish woman at that time. Two of my children are half-Spanish. So I was in a situation very similar to that of the fisherman with his daughter. Furthermore, my marriage was breaking down at the time. It only lasted another few years—I was divorced in 1990. In *Badis* that idea of the mixed marriage comes up in two ways—in the impossibility of the relationship between the soldier and Moira and the impossibility of such a relationship a generation earlier between Moira's father and mother. Then, you could probably also see me somewhat as the owner of the café who is away, working in another country; perhaps even as the teacher with his authoritarian side.

So, the mixed marriage, children of mixed marriages, to say nothing of a marriage that was nearing its end, and these other aspects—I was certainly going through a lot of things in my life that were reflected in the film and that perhaps came out of my subconscious, and I guess you might call that "coming from the guts." [Laughs at the understatement.]

In fact, that's the way it should be. When your creation comes from your guts your sincerity is perhaps the most complete, perhaps that's when you are most truly yourself. After all, it's just not worth spending the years it takes to make a film unless you really feel the thing deeply—perhaps it's something you lived through intensely or are actually living through at the time. Of course, you yourself may not see the relationship between the work and your life and it often takes someone else to point it out.

On a completely different level of involvement, I was very strongly attracted to the area, probably because I had lived in the countryside for many years when I was young. I'm someone who tolerates cities only with great difficulty. My greatest pleasure is when I'm on the bank of a lake or on a snowy mountain, or at the seaside or in the green countryside, and so on. I'm not made for the urban environment. So, the sober country life held some nostalgic attraction for me—the sobriety, the lack of malice, the lack of deceit. People, instead, are rather transparent.

K. With the film coming in part from the turmoil you were living through, did you have the feeling, once you'd finished it, not necessarily that you had resolved the problem but at least that you were less uncomfortable with the situation?

M. In some cases, I think that creating can be like going to a psychoanalyst. When you go to the psychoanalyst, it doesn't mean that he's going to cure you, but at least it's one way to get the problems out. Then, at least, you're somewhat relieved. Things that are deeply hidden inside you, that are opaque, that are part of your life, somehow work themselves into the artistic creation—it's not simply a deliberate transposition of things onto the work. That, I think, is what creation is all about.

"ADDING A CERTAIN FEMININE SENSIBILITY"

K. Given how tightly interwoven your life and this film's story were, how did work on the screenplay proceed, because you, Noureddin Sail, and Farida Benlyazid were all involved?

M. Noureddin Sail agreed to write the screenplay, based on the setting and the research I had done. Noureddin has a great facility in writing; I don't, but I do know how to tell a story. At one point he said, "It would be good if we had a feminine sensibility contributing to this." He likes Farida Benlyazid's work a lot and suggested that she go over the screenplay once he had finished with it. Farida did in fact enrich the script greatly, adding a certain feminine sensibility to it. This kind of enhancement is of enormous benefit to a film and that's why I wouldn't like to direct my own screenplays, to be limited by them. You need the contributions of others, especially when they are specialized in the particular activity and they can add their own sensibility.

ACT THREE: TRANSGRESSIONS COMMITTED AND EXPOSED

One evening some days later, the café owner is serving wine to the postman in her home. He tells her that each day the soldier and Moira spend at least a half-hour together at the well, and that the teacher has something other than a teacher's interest in the young woman. He puts his arm around the café owner but she pulls away, laughing, offering him another drink.

At Touria's home the teaching situation has been reversed: Moira is giving Touria lessons in Spanish dance. A noise comes from the doorway and both women abruptly resume their studious poses—Touria teaching Moira Arabic. The teacher enters, sits, and begins to read his newspaper while observing the two women.

Early the next morning the postman, looking through binoculars, observes the Spanish soldier leading donkey and cistern toward the well. A little later, at the well, Moira is telling the soldier her story, in Spanish. Her parents had met while her father was working in Spain. After Moira was born and the family came to his hometown of Badis, Ba Abdallah wanted his Spanish wife to behave like a Badis woman. They argued all the time, sometimes he beat her. Moira hated him for this and concurred when her mother decided to run away while her father was at sea. The soldier promises to help find her mother and gently tries to take Moira in his arms. "Are you crazy?" she says. "If someone saw you. . . ." He implores her to stay but she leaves, promising to return the next day.

In the school, the teacher is giving an exam, walking around the room and nastily twisting a child's ear here and there. He questions the pupils on some matters of Islamic law.

One morning soon after, Touria welcomes Moira to her house with words of caution: "He's sleeping, be careful." Touria asks, "Did you see the soldier?" And Moira answers, "Yes, and he tried to kiss me." Both women laugh but waking noises from the next room call them to order, as Touria says, "I hate him, I can't stand him." The teacher wakes, performs the morning prayer. After he leaves the women breathe a sigh of relief, smile, and say, "How peaceful." They take up their dancing lessons again.

In the café, the postman sarcastically asks the teacher how the new "student" is progressing, then adds, "You're wasting your time with her." When the teacher protests, the postman continues, "I know what I'm saying. If you want to know what she's really up to, meet me at 6 A.M. tomorrow morning." The following morning, Moira is washing clothes at the well. The soldier arrives, they run toward one another and hold hands. From a short distance away, the postman and teacher are spying on them; the teacher, overcome with emotion, starts toward them but the postman holds him back.

Fourth Motif: Character—Manicheanism, Absence of the "I," Fate

By now, the two transgressing relationships have been cemented, Moira and Touria uniting in their struggles and Moira and the soldier meeting regularly at the well. But the postman—who correctly gauged the teacher's desire for Moira—now manipulatively raises the stakes: he exposes to the teacher the explosive relationship between Moira and the soldier.

At this point in the film, with conflict threatening to break into the open, the spectator's sympathies go strongly toward Moira and Touria, whereas both teacher and postman appear contemptible. I wanted to talk about these characters and about character in general.

Maribel Verdu (Moira) and Zakia Tahiri (Touria) rehearsing the dance scenes

I focused first on the teacher, and this led us into a broader discussion of notions of the human person.

"Linear" characters

K. The mood of this film reminds me very much of a Greek tragedy. First, there is a unity of place. There is also a certain unity of time—although there are a number of simultaneous actions and the tempo is marked by crosscutting and parallel editing, there are no flashbacks and there is a clear forward momentum. I also think of Greek tragedy because from the outset the characters seem quite fixed and change little if at all in the course of the story.

M. That's right—each character is rather linear and has his or her own particular story. The café owner is thinking about building a tourist hotel with the money her husband sends from abroad, the postman is looking forward to a transfer, the teacher is trying to punish his wife, the fisherman wants to keep his half-Spanish daughter on the straight and narrow. Within the setting that brings them together, each has a line to follow and they don't deviate from their paths as they go forward.

The lure of caricature, the reality of ambiguity

K. Let's look a little more closely at the teacher's character. In the classroom, the teacher gives a lesson on Islamic law. Did you envisage him as being cruel toward the pupils in the school scene?

M. Absolutely. He twists their ears as he walks around the classroom, he pretty well makes them tremble. Also, his questioning—"What does it mean for an act to be 'forbidden'?" "What does it mean for an act to be 'permitted'?"—helps to portray his authoritarian, sharp-edged character and hints at the kind of Manichean vision he has of the world.

K. The Manicheanism you just referred to runs throughout this film. I remember this was one of the criticisms made of *The Big Trip*.[19] Taking both films together, we can see a kind of Manichean vision informing all the main characters: there are good people and bad people, and very rarely people whose characters are ambiguous or mixed. Furthermore, these people don't seem to change as the film moves forward. Is this something that responds to your vision or that of Noureddin Sail, who wrote the screenplays for both films?

M. In any event, this is partly a reaction to the reality around us: in society there is a lot of ambiguity—someone gives you the impression that he's good, that he's on your side and then behind your back he's exactly the opposite. In reaction to this, the film shows a person with his true face, rather than with all the ambiguity. This way we, as spectators, don't have to go through all that analysis to find out if the person is good or bad, we know that almost from the outset.

But also, I'm not sure I agree with you that the films show people as either good or bad. There are also some people who are neither good nor bad. Take the case of Touria, the teacher's wife— she's more a victim than anything else.

K. Yes, she's a victim, but she's a victim who is good, we don't get to see her faults. Possibly she was unfaithful to her husband, but she denies it and her denial is rather convincing.

M. Well, maybe you're right that the vision is Manichean. It's an interesting question as to what extent this comes from Noureddin or from me. We should also consider Farida Benlyazid's contribution to *Badis* and then to *Looking for My Wife's Husband*.

K. Actually, I was coming to that, because in your next film, *Looking*, the characters seem less Manichean.

M. But it also depends on the situation, on the milieu—these influence the kinds of characters you show. In the environment of Badis, with a sobriety so thick you can cut it with a knife, with its sharp contours, it's difficult to introduce characters who are ambiguous although, obviously, some exist.

K. The postman is so terribly evil—isn't that somewhat too Manichean?

M. He *is* evil and he's the source of much of the trouble. Or, rather, he's the catalyst, because much of what happens might have happened without him, but not as quickly. Certainly he's a nasty character and he's quite pleased to see how the things he has set in motion grow increasingly ominous.

K. I wonder whether some of these extra flourishes—such as later, when the postman smiles with satisfaction after behaving in a particularly abject manner—aren't perhaps a bit exaggerated?

M. Well, there's always the danger of falling into caricature, that *is* a real danger. Even when you stay close to reality in portraying a character, it sometimes can appear as caricature because the person is a caricature in reality, in daily life. That's where the unrealistic and the realistic merge. It's very difficult to portray certain kinds of characters and get past this danger.

On the other hand, life as a whole is riven with ambiguity— every individual has it, so do religion, society, and all sorts of economic, social, and political practices. It's something we can't escape. In part it's because of this overwhelming ambiguity that characters in a film have to be more clear, or at least clearer than the environment they live in.

K. You're saying that the transparency of the film's characters should be seen as a kind of reaction to the opacity of society?

M. Yes. In our environment almost everything is ambiguous; if you make the characters just as ambiguous, well, then, the spectator will be lost in a haze of suppositions.

Do CHARACTERS "DEVELOP"?

K. Another aspect of character is related to what you have called "linearity": these characters don't "develop," they don't evolve over the course of a film.

I was talking to a Moroccan friend of mine the other day—he was reading the first volume of Edward Said's autobiography. I mentioned that I couldn't recall any Moroccan film that showed character development the way an autobiography or a bildungs-roman does, and I asked whether this was also the case in Moroccan literature. He answered, "Here, autobiography is a genre that is more or less absent."[20]

M. It's because speaking of oneself—what we call "egotism" [Ar. 'an-aniya]—is seen as out of place. But I think it's essential to speak of this "I," of the subjective element. How else can one come to understand one's own efforts—for example, mine to escape from Fez society, from a certain kind of bourgeoisie and social class?

K. But in your films the characters don't change, they appear set once and for all. I was thinking a moment ago of *Citizen Kane*—it has a strong psychological undertone and we see a character go from youth to old age, battling with himself and with the society around him and changing significantly over the course of the film. Have you ever thought of making a film in which characters do develop?

M. Not really, but I haven't actually given it any thought. My approach to a screenplay, whether it's an adaptation from an existing work or my own idea that a screenwriter then develops, is to work from situations, from the idea that governs the story and from the themes that the film might treat based on that story. But what you're suggesting, where the characters would change and develop in the course of the story, is a good thing to think about.

K. The story of an individual's battle with him- or herself and with society, to improve as a person, is one of the great themes in world literature as well as in cinema. I certainly haven't seen all Moroccan films, but none of those I can recall has that as a theme. I wonder why. Do you think it might have something to do with what we were talking about earlier, the reluctance to show intimacy? This would perhaps then go along with a difficulty in probing deeply into a character and showing its psychological evolution.

M. But intimacy as a notion is rather ambiguous, it doesn't seem very clear to me. Perhaps part of the explanation may have to do with Islam, because we may be guided by a certain notion of the predetermined fate of the person, the idea that people have a destiny traced for them, that they aren't in control of their future but that this is controlled by the Creator. I think this plays a role in our unconscious. Although there is also the other idea, that it is possible to do things, like going on the Pilgrimage to Mecca, that enable you to attain salvation through your own acts. This is what I meant earlier by religion, too, having a kind of ambiguity.

In fact, going back to the Manicheanism you were talking about, perhaps this also has some relationship to religion. In the Qur'an we hear repeatedly of believers and unbelievers [Ar. *'al-mu'minun wa al-kaffirun*]. I'm sure that the Manicheanism we come across repeatedly in our religious teachings has some influence on our subconscious.

ACT FOUR: LOVERS SEPARATED, WOMEN CURBED

In the café, with the TV in the background showing Vietnam War scenes and U.S. president Nixon talking about honesty in politics, the teacher says to Ba Abdallah that politics and ethics must go together and that Nixon should resign because he lied. Ba Abdallah counters that politics is a winding path, what's important is winning, and "you don't tell a kitten what you're going to do with it when you go fishing."[21] The teacher, patronizing, answers that he is not a fisherman. Ba Abdallah replies that he ought to become one if he wants to understand politics. The postman scornfully observes the teacher's moralizing.

The teacher has called a village meeting at the school. To implement his plan to separate Moira and the Spanish soldier, he tells the villagers that the soldier has been seen urinating into the well and must be forbidden entry into the village. Shocked, some villagers are

The teacher, Ba Abdallah, and villagers get ready to bar the Spanish
soldier's passage

prepared to become violent, but the teacher counsels calm, reminding
them that the fort is a Spanish colony and proposing that they simply
inform the Spanish authorities that the soldier is unwelcome.

Early the following morning, the teacher and Ba Abdallah lead
men and children to bar the Spanish soldier's passage. At the border
crossing, Ba Abdallah tells the soldier he will no longer be allowed to
enter the village and dirty the fountain. The soldier, without a word,
turns on his heels and reverses direction.

At the well Moira waits in vain for the soldier; crestfallen, she
walks slowly home. From a vantage point she looks on, baffled, as the
men mill about in the distance. When she reaches Touria's home,
Touria whispers that she will explain everything but they must now
remain quiet because the teacher is watching them. The women begin
their lessons under the teacher's eye and he says, "Now that she can
read the Qur'an, she should start to memorize it. Here, let her use my
copy."

Fifth Motif: Three Political Positions

The colonial theme, which Tazi often referred to, here reaches a
climax: transgressing the boundary between foreign and indigenous

has led to retribution and contact between Moira and the Spanish soldier has been sundered. Tazi certainly meant this film to be a criticism of the colonial presence and this raised a more general question: What political stance were this film and he behind it expressing? I used as a springboard for the discussion the various political positions that had been adopted in the café scenes.

"INTELLECTUAL . . . CYNIC . . . REALIST"

K. In the course of the film, there are several political discussions set in the café. Three positions seem staked out. There is the postman's position, "This isn't my field."

M. "I'm not interested in politics."

K. Then there is the teacher's. In an early scene he argued for Arab unity, deplored the situation in Palestine, and so on.

M. Yes, he takes the stance of an intellectual.

K. And then there is the fisherman, who says that politics is like fishing—in effect, it's a battle between fisherman and fish and what counts is who wins, not how you carry out the struggle.

How do you view these three different stances?

M. Well, the postman stands outside of it all—he's a bon vivant and doesn't give a damn about these issues. He's a cynic, he's blasé. Perhaps he used to be involved in politics, but now he no longer believes in political action. In fact, a lot of people adopt this stance—if you start talking politics they say, "Please, not that again. . . ." They're saying, in effect, "Look, this kind of talk is meaningless, it's just dinner-table conversation that leads nowhere. Why bother?"

Then there's the teacher, always instructing, very didactic, always appealing to reason, patriotism, nationalism, ethics—all the great principles. But you certainly can't say that his behavior is in accord with these great principles.

Finally, the fisherman is the realist.

Above and beyond these positions, you should notice that Nixon's TV speech is the element that triggers their last discussion. The idea here is that local and regional politics have to be seen in the context of international politics, or Western politics, or American politics. Even in Morocco today, when we talk about the Moroccan economy it's always with the aims of the World Bank or the International Monetary Fund in view; we can only see our own economy on the basis of its relationship to the World Bank.

[Laughs sarcastically.] It was in this spirit, too, that the scene was shot.

ACTIVISM OUTSIDE A POLITICAL PARTY

K. Where do you stand and how do you see your films with regard to these three political positions?

M. Well, one always would like to believe that one's film has a critical social function, even while not wanting to push beyond certain limits. There are two extremes: those who have nothing to say and admit it—the postman's position—and those who want their films to be politically militant. This last isn't my case but, of course, I'm not like the postman either! [Both laugh.]

I know you have to be an activist and I'm militant for a number of things. But for me, activists often tend to become like watchdogs, making sure that actions follow a particular party line or a particular orientation. My approach is more to act in the service of certain principles—like democracy and human rights—but not to do this within the framework of any particular party. When I can express these ideas in a film, so much the better. In fact, someone once said—I don't remember whether it was a sociologist or a feminist or a critic—that *Badis* and the discussion it generated had more impact than all kinds of lectures, seminars, and debates.

ACT FIVE: RUSH TOWARD FREEDOM

A considerable time has passed and a new equilibrium has been established: fishermen continue to go out to sea, the fort sounds reveille, a different and much older soldier guides donkey and cistern, and Moira now reads fluently from the Qur'an, much to her father's pleasure.

The postman gets an important letter, "finally . . ."—he has been transferred. He seeks out Moira and gives her a stack of airmail letters he has been keeping from her. Later, Touria reads Moira these love letters from the soldier. He wants her to join him and Moira says she must go, but how? Touria answers, "We'll leave here together, but we have to be patient."

Some evenings later, the teacher is sick in bed. Carefully, Touria makes him an infusion, spiking it with several Valium pills. Later the postman, having spent the night with the café owner, leaves her at dawn, unstable from too much drink and stumbling down her stairs. She assists him; then, as she returns home, she notices Touria in the distance carrying a suitcase. Touria reaches Moira's home, tells her to move quickly, they must leave before the village wakes. Moira and Touria begin a long march toward the fort over rough, rocky terrain.

In the café that morning, the café owner tells the postman she thinks Touria has fled. He rushes to wake the drugged teacher, tells him his wife has gone and then tells the village children to inform the men that the two women have fled. Having set this action in motion, he pauses to light a cigarette and smiles with satisfaction.

Search parties are sent out by land and sea as Moira and Touria continue their trek. Suddenly, Moira realizes that a boat is catching up to them and the two women stop, knowing they are caught. The men land and approach threateningly, and the women are taken aboard. The boat returns to the village beach where the men are waiting menacingly. The women disembark, rush past the men, and look backward at them in fear. Moira and Touria stop within a large circle of white stones as the men, at the circumference, surround them. The postman and café owner look on from the café. Birds are squawking in the background.

Defiantly, Moira loosens her hair and starts to dance within the circle. Touria tries to stop her, but Moira continues, looking brazenly outward at the men. Several village women approach the circle. One steps inside it, bends down, grasps a rock, and throws the first stone. Other villagers now begin to throw stones but Moira continues to dance. Ba Abdallah and the teacher rush into the circle to stop the incident but just then a stone hits Moira flush in the face and she falls to the ground, blood appearing at her temples. Touria, bending over Moira as stones continue to rain down, is struck too and falls upon Moira. Neither woman moves.

The camera pulls back and the villagers start to withdraw. The teacher staggers away in shock and Ba Abdallah walks off too. As the camera pulls back even farther the two motionless, apparently dead women lie in the foreground, a white wall stands behind them, the men walk away behind that, and the mountains appear in the distance.

Later that evening, taps sound at the fort. The postman has already left in the minivan; Ba Abdallah is sitting motionless outside the café. The teacher is again in the circle, throwing pebbles to the ground, as his jacket slides off his shoulders. The camera stops, freezing the

Moira, blood at her temples

teacher about to throw another pebble, with sea and mountains in the background.

Sixth Motif: The Controversial Ending

The tragedy of the two women and the power of the final scenes led to much discussion and to controversy over whether the situation of women had been illustrated in a way truthful or appropriate to contemporary Morocco. Before discussing this, I needed further explanation of several aspects of the scene.

"KILLING . . . AGAIN AND AGAIN"

K. At the end of the film, we witness scenes of defiance, tragedy, and pain. Moira's dance seems meant to defy the village by showing her own essence and her difference from those around her.

M. Yes, first of all the dance is a challenge. Normally, when Moira moved about the village the men would look at her furtively. Now, through this dance she is saying to them, "You wanted to see my body? Well, here it is, and here is the way I want to show it, in what I love, in what I am." It's her way of expressing her identity.

K. After Moira is struck, Touria comes over to her and is struck, too.

The circle of stones and the white wall

The postman, his work completed, leaves in the minivan

M. Yes. But one might suppose that the stone isn't aimed at Touria. She's an outsider, not part of the village, she's struck by accident because she's trying to protect Moira. Moira is the one who has to be disciplined.

K. After the stoning the teacher, in something of a trance and with the sun setting, stands in the circle and throws pebbles to the ground. Is this an allusion to the moment in the Pilgrimage to Mecca when the pilgrims throw pebbles to ward off the devil?[22]

M. Yes, this association is unavoidable. When we say, "This is the devil's work" [Ar. *Hada min-ʿamal ash-shaitan*], meaning "one is not responsible for one's acts," it is understood that it is the woman who has led the man into sin, on the Eve and Adam model. The teacher is convinced his wife has been unfaithful, he has developed a kind of hatred for her and an injured pride. At the same time, he thinks of his wife as his property, as someone he can treat with cruelty—as he says early in the film, "I'm going to kill you little by little, for the way you made me suffer." For him, this woman represents Satan and this scene can certainly be interpreted in the way you suggested.

But my own idea of this scene is that the teacher is someone who exists solely to carry out revenge on this supposedly unfaithful woman. When he throws these stones, it is a symbolic way of killing his wife again and again, a repetition underlined, in the background, by the cistern passing, which is another repetitive movement. Also, a passive Ba Abdallah is sitting in front of the café, watching this performance in a vegetative way, with resignation, as though he witnesses this scene every day.

AN "OPEN" ENDING?

K. You talked earlier about how you like all your endings to be ambiguous, open to further developments in the story and open to further interpretation. This is the case in *The Big Trip* and also clearly in *Looking*. In *Badis*, however, this doesn't seem to hold true.

M. You mean that just because a person dies there is no ambiguity, no continuation? [Laughs in disagreement.]

K. Well, let's say that the ending of *Badis* is quite a bit less ambiguous than in your other films.

M. But we don't know what happens to the teacher, and we don't know what will happen with the postman—who knows what kind of disaster he is going to create elsewhere? And the café owner—she's still there. And what will happen to the village of Badis after all this? There are a lot of things we don't know.

K. Yes, but two of the main characters, the two women with whom the audience sympathizes, have no future at all! To say that the ending of *Badis* is open in anything like the same degree as the others seems to me to be pushing things a little.

M. OK, the ending is less open.

K. I'd even say it's hardly open at all, it's almost completely closed.

M. I'll just say it's less open. Again, it's not just because the two women die that the ending can be seen as completely closed.

Too "cold" a scene? Symbol and emotional impact

K. The lapidation sequence generated a lot of discussion and criticism—criticism phrased sometimes in terms of style, sometimes in terms of substance. The former first: one commentator said, in effect, that you so feared falling into melodrama that you erred in the opposite direction, making the scene colder than it ought to have been, weakening both its symbolic and emotional impact. When you filmed this scene, did you want it to appear as somewhat distant, cold?

M. Regarding the symbolic aspect, for me this was a very symbolic scene and I think many of the critics missed that. It's not that the use of the symbols leads us to a key to the scene, but elements like the white wall—the place of prayer [Ar. *msella*]—and the symbol of the circle outlined with stones gives the event more resonance.

As for the scene being too "cold," there are a lot of factors involved. You remember I said I would have liked to use a helicopter to shoot *The Big Trip*'s final scene of Omar in the boat? I wanted to do that for the end of *Badis* too, but I didn't have the budget for it here either. Obviously, that would have created a different effect. Also, I had difficulty assembling a large number of extras. You know, there are specialists who organize things like fight scenes and so on.

K. Perhaps even specialists for stonings? [Laughs.][23]

M. Certainly. [Laughs.]

It's easy to imagine shooting this scene differently with a larger budget—giving it more grandeur, more suspense, more stones thrown, more blows, more blood. I know this could have been made into a kind of apotheosis. But I don't think this would have fit in with the rest of the film's rhythm and mood, with its overall sobriety, with its lack of artifice. In fact, I don't think this scene required more than we gave it.

You know, a similar point about sobriety could be made concerning the film's music. Originally, I proposed the idea to a very well-known Moroccan composer who lives in Paris, Hmed Siyyad, who wanted to have the orchestra of French Radio and Television play his composition. For my budget this was completely out of the question. So, with the shooting finished, the editing coming up, and still no composer, what was I to do? I contacted an architect friend of mine who composes in his spare time. I showed him parts of the film and explained that I wanted the music in the film to express the idea of the meeting of Spanish and Moroccan cultures and the exchange that existed between them. He came up with the dialogue between two guitars, alternating between a flamenco style and the classic Moroccan Andalusian style. I loved the simplicity of it and the choice of the two instruments for many reasons, not least of which was budgetary! [Laughs.]

The music had a certain purity. Music must be discreet; it must follow, not impose itself. Unfortunately, we now find most films with music we call "illustrative" [Ar. *teswiriyya*], which tries to express the tensions and emotions. I'm against that. The music must be there without being noticed. Here, with just a few strums on the guitar, we remained very much in the tempo and spirit of the film's clarity, without the grandiose orchestrations that we might have had otherwise.

K. I found the music in *Badis* very effective. Sembène would certainly agree with you—I remember him criticizing elaborate music and saying that the best kind of music was music that went unnoticed.[24]

CRITICISM FROM TWO WOMEN

K. I've talked to a number of people about the substance of this scene, among them Fatima Mernissi [the well-known Moroccan feminist sociologist and writer] and Farida Benlyazid [the screenwriter on *Badis* and also a filmmaker]. Both criticized the ending.

Fatima told me that *Badis* "shouldn't have ended in that defeatist, pessimistic manner, because the film was made at a time when Moroccan women were starting to take their lives into their own hands." And Farida's view was rather similar, that women have many more resources to use in their struggles than were shown in the film.[25] What's your reaction to these criticisms?

M. Well, what Fatima says is the same as saying that every film should carry a message that fits in with a certain well-defined partisan commitment.

I think the first thing to point out is that one of my aims in this ending was to sound an alarm. In my workbooks preparing for the film I had many cases, in Iran for example, where women had been stoned for having betrayed their husbands or been suspected of it. I was sounding an alarm that if we didn't stand up to that kind of obscurantism, that kind of interpretation of Islam, we could end up with events of the same nature. But also, stoning isn't necessarily specific to Islam, it's something that belongs more to the Mediterranean area, it existed among the Romans and in Greek civilization—you can see it in the film *Zorba*, for example. Here, women try to flee a village and violate tradition. Therefore, they have to be disciplined and that's why the men gather, not to stone them.

Coming back to Fatima: I had actually given her the screenplay to read and she reacted, "No, no, no—that ending is absurd, it's horrible." I told her, "But look, you have to recognize that woman is the enemy of woman, we're living through this now." It's only when that first village woman throws the stone that the men start to throw stones. And the woman who throws the stone is doing it, in a way, to protect the girl, to protect the family, to protect women as a sex. She's not throwing it to punish but to stop this girl's indecency, to stop men from being bewitched by the spectacle. Some people have even suggested that it was the girl who provoked the stoning. But for me, the people haven't come together in order to kill the girl. At the beginning they were transfixed by the spectacle, then they got caught up in the mass frenzy and started to throw stones themselves.

As for Farida, I remember those were her feelings. She wasn't present during the shooting to voice her criticisms but Noureddin Sail was, and he tried to dissuade me from the ending, even during the shooting. But I had a vision for the film, and I brought people into it as a function of their talent and competence, but I kept my vision. So I kept firm on the ending I wanted, and I'm not at all sorry.

But it is true that there was a lot of criticism of this ending, especially on the part of women committed to progress and to women's liberation, both because of the fact that it was a woman who threw the first stone and because they would have liked a happier ending, one where the women manage to escape. But, this was *my* ending and I was convinced that this was the ending the film needed.

"I COULDN'T IMAGINE CHANGING IT IN ANY WAY"

K. Why were you so wedded to this ending—admittedly a powerful one—but challenged by people during the shooting (as well as afterward), by men as well as women?

M. Despite the many people, among them the two screenwriters on the film, who tried to convince me to change the ending, I couldn't see any ending other than this tragic one. I was very attached to that ending. I knew it was brutal. But here I couldn't imagine a "happy end" [in English in the interview]. The women couldn't escape.

For me this ending is very symbolic, and the film had to tie things up in that way. Think, on the symbolic level, of the circle of stones, where the village comes together to treat important problems; of the white wall, which exists in all our Moroccan villages as the place of sacrifice, where, when we slaughter a ram on the Feast of the Sacrifice, we re-enact Abraham's obedience to God's call that he sacrifice Ismail. It wasn't at all accidental [laughing, as a rebuke to his critics] that we have a circle, the white wall, the sacrifice, and all that. This ending was so well nurtured by everything in the film that preceded it that I couldn't imagine changing it in any way, even if *nobody else* was happy with it.

Seventh Motif: Filmmaker and Village, Part Two—Showing **Badis** *to Badis, the Dilemmas of Representation*

The power of the final scenes—convincing and cinematically "real" in the way that good films so effectively are—raised for me another question: What kind of representation may one legitimately make of an existing community? Badis is an actual village, its name was used as the film's title, its villagers were given roles to play—all in a story that Tazi and the screenwriters felt was relatively faithful to the way villagers led their lives. What responsibilities and limitations does a filmmaker face in ascribing fictional events to that community?

As first steps in exploring this question, we might ask to what extent the villagers felt "at home" with the story and in their roles as actors; and, with Tazi having promised to show the film to the village, how had villagers reacted to the finished film?

BADIS VILLAGERS IN *BADIS*

K. How did villagers respond when you began to tell them the story you had in mind?

M. When I told them the love story between the soldier and a village girl, that was a big shock! They warned me right away, "We're quite willing to work with you, you can film us and everything, but there is absolutely no question of filming even one woman from our village or one of our girls." I said, "Fine, that's no problem." And we respected that agreement.

K. But I noticed quite a few shots of women in the film, carrying wood, going to the well, and so on.

M. Some of the women in these scenes were brought from other villages and, when we were away from Badis, we sometimes took candid shots—when you see women off in the distance, for example. But the women who encounter Moira at the well or elsewhere were women from other villages who agreed to participate. And then, of course, as a village woman we also used Naima Bouanani. [Both laugh.][26]

So, as far as filming Badis women is concerned, we kept our word.

K. Why were women from other villages more disposed to having their pictures taken?

M. We sought out villages where there was electricity, where there was television, where there was a school, and so on—places that would be more open, more tied into the hustle and bustle of the wider world.

K. Perhaps they would also be more involved in a cash economy?

M. No, it wasn't a question of their wanting the money. It had more to do with knowledge—they had seen TV, they knew it wasn't shameful, it wasn't like prostitution, it all wasn't such a serious matter. They just had a different view of such things.

K. How did villagers react when you told them the ending?

M. I just told them, "The women are going to be disciplined, you're going to throw stones at them to discipline them." They liked the idea of this ending, it fit well with their views—these women can't just up and leave the village without some kind of retribution. But I didn't actually tell them the women would be stoned to death, I didn't speak of death.

K. How did they take to their acting roles?

M. If anything, the acting was often *too* realistic. For the scene where the men catch up to the women and are taking them into the boat, I had explained to the two villagers—the younger one and the old man—what I wanted. But it was as though they were playing themselves, there wasn't much need to explain things to them, to the extent that the actress playing Touria said to me, "He's really hurting me, he's really grabbing me very hard!" [Laughs.] They were so into their roles that they really wanted to hurt her a little.

And, in an earlier scene, when they are in the boat still looking for the women, I had told them to imagine what they would say if two women from the village ran away, and they started discussing it spontaneously, "What! We, the men of this village, and our women have left home!" I recorded exactly what they said, it's dialogue that I didn't direct at all, and it's in the film.

There are lots of cases like that, where reality goes beyond your imagination, beyond what you were intending to show. Someone once said, I don't know who, that every Moroccan carries an actor within—and it's true. You just have to put them in the situation, explain to them the situation, very simply—of course it's very important to be able to do this—and then things just go by themselves. It's unbelievable.[27]

A LEAD ACTRESS REACTS

M. I had promised the villagers at the very beginning that, once the film was finished, it would premiere for them. That's what I set about to do when the film was completed.

We had a small showing before that in Madrid, for the crew, a few friends, and some critics. Let me say something quickly about the reaction of the Spanish actress, Maribel Verdu. During the showing, I noticed that she was crying for what must have been a good quarter of an hour. I asked her what was the matter and she answered, "You know, the story is really touching. Even though I acted in the film, I only saw my part and didn't realize all the other elements that were going into it. But beyond that, people wanting me for films now all want to show my body, my legs, my breasts. But in your film it's not a question of my body, it's a question of me as an actress. That's why I was so touched."[28]

BADIS REACTS

M. After that first projection I came back to Rabat to find a projector and an electric generator that I could take to Badis. This turned out to be very difficult so I adopted another plan—showing the film in a cinema in al-Hoceima and sending a minibus to Badis to bring as many of the villagers as possible. In al-Hoceima, we publicized the showing of the film, sending a car with a megaphone around the city announcing, "Free entry for the showing of a film made in this region." We projected the film in a large movie theater and the theater was full—there were probably between seven hundred and a thousand seats in it. However, among all those people, there were about twenty who had made the trip from Badis, none of them women, of course. In fact, there were only two women in the entire audience, one a member of a woman's association, another the wife of an official.

When the film ended, there was absolutely no applause, nothing at all. Like every director, I waited at the exit to gauge reactions, to see whether people were smiling, angry, or whatever. As the crowd started filing out, I looked them over and they looked back at me with a nasty look. Really, that's how they came out. I couldn't explain it. Afterward, I asked some people, mainly local officials and people involved in the cultural field, "Why were they looking at me with such anger?" The answer, in effect, was "Because you stuck your nose into their lives, especially into their relationship with women. They're so protective of their traditions that they don't want other people putting these on display."

For me this was inexplicable, illogical. I would have thought they'd be proud that a film had been made in the region, that it expressed the atmosphere of the region, that it told the story of this island still under colonial control. I would have thought that they'd be proud of this—even if only out of patriotism and nationalist feeling.

THE ETHICAL CLAIMS OF "REALITY"

Much of what Tazi had said in the preceding discussion of *Badis* was directly relevant to the anthropological problem of how to "represent" living human communities. In this regard, I was struck by how the villagers who made the trip to al-Hoceima reacted to Tazi's representation in ways that were both different from and similar to the response of the "progressive" women. A difference lay in the fact that the "progressive" women felt that the great advances women in Morocco had made were not faithfully represented, that the film, therefore, was not "documentary" enough; villagers, on the other hand, seemed to feel the film was too much a documentary, exposing their private practices to a broad public. Yet, underlying this difference, both groups were challenging the artist's "freedom" to represent a living community—in one case the community of women, in the other the village community.

When we represent a complex human community, we necessarily take certain liberties in what we select, adapt, emphasize, attend to, turn away from, or simply fail to notice. Although taking such liberties is inevitable, all such liberties are not equal; different genres—documentary, fiction, ethnographic film, anthropological ethnographies—systematically take different kinds of liberties in constructing their particular kinds of representation. At the end of the process, it is not always easy to discern the line that separates portraying a "real" event from creating a new one. Along these lines, I wondered, for example, whether the negative response of the villagers might have been attenuated if their identity had been better protected by, say, using a different name for the village in the film.[29]

K. Was it a good idea to use the true name of the village, implying that what was represented in the film were real facts, real events?

M. I never thought of using another name. First of all, as I've said, the name "Badis" carries so much with it—historically, geographically, politically, and socially. Also, it's an anachronism that this place, just an area of a few square meters, is still under foreign control. Perhaps the name "Badis" doesn't mean anything to most people, but once you explore a little further you open up all that history.

K. That has to do with the historical reality of the place. I'm thinking more of its contemporary reality. Let me ask this in a different way. I remember, years ago, seeing the Michael Cimino film on the war the Americans waged in Vietnam, called *The Deer Hunter* (1978). The film shows the Vietcong forcing U.S. prisoners to play Russian roulette, something that never happened in reality. My reaction to this? Perhaps this made a powerful film moment but it also did a great deal of violence to the Vietcong and its historical reality, taking a fictitious event, something so dramatic and cruel, and attributing it to them.

M. I know the film. In France it was called *Voyage to the End of Hell* [Fr. *Voyage au bout de l'Enfer*]. So you're asking whether, in talking about Badis and the relationship between the mainland and the little island, I falsified reality somewhat?

K. Not that so much but, more concretely and more strikingly, putting the stoning in a village you call by its true name may lead the spectator to believe that this kind of thing really happens in that particular place.

M. But the scene is meant to be symbolic! But, I guess that on one level you're right, because that explains why part of the Moroccan public reacted by saying, "But these things don't exist here." Yet it was meant as a parable.

K. OK, but the question is the relationship between the symbolic and the real. Perhaps this relationship tends to be misunderstood when you use the real name of places and of existing people.

M. Yes, yes. But I believe very much in the power of the spectator's imagination. You know there are people who, every day just before sunset, go to listen to stories told by storytellers in public spaces. They imagine themselves so fully in the story that when the storyteller makes a sweeping motion with an imagined sword—his hands are actually empty—the listeners lower their heads to avoid having them cut off. The spectator has great imaginative power and this enables him to understand that this is not a lapidation that actually happened in that specific place.

Lapidation certainly existed in the Mediterranean region, in Greco-Roman civilization, but the spectator can understand that the film presents this event as something symbolic. And, as I've said, I was also sounding an alarm. This is the way I felt it had to be expressed.

K. So, this has to do with your confidence in the public—that the public would be able to understand that this didn't represent a real event but was a symbolic form of expression—and also with the fact that the film itself encouraged this kind of symbolic interpretation.

M. Exactly. But of course I was wrong—wrong insofar as it is difficult to talk about the interpretive capacities of the Moroccan public for symbolic and imaginative expression, when a film-going public for Moroccan films didn't even exist yet![30]

Interlude

Telling a Story—Narrative and Symbols

One of the qualities that critics and viewers singled out when discussing *Badis* was that it told a good story very well.[1] Tazi has already spoken here of how closely the story was connected to his own situation and how organically related it was to its symbolic elements. He invoked both these dimensions—narrative and symbolic—when he insisted on adhering to *his* ending, demonstrating how strongly he felt about narrative power vis-à-vis other aspects, such as a film's "ethnographic truth" and its "social" and/or "ideological" implications.

I wanted to focus more specifically on how Tazi conceived of narrative, how he filmically shaped and expressed the story, and how attached he was to symbolic expression. We will explore each of these in turn. I opened the discussion by referring to a visitor he had received a few days previously.

Narrative
PROXIMITY, SIMPLICITY

"AVOID TOO MUCH EXPLANATION"
K. That fellow who came here the other day asking, "Are there some books for writing screenplays, are there some recipes for this?" reminded me of books on screenwriting I've seen that are indeed

full of recipes, along the lines of, "the first small, strong moment should come after ten or fifteen minutes."

From your point of view, what gives something a good narrative structure? Do you have a mental guide for what constitutes a good screenplay—for example, when the strong points should appear, how much time should be spent on exposition, and so on?

M. My strong belief is that in order to end up with a good film you have to start with a good screenplay [laughs at how obvious this is]. I don't think you can talk about recipes but I think there are certain elements that are indispensable. First of all, there's the need for proximate images; that's very important. Nowadays, spectators are stuffed full of images coming from outside and they'd very much like to see their own images on the screen.

As far as narration is concerned, I don't think it's appropriate for Moroccan films to narrate in the style of Bergman or Antonioni. I think simplicity is primary—we don't need to create a complicated scheme in order to construct a narrative. We need a linearity in narration, in telling the story. Obviously, though, you can't follow this form of writing in a stagnant manner, because today's spectators view images from all over the world and have become familiar with certain forms of writing, transitions, and rapidity.

I also think that we shouldn't make our images too symbolic, or use litote too often, or strive for explanations between the lines. When the discourse is simple rather than sophisticated, I think it is much more powerful and gets to its destination much more effectively. And this is true not only in Morocco but everywhere.

And you have to avoid too much explanation. In the case of *Badis,* I dropped some scenes that had long discussions of Franco. In fact, that's why I introduced the TV into the café—there was no TV in the real village—to help launch the political discussion without having long explanations. There was other dialogue I didn't shoot at all, for similar reasons—too much talk, and it didn't correspond to the rhythm of the film.

PLOT AND RHYTHM, "WESTERN" AND "ORIENTAL"

"I DON'T HAVE A METHODICAL ANALYSIS"

K. When I asked about narration, I was also thinking of the fact that, in *Badis,* we're already some forty-five minutes into the film when the plot is launched, when the postman leads the teacher to discover Moira's affair with the soldier. A similar example: in *Looking*, the third repudiation comes some twenty-five minutes into the film, but what really launches the story, for me at least, is when Hajj Ben Moussa visits the religious judge [Ar. *qadi*] and hears what he must do in order to get Houda back. That takes place after fifty minutes.

Taking these two films together, with their action gaining momentum only after a long period of preparation and contextualization, makes me wonder whether you think you have a certain amount of time to establish the situation, a certain amount of time to capture the spectator's interest.

M. No, I don't do this kind of analysis, creating a sort of curve that specifies where the action ought to take off, when it ought to reach a high point. My concern is to tell a story that can carry the spectator visually through its various turns.

In fact, I think "plot" is something of a Western notion. In Arab literature—and I don't mean *The Thousand and One Nights*, which is often taken to be Arab but is in fact Persian—and I'll take *Sayf Ibn Dhi Yazan*, which is truly Arab, as an example, you encounter some marvelous descriptions and the story doesn't need tension or plot to carry the reader along.[2] My main concern is to capture and carry the spectator along; the plot or suspense is secondary, as is the element of the unexpected—I think the unexpected is minimal in my stories, the storyline doesn't develop as it does in Hitchcock, you know. [Laughs.]

K. Nor does anything like a deus ex machina seem to enter into it and change the course of the story.

M. That's right, absolutely. Each person's role doesn't change much, it's rather linear. In this linearity things happen—some more important than others—that change the situation. In this way the story develops. But I don't have a methodical analysis of where to place this and that in the plot as a whole.

"Too slow"? "but languor is part . . . of the pleasure"

K. Let's look at the question of narration from another angle. You've often said, "I don't think in a Western way, the narrative form in my films is Oriental." Can you tell me what you mean by this?[3]

M. Yes, absolutely. In the Western manner, you begin a story by saying, "Once upon a time." In Oriental narration there is a much longer introduction, "*Kan hetta kan, fi qadimi zaman, al-hbeq wa as-*

sussan."⁴ This is not only longer but, more importantly, it establishes a certain rhythm. That's the crucial distinction: between an Oriental rhythm and a Western rhythm—the two are completely different. That's one of the reasons our films are often judged to be slow.

K. I remember a critic taking *Badis* to task for being too slow. You answered, "I would have liked it to be even slower."⁵

M. Yes. Here, in an Arab-Muslim society, we have a different approach to time, we don't calculate it in the same way. Here, people think there's no sense hurrying, that many things should be experienced slowly. Perhaps it has to do with the desert, with mirages, with slowness, all of which don't correspond to a Western sense of rhythm. If you had an Oriental story told by a Westerner, it would probably take half the time. A feature film would become a short! But with us the languor is part and parcel of the pleasure of telling and listening. And this also comes from the richness of the Arabic language and all the adjectives it has to dress things in—you might have a phrase that can be said in two words but will give more pleasure in forty words, pleasure both for the teller and for the listeners.

In a film as well, there are slow moments that give pleasure, scenes that require a leisurely pace so that the passage of time can be expressed, expectations can be developed, and so on. They would lose a lot if presented like telegrams. When you look at Western films there are indeed scenes that are long and slow, but these tend to be erotic or pornographic ones, that are made lengthy in order to attract the public.

"GAIT . . . GESTURE . . . SMILING"

K. Besides rhythm, what else might distinguish Western from Oriental narrative forms?

M. It's the ensemble, really. For example, the Spanish actress who played Moira in *Badis* was Maribel Verdu, she's Western of course. I realized early on that her gait, her gestures, the way she turned her head and many things of that sort didn't correspond to the society she was supposed to be part of. We had her live with villagers for about ten days by which time, with her quick intelligence, she was able to assimilate all this.

So I think that the difference is also noticed in such things as gestures, stance, even the way of smiling. A multitude of such things go into making the difference between Orient and Occident. But as far as narration itself goes, I think rhythm constitutes the essential difference.

THE USES AND MISUSES OF "ORIENTAL"

K. You're using "Oriental" in a rather broad way. Between Morocco and Tunisia or, better yet, between Morocco and Egypt, are there differences in narrative form?

M. [Pause.] Well, that's difficult to say, especially because I have cinema in mind rather than literature. But as regards Egyptian cinema, some narrative styles—as in the films of Salah Abu Seif, or Tawfiq Salah, or Youssef Chahine—interest me more than others, because their characters aren't so . . . out of control; there isn't such a strong . . . I guess I have to say "Oriental" aspect, with all that singing and dancing and so on, which I find very boring, very heavy. These last elements do distinguish Egyptian from Moroccan cinema.

Between Tunisian and Moroccan cinemas the differences are much smaller. I think many of the social subjects are treated in a rather similar fashion in the two countries. For example, I think the Tunisian director Nouri Bouzid's films—at least those that were shown in Morocco—can be approached more or less like Moroccan films. I can't speak for what the corresponding response might be in Tunisia, because Moroccan films aren't released there.

Also, when I contrast "Oriental" to Western narration, I'm not really referring to certain Oriental influences that we in Morocco were spared—by that I mean mainly the Turkish influence, which went into Tunisia and Algeria but didn't reach Morocco—although some of these influences did indeed reach us, especially through music and song, which already conveys an Oriental pace and mentality and where, as you know, one song can take an hour and a half.

Remember that Morocco is quite special in that there are a number of elements in play here, in addition to the Oriental: those coming from the Berbers, from Andalusia, and from Africa—because Morocco was a land of transit for people, merchandise, caravans, and also a land of slavery. There is a definite blending here, resulting in a muting of Oriental aspects that are much stronger in Egypt, Syria, Iraq, and so on. Our mentality is more Mediterranean.

It's related also to something I was trying to show in *The Big Trip:* here we are not a society of the word, unlike Arab society in general and Egyptian society in particular, which place great

emphasis on the beauty and the majesty of language, of vocabu-
lary. Here, our spoken Arabic dialect—I'm not talking here of the
Berber language—is rather impoverished, in that it takes over
many foreign words to express things. This isn't true in Egypt or
Syria, for example, where, although people speak their dialects,
these dialects have been constantly enriched, are still evolving,
and are used in films, in songs, and elsewhere.

VOYEUR AND DECENCY

"THERE'S NO POINT IN DOTTING ALL THE I'S"

K. You've emphasized your preference for narrative simplicity, for
linearity. In one of your interviews, you speak of not wanting to
have a camera that is very voyeur, saying that this hurts the story.[6]
Why do you privilege narration to such an extent, over and above
the other attractions film has, such as voyeur appeal?

M. I suppose there is a kind of realism that I'm trying to achieve in
my films. But also, when I spoke of my aversion to a voyeur cinema, I think you have to bear in mind that I'm in an Arab-Muslim
society where the notion of decency [Ar. *ḥeshma*] is strong. I don't
believe in pushing scenes toward the erotic and certainly not into
pornography, simply because it's shocking and can attract an audience.

K. Is this related to what you told me earlier, that you might have
showed more blood when Moira is stoned to death?

M. Absolutely. Yes, that's the same thing, showing a lot of blood or
showing a lot of her body. Why show a lot of blood? There's no
point in dotting all the i's. I've always been against showing certain kinds of images that recur frequently in Moroccan films—
showing the suffering of a bird as was done in *Weshma;* or, showing the slaughtering of a ram with the knife cutting the throat
again and again, the blood gushing out, and so on. For me this is
a kind of self-indulgence, a form of violence out of control.

"PLEASING THE PUBLIC"?
PUTTING IN "WHAT
HAUNTS ME"

"THE SPECTATOR IS VERY UNPREDICTABLE"

K. Taking all this together—the desire to show proximate images,
simplicity in narration, linearity in story and characters, what

you've called an Oriental rhythm, avoiding stereotypical scenes, adhering to a cultural notion of decency—I don't suppose you've come up with some kind of recipe that helps you to mix them in the right proportions?

M. Absolutely not. If you're going to have pleasing the public as your primary aim, then obviously there are recipes. But the spectator is very unpredictable for us filmmakers. The only time I really had the spectator in mind was when I started to make the sequel to *Looking*. It wasn't my concern before that, it's not my concern now, and I hope I'm still far from having that become my concern again! [Laughs.]

Pleasing the spectator does indeed become a concern as soon as other functional elements in the film sector begin to have a say—the distributor, the exhibitor, the producer, and so on. This can go to great extremes: I know there are now computer programs in the United States that tell you which elements will grab the spectator better than others—should it be a BMW instead of a Mercedes, a settee of such and such a make, or a suit, or makeup, or whatever.

I'm still able to be my own producer, so I don't have to think too much about how to please the spectator in these kinds of ways. I'm still at the level of ideas and things that concern me and that I want to express. Being my own producer also allows me to put in things simply because I want to, to put in what haunts me. Emigration is one example, having the sea in my films is another.

"THE SEA NOURISHES . . . BUT TODAY WE JUST USE IT TO CARRY US AWAY"

K. Yes, I've noticed that in each of your films you give at least a nod to the sea. *The Big Trip* ends in the sea as does *Looking*. In *Badis* the sea is all around and plays a very important role. Your fourth film, *Lalla Hobby*, opens in the sea.

M. I feel a kind of faithfulness to the sea. As far as our human species goes, it is the sea that has the last word—you know, the story of Noah and the ark, the flood, and so on. Also, one of the particularities of Morocco is that it has some 3,000 km of coast, with both a Mediterranean and an Atlantic shore. This gives us a country bounded on two sides by water, and the water thus is connected to the desire to leave, to emigrate.

You know, before we knew the earth was round, the Atlantic was referred to in legends as the Sea of Darkness [Ar. *baḥr al-*

zulumat]: we knew nothing of what was beyond it, we knew nothing of what might arrive by way of it.[7] This idea resonates even today as far as the Mediterranean is concerned—we don't really know what lies beyond it, despite having this windowlike coastline and all the TV channels that show us the West in such an attractive way. The Sea of Darkness implies the idea of escape, but it also suggests the danger of being engulfed, swallowed up, which is exactly what happens to many clandestine emigrants.

But this has led me to another idea. Now, there are so many people risking their lives in order to leave—they embark on these boats of death, only then to drown or be arrested or be shot at by *la guardia civil* [in Spanish in the interview] like pigeons. Well, the day may arrive when these people begin to say, "Instead of risking my life by leaving, I'm going to risk my life staying, in order to build a better country." At that point, who knows what will happen? The will to change things may become so strong that things could get violent.

K. Would you say that for you the sea is more a barrier, or a means of escape, than something to be used to advantage? In *Badis*, although you see the men coming back from the sea, you don't really see them benefiting from the sea's wealth.

M. The fact is—and I show this in *Badis*—that although the sea *is* a source of nourishment, the fishermen come back with very little to show for their efforts. That's because, to all intents and purposes, we've sold our coastline and sold out our fishing. There are Japanese freezer boats that now troll our coasts and whatever little our own fishermen catch has become so scarce, and therefore so expensive in the market, that people can't afford to buy fish any longer. Instead of exploiting this wealth we're selling it for foreign currency, for what turns out to be one-tenth or one-twentieth of its value if we were fishing it ourselves.

For me, the sea nourishes, it nurses us, it's a source of extraordinary wealth. But today we don't benefit from it, we just use it to carry us away, not to carry things to us.

Symbols

Tazi's discussion of the sea—the meaning it holds for him and how he has used it in his films—raises the question of how he employs symbols in telling his stories. On the one hand, he had said earlier, "I also think that we shouldn't make our images too symbolic . . . we need simplicity"; on the other, he had stressed how full of symbols *Badis* was. I wondered, on a general level, what his approach to symbolic expression was—what functions he felt symbols performed in films, how he used them, what he thought about them. There was also a larger question: What might be the societal conditions that encouraged or discouraged symbolic expression?

WHY USE SYMBOLS?

"READ BETWEEN THE LINES . . . TREATING
SPECTATORS WITH RESPECT"

K. In general, what is the importance of symbolic expression in your films?

M. First of all, symbols allow you to cut down on explanation and allow spectators to read between the lines. These symbols often have a precise meaning in the context of a particular society and in this way you're treating the spectators with respect, not as though they lacked the culture to understand the symbols.

Obviously, *Badis* is very relevant here because of its many symbols: the circle has a universal meaning that doesn't require explanation; the white wall is a very precise symbol here in Morocco, referring to the sacrifice; and so on. Or you could take the end of *The Big Trip*, where Omar starts to row. Rowing, too, is a symbol—a symbol of rebirth, learning to be a new kind of man. There are a lot of symbols like these.

Symbols and signs are strewn throughout our society and they are very useful in communicating through sound and image, rather than having to continually explain things.

SOME PROBLEMS WITH SYMBOLS

K. What do you mean when you say that symbols and signs are strewn throughout our society?

M. You don't have to look very far—just take the example of women's makeup and you find tattooing, designs with henna, things like that. Many of these are pagan survivals—signs and symbols that invoke maternity, fertility, or some such notion. What is popularly called "the hand of Fatima," the "five"—everything that is related to the evil eye—is a symbol that runs throughout our society. There's also incense and other things that are meant to get rid of demons and other spirits. All of these are signs and symbols we grow up with from the earliest age.

K. Orson Welles said something similar about life being full of symbols. But, at the same time, he was opposed to deliberately employing them.[8] What's your reaction to that?

M. I think the symbolic dimension can be helpful in emphasizing certain things, even when it isn't absolutely necessary. When I look back at *Badis*, I know that I was trying to have the teacher serve as a symbol for authority. When he goes through the lineup and then orders the kids into the school, when you see him in front of the classroom, when he roams around in silence during the exam—all this, for me, was a symbol of authority that I found it essential to express. And this explains the fear the students had and the way they behaved. On the other hand, it's true that sometimes people read as symbols things that aren't symbols at all.

But I don't agree with the general contention that it's a mistake to use symbols. I think this depends to a large extent on the kind of society you're in. Each film is a product of the time and place of its making. When society places great limits on freedom, you have to find a kind of symbolic expression to disguise your idea. You may not be able to say, in a direct manner, "We're in a dictatorship" or "Our religious system is such and such," but you still can find ways to express these things through symbols, litotes, and other techniques, hoping that the spectator will be able to understand what you mean.

DIFFERENT USES OF SYMBOLS

SYMBOLS: PRECISE OR ALLEGORICAL

K. Each of your films seems to use symbols in a different way. In *Badis* symbols appear in a rather direct manner. For example, throughout the film the women have a particular rapport with birds and chickens. Moira feeds the chickens and talks to them, Touria reads a book called *Birds Hide to Die* and not only doesn't cook the chickens but sets them free. Ba Abdallah, on the other hand, slaughters them for dinner.

Here, the bird as symbol is associated with something precise, in this case the women. Another way to use symbols is in allegory, where two or more levels of meaning run parallel to one another through the work, and where the more literal level is a metaphor for a more general meaning. *The Big Trip* can be read as an allegory: the literal metaphor of travel from north to south reflects the more general process of Omar's progressive dispossession. One critic even said that the film was so allegorical that if one read it on the most immediate level, in terms of characters and plot, it was an unsatisfactory film, but a reading on the second or third levels, as allegory, turned it into a very important film.[9]

M. In *The Big Trip*, the symbolic dimension involved a level of meaning where the farther north one went the greater the cacophony, culminating in Tangiers where Omar no longer understands much of anything at all. You could extend this metaphor into today's world: in the context of growing globalization along liberal lines, dominated by organizations like the World Bank, the IMF, the World Trade Organization, citizens in countries like Morocco become more and more confined to the role of consumer, people who consume meanings rather than create them. I think this kind of allegorical structure was very evident in *The Big Trip*.

In *Badis* the symbols were more limited, more emotional, directly related to human traits and relationships. Touria feels her lack of freedom and naturally tries to act in a way opposite to her oppression. That's why she treats the chickens as she does, that's why she develops a protective attitude toward Moira. It's as though she has swallowed things and then ruminates to make something of them that will lessen her pain. The symbols in *Badis* are often on that immediate emotional level.

Of course, there are more general symbols too—for example, the minivan as a symbol of departure, symbols referring to the nation, to colonization, and so forth. Also important in *Badis* are symbols that indicate cyclical, repetitive motions and recurring time, which we've discussed before. Then too, there are the symbols pointing to politics. And don't forget the scenes where you see ten or twelve children coming from school, and on the road they see a girl shepherding a flock of goats—that too is a symbol.

PARABLE AND ALLEGORY

K. You mentioned earlier that you saw *Badis* as something of a parable. Is there also an allegorical level to this film?

M. If you wanted to look for that, I suppose you could find it in the impact of the community, symbolized by the circle of stones. The allegory would be that the community structures the individual's behavior, that in this society the collective spirit is very strong, the individual is subordinate to the collectivity, and the community dictates the conduct and rules to follow.

K. Does *Looking for My Wife's Husband* have a symbolic dimension? It's not clear to me that it does.

M. Well, sometimes you're dealing with one subject overtly but your unconscious is working out other issues through certain symbols. No doubt *Looking* also has a symbolic level of that sort. [Long pause, as I waited for him to elaborate.]

K. I don't really see much of a symbolic dimension in it.

M. Perhaps there isn't—I can agree with that. I said earlier that symbols are there in part to push us beyond the immediate image to search for an additional explanation—reading between the lines, I called it. But *Looking* is a rather banal story of a man with three wives who divorces one of them for the third time. So, in its banality, we don't need symbols to help us understand things. And I think the sequel is in the same vein as *Looking.*

MORE SOCIETAL FREEDOM, FEWER SYMBOLS?

Controlling "the two policemen"

K. With regard to forms of symbolic expression, can we see an evolution in your work, along the following lines? *The Big Trip* is an allegory from beginning to end. *Badis* is full of symbols that are direct and immediate, and the allegorical level is much less strong. Finally, in *Looking* and then in *Lalla Hobby*, the symbolic dimension hardly exists at all, neither allegorical nor direct. Do you think the reduced use of symbolism in *Looking* and *Lalla Hobby* might have something to do with changes in Moroccan society over the past two decades?

M. Yes, I think so, I really do, especially if we remember that *Looking* was filmed and came out over 1993–1994, at a time when the women's movement was becoming much stronger and pushing for changes in the Mudawwana.[10] Along with this, religion was no longer a taboo subject and you were able to discuss many issues you couldn't earlier. When I think back to when we were children and what we suffered from our teachers and parents whenever we raised questions like, "Can you prove to me that such and such a thing exists?"—we were asking not in the spirit of doubting our religion but just trying to understand it—we were treated like we were blaspheming. It was very painful.

Being able to ask such questions is a sign of a democratizing society in which freedom and the individual are growing stronger, a society that is showing greater respect for human rights, even if there are still limits regarding what we call "the sacred institutions"—God, the king, and the nation. That's a vast domain to be off limits, certainly, but within these institutions there are many rubrics, and you can find a number of them that can be treated and criticized.

Things are moving forward as each day passes and in the last four or five years the changes have been very rapid. There are a number of issues I handled with kid gloves in *Looking* that I would be able to treat squarely today. For example, I could have presented the *qadi*'s discourse in *Looking* in much cruder language, I could have made him appear much more ridiculous. Remember when we talked about *The Big Trip* and not being able to show a policeman's uniform?

K. Yes, and if you look at Abdelkader Lagtaa's film *Casablancans* (1999), you not only see policemen in uniform but the policemen themselves are portrayed very negatively.

M. Yes, this was unimaginable in 1980 or 1981.

K. With Moroccan society and culture moving in this direction, do you think your future films will be less likely to depend on the symbolic dimension?

M. I think so. In the project I'm currently working on, the procedure will be similar to *Looking*, where I was able to establish a kind of "atemporality" that allowed me to place the film in the past and perform a critique of the present. In this way I'll have great latitude in criticizing society and the power system, without having the two policemen inside my brain, one for each lobe, saying, "Watch out, you're getting too close to such and such a problem."

Given the current situation of greater freedom of expression and the kind of film this next one promises to be, I'd be pleased if I could do away with symbols entirely! [Laughs.]

Chapter Five

The Other Side of the Wind, Almost

Introduction: Two New Hurdles

By the mid-1990s, Tazi could look back with pride upon his two most recent films: *Badis* had been a great critical success (although at a moment when it was still difficult for a Moroccan film to have wide national distribution) and *Looking* had become the most popular film in Moroccan cinematic history. One might have thought that, just a few years past his 50th birthday, he had every right to look forward to a filmmaking career full of new and interesting projects and many more films to be completed. After all, at the age of 50 Robert Wise was still to make about ten films, among them *The Sound of Music, The Sand Pebbles,* and *Two People;* and John Huston (admittedly, a far from typical example) was still to make some twenty-five, including *The Misfits, The Night of the Iguana, Fat City, The Dead,* and, as we have seen, *The Man Who Would Be King.*

This hope might be a realistic one were the structure of Moroccan filmmaking more "industrial"; were there substantial integration among production, distribution, and exhibition; and were there an effective state policy to ensure continuity of production, train a full complement of technicians, and encourage the emergence of new filmmakers as well as provide some artistic safety net for established filmmakers who had already proven their worth.

By the mid-1990s Morocco had taken some significant steps in these directions but one cannot say it was near reaching these goals.

For Tazi to have hoped to direct a feature film every couple of years would have been unrealistic ("utopian" is the term he prefers) and would have meant ignoring the basic context within which he works—an unprofitable national film sector, a global situation that makes it almost impossible for Moroccan filmmakers to have success abroad, and the need to devote considerable time and energy to activities other than making fiction films simply to earn the income to support a family.

Following the success of *Looking*, Tazi himself did not appear to have been unduly sanguine. As he said to me,

M. After all the hubbub around the premiere of *Looking* I still had few illusions. Knowing the situation of the Moroccan filmmaker and the structures within which he operates, I was certainly not saying to myself, "Ah-hah, this film is really doing well at the box office, now all doors will be open to me and I'll be able to make other films with much less trouble." I knew that I would still have to battle as I always did—the only improvement I could hope for might be with regard to distribution.

I was already working on another project, one that is still on my mind, treating Raissouli, an important figure in Moroccan history at the end of the nineteenth and beginning of the twentieth centuries. For us he's a character somewhat like Fan-Fan the Tulip, although many Moroccan historians contest this and see him only as a bandit, a highway brigand. But, really, he was a character who struggled against central authority, who was against the colonization of Morocco—a kind of popular hero. I wanted to show, from an intimate perspective, how such a character develops, how he becomes a revolutionary or a brigand—depending on what you want to call him.

Also, I still had my other activities—making documentaries, doing advertising work, and so on. In any case, in our society to hope to make a living from feature films is utopian.

Although not expecting things to grow much easier, Tazi could not know how difficult they were about to become. At a first stage, *Looking*'s success had sharpened the ambitions of many people in Morocco's film world who, having suffered through years of frustration, now wanted that success to breed another one. Pressure for a sequel climbed to the bursting point and it fell to Tazi to try and channel that pressure.

At a second stage, were such a sequel to be carried forward, *Looking*'s ending—Hajj Ben Moussa setting off in a boat bound for Europe in an effort to retrieve his ex-wife's husband—dictated that the film follow the Hajj into Europe. Yet no Moroccan filmmaker had ever filmed most of a feature in Europe. Morocco greatly encourages Western producers to film in Morocco, but what kind of a welcome will Europe offer a Moroccan filmmaker who tries to turn the camera 180 degrees and film in the West? Tazi was not a novice in this area— he had already lived in Europe and had filmed abroad—but the hurdles such an effort faces and Tazi's attempts to surmount them provide a telling commentary on relations between North and South and, not surprisingly, have a noticeable effect on the film that resulted.

The spectacle of a Third World filmmaker shooting a film in Europe draws our attention to a broader issue: What are the various aspects of such a filmmaker's encounter with the global marketplace? Shooting a film is but one moment—perhaps the most direct one—in this encounter, but there are other aspects as well that we are going to touch upon in this chapter: obtaining rights to literary works, gaining financing, associating with other producers abroad, postproduction, securing a film's distribution, and obtaining the fees and payments that, by right and contract, one is due.[1]

Taken together, the domestic pressures building toward a sequel and the effort of a Moroccan filmmaker to go "international" might be taken as signs that people in the Moroccan film world, having had several relatively successful years since the early 1990s, now believed that a big leap forward was possible and that the moment should be seized. Perhaps they were signs, too, of the deep-seated optimism of a filmmaker who had already made three films in very difficult circumstances, who was strongly motivated to create and construct, and who believed that intensity and hard work could conquer almost any obstacle. Ambitions had grown, but had they outgrown capabilities?

To get a better sense of both Tazi's and his Moroccan colleagues' capabilities in these regards, let us follow, first, the mounting pressure for a sequel to *Looking*; then, we will explore some of the experiences Tazi has had abroad, with respect to shooting, commissioning, financing, distributing, screening, and, not least in importance, being paid. This will help us better understand why the experience of making *Lalla Hobby* almost ends in tragedy.

Pressure for a Sequel
"THERE WILL BE NO SEQUEL"

Following the success of Abdelkader Lagtaa's *A Love Affair in Casablanca* in 1992 and the even greater success of *Looking,* the hopes that many in the Moroccan film world had that Moroccan films would now be distributed widely throughout the country and the Moroccan public would eagerly turn out to see these films were, to a significant extent, fulfilled. More ominously, however, *Looking's* success led to the expectation that it would be relatively easy to follow the first success with another, an expectation that led to demands for high fees and requests for special indulgences and other emoluments on the part of the first film's participants.

Immediately after *Looking's* success, Tazi had foreseen some of the problems a sequel would generate and clearly stated his opposition to one. What made him change his mind?

"*LOOKING'S* SUCCESS WENT ON AND ON . . . I BEGAN SAYING TO MYSELF, 'AFTER ALL, WHY NOT?' "

K. In an interview you gave in mid-1994, some six months after the release of *Looking,* you clearly said there would be no sequel—in fact, the title of the article quoted you saying "There will be no sequel to my film."[2] Adding to the irony, you gave several reasons why making a sequel would not be a good idea: a sequel is always a qualitative disappointment, expenses for recreating the sets and for paying the actors would quadruple, you would have your hands tied because of having to depend on the same actors, the same objects, the same extras. All that sounds quite convincing, yet you went ahead anyway. Why?

M. *Looking's* success went on and on and on. The main actor as well as several of the others—all of whom had now become stars sought out by everyone—wanted to take this success one step further and implored me to make a sequel. I won't say I fell into a trap because this is my responsibility and I assume it, but I let myself be persuaded, even though the project wasn't very dear to me. Also, I knew that sequels posed serious problems—every spectator has his or her own idea of what the original was and what a sequel to it should look like. A director will always have great difficulty fitting his own idea into the imaginary of each of the spectators.

But I let myself go in this direction. I began saying to myself, "After all, why not?" And I started to imagine a sequel imposed by the ending of *Looking:* the Hajj has set out in a small boat, so now we can follow him into Europe.

What's even more ironic is that this ending, which gave some people the idea that a sequel would follow, was really put there just to cast a glance at the acute immigration problem. I also put it there because, as I said earlier, I like to give a nod now and then to the sea. I had absolutely no idea of a sequel. It was only afterward, with the open ending and with people saying, "We have to have a sequel, what will the Hajj find when he gets to Europe?" that the idea for a sequel really began to become a concrete possibility for me.

"[WE'VE] EATEN OF THE RABID COW . . ."

OTHER PEOPLE'S DESIRES

K. When you did finally decide to go ahead with the sequel, you had to do without some of the original's actors as well as the screenwriter. Why was that?

M. Well, after *Looking* some of the actors considered themselves big stars and made some exorbitant demands. Bashir Skiredj, who played Hajj Ben Moussa, not only made major financial demands but wanted significant changes in the screenplay, on the order of, "Now that I'm the biggest star in Morocco, I can't play a role where at one point I become a prison inmate."

For the screenplay, I first went to Farida Benlyazid, who had done the screenplay for *Looking* and whom I really like to work with. I gave her the idea and the synopsis and she put things in shape, which really helped me out. But then she asked for half of her fee up front. Her words were, "All of us filmmakers have eaten of the rabid cow all these years; now that there is some cake we all have to share it" [meaning, "we've been so starved we've had to eat rabid meat"]. As though I had made millions on *Looking*.[3] I couldn't satisfy that kind of demand.

Changing the screenwriter is similar to changing the actors. Farida has a certain style of writing and gives a special coherence to her screenplays; a sequel should have a similar style and coherence. With a change in screenwriters, you're inevitably going to have a change in sensibility, in approach, and in situations.

All this upset me quite a bit. What's painful is that everyone here in the film world knows how little money filmmaking actually brings in. But still, as soon as a film has some success they begin to think like the public, which, seeing lines in front of a movie theater, believes that we're making millions. Even though they know that a film on the Moroccan market will rarely earn more than one-third of its budget. What hurts even more is that I'm one of the filmmakers who pays actors and technicians the highest fees—especially with regard to the actors and the screenwriters. You should see what the others pay.[4]

K. So, with Farida out of the picture, how was the screenplay written?

M. I turned to my constant friend, Noureddin Sail, and he agreed to write the screenplay. And, as with *Looking,* el-Alj wrote the dialogue and Abdelwahab Doukkali did the music.

K. It sounds as though this project was determined more by other people's desires than your own.

M. Yes, that about sums it up. We were still writing the screenplay and already people were elbowing their way forward, wanting to help finance the film as co-producers, with some actors pushing from behind because it was in their interest to have a sequel made and continue their momentum toward "stardom." And the public too, "So, what about the sequel, how about a sequel?" It became so repetitive. And later, while we were filming—now I'm jumping forward a bit—I was visited by distributors and exhibitors who wanted to book the film for its Moroccan release.

My feelings became, "I've got to get this film over and done with, I've got to get it behind me." It was like being pregnant, you wanted to give birth as rapidly as possible. [Laughs.] And then, once we were into production and into the shooting, I realized that I was really drained and was being swept along by events beyond my control. One symptom of this is that the period between *Looking* and *Lalla Hobby* was relatively short, just two years. Given our conditions of production in Morocco, I think I need a minimum of three years between films.

So, this was very much a film made for other people, including the public. There was a certain complaisance on my part, even though I was still able to express many of the things I wanted to in the film. Perhaps we should see it as a small detour, a pause, with regard to the direction I would like to follow in my films. It reinforces the idea that it's very important to make the films that one feels most deeply about—films, as I've said before, that come from the guts.

Also, making the film turned out to be a constant challenge. In addition to the demands made by some of my collaborators, there were also the daily challenges. For example, I needed the same inlaid table I had used for the first film, when I had paid 100 DH a day for it. This time the owner wanted 5,000 DH per day! After all, he knows the film is launched, knows I need the table, knows that I'm at his mercy. When you have this cast of mind all the way from the guy renting antiques up to and including the actors, it becomes a daily challenge, a kind of test. This pushed me into another frame of mind—that no one is indispensable, that I can still make this film, and that I can make it without those people!

Going Abroad

When a Third World filmmaker begins to look beyond his or her own borders, problems may arise at any (or all) stages of the filmmaking process, from acquiring rights to a filmable property, through securing financing, during the shooting, then to postproduction, on to distributing and exhibiting, and, finally, up to and including actually receiving the compensation that one is due. Tazi had experience in most of these areas.[5]

FILMING ABROAD

THE PILGRIMAGE IN SAUDI ARABIA

M. My first experience filming abroad took place in the early 1970s, when we tried to make part of a feature film in Saudi Arabia. Abdelaziz Ramdani, one of our first Moroccan directors, intended to shoot in Saudi Arabia at the time of the Pilgrimage.[6] We were more than twenty people in all, technicians and actors included. Before laying out the money for the travel, we'd taken all the necessary precautions and satisfied all the formalities with the Saudi embassy and all the ministries responsible for those sorts of things. But upon our arrival in Saudi Arabia all our equipment was sequestered and no official could be found anywhere to help us, because everyone was involved with the Pilgrimage. Not only that, but we couldn't even retrace our steps because during the Pilgrimage period all the planes are booked solid.

It was the start of this film's shooting—we wanted to get this part wrapped up and then continue the rest of the shooting in Morocco. But we were completely blocked. Of course, we had suspected that things might not go smoothly, because we knew the Pilgrimage was a source of enormous revenue for the Saudis and that filming it—perhaps demystifying it somewhat, showing its disorganization or other problems—might not make them very enthusiastic, to say the least. As it turned out, all the permissions and authorizations they gave us on paper were only a facade. We couldn't shoot and we couldn't turn back either, so we were more or less caught up and buffeted about by all the goings-on of the Pilgrimage. Eventually, the entire project had to be abandoned.

Even though we couldn't do the filming, we were still forced to stay on in Saudi for some time, because we couldn't get planes out. The fact that the three of us—that is, the Sigma 3 group (Ahmed Bouanani, Muhammad Seqqat, and myself)—couldn't actually get started on the filming meant that we became rather critical observers of what was going on around us. I had a still camera but somehow, every time I wanted to take a picture, our "guardian angels"—people from the security services, of course—always managed to push me or bump me at just the wrong time (or right time, depending on your perspective) so that the pictures were never good ones. These were really rather unsubtle techniques. But what we did see—although we were never able to film it—regarding the exploitation of the religious ceremony, everything related to the sacrifice of the ram, the way money is pumped out of the pilgrims . . . well, it's really unimaginable.

This was my first experience of all the difficulties that can arise when you try to film abroad, and they gave me a foretaste of the kinds of problems I was going to have some twenty-five years later when filming *Lalla Hobby*.

In fact, this wasn't the only occasion I had problems in Saudi Arabia. Toward the end of the 1980s I was approached by CBS to do a documentary on the Pilgrimage; after two years of trying to get permission and authorizations, I gave up. Even today, the Saudi authorities are not interested in that kind of film.

FAITH HEALING IN THE PHILIPPINES

M. Filming in the Philippines was a different experience altogether. In 1977 I was asked to direct a documentary that would shed some light on the phenomenon of "faith healers" [in English in the interview] in the Philippines, some of whom seem to be surgeons with their bare hands. Our group consisted of a magician— and he was the "Oscar" of magicians at that time, a Tunisian who performed in Paris—and a French cardiologist who had also done training in acupuncture in China and Hong Kong. The cardiologist was very well known, in France he had invented a ring you put in your ear to help you stop smoking. In fact, he specialized in what is called auricular acupuncture, which focuses on the ear— the ear is said to have the form of a fetus and each part of the ear represents one part of the human body. He had also written a book that he gave me as a gift, together with acupuncture needles, saying "With these you now have all you need to become a practitioner yourself." I'm still in touch with him, he's a very interesting guy. That's one of the things I love about film work—you come across all sorts of interesting people, whether they be professionals, intellectuals, or people off the street—it's kind of a continuing education, a sociological lesson day after day.

So there we were, leaving Paris for the Philippines, with a stopover in Thailand, which we had trouble getting out of, by the way, because of some sort of coup d'état. We finally reached Manila and from then on, for about twenty-five days, we went all over the Philippines looking for faith healers. The documentary I made from this experience has, I think, a certain claim to priority, because it was one of the first to deal with these bare-handed healers who, at that time, had become something of a fad, with a lot of people flying to the Philippines to be cured, especially from Canada, the United States, and Europe. When I started the trip I knew nothing about this phenomenon, so the film became a kind of day-by-day personal inquiry as I learned more about the subject.

K. Who commissioned the film?

M. The cardiologist was King Hassan's cardiologist, and I suppose he had spoken to the king about this at some point and the king became interested.

K. Do you think the king was looking for new healing techniques?

M. No, but the film was to be made in the spirit of finding out what was really going on, whether these bare-handed healers actually cured people, what kinds of ailments they treated and how they did so. That was the guiding spirit, and that's why we had a cardiologist/acupuncturist and a magician, so we could figure out whether this was something more than a bag of tricks. And I think we carried out this task very well.

K. Did you have any problem getting authorization for the filming?

M. No. We went through the medical establishment in the Philippines and they made the necessary contacts. In fact, we were giving the healers in the Philippines a good deal of free publicity; we were tolerated and we could film openly. Of course, this wasn't true absolutely everywhere, but it was true for the most part.

Among the most striking aspects of this phenomenon was to see the chartered planes coming from Canada, from Belgium, from France, full of sick people, hopeless cases from the point of view of classical medicine—people with cancers, with diabetes, with multiple sclerosis, and so on. We took a chartered plane from France and we became part of the group—the cardiologist even passed himself off as a sick person and I was able to film two or three operations that were performed on him.

The magician too had his role. While a healer was using different curing objects, the magician would make some of these objects "disappear," and then we'd be able to examine those objects that evening. For example, when the healer would use a cloth that had some blood on it, the magician would make it disappear—then the healer would be looking all over for it and not finding it. [We're both laughing.] The healer had no inkling of the tricks that the magician was performing! [We continue laughing.] It was really amusing to have the magician around—you'd shake his hand and your watch would disappear. I still don't know how he did it.

In fact, that's how we ended the film, with the magician himself performing an operation!

K. What kind of conclusions did you come up with?

M. Basically, that the whole phenomenon is a scam—it's 100 percent trickery, there's no surgery, no opening of the body, no blood flowing, nothing at all. You know, you can lie to the eye but you can't lie to a camera—we can adjust speeds, see what's happening frame by frame, image by image. I saw operations to heal eye cataracts where, supposedly, worms were extracted, or small lenses. When you looked at the film frame by frame you could see how the healer inserted the object before he extracted it.

But I did see some amazing things in the Philippines. One time we were far from Manila, far from civilization, and I saw a woman in a weekly market healing hemorrhoids, those large boils that form in the buttocks. People wouldn't give her money, they'd just bring her a chicken, or eggs, and she healed them. Even with the camera—we filmed these operations on the buttocks—and going over the film frame by frame, it was impossible to see how she healed the hemorrhoids. And the patients had no pain or suffering. For me, that still remains an extraordinary scene.

K. Was the film ever shown?

M. Yes, it was shown a couple of times on the French television channel Antenne 2, in 1978 I think, and there was a lot of discussion over it. That's why I think this film had a certain priority. There had been a couple of French and American films on the subject that had taken a rather credulous position. But my film really exposed the complete dishonesty of the phenomenon—that things were accomplished through prestidigitation, with great rapidity, but they were fundamentally dishonest—exposed this to such an extent that I was persona non grata in the Philippines after it.

I think the incident that brought this home to greatest effect concerned a young woman of 18, a Belgian girl with multiple sclerosis whose mother's only wealth was a small grocery shop that she had sold so she could make this trip to the Philippines to cure her daughter. In the Philippines, at the very beginning, the girl had great difficulty breathing and had almost died because of the mountain altitude. Then, on the return home, she died in the airplane, again altitude was the problem. And there was another woman with a bad case of diabetes, who stopped taking her insulin because the healer had said, "Your disease is cured, you should stop taking the medicine." This person didn't die, at least not by the time we left her.

In the film I showed these things saying, in effect, "Watch out—these people are neither doctors, nor healers, nor surgeons. They are charlatans, and you have to beware of them."

OTHER VENTURES ABROAD

ACQUIRING RIGHTS

"THE CONDITIONS WERE VERY ONEROUS"

K. Looking at your experiences abroad other than filming, perhaps you could give me an example of an effort you made to acquire rights to a property you wanted to film?

M. Certainly. Some years ago I read a novel by the well-known Moroccan writer Driss Chraibi, *An Investigation in the Countryside*. I found it very interesting and got in touch with Chraibi, who loved the idea and said, "As far as I'm concerned you can have all the rights to this at no charge. But of course, you have to get the permission of the publisher." I got in touch with the publisher, the French publisher Le Seuil.

Here I had a lot of problems. First of all, they wanted an enormous sum of money just for the rights to adapt it—some 200,000 to 300,000 DH, which may seem normal in the West but for me is an exorbitant amount. Furthermore, they then wanted rights concerning distribution and other aspects. I drew up a contract but the conditions were very onerous for me financially and we couldn't carry it to completion. I'm really sorry about that, because it was a subject that I found fascinating, the book is full of humor and really a very fine work.[7]

SCREENING: CHICAGO—LOCARNO—ST. MARTIN— CALCUTTA—OUAGADOUGOU

BADIS—"THE SHOCK OF THE FILM"; LOOKING—"DIALOGUE BETWEEN THE FILM AND THE PUBLIC"

K. When we talk about international distribution and exhibition, we should probably distinguish between the audience's response and the question of commercial benefits. Perhaps you could start by telling me of some of the experiences you have had exhibiting your films internationally, and then we can move on to the problems you've had commercially.

M. I've had a number of very positive experiences showing my films internationally, experiences that have really touched me.

Let's take the case of *Badis* first. I was at a showing of *Badis* in Chicago where, without exaggeration, for one minute after the end of the film, with the lights having gone on, there was total silence, everyone stayed in their seats. Then, after that very long moment when people were still under the shock of the film, a great burst of applause broke out. At the Locarno Festival in Switzerland, where the film won the Jury Prize, *Badis* was shown in the open air, at the public square, and there must have been ten thousand spectators there. Everyone's reaction—the public, the critics—was fantastic.

I also projected the film on a small island in the Caribbean, called St. Martin, that is divided between the Dutch and the French. The island had all kinds of TV channels coming from the United States and elsewhere, but there wasn't one movie house. So a festival had been organized to introduce filmgoing to the island and this was the occasion to build the island's first movie theater. I showed *Badis* in this new theater—there were some five hundred to six hundred seats—and the house was full. *Badis* was shown at 3 P.M., another film was to be shown at 5, another at 7, and so on. When the 3 P.M. showing of *Badis* was over, a lot of people who left the theater promptly got on line again. When the title of the next film was announced, quite a few people said, "No, no, we want to see the film we just saw again, you can just postpone showing the others." This was really their first contact with filmgoing and they wanted to see the film three or four times to understand it better. I thought that was a very interesting response on the part of people who had no film-going experience.

To go from that small island to the other extreme, I also projected *Badis* in India—in Calcutta and in one other city. For me, simply to see the theaters in India with four thousand or five thousand seats—you can imagine my reaction, just to conceive of a film-going public that immense! Obviously, that goes together with their very high production numbers. This projection was at a festival that took place in 1990 or 1991, at the time of the Gulf War. The response was very, very warm.

As you can see, as far as *Badis* is concerned, I had wonderful responses from all over—India, Europe, the United States, Canada. Also, the Spanish TV co-producers distributed the film throughout the Spanish-speaking world, and I had wonderful echoes from the press in Mexico, Chile, Argentina, Uruguay, and so on. On the whole, I was really overwhelmed that this simple story, a story that happens, so to speak, right around the corner from where I live, could get such a strong and unanimous response from a public coming from so far away, from all over the world.

I really understood then that, starting from particularities in your own history and milieu, you can still reach the general, the universal.

With *Looking* I had good experiences too. For example at FES-PACO [the acronym stands for the French *Festival panafricain de cinéma à Ouagadougou*, held every two years in the capital of Burkina Faso], where I saw it in two different venues, people were laughing all over the place—I had the impression I was back in Morocco. There was a real dialogue between the film and the public.

COMMERCIAL PROBLEMS: CANADA, THE UNITED STATES, FRANCE

"I NEVER SAW ONE PENNY"

M. On the other hand, when you start talking about the commercial aspects of international distribution and exhibition it's another matter entirely. I had a problem in Canada that was really very simple. *Badis* was distributed in Montreal and for some time it ranked second in the box-office receipts, right after *Rain Man*. For weeks and weeks I was getting good reports on the box-office results, but I never got a centime from any of that—it was complete robbery. What made things even worse was that later, that same distributor sold *Badis* to a TV channel in Toronto for something like $20,000–$30,000, and to another channel for $15,000–$20,000. And I never saw one penny of this money. It's money that he simply took and put in his pocket. After that I was pretty mistrustful of distribution across the Atlantic.

In 1991 or 1992, I was invited to present *Badis* at an Arab film festival in Seattle, along with Farida Benlyazid who was presenting her film [*A Door to the Sky*, 1988]. During the festival a woman distributor introduced herself to both of us and wanted to buy the rights to our films for what she said would be university and video distribution. It seemed like an interesting arrangement. She would take the festival copy, which already had English subtitles, she would make the videocassette copies, and then, every time the film would be shown at a university or when a cassette was sold, we would get a percentage. It was economical for her too, because she wouldn't have to pay for her own copy of the film.[8]

Farida signed a contract with them right away but I said that I wanted to take the contract back to Morocco, look it over, and then I would decide whether or not to accept it. When I got back to Morocco I began to think, "How am I going to check on what's happening with the film?" It's a question of trust, and I didn't have any at that point. So I stopped right there and didn't make the deal.

A few years later I saw Farida and asked her how it had turned out. She said, "That's enough, I don't want to hear any more about this matter!"[9]

K. So, as of now, no one in the United States has rights to your films?

M. Absolutely no one. In fact, there was a lot of interest in *Badis* and *Looking* and some people went to substantial lengths to obtain the rights, but I refused to go ahead. I said to myself, "I've lost enough time and money on this, had enough stress and pressure." I prefer to keep my film right here in its can, rather than knocking myself out trying to discover whether the guy who's got my film is in the process of making money on it and not giving me what I deserve. If I can't verify what's going on I'm not going to get involved. If someone comes up to me and says, "Look, I'll buy the rights, here's a healthy sum of money for them," that's fine, then he can do with the film what he wants. But someone who says, "Here's $2,000 to pay for the copy, and then I'll be sending you some small amounts, $500 here, $200 there," and then even that doesn't reach me—well, it's better to avoid the whole thing altogether.

"THERE ARE A LOT OF WOLVES OUT THERE"

M. In France, I had a problem similar to the one in Canada, although this time with *Looking*. I was at a festival—I can't remember whether it was in Amiens or Nantes—and a woman distributor came up to me saying, "I really loved your film, I'd like to distribute it in France." I asked her what she had distributed recently and she said *La Isla* [*The Island*], a South American film I had liked a lot and that, thanks to her, had been well distributed in France.[10] On that basis I agreed to give her *Looking* and she had the good sense to advertise it on Radio Shalom and Radio Beur, an excellent way to reach the North African communities. The film came out in three different theaters in Paris and over three weeks had about twenty-three thousand spectators, which is very respectable for a film from the South.

But, when I asked to see the accounts, she was never available, always too busy. Finally, it became very difficult to contact her at all. I eventually had to hire a lawyer. As a result, not only did I not get a peanut from the distributor but I actually had to spend 25,000 francs[11] on the lawyer! But at least that enabled me to void the contract that allowed her to sell the film to television. Getting those rights back and being able to deal with the television stations is very important, because stations like ARTE or the Turkish or Belgian stations can come through with interesting offers.

This all reinforces my view that you have to think first of your own public. There at least you can keep an eye on things, you're dealing with people from your own society. There are lots of wolves out there and you have to protect yourself. When you have a small film you can't in any case hope to get wide international distribution. All you really can hope for is that the distributor treats you honestly.

ARAB EXPERIENCES—EGYPT: "WE WEREN'T ON THE SAME WAVELENGTH"

Other than his filming problems in Saudi Arabia, Tazi hadn't mentioned dealings with Arab countries, where there are some particular difficulties. On the one hand, since the 1930s Egyptian films have been widely distributed throughout the region, making it very difficult for productions from other Arab countries to penetrate.[12] On the other hand, these films have helped to turn Egyptian Arabic into something of a regional lingua franca, reinforcing the marginalization of other Arabic dialects, such as the Moroccan. In addition, Egyptian distributors, while strongly promoting their own films throughout the region, have little to gain from promoting non-Egyptian Arab films domestically, which has the effect of keeping this large market off limits to other Arab producers. Despite these difficulties, Tazi had initiated efforts in a number of areas.

"THEY WERE WATCHING A FOOTBALL MATCH!"
M. In 1991 or 1992, I was invited to the International Film Festival in Cairo, to show *Badis*. I was supposed to either send the copy by diplomatic pouch, which is something I try to avoid because I've lost copies that way, or send it by a normal shipping agent, which also poses problems, because it is sometimes difficult to repossess your own film, especially when you're leaving the country. So, for a long time I've had the practice of taking my films

with me as accompanying baggage—the films are with me in my suitcase and, depending on the country, I either declare them or not. Then I go out the same way, with my films as baggage.

In Egypt I did things the same way. When I arrived at the Cairo airport, the officials who had come to welcome me asked me where the film was. I told them not to worry, it was in my suitcase. Unfortunately they showed that extra bit of solicitude, or perhaps fear, toward the customs officials and told them about the film. Customs immediately took the film into their possession. "Don't worry," the festival officials said, "all it takes is a form and we'll have the film in twenty-four hours, at the very latest." Six days later I still hadn't gotten the film, and now I was two days from leaving the country. The film was still arrested, so to speak, at airport customs. I even made an announcement to the press, inviting everyone who wanted to view the film to come to the airport, because that's where the film was to be found.

I managed to show the film at the festival in video format. Following that, there were a number of articles about the film and a few distributors showed some interest. Six or seven of them asked me to give them a private video showing, which I did, in a room at the Nile Hilton. It was a small room, and five minutes or so after the cassette projection began I left the room, intending to come back, say, ten or fifteen minutes before the end to get the reaction.

When I got back I was very agreeably surprised to see a room full of people, all glued to the TV screen, craning their necks to look at the screen, which was above eye level. When I got a little closer my surprise turned to embarrassment, because I saw they were watching a football match! I can't say how long they had continued to watch my film, all I know is that for them the match was much more interesting.

The distributors tried to justify themselves, saying that this was an important match, it was being transmitted live, it was taking place abroad, and so on. But what I understood was that all this talk about an "Arab market" refers to something existing only on the level of television, not on the level of movies or movie theaters. For movies there is always some kind of excuse—other Arabs supposedly don't understand our spoken Arabic, or they don't understand our society, or even that Maghreb filmmakers make films aimed at the West rather than at the Arab world.

There's always some excuse. At least this experience wasn't a total loss, because I was able to retrieve the copy of my film on my way out of Egypt!

So, despite all the talk about reciprocity and the free market, we have a lot of difficulty getting into that market, even into the Arab market. But I will admit that I have now put some water in my wine on this issue, to the extent that I would no longer refuse to subtitle or dub my films for the Arab market, as I did for a long time. If that's what's necessary to reach that market, why not?

"Nothing more than a mise-en-scène"

K. Have you had any experiences in this area more recently?

M. Well, in the context of cultural exchange between Egypt and Morocco, we had an Egyptian Film Week in Morocco in November or December 1999. The counterpart to this was a Moroccan Film Week in Egypt during the second semester of the year 2000, organized by the CCM and the film institution in Egypt. I went to Cairo with four or five other Moroccan filmmakers and public projections of our films were programmed.[13]

To explore the practical possibilities, I planned to propose a specific co-production within the framework of the signed accords that already exist between the two countries.[14] Before the trip, I had prepared the groundwork somewhat by mailing some material to the director of the Egyptian Film Center, informing him that I would be in Egypt that week and that I would be very pleased if we could find a way to put these co-production agreements into practice.

During our visit we had many meetings and signed further agreements, mostly theoretical ones, I should add. Of course, TV cameras were all around, filming every signature. But I didn't see any practical results coming out of this so, at one point in the middle of all the blah-blah-blah, I suggested, "Let's be practical and see if we can implement all these beautiful principles we've been spending most of five days discussing. We all know that once these festivals are over you usually hear nothing more about these grand principles. Why don't we get practical and discuss the possibility of an Egyptian co-production for a Moroccan film or a Moroccan co-production for an Egyptian film?"

An Egyptian producer—and not a minor one, I might add—said he was very interested and that he would send his driver for me the next day to discuss the project. At his office the next day, the producer had as his starting point a series of conditions that had to be met if he were to be a co-producer. These included: the film had to have Egyptian stars, dialogue had to be in Egyptian Arabic, a major part of the film had to be shot in Egypt, and so on. What interested him, he said, was reaching the public, these were his conditions, and that was that.

Well, it seemed impossible to have a dialogue on that basis; we weren't on the same wavelength at all. Obviously, his overture to me at that earlier meeting was, I'm sorry to say, nothing more than a mise-en-scène for the benefit of all the officials present. So I packed up my papers, so to speak, and left.

MAGHREB EXPERIENCES: "ONLY YOUR OWN NAIL CAN SCRATCH YOU"

The three main Maghreb countries—Morocco, Algeria, and Tunisia—share varieties of spoken Arabic that allow mutual comprehension (with some small degree of difficulty) and have a total population of approximately seventy-five million, traits that might compensate for some of each national cinema's inherent disadvantages, such as a relatively small market and the use of "local" languages.[15] But Tazi's experiences of regional cooperation turned out to be largely negative.

"ONLY POWER RELATIONS ARE RELEVANT"

M. After *Badis*, around 1992–1993, I tried to mount co-productions with Algerians and Tunisians. Working with Algerians turned out to be impossible, given the conditions in their country. We have had some co-productions with Tunisians, but this has only involved financial matters where a Moroccan company will share in the production of a film made by a Tunisian director, or vice versa, by providing some of the materials or some technicians.

But as far as actually working with Tunisians is concerned, I could write a book about it. Suffice it to say, I realized soon enough that, as our Arab proverb has it, "Only your own nail can scratch you." [Laughs.] These efforts at cooperation failed for many different reasons, and it led me to a simple conclusion: I no longer believe in co-productions, neither vertical nor horizontal ones—only power relations are relevant. The day that I have a project that is designed for an international audience, at that point I'll be able to find foreign financing because I know the film will be interesting for particular publics. But you have to have that idea in your mind at the very outset, rather than coming to it because of the co-producer.

To show you what I mean, let me tell you of one experience I had with Tunisians. Here the problem had to do with distributing *Looking*. At the Carthage Film Festival, probably in 1994, a major Tunisian producer introduced me to one of the biggest distributor-exhibitors in Tunisia. He wanted to distribute *Looking* and asked me to provide two copies of the film, as well as posters and stills. We signed a contract, stipulating that he'd pay me 50,000 French francs for all distribution rights in Tunisia. He'd use the copies, keep the rights for two or three years, and then return the copies to me. When I got back to Morocco I sent him everything we'd agreed to and the film came out in the Tunisian theaters. The distributor even got the pay-TV satellite channel Canal Plus Horizons to advertise the film in Tunis and to push back its telecast of the film. But from all this I have never received a peanut.

But matters didn't end there. To try to get what I was owed I went to see the Tunisian ambassador in Morocco, who directed me to the ministry of culture. I wrote to the Tunisian ministry of culture several times, but they never answered. Then I went to the offices of the Arab Maghreb Union, again to no effect. I was sick and tired of the entire affair.

A couple of years ago I was invited to the Hammamet Festival in Tunisia. At some point, out of nowhere, there was the distributor, standing right in front of me. Luckily, people held me back, because I was on the point of putting my fist in his face. I did attack him verbally, "You're unbelievable, you're rolling in the money, you've made money on my film, some of that money's mine and I can sure use it!" He claimed that the film didn't do well. But several people told me that it showed in two or three theaters and did very well. In any case, we had a contract and you've got to honor that.

And the story isn't finished. When I was in Hammamet, I asked the producer who had introduced us to tell me who was the best lawyer in town, so that I could go and file a suit. He gave me a lawyer's name, I made an appointment, and took a taxi from Hammamet to Tunis to meet him. I told him the whole story, it must have taken almost a half-hour. At the end of it all he said, "I'm sorry, I can't do anything, I'm the distributor's lawyer."

K. Tunisia is very small!

M. And you can't believe how long that guy held on to the copies of the film! We'd given him those copies for nothing—we had something like eight or ten copies in Morocco and after they'd been shown around the country two were still in good shape, and those were the two we sent him. He didn't want to make his own copies—so he got the copies for free, made a lot of money, and never paid me a centime.

I said to myself, "This is just like the mafia. It's really a mafia." Finally, in January 2000, I got the copies of the film back. But, believe it or not, I had to pay all the transportation costs, another $100!

The *Lalla Hobby* (1997) Experience

Tazi's experiences on *Lalla Hobby* constitute one particularly eloquent example of what can happen when a Third World filmmaker ventures abroad; we discuss these in detail here and then turn, in the interlude, to examine the film itself.

COST ESCALATES, CO-PRODUCER EVAPORATES

"THE PROBLEMS ALMOST SUBMERGED US"

K. I know your effort to shoot a feature film in Europe led to some major problems. Am I right in thinking that *Lalla Hobby* is the first Moroccan feature filmed largely in Europe—although perhaps not the first filmed abroad?

M. Yes, it is. Souheil Ben Barka had filmed a few sequences, perhaps four or five days' worth, of his *Drums of Fire* (1991) in Spain. Another Moroccan filmmaker had earlier done some filming in Libya and Moumen Smihi went to Egypt to film his *Woman of Cairo* (1991).[16] *Lalla Hobby* is innovative in that it was, as you say, the first Moroccan film to be shot mainly in Europe.[17]

I should start by saying that my decision to make this film in Belgium had nothing in particular to do with the special characteristics of Belgium. Belgium was simply imposed by the ending of the first film. Otherwise, I could just as well have filmed in Spain, France, or Portugal. But having Houda's new husband working in Belgium had been a realistic choice in the first film, because Belgium has a large Moroccan community; also, Belgium makes it very difficult for Moroccans not already there to obtain visas, so it was a realistic choice in that respect, too.

In addition, there was another very important reason for filming in Belgium: a Belgian producer, with his own production company, with some experience in the field, seemed very eager to become co-producer—we hoped this would facilitate many aspects on the Belgian side. So we started out with a co-production involving three countries: my own company in Morocco, Ciné-Téléfilms in Tunisia, and the Belgian company ERIS. The contribution of the second was minimal; the Belgian's contribution was a true calamity.

You'll see the problems as we go along but, in essence, it comes down this: up until the very moment of my arrival in Belgium to start the filming, the Belgian co-producer played an active role. However, as soon as I arrived he just disappeared, evaporated, as though he had gone into hiding. As a result, I found myself in a country with no help on the production side—I had some contacts, some friends there, but none of them had experience on the production side of filmmaking.

For financing, I got some money from the Fonds Sud, some more from the French Agency for Cultural and Technical Cooperation,[18] and the TV channel Canal Plus Horizons came through with an advance on its purchase of distribution rights for the film. Therefore, as far as the money was concerned, I should have been relaxed. But because much of the shooting was going to be done abroad, the budget was higher than usual.[19] Given the higher wages and all the other costs, a day's shooting in France or in Belgium will cost as much as a week's shooting in Morocco.

So I can certainly understand how a film we make in Morocco for four to five million DH would cost five times that in Europe. In fact, nowadays there's hardly a film in France that is made for less than fourteen million francs [approximately two million dollars]. Prices are just so much higher there. Filmmaking in Europe is an industry and the technicians and actors all benefit from that. For me, coming from Morocco, the prices and fees were extremely high. And not only did I have to pay a French or Belgian actor's high fee but I also have to add 52 percent to that for the various social benefits.

Another problem was the attitude of some Belgians. Here I am, coming from an Arab country, making a film. For the Belgians, this means I must necessarily be a rich Arab. On the other hand, Belgium has a large Moroccan community, known mostly for its manual workers, but also, as is the case with many poor communities, for its scheming, robberies, and other sorts of illegal activities. I'm a Moroccan, so for some Belgians I was part of that category. My situation was somewhat paradoxical.

K. So people would put you in one pigeonhole or the other.

M. Or sometimes both at the same time!

K. You mean, like a rich Arab who's trying to swindle us! [Both laugh.]

M. Yes. And this had an effect on the Belgians around us, to the point where the Belgian technicians demanded to be paid in advance, contrary to the normal practice in all countries of paying at the end of the week. And it was the same thing for all the equipment—I had to pay for all of it in advance.

For example, we had a bad experience with the canteen—the trailer was providing us with absolutely terrible food at exorbitant prices. I wanted to send them packing but couldn't do this immediately because, again, we had paid them in advance. But to show them how bad I thought the food was and to let them know a week in advance my intention to dismiss them, I went on a kind of hunger strike and didn't eat there for five or six days.

All of these kinds of things made the work difficult but not impossible. What really made the problems acute was that a significant portion of our expenses in Belgium was supposed to be financed by the Belgian co-producer. When he disappeared, the problems almost submerged us. He normally would have handled all these problems—payments, canteen, and so on. But here I was being asked to pay everything in advance, at prices that were prohibitive, without a Belgian co-producer anywhere in sight. These were enormous problems and I spent more energy trying to solve them than I did on the film itself. I don't wish these kinds of filming conditions on any filmmaker from the South.

OBTAINING AUTHORIZATIONS; MOROCCAN COMMUNITY SUPPORT; SHORTENING TIME IN BELGIUM

"IT TOOK ME A MONTH . . . TO FILM FOR TWO HOURS"

M. Then there was also the problem of permissions and authorizations for shooting. In Morocco, when you get an authorization to shoot, it's an authorization for the entire shooting. I thought the same would be true in Belgium. But in Belgium, authorizations are not even done by city—they're often given out only for a particular part of a city and, in addition, by sector. That means that you have to get one authorization from the railroads, another for shooting on the street, and so on. I'm sure this is all very well organized and very systematic, but it requires so many different steps and so much time and effort. Of this the Belgian co-producer had never spoken and there I was, alone, trying to handle these kinds of problems.

I'll give you a couple of examples. Just to film for two hours inside a train compartment, it took me a month to get all the authorizations needed—going to the railway offices almost every day, or sending someone, paying all kinds of money along the way. Finally, filming for those two hours cost me something like 20,000 DH. To top it all off, the train technicians were always on my back, saying, "Don't mess with this, you can't use the electricity here, don't touch this or that." Really, that was some lesson to learn.

Then, I needed an authorization to shoot at night in one section of the city—this was for a fight scene where the Hajj is attacked by skinheads. Again, all sorts of procedures to follow and a large sum of money to pay. And finally, right in the middle of filming, the police came along to stop us because someone had complained of the noise, even though we were quite restrained. There we were, with an authorization for only that one night, for shooting only between 8 P.M. and midnight, and we were being stopped from shooting before the scene was fully finished. The film *absolutely required* this full scene—it was an essential scene not only because that's where the Hajj meets the woman who will help him but also because it referred to a true event in which a Moroccan was attacked in Paris and killed.[20] But the police were on us, "Hweet, pack up your things, you're finished here!" Some of the scenes were therefore shorter in the film than I would have liked and some we had to completely eliminate.

"IF OUR HEADS FIT . . . YOU CAN USE US"

K. Given all the difficulties you had filming in Belgium, was there at least some compensation for this as far as help from the Moroccan community there was concerned?

M. Yes, there was. One old Moroccan friend of mine in Belgium helped me out quite a bit when I shared with him my predicament. He had many friends and, as a result, a number of Moroccans gave me their support. That's how I got the BMW you see in the film—a person had heard I was looking for this kind of car and he contacted me, saying, "Listen, I have a BMW like the one you're looking for. Come and get it and you can use it for as long as you need it." I found that absolutely extraordinary. And there were many others who said, "If our heads fit what you're looking for, you can use us as extras, at no charge."

But there were lows as well as highs. There was one Moroccan who agreed to let us use his café, but then his fee doubled, tripled, quadrupled. And then, regarding the fight sequence I just mentioned to you—who do you think made the complaint? It turned out to be a Moroccan restaurant owner. He was trying to show he was more Belgian than the Belgians, obviously wanting to be on the good side of the police. Actually, he was just being an informer, plain and simple.

But, in general, I had some very good support from several members of the Moroccan community, people who helped out either by acting as extras or furnishing some props or providing a vehicle. One Moroccan, owner of a rather classy restaurant, suggested that I could shoot inside his restaurant. Others offered their homes. And there were many offers of assistance that we never were able to exploit—the use of houses, cafés, restaurants—because although these scenes were initially planned for filming in Belgium they were eventually filmed in Morocco, because I had to cut short the Belgian filming.

The way we had planned it, half the film was to be shot in Belgium. But with all these difficulties, I decided that all the interiors I had intended to shoot in Belgium I could shoot in Morocco. There are five or six sets of this sort that we eventually shot in Morocco—one, for example, is the scene in the mosque. This meant a lot of work reconstituting a number of sets to create the impression that they were filmed in Belgium. But, we did manage to shorten the time spent shooting in Belgium by almost ten days. The situation there had become intolerable and we no longer had the money to keep going. The co-producer's disappearance at the beginning of our filming completely changed our circumstances. We had to choose: either we just turn around and abandon the project or we try to film the minimum in Belgium with funds we

could somehow get out of Morocco. We took this second course
of action.

SUMMING UP

CO-PRODUCTION: "YOU HAVE TO BE VERY SUSPICIOUS . . ."; SUPPORT FROM TV

"THE CIRCUMSTANCES ARE TOO UNBALANCED, TOO STACKED
AGAINST US"

K. How would you sum up this particular experience?

M. Well, remembering that the reason I shot this in Belgium was
because I thought the co-producer would make things easier, the
first lesson I learned is that you have to be very suspicious of a
foreign co-producer. It's an illusion to believe that such a person
is really interested in the cinema of the South. Let's be clear: almost all the financial support for films from the South comes from
official institutions, from the French Le Fonds Sud, from ACCT,
and so on. If a foreign private producer shows up wanting to help
produce a film from the South it can mean only one of two things:
either the film is going to be pushed in the direction of satisfying
the Western desire for exoticism and Orientalism, or there's some
kind of scam involved. [Laughs uncomfortably.] I suppose there's
a third possibility—that the person is really an idealist and on the
level—but that is very rare.

   As for this Belgian so-called "producer," I know for a fact that
he wasn't in the third group. He wanted to co-produce only in
order to obtain funds from his own country's official organizations. That was the long and short of it. He wasn't putting a centime of his own money into this, and that's something I couldn't
know beforehand. When he presented the proposal to these organizations, he didn't even present it properly—he failed to follow
some of the rules and satisfy some of the criteria—and the proposal was rejected out of hand. And then he completely disappeared, I never saw him at all during the shooting until just before
the end of it.

K. Was the Belgian co-producer someone you knew previously?

M. No, but he was introduced to me by a fine Belgian filmmaker
who's a very good friend and whom I trusted. As it turned out,
the aim behind the introduction was more to help out the Belgian
producer, whose company was in a catastrophic financial situa-

tion, than it was to provide me with a capable co-producer. He hoped to use my film as a way to get funds from the Belgian government and allow him to get back on his feet. His becoming my co-producer was really supposed to breathe new life into him but, as it turned out, it almost took the life out of me.

He did reappear at the very end of the shooting, turning up with a cameraman, an assistant, and a camera, sort of begging for money because of his situation. He was trying to show that, despite his problems, he was capable and willing to work. There I was, having thought of him as a co-producer and then finding myself face-to-face with someone asking for a handout. We did give him some money for his one day's work, but I must say I had no respect for him after that. He hadn't been honest with us and, in fact, had been using me as a pretext. After this experience I told everyone that I no longer had any faith in shooting abroad and that I no longer believed in co-productions because the circumstances are too unbalanced, too stacked against us.

But I should point to one of the positive aspects in producing this film, and one of the innovations: for the first time a Moroccan feature film had Moroccan TV as a co-producer. Although the financial contribution was small, really just symbolic, it was very helpful to have the contribution of some of their technicians, equipment, and material. In addition, we had the benefit of their prime-time advertising spots. In fact, there is now a directive from the ministry of communication to the effect that the television must provide free advertising time for Moroccan films. This is very important because TV advertising time is normally too expensive and beyond the capacity of a Moroccan film's budget.

For the TV co-production, I signed contracts with Moroccan TV and with Canal Plus Horizons, allowing them to show the film one year after its release in the theaters. This, in effect, freed me from looking for foreign distribution for the film. In fact, I never tried to find a foreign distributor and there never was foreign distribution.

THE PUBLIC'S REACTION; INTERNATIONAL FESTIVALS

"SUCCESS WAS MODEST"

K. Regarding the film's reception, the figures I've seen show that there were about two hundred thousand spectators in Morocco, which is respectable, up among the leaders in the last few years.

M. Yes, two hundred thousand spectators is not bad at all. Of course, it was always hedged with, "But compared to . . ." Obviously, compared to *Looking, Lalla Hobby*'s success was modest. The public and critics had high expectations and it had some good reviews. The articles that took the film seriously and addressed the problems it raised gave me some pleasure. But there were also some quite negative reviews.

Keeping in mind my very disagreeable experience of *Looking* being pirated so widely, I responded by trying to sweep very rapidly through the theaters with *Lalla Hobby.* We put a large number of copies—eight or ten—into circulation and tried to open simultaneously in the big cities like Marrakesh, Casablanca, Rabat, Fez. Within two months we had pretty much covered the entire Moroccan market.

"THE FESTIVAL PHENOMENON TODAY IS NO LONGER WHAT IT WAS"

M. Internationally, I didn't have to worry about distribution because, as I said earlier, this was taken care of by the co-production deals with television. I was invited to half a dozen festivals and I accepted two or three. After that I declined, partly because I had some health problems and had to recuperate but also because some of the festivals don't hold much interest for me any more and, as I've said elsewhere, I'm tired of being taken for a camel showman.

The festivals that still interest me are those that have an important African component or are important for the art of cinema, like Locarno, Berlin, Venice, Ouagadougou, the Three Continents Festival in Nantes, and the Amiens Festival. FESPACO in Ouagadougou is particularly exciting. It's marvelous to show your film there, because the public is like it was in Europe in the 1950s, when you went to the movies with heightened emotions, high interest, and intense concentration. In Ouagadougou, it's *really* a festival in the true meaning of the term.[21]

But the festival phenomenon today is no longer what it was. Now there are literally hundreds of film festivals and there are plenty of NGOs [non-governmental organizations] that live off this structure. In fact, you often get the feeling that the reason for the festival isn't so much to show the films as it is to give a source of revenue to a group of NGOs.

COSTS EMOTIONAL AND PHYSICAL

"IT'S LIKE WITH CHILDREN . . . SOME YOU . . . REALLY DESIRED, OTHERS CAME ALONG SOMEWHAT ACCIDENTALLY"

K. After all the problems you had with this film—the exaggerated demands of former collaborators, the logistic problems of filming in Europe complicated by the disappearance of the Belgian co-producer, the high expectations of the public, and then the somewhat lukewarm response on the part of both public and critics—I would certainly understand if this left you with a bitter aftertaste and even created for you something of a professional crisis.

M. First of all, you have to understand that, even with all these difficulties, this is in no way a film that I disown. To the contrary. This film has its own significance, and it is also important with regard to my own development and my own concerns. I managed to express a number of things related to current events—the entire theme of emigration, the reference to the racism of the National Front in France in the scene where Hajj Ben Moussa is attacked by skinheads—things like that.

It's like with children—some you want and have really desired, others came along somewhat accidentally. [Softly laughs.] *Lalla Hobby* is one that wasn't desired so much. But that doesn't at all mean you reject it. It required a different approach, that's all. It didn't come from my guts, except concerning the themes of emigration and demystifying the West.

But, let's face it, all of the problems we had with this film had a very high cost. When you get only four or five hours sleep over a long period of time, when you have to accept things that you'd rebel against in your normal life, when you have to postpone things because something unexpected has come up, when you have to put certain key people at ease and keep them happy when normally you wouldn't give them the right time of day, this really creates a lot of stress.

These incidents can be incredibly trivial, like the time an actress came to me just as we're starting to shoot and hands me an envelope. I look inside and see a couple of small receipts—two DH for parking, a receipt for gas to drive her car to Casablanca, a couple of things like that. You look at her—you're supposed to start shooting her in a scene—and she says, "You've got to pay me for these." She behaves like she's blackmailing you! And I swear, this really happened, and with a receipt for two DH for parking!

When you take all those things together, well, it can even lead to a heart attack! [Laughs sardonically.]

PROBLEMS OF THE HEART

Tazi was not being flippant with this last remark, for he had indeed had a heart attack some time after the release of *Lalla Hobby*, something he had alluded to earlier when he said that the co-producer's disappearance "almost took the life out of me." Over the period of our interviews he seemed to harbor no ill effects from this attack and maintained a very heavy work schedule, but he did go to France once a year for tests and some monitoring. A person well known for the pace and intensity of his activity, Tazi told me at one point that it annoyed him immensely when people he hadn't seen for a while immediately asked about his health. I took the hint and hadn't raised the subject before, but now that he had opened it, I pursued it.

K. To what extent do you think the problems related to *Lalla Hobby* actually caused the heart attack?

M. I had already finished postproduction and *Lalla Hobby* had just been released when I had the attack. But there's always that extra drop that causes the overflow. My doctor said, "70 percent of the problem with your arteries has to do with stress and with the rising levels of adrenalin." From that, I understood that the attack came from things that had been accumulating for years, throughout my whole life in fact. But, still, *Lalla Hobby* was the apotheosis of everything that creates stress and causes overflow. Who knows, perhaps *Lalla Hobby* was a lucky experience—I say "lucky" because I felt the malaise and was able to do what was necessary and get it taken care of right away. If it had happened at another time, under an accumulation of even more stress, I might not have realized what was happening and it could have been a real heart attack, perhaps a fatal one.

But when you think of the kind of stress you can have, particularly with some of the actors, it sometimes really goes over the top. Have an argument with Bashir Skiredj, for example, and he immediately gets sick, you have to take him to the hospital and start filming something else. And he couldn't care less, it's as though he does this on purpose. At any moment you can run into an actor who tries to impose his will, to make believe he's a star and so on. But after all, that's part of the job, it goes more or less with the territory.

Perhaps there's a lesson to be learned here from Scorsese. He used to be so close to the filming process but now we see that he arrives on the set at the last minute, sits down in his chair, and says, "Shoot." There are times when you have to put some distance between yourself and what's going on around you and not plunge into the middle of things at every moment, not have to know about every little thing that's going on, from the parking expenses of one actor to the little car accident of another. I can't count the number of times I've had to go to the police station at nine or ten o'clock at night to get an actor released because now that he's in a film he's a star, and either he's made an idiot of himself after two drinks in a bar, he's insulted or been aggressive toward someone, had a fender bender, or something of the sort. Perhaps some of these people are calm and tranquil in their normal lives but once they get near a movie set they not only act on the set, but they start to act up off it.

"A MORE SERIOUS AND DEEPER FILM THAN THE FIRST"

"PEOPLE ARE DYING ALMOST EVERY DAY"

K. In light of these difficulties, to what extent did the film turn out differently than you would have wished?

M. I think I kept it pretty much on line. Even with all these truly enormous problems of administration, supply, and production, and even with all the changes in personnel, I still think I kept it on course, I made the kind of film I wanted to make. I have a certain esteem for the film, in that I was trying to move from *Looking*'s comic mode—based on circumstance, grimaces, and clowning—to the much more serious themes of immigration, racism, and the malaise of our own people.

As far as the main theme of emigration is concerned, it's now several years since the film's release and the problem is no closer to being solved. Many of our youth want to emigrate, Morocco is still being used as a way station, people are dying almost every day trying to cross the Mediterranean in these boats of death, and the media are hardly even addressing the issue. We have to find a solution to this problem. And by we I mean Morocco and Europe, together. It's not enough for Europe to send us money or foreign aid to buy up the kif grown in the north. That's not a solution. There has to be a policy leading to new industries, new businesses, things that will keep people at home. This is the problem that haunted me then and it still haunts me now.

So, whereas *Looking* can be seen as a conservative film, *Lalla Hobby* is a film that tries to demystify the paradise that so many people believe the West, the North, to be. *Lalla Hobby* is a more serious and deeper film than the first, I have no doubt about that.

Interlude

Lalla Hobby—The Film

Lalla Hobby—Summary

[In *Looking* Hajj Ben Moussa, a well-off jeweler from Fez, repudiated his youngest wife Houda for the third time, making the divorce binding according to Islamic law. Regretting his rashness, he wants to remarry her but can legally do so only if she first marries another man and then gains a divorce from him. Houda's marriage to a new husband is arranged and consummated but, before the divorce can follow, the husband has to flee Morocco for Belgium. As *Looking* ends, Hajj Ben Moussa, desperate to find the husband and then regain Houda, sets off in a small boat for Europe, in the company of other clandestine emigrants.]

ACT ONE: FROM BOAT TO PRISON TO BELGIUM

Hajj Ben Moussa, crowded uncomfortably in a small motor-driven boat, angers quickly (again!) at a mild insult and stands up, wanting out as though he were simply riding a bus. Chaos ensues, Hajj Ben Moussa falls backward, the screen goes black and the titles roll up. The dedication reads, ". . . to those who risk their lives every day in the straits of Gibraltar."

In a Tangiers prison, Hajj Ben Moussa is being photographed, fingerprinted, and put into a cell; some of his boat mates have died, others have been fished out of the water and incarcerated as he has

Hamidou as Hajj Ben Moussa

been. In Fez, the Hajj's wives learn of his whereabouts and the eldest, Lalla Hobby, decides that she and Hajj Driss, her husband's fellow jeweler, will go to Tangiers to see him. Meanwhile, the young ex-wife Houda, unhappily living with her new mother-in-law in her absent husband's apartment, is seeking a divorce for abandonment so she can remarry the Hajj.

Lalla Hobby and Hajj Driss reach Tangiers to learn that Hajj Ben Moussa has just been released. At that very moment he is in a gypsy camp in Spain, enjoying an evening of dancing and singing, and he will soon be boarding a train bound for Belgium. Arriving in Brussels, saying halfhearted good-byes to two fellow Moroccans he has met on the train, the Hajj suffers some petty humiliations and is on the verge of despair when he finally meets his contact and receives the money he had advanced in Morocco.

ACT TWO: THE HAJJ IN PURSUIT, LALLA HOBBY IN BUSINESS

In Tangiers, Lalla Hobby and Hajj Driss continue looking for Hajj Ben Moussa. Reaching a beautiful mountain setting by the sea, they are taken on a tour of a thriving business enterprise that organizes clandestine emigration, and they learn that Hajj Ben Moussa has been in Belgium for three days.

Evening in Brussels. The Hajj finishes his prayer and leaves his hotel, wearing a *jellaba*. Three young men coming out of a bar eye him aggressively, then insult and attack him. A girl tries to intercede but they throw her to the ground next to the Hajj and run off as police sirens sound. The next morning the Hajj wakes up in a strange bed— Marquise, the girl from the previous night, has taken pity on him and brought him home with her. Over coffee he explains that he is "looking for his wife's husband." She bursts into sympathetic laughter and says she will try to help him.

Returning to Fez, Lalla Hobby recounts her Tangiers adventures to the family, saying it is now up to all of them to ensure that everything runs well in the Hajj's absence. She herself will take charge of the jewelry store. Her first sale at the store is so skillfully done that her jeweler colleague Hajj Driss intones what will become a refrain, "Hajj Ben Moussa, you've been outdone!"

In Brussels, Marquise and the Hajj are having no success in locating Houda's husband, who is thought to operate in one of Belgium's three automobile markets. The Hajj heads to Antwerp to enlist the help of one of the Moroccans he met on the train. This friend introduces him to the local mosque and, hoping the congregation will help him solve his problem, the Hajj begins to participate actively, becoming its prayer caller.

ACT THREE: THE HAJJ GETS HELP, LALLA HOBBY SHOWS HER METTLE, HOUDA MEETS HER LAWYER

Walking with his friend along an Antwerp street, the Hajj comes upon the diamond market. Still wearing his Moroccan *jellaba*, the Hajj tries to enter but a guard turns him away. Not to be defeated, the Hajj returns in a black overcoat and black fedora and this time easily gains entry. On a storefront he recognizes the name of a former colleague from Fez, a Jewish jeweler. After warm greetings, the jeweler offers to take the Hajj to another automobile market, on his way to a town where Carnival is being celebrated. As they ride in Mr. Cohen's black BMW, they sing and grow nostalgic for their youthful times together in Fez. Reaching the automobile market, they search in vain for the disappeared husband and are rebuffed by a Moroccan who says he's there to sell cars, not to sell out people.

The Hajj in Antwerp, drinking with his friend, a Jewish jeweler from Fez

Houda (Samia Akkariou) receives a phone call from her lawyer

Lalla Hobby is now a practiced shopkeeper and even outsmarts her mentor, Hajj Driss. Meanwhile, Houda learns from her lawyer that if her husband makes no appearance within the month, she will gain a divorce for abandonment. The lawyer invites Houda for dinner in Casablanca and she agrees, but this is a rendezvous she will not keep.

ACT FOUR: THE HAJJ'S COMEUPPANCE

Hajj Ben Moussa and Mr. Cohen part company briefly during the Carnival celebrations. The Hajj, wandering freely, catches a glimpse of Houda's husband across the road but loses him in the crowd. Later, in a café with Mr. Cohen, the atmosphere grows raucous. The Hajj becomes the butt of some violent buffeting and his anger bests him yet again. Later, in a police station, the Hajj is accused of having attacked someone in the café. Worse yet, the officer notes that his visas are forged. Mr. Cohen pleads on his behalf but to no avail. Hajj Ben Moussa is to be expelled from Belgium and repatriated immediately.

The Fez household is in commotion as the entire family readies to go to the airport to welcome the Hajj. Meanwhile, in the airplane, the Hajj is seated next to an attractive blond woman and chatting with her—she is the Belgian customs officer accompanying him. As they prepare to land, she handcuffs him to her saying, apologetically, "Regulations, you know."

Gathered on the observation terrace, the Hajj's family watches the passengers descend from the plane. They see him and begin to wave and shout. The Hajj lifts his hands to wave back and with them lifts the handcuffed hand of the blond woman. Lalla Hobby exclaims, "Now we're in deep trouble. God preserve us, he's come back with a European woman!"

The screen goes black, music and credits come on, and an upbeat song breaks out, "Lalla, Lalla Hobby."

Lalla Hobby—Issues and Scenes

The sequel to *Looking* raised a number of interesting issues. One was a set of problems common to all sequels—how much knowledge of the first film can be assumed for the second and to what extent characters are consistent from one film to the next. This second issue was made particularly acute in this case since new actors were playing two of the main characters—Hajj Ben Moussa and Houda.

The Hajj during Carnival

Lalla Hobby tries on European clothes, preparing to greet the Hajj at the airport

The film is suggestive in other ways too: unlike Tazi's earlier films, this one seemed to begin more from an idea—the problems of emigration and the situation of the Moroccan abroad—than from a visual or nostalgic stimulus; its humor had a very different tone from its predecessor's; and the filming of some scenes raised either thematic or practical questions and sometimes both. On the practical side I was most interested in the difficulties of filming abroad.

STIMULUS:
GOING BEYOND THE PLOT

"CLANDESTINE IMMIGRATION . . . THE FANTASY ABOUT THE WEST THAT PEOPLE HAVE"

K. One of the things that struck me about *Lalla Hobby* is that, unlike your other films, this one seems to grow out of an idea. Regarding *The Big Trip*, you've talked about the visual mosaic of moving across Morocco from south to north; for *Badis*, you were very taken by the beauty of the village and its surroundings; for *Looking* you were trying to recreate the feeling you had as a child.

M. Yes, that's true. With *Lalla Hobby* the point of departure was not so much an idea as a very important phenomenon, that of clandestine immigration and the entire question of immigration, with the boats of death—*las pateras* [in Spanish in the interview; Ar. *fluka*, meaning "small boats"]—which is a daily phenomenon here in Morocco.[1]

   Obviously, the plot exists on another level—we have a man looking throughout Belgium for his ex-wife's husband so that he can bring him back to Morocco, secure a divorce, and remarry the ex-wife. You could make a film based simply on that and go no farther. But that wouldn't have interested me at all. Also, another theme here interested me, in addition to the theme of immigration: a man, with no warning or preparation, leaves behind an entire family in Fez. This could turn out to be a very serious matter indeed because, after all, these women are considered to be "minors" in a certain sense and their needs—financial and otherwise—are supposed to be taken care of by their husband. But in the film we see that they manage very well on their own; in fact, in some ways they manage better than the Hajj did. So one of the aims of the film was to show that women are fully capable of performing jobs—like that of the jeweler—that they are usually excluded from. As an aside, I should add that a recent meeting of the Ministerial Council decided that women could deliver the mail, something that until now they have not been allowed to do.

So, I wanted to concentrate on these very important themes in today's Morocco: above all, the question of clandestine immigration; then, the fantasy about the West that people have and to show what that reality is really like; and also to show how women can seize hold of a business and run it perhaps better than their husbands can. All of these are very current issues.

HUMOR

"I DIDN'T WANT SIMPLY TO TICKLE"

K. One of the great innovations of *Looking,* as far as Moroccan films go, and one of the most important reasons for its success was how much it made people laugh. To what extent did you think that *Lalla Hobby* should continue along this line?

M. There was certainly a need to continue in the humorous mode but this was also where I needed to break with the first film. In the first film the main character was a comic one, the situation was comic, and there was a gestural humor that I hoped wasn't too burlesque. That kind of humor worked in *Looking* because it fit the situation of the harem, a limited and enclosed space, and the film just moved back and forth between there and the Hajj's store. That's one of the reasons I've always called that film a conservative one.

But in *Lalla Hobby* we move out of that environment—we leave the home and we even leave the country—we're outside, abroad. I wanted to move toward a more thoughtful kind of humor. I didn't want people to laugh at just anything, I didn't want simply to tickle them.

"THE COMIC SITUATIONS ARE VERY DIFFERENT"

K. The humor in *Lalla Hobby* is certainly more somber. At times you gnash your teeth, saying, "This isn't very funny" but every so often you find yourself laughing because the scenes are played for humor. How do you see this?

M. Well, first of all, the main character, Hajj Ben Moussa, the pillar of the film, changes significantly from the first film to the second. Whereas in the first he is mischievous—even physically he conveys that trait—the spectator nonetheless feels, "There's no reason to worry about this guy, nothing really bad is going to happen to him." But in the second Hajj Ben Moussa goes into situations with naïveté and innocence and becomes a victim because of these qualities. For example, in the automobile market, the Hajj starts asking a series of questions, showing too much naïveté. So the comic situations are very different. Whereas the first Hajj Ben Moussa creates comedy through his mischievous nature, the second is a pathetic figure who calls forth pity. I think you become much more attached to him and develop much more concern for him.

K. You certainly become more worried about his fate—whether you become more attached to him is a difficult question that requires some discussion of the change in character between the two films and, therefore, of the change in actors. This brings us to problems related to sequels.

PROBLEMS OF SEQUELS

Two Independent Films?

K. I suppose one of the main problems was to what extent *Lalla Hobby* was to be filmed as independent from *Looking*.

M. That's true. In fact, I think that may be one of the mistakes I made—every film has to be seen as an independent product and perhaps I didn't detach the characters of this film sufficiently from the first film. The mistake was in making the second film assuming everyone had already seen the first. I think there are a number of places in *Lalla Hobby* that are incomprehensible if you haven't seen the first film.

Changing Actors, Shifting Characters

The Hajj: from "mischievous" to "naïve"

K. A key difference between the two films has to do with the change in actors and shifts in character of two main figures, Hajj Ben Moussa and Houda. For the first, it's difficult to imagine how the "mischievous" Hajj Ben Moussa of *Looking* would get very far in Europe. My feeling is that he would be immediately picked up by the police—he would do something stupid like he did when starting a fight in the boat—and either quickly be expelled back to

Morocco or imprisoned for a very long period. He's someone who's fine as a spoiled child in a protected environment but, in the wider world, his whims and tantrums wouldn't be tolerated.

M. Absolutely right. In fact, that's why I sent him to prison at the beginning of the second film, to allow me to introduce the new character; the sequence shortly afterward in the gypsy camp in Spain, where he adapts easily, like a child might, dancing and drinking, serves a similar function and shows that he's a likable person all in all. Here he's still close to the Hajj Ben Moussa character of *Looking*. But once he gets out of the train in Brussels we are with another character entirely.

"A BIG INTERNATIONAL CAREER . . . [BUT] HERE HE WASN'T REALLY IN HIS ELEMENT"

K. It must have been difficult for the second actor, Hamidou Ben Messaoud [commonly referred to simply as Hamidou or Amidou], to follow Bashir Skiredj, who played the Hajj in *Looking*. What was Hamidou's contribution to the character?

M. Obviously, the way a role is played is a function of the person who plays it. Bashir Skiredj was known as a clown, that's his forte; Hamidou had never played a comic role. So the screenplay, which had been written with the first actor in mind, now had to be re-examined, taking into account the different personality of the new actor. Hamidou is a guy who has had a big international career—he's had major roles in films with some of the world's best-known directors, with William Friedkin in the remake of *The Wages of Fear,* with Claude Lelouch in *Life, Love, Death* (1969), with John Huston, and he's won a major acting award. Often, when he's in the street—I saw this happen in Belgium—he's mistaken for the big French star Jean-Paul Belmondo.

Hamidou did make some important contributions. First of all, he's a serious athlete and has attained the highest karate level. He got very involved in orchestrating the scene where he is attacked by the three skinheads and was really in his element there. On the other hand, there were some negative aspects. For example, I think this was the first time that Hamidou had ever acted in traditional dress. Here he wasn't really in his element, he wasn't comfortable with the traditional clothes. Sometimes, when I was trying to figure out whether I needed a second or third take for a scene, I'd turn to him and in the few seconds that had elapsed he'd already taken off the *jellaba* and put on Western clothes, along with his sunglasses. I think the question has to be asked, whether he really felt the role.

Then, the response of the public and even other professionals toward Hamidou was rather reserved. I've never been able to explain this. He's an actor with great talent, he's known by professionals, he's acted in a lot of films in many different kinds of roles. I really didn't think this would be a problem.

HOUDA: FROM NAÏVE TO CUNNING

K. A different actress plays Houda and here too the role is played somewhat differently. In *Lalla Hobby* Houda is more verbal, less naïve. How was this character constructed?

M. Houda in *Lalla Hobby* was played by Samia Akkariou, a recent graduate of our Higher Institute of Dramatic Arts and Cultural Activities and this was her first role in films.[2] She was a newcomer and in a very difficult situation. It's a very delicate matter, trying to take over a role played by someone else. Even Hamidou, with all his experience, had this problem. When you make a sequel, it's as though the spectator approaches it with a somewhat negative, "show me" attitude, thinking, "This will never be as good as the first."

K. The new Houda is much more worldly and cunning. This comes out in one of her scenes with the lawyer.

M. Where the lawyer tries to pick her up.

K. Exactly. This scene raises some questions about a woman's behavior that are similar to those that came up when we discussed *Looking*. I'm thinking particularly of how Houda, in the first film, is somewhat compliant when she is approached by men as, for example, in the café scene. There, the explanation was that Houda was rather naïve. Here, when she agrees to the lawyer's overture, naïveté doesn't seem to be the explanation. In fact, she doesn't keep the rendezvous. What was the idea behind this scene?

M. First of all, Houda's husband is absent. Spectators might be thinking that her morals were somewhat "easy" and that if an interesting opportunity were offered to her she might very well accept it. I wanted them to understand that Houda wasn't like that at all.

Inviting her to meet him in Casablanca, the lawyer is saying, in effect, that he's won the case for her and now would like some extra form of compensation. So, the scene was also there to show the kind of attitude a lawyer might have in this situation—here's a woman getting divorced, she's young, she's beautiful, she's wearing a minidress. For him this may even seem a little provocative. He thinks, "Why not, I'll try it and see what happens." After all, he's human.

K. You can tell from Houda's close-ups as he moves toward her in his office that she really is in no mood for this. Yet she agrees to meet him in Casablanca, he waits for her there, but she never arrives. Why doesn't she find some way to turn down his invitation rather than put him to all this trouble?

M. Well, have you ever seen people here in Morocco give you a straight yes or no? People always respond indirectly.

You know, I've seen situations right on the street, in broad daylight, where a guy in a car thinks he just has to open the door and every woman in the world will rush to jump in there with him. He insists and insists and when the woman really says no, definitively, he gets very aggressive and may even strike her. A lot of men just can't take rejection from a woman—she's like game and he just has to keep on hunting.

Well, this lawyer isn't that crude. Also, Houda likes to play a bit with people, that's in her character. So she lets him believe what he wants, "Oh sure, Casablanca, that's great, I'm going to be there anyway, fine, I'll meet you there."

K. Suppose you were filming a further sequence: after she misses the rendezvous she meets the lawyer in the street. What would she say to him?

M. "Oh listen, I'm terribly sorry, I got there half an hour late and you were gone." Or, perhaps, "My father fell ill, I couldn't get away." You can always find something to say.

K. So it's easier for her to feign agreement.

M. Yes, that's easier than refusing outright. And who knows, perhaps the legal matter isn't really settled. She can't be sure of that until she has the papers in her hands. Until then, she should keep on the lawyer's good side.

DIFFICULTIES AND RUSES

Tazi had already told me in passing of difficulties in filming a number of scenes—the fight scene, for example, which had to be shortened because the police put a stop to the filming. He also had mentioned how regretful he was that it had been impossible to shoot inside the Antwerp train station, which he termed "extraordinary, beautiful, a certified landmark." The cost for an authorization was prohibitive and it was impossible to shoot with a hidden camera because the hall's darkness required setting up light projectors. What Tazi called "one of our biggest problems" arose in filming scenes in the diamond market.

THE DIAMOND MARKET

M. This scene was absolutely central to the film. In Antwerp there is a section of the city where all the diamond merchants work, it's a very well-policed area, and it's hard to gain access to it, to say nothing of doing so with film equipment. When I asked for permission to film there I was refused outright. After all, it's a very rich community, very important, and very closed.

But I had to find a way to shoot some scenes there—the ones where the Hajj tries to gain access to the area but is turned back—even if it meant taking some risks. Anyway, you can't avoid risks in this line of work. Obviously, in your own country you can take greater risks and take them more easily, because you can usually come to some kind of arrangement if you're caught. But in Belgium people are colder, they have no taste for discussing the problem or coming to an arrangement.

The ruse I used involved renting a Belgian policeman's uniform in Brussels and placing an actor in this uniform at the entrance to the market. We had the camera in a car across the way and we were filming secretly from there. So the policeman who initially refuses the Hajj entry is that actor playing the policeman at the real entrance.

K. Then the Hajj changes into European clothes and is waved through by the true entrance guards?

M. Right, but those clothes aren't European, they're typically Jewish. These diamond merchants are almost all Jews. When he came to the market the first time dressed as an Arab, the police were mistrustful and would never let him enter. But when he comes back dressed as a Jew, access is no problem at all.

We filmed all this with the hidden camera. If they'd discovered us, that scene would have cost us a lot of money. As for the scenes in the jewelry store immediately following his entry into the market, they were among those scenes that I wanted to film in Belgium but, because of all the difficulties, I eventually filmed in Morocco.

"THIRD WORLD STYLE"

M. There's another sequence related to this one that I should mention. With permission to film in Antwerp refused, everything there had to be filmed with a hidden camera. I needed a long traveling shot, where the Hajj recounts his problems to his friend as they walk toward the diamond market. The cameraman, a Belgian, wanted to use a dolly but I told him we'd immediately be noticed and picked up by the police. So I asked him to film it in "Third World style," sitting in the trunk of a car with the camera on his shoulder. He categorically refused. So I had to shoot it myself, and for me, this shot is very successful, it's impeccable.

Compare this attitude to that of Ribès, the Spanish cameraman [Federico Ribès had been the cinematographer on *Badis*]— adaptability was one of Ribès's great qualities. Remember the scene in *Badis* where the women are fleeing toward the fort? There's a traveling shot on unpaved ground, just dirt. That sound camera is pretty heavy, between twenty and twenty-three kilos, but Ribès can carry it on his shoulders while shooting the traveling shot. His adaptability is wonderful, which isn't true of some of the other cinematographers I've worked with—Europeans too, some of them, who work on such a level of technical comfort that they insist on things that are often beyond our means. You tell them to use a handheld camera, they answer, "Oh no, I can't, I need a Steadicam, or traveling tracks," or something of the sort. But Ribès knows both your technical and equipment limitations and he adapts, he finds the solution. A cinematographer has to be able to adapt to different conditions. When something is impossible, you feel it yourself, and he'll just say, "No, can't be done." But that's very rare. There's always a way to do things.

STRESS

K. It must be tremendously stressful to film with a hidden camera, always looking out for the police, and so on.

M. The police are not the main problem. In Europe the police aren't all over the place and they're not onto you so quickly. The only place in Belgium where we really had to worry about the police was in Antwerp because there our request for authorization had been refused. That made everything more risky. The problem is actually worse here in Morocco, but not because the police are everywhere; it's because there's such a strong Makhzen spirit that people think it's their role to go and tell the police that you're setting up a camera. As a result, in two minutes the police are on your back.[3]

But, you know, we're not hiding the camera simply because of the police. We hide the camera mostly so we can film more naturally, so people will behave normally and not stare at us.

A bigger stress comes from people who change the rules regarding prices as the filming progresses. In the auto market sequence in this film, for example, we had to keep renegotiating because the price doubled, tripled, quadrupled, as we were filming. I'm sure we ended up paying three times the initially agreed price. That's what's the most stressful. In the beginning someone gives you his word but then, when he sees the camera, the actors, the makeup, the sound and other equipment, he gets bewitched and the price climbs.

This kind of thing happens wherever you film, in Belgium or in Morocco. I can't count the number of times we were filming a foreign production in Morocco and we'd agreed on the price for using a house, even signed a contract for it, given the owner an advance, and so on. You show up in two weeks, planning to shoot for three days. The first day, everything goes without a hitch. The second day you find the door to the house is locked, the owner nowhere to be found. You finally hunt him down, he tells you he's changed his mind. "But listen, you've signed a contract, you've got to honor the contract." Now he's become absolutely indispensable and he knows it. "No," he answers, "I've changed my mind. You can sue me if you want." What happened to make him change his mind? Well, after signing the contract he went to the café and people told him, "This is a film. Let them get something in the can and then you can get the price you want."

This is true for actors, for extras, for prop people. And they don't care whether you're making a foreign production or a Moroccan film, they don't give a damn, it's really terrible. For them, making a film means throwing money out the window and they want to catch some of it.

TWO KEY SEQUENCES

THE FIGHT; WOMAN AS "OASIS"

K. I'd like to discuss just a couple of what seem to me to be key scenes in relation to the film's themes. The crucial plot element

in the scene where the Hajj is attacked by skinheads is his encounter with the girl who befriends him, takes him in, and then
helps him pursue his search. The way she appears on the scene
reminded me very much of the arrival of the girl in your first film,
The Big Trip. In both, the main male character is in dire straits and
the girl comes, in a certain sense, out of nowhere. I found these
incidents a bit too coincidental in both films.

M. OK. In the case of *Lalla Hobby,* when the girl tries to intercede on
the Hajj's behalf, she's also attacked by the skinheads and finds
herself by chance connected to this Moroccan. It's true that this is
a similar kind of event to the one in *The Big Trip,* an unconscious
similarity.

K. Of course, both films have the same screenwriter. In fact, even
though the context is very different both films have a very similar
structure: the main character has just left home and travels north.
On his trip he has a series of experiences in which he is humili-
ated, dispossessed. The endings are different—in *The Big Trip* the
ending is open, Omar is adrift at sea and we don't know what will
happen to him; in *Lalla Hobby* Hajj Ben Moussa is expelled from
Belgium and returns to Morocco, and we can suppose that his life
will continue rather as it was before the break with Houda. But,
on the whole, the movement of both films seems very similar.

M. Perhaps. But you could also look at it in another way. Both Omar
and Hajj Ben Moussa are under a kind of escalating pressure and
stress. At a certain moment an incident happens that leads to a
sort of pause, a moment of reflection, and that comes with the
arrival of a woman. The idea in both films is that of the woman
as an oasis, allowing the man to regain his strength so that he can
continue onward. Of course, whether he's going to succeed depends on his own character—whether Omar will get to Europe,
whether the Hajj will find his wife's husband. But the woman is
the one who puts the man back on track.

K. That reinforces the similarity between the two films.

M. Absolutely. I suppose that comes from both films having the same
screenwriter, and also from the fact that Noureddin and I both
have the same strong concern with movement north. Even in Belgium the farther north the Hajj goes—Antwerp is in the north of
Belgium—the more disoriented he gets, the more he loses the
ability to communicate.

K. Did you and Noureddin ever think of creating a more natural
encounter between a man and woman—perhaps where the man

meets a woman, they begin a conversation, develop a kind of rapport, leading to a relationship—rather than an encounter where the woman is, so to speak, thrown at the character?

M. But Hajj Ben Moussa is not the kind of character—nor was Omar for that matter—who would go into a bar and casually begin to chat with a woman. When Hajj Ben Moussa is at a gathering, a celebration, he can certainly have a drink or two, or even more, but he's not going to go and meet women just like that.

Remember, too, that Hajj Ben Moussa is a foreigner, a clandestine immigrant. He's only going to meet people in the kind of environment that he's likely to be in—railway stations and so on; he's not going to meet people at receptions, or at family gatherings—he's not in that kind of situation. And that's why the girl has to fall on him out of the blue.

THE "TRAINING CAMP"

"TAKING THE VEIL FROM THE VIEWER'S EYES . . . WITHOUT BECOMING DIDACTIC"

K. Let's return to the film's main theme, clandestine immigration, and to what was for me the most interesting and inventive sequence in the film: the encampment outside Tangiers where Lalla Hobby and Hajj Driss go to inquire about the fate of Hajj Ben Moussa. How did that sequence develop?

M. This was a sequence that I was very attached to and that was completely my idea. It brought together all the subthemes: the exodus from this country, *las pateras* or boats of death, the clandestine nature of immigration, even the unemployment that is a cause of so much of it.

The basic aim of this sequence was to portray the kind of organizations that exist in Morocco today and that have as their business trafficking in people, making money off people's desperate desire to emigrate. One thing to note is that we see assistants, lieutenants, and staff, but we never see the boss. This reinforces the idea that the entire operation is clandestine; it's a kind of mafia. The idea was to show this reality, taking the veil from the viewer's eyes on this subject, but to do this without becoming didactic.

I tried to give it a realistic tone, to the point of hiring as extras people—including some Africans—who had already tried to make that trip two or three times. I also put in a few comic touches—

the calisthenics they do to get in shape for the ordeal, putting a dwarf in as one of the trainees. And I put in a few messages, such as the one about unemployment where the staff member says, "This country here is magnificent, yet everyone wants to leave. I just don't understand it. Obviously, unemployment is a horrible scourge for any country."

What really helped me visualize this sequence was a segment directed by the Tunisian Nejia Ben Mabrouk in the film *The Gulf War*.[4] This had scenes of Americans preparing for desert war and you could see the kind of training they went through. If I'd had the budget I planned to develop this sequence even more: I was going to show people taking Spanish language courses, learning how to avoid *la guardia civil*—the Spanish police—and how to deal with them if you ran into them, and so on. The idea was to parody the way the Americans trained for the Gulf War. As it turned out, with the budget restrictions the sequence was reduced—we just get to see them learning to row the boat, there is talk of "sending the merchandise across," there's the calisthenics.

K.   Given the realistic style, I wonder whether anyone contacted you to get the training camp's address? [Laughs.]

M.   No, not yet in any case. In fact, most people thought this was pure fiction, a wild exaggeration, that such a thing wasn't possible at all. But I assure you that what I showed understated the reality of things.

It's such a tragedy. Just think of all those people trying to go abroad illegally. They've been saving painstakingly over the years, or perhaps they've sold their cows or even everything they owned in order to get that money. And then think of the shady people making money from that. There are even stories of people embarking under cover of night and waking up the next morning to find they've been deposited somewhere farther up the Moroccan coast, not unlike Omar in *The Big Trip*. You have to denounce the way the naïveté and trust of these desperate people are exploited by others. If some people think what I've shown is an exaggeration, well, that's their problem.

BALANCING HUMOR AND THE SERIOUS: "HERE, ALL YOU HEAR ARE INSULTS . . . SOMEHOW, WE HAVE TO RECAPTURE THAT ENTHUSIASM"

K.   I thought this sequence was very effective in maintaining the delicate balance between the humorous and the serious, a tone you established early in the film when Hajj Ben Moussa is captured and inducted into prison.

M. It's the comic that helps the viewer swallow the pill.

Balancing the comic and the serious was a main idea from the outset: we wanted to denounce certain injustices in society but not to do it didactically, because then it becomes a kind of provocation. With humor and comedy you can convey the message more effectively. So we dressed the social criticism in humor. And the viewer takes it in better that way—you give the viewer all the elements to draw the conclusions, rather than hitting him with the message like a punch in the face.

This whole sequence is also a way to talk about the shocking devaluation we see today of everything Moroccan. If you think back to the period right after independence, there was enormous patriotic feeling. In cultural expression at that time we created our best songs, our best theater—of course, there was no filmmaking yet, so we can't speak of that. But everyone was trying to do something to make the country better. Now, more than forty years later, everything is devalued. You can't talk to anyone—from whatever social class—without hearing the country insulted. People are unhappy, disillusioned.

Look, when I'm in France, people are very quick to criticize things. But still, they're proud to be French. In the United States it's the same. But here, all you hear are insults: Moroccan products are no good, you can't take a Moroccan at his word, and so on. There's this devaluation across the board, and it's painful to live in this kind of situation. Somehow, we have to find a way to recapture that enthusiasm of the early 1960s.

Chapter Six

Reflections and Projections

Introduction: Approaching a Crossroads

Toward the end of our interviews I wanted Tazi to take a synoptic view, to draw upon his four decades of professional experience, look back over his career as a whole, assess some of the major changes he had witnessed, and speculate on what the future might hold, both for Moroccan filmmaking and his own role within it. This discussion will lead the two of us to a crossroads and a parting of our ways: Tazi's career will veer in a new direction and I will abandon the direct dialogical encounter to offer, in the concluding chapter, some thoughts of my own.

Before we reach this crossroads, we need to explore the role that two different groups play in Morocco's film world: first, filmmakers themselves, to the extent that they have been able, as a professional interest group, to influence the film sector; second, the audience and its changing demographics and tastes. If we have left these two groups unexamined until now, it is not because they are unimportant—to the contrary, they are key to understanding Moroccan cinema—but rather because both groups have been largely ignored over most of the more than four decades since independence, although for dissimilar reasons. It is only within the last decade that each becomes a force to be reckoned with, to very different effect.

Filmmakers and Filmgoers

THE PROFESSION

STATE DISINTEREST, ORGANIZATIONAL IMPOTENCE

In allowing the cinema's distribution and exhibition sectors to operate freely and intervening only minimally in the production sphere, the Moroccan state was consistent, over the first decades of independence, in its lack of interest in Moroccan feature films. Even when the state began to show some concern for Moroccan film production and instituted the Support Fund in 1981, the small sums it allocated in this direction were never accompanied by measures to encourage the distribution and screening of Moroccan films, with the result that these films had no chance to become financially viable. This disinterest sat comfortably with the state's laissez-faire attitude toward the big screen's foreign backers—those shooting foreign productions in Morocco and the main foreign-based distribution companies whose products dominated Moroccan theater programs. It also sat comfortably with the state's greater interest in the big screen's little brother, television.[1] Although within the last several years the state has shown greater commitment to Moroccan film production, no significant state initiatives or legislation have yet been implemented to address distribution, exhibition, and other infrastructural problems.

One of the reasons the state was able to refrain from adopting measures to support Moroccan films effectively is that those in a position to benefit most directly from such measures—the filmmaking professionals—did not form a cohesive unit that might apply significant pressure to influence government policy. In the late 1960s and into the 1970s, the Moroccan Filmmakers Association (*Association des cinéastes marocains*—ACM) acted in a rather unified manner but it was a small group and its entreaties were easily ignored. Then, in the late 1970s, new statutes governing the profession came into effect, reinforcing the power of the CCM. Under these new statutes, a film director wanting to make a film had to form a production company and the ACM was reorganized into a more inclusive Producers' Guild (*Chambre des Producteurs*) that brought together in one entity three factions with divergent interests—service providers for foreign productions, those who had primary income coming from outside the sector and for whom filmmaking was a secondary activity, and those whose living came primarily from filmmaking and related audiovisual activities. Although formally numbering in the hundreds, the guild's active membership comprised only about thirty people, divided roughly equally among the three factions, and it was able to show unity only on rare occasions. Weakening the guild further was the fact that all its proposals passed through the CCM, which often reformulated them so as to increase its own control and authority.

Tazi was frequently at odds with the guild. He was disappointed that it didn't push to have foreign productions aid national production—perhaps by obliging them to provide employment for a specified number of local technicians, or by imposing a percentage tax on the foreign film's budget for the support of national production, and/or other measures. But, as Tazi put it, every time he raised the issue, he heard responses along the lines of, "But we have to wait until foreign production becomes a tradition here, then we can institute new legal texts." He continued, "But nothing has been done. For the foreign producers Morocco is just a way station; they do what they want, bring the technicians they want, and so on." What saddened him, in general, was that "the guild seems to care more about *filmmaking in Morocco* than about *Moroccan filmmaking*. The problems of our own national cinema are secondary." Another difference Tazi had with the guild was on the question of film training. As he put it, "One of the problems that I see as crucial and in which the guild has shown no interest whatsoever is the problem of training."

Tazi's view that the tensions within the guild would soon erupt was borne out when, during the summer of 2001, he and some twenty colleagues left it to form a new association, the Group of Writers-Directors-Producers (*Groupement des auteurs-réalisateurs-producteurs*— known by its acronym GARP). GARP, of which Tazi later became president, brought together many of Morocco's most accomplished filmmakers as well as a number of the most promising younger ones.[2] Its charter pointed to a number of Moroccan cinema's advantages, including having a public that both appreciated the national cinema and was supporting it at the box office, but then went on to highlight its liabilities, stating that the sector was characterized by "Too many internal quarrels. Struggles for power. Personal interests taking precedence over collective ones. An inadequate legal framework. A completely unstructured national film market. A lack of political will to organize the film sector. A lack of commitment and organization among film professionals. A scarcity of groups representing the different filmmaking specialties."[3] GARP argued, in another statement, that

Moroccan cinema's three most urgent needs were reforming the Aid Fund so that it rewarded quality, providing better protection for artistic rights (Fr. *les droits d'auteur*), and establishing an institute to train people in the various audiovisual specialties. More broadly, GARP was seeking to create a "coalition for cultural diversity," with the aims of "pursuing the struggle for freedom of expression and opposing efforts to commodify artistic and cultural production."[4] It was also hoping to inject new life into the National Film Federation (*Fédération nationale du cinéma*)—an organization that brings together all film professionals working in distribution, exhibition, and production—in order better to promote the national cinema economically, politically, socially, and culturally.

The question of training had long been one of Tazi's hobbyhorses. To pursue this aim GARP joined a broader group—the Moroccan Association for Film and Audiovisual Producers (*Association marocaine des producteurs audiovisuels et de cinéma*—AMPAC), hoping to give more force to AMPAC's long-standing aim of pushing for the creation of a higher institute (a structure on the level of university) for film training, as already existed in some other professions, such as the dramatic arts and journalism. Tazi was optimistic that this intention would soon become a reality.[5]

"AUDIOVISUAL STRESS"

The long-standing weakness of filmmaker organizations, the unwillingness of the state to play an active role in supporting the distribution and screening of Moroccan films, the absence of supportive legislation: these not only discouraged production but, inevitably, had demoralizing effects on the creators themselves. When I asked Tazi how the structure of the profession affected his own outlook, he began with a sardonic laugh and then went on:

M. When you ask me about this you're referring to what I call "audiovisual stress!"

I think a lot about such problems these days and I can't avoid seeing a shortened horizon and feeling pessimistic. As a filmmaker, if your machine stops running at the age of 56 or 57, you have nothing to support you. Basically, the state leaves the artistic sector alone and you're therefore in a very precarious position. There's no pension or anything like that. So you can't help thinking, "Either I'm going to have to hold the camera in my hands and work very hard, like a craftsman, to the end of my days, or

I'll die hungry like Meliès, the founder of cinema." You might not think about such things until you reach the age of 50 or so but then, when you're faced with some kind of misfortune or a little health problem, you start to ask these questions. The answers aren't encouraging. We don't even have something like an Academy of the Arts here where, at the age of 70, you might be able to count on a seat and perhaps receive a small allowance. So, someone who's had a career over thirty or thirty-five years gains absolutely no benefit from being a citizen, absolutely none. In another country perhaps I'd have the benefit of a public health service, or at the very least an efficient public transportation system!

Here, it's all very stressful. We're like discards. When you're sick, when something happens, you can die without anyone lifting a finger. The only social security system we have, if you can call it a system, is the one that comes from the king, and it's neither a right nor an obligation. But at least we had that: each time an artist had a health problem, King Hassan II himself took care of it. But to help you the king had to hear about it, and sometimes he didn't. I just hope this will continue with his son.[6]

K. Did you benefit from this when you were sick?

M. Absolutely!

The question I now face is, how long can I go on at this pace? It gets more and more difficult. The cost of living is rising all the time. And of course this takes a lot of time and energy that you could otherwise be devoting to creative activity. Your daily needs come first and you have to satisfy them even if it means just taking an artistic photograph, or filming a door, or making a multimedia CD, or delivering a lecture. And that risks pushing aside the kind of activity you really want to engage in.[7]

CHANGING AUDIENCE, CHANGING TASTES, CHANGING FEATURES

As we saw in chapter 1, the initiative taken by one distributor in the early 1990s to distribute a couple of Moroccan films in a truly commercial way was a crucial factor in enabling Moroccan audiences to turn toward their national films. Perhaps this distributor's success with the two films was simply luck; more likely it came from his accurate, if intuitive, reading of the changing demographics and changing tastes of Moroccan filmgoers and his recognition that the filmmakers were beginning to make different kinds of feature films. On a broader level, this striking change in the habits of the Moroccan film-going public is no doubt a reflection of the audience's growing desire to see themselves and their own society represented on the large screen rather than yet more representations of life in the West.

Who is attending these films now and who is likely to attend them in the future? How can we characterize their tastes? How do the Moroccan films that emerged in the 1990s compare with films from earlier decades and to what extent do they reflect changes in the audience?

According to a survey done in the early 1990s, just as the public was turning toward Moroccan films, film spectators were almost exclusively in their late teens or young adults (one-quarter of whom were female, mostly on the young side), and a good three-quarters of all filmgoers had competed secondary school at least. Only 1 percent of people at the management level frequented the cinema (Jaidi 2000: 162), a sign perhaps of the lack of suitable theaters.[8]

The survey also gives us some insight into audience tastes. The largest percentage of the audience sought out films that provided laughter (43.5 percent), followed by action, suspense, deep emotions, and escape. Spectators ranked adventure, comedy, and sociopolitical films as the most preferred genres (Jaidi 1992: 47–48, 51).

As far as national origins of films are concerned, a higher proportion of women than men (12 percent to 8.5 percent) favored Moroccan films (the difference is even greater, 17 percent to 6.5 percent, with regard to Egyptian films), whereas men and women preferred American films in roughly equal proportions. Students attended significantly more Moroccan films than did individuals in other categories, but only among the unemployed were the numbers seeing Moroccan films low (a phenomenon that may have as much to do with ticket price and theater location as with taste preferences).

There is a significant discrepancy between the national origins of films shown and spectator preferences, with the strong demand for Moroccan and Egyptian films outstripping supply, pointing once again to the dominance of distributor and exhibitor economic interest over the national audience's desires.[9]

These trends and figures suggest that the portion of the film-going public wanting to see Moroccan films is likely to continue growing: a higher preference for Moroccan films correlates with higher educational levels and the Moroccan population grew considerably more educated in the 1990s; women prefer Moroccan films more than men do, and the proportion of women filmgoers should increase due to greater schooling of women and the growing number of single women and those who have not yet borne children (because of later marrying age and later first births). Another trend that might support a growth in women's attendance would be the creation and expansion of better-appointed theaters and multiplexes, because the survey also shows the proportion of women's attendance to be significantly higher in such venues.[10]

How have Moroccan filmmakers responded to or reflected these audience tastes? Recall the distributor again, and his mentioning that one element in the commercial attraction of Abdelkader Lagtaa's *A Love Affair in Casablanca* was its shift from the more usual concern with the less well off to a focus on more privileged social classes and situations. In fact, into the 1980s Moroccan films typically were set largely in a rural or lower-class urban milieu, almost always among the poor or very poor. Many of the films of the 1990s, to the contrary, establish themselves primarily in urban settings and deal with white-collar workers and sometimes the quite wealthy bourgeoisie. Also, many films of this decade concentrate on young rather than mature adults, individuals who are early in their working careers and/or marriages. A focus on woman characters was already important during the 1980s but this, if anything, increased during the 1990s.[11] One of the constants throughout the history of Moroccan cinema has been a concern with social issues—what Tazi often refers to as "a sociological cinema."[12]

In addition to continuing the focus on women and the "sociological" approach, the films of the 1990s also fit in with the changing audience tastes just outlined and also with the broader changes in Moroccan society: humor—still somewhat rare in films—has brought in the crowds in the few films that have employed it; a number of daring and provocative films have been shown in the theaters; greater narrative thrust and use of suspense has been in evidence; and there is also some significant use of what might be termed a televisual style.[13]

Looking Backward and Around

Over the length of his career, Tazi had seen the birth of Moroccan feature film production and its growth to current levels, developments that went along with the film sector's changing technical capabilities and with changing Moroccan tastes. Before asking Tazi how he situated his own work I wanted his views on these aspects—how he would assess the changes in film technology and technical capacities in Morocco and what his thinking was concerning the formation of taste, first with regard to Morocco generally, then with regard to his own taste, and finally how the tastes of the society around him might be changing.

TECHNIQUE, TECHNOLOGY, COMPETENCE; KEEPING UP-TO-DATE

"TECHNICAL POSSIBILITIES ARE IMPROVING DAY BY DAY"

K. If you look back over your experience in filmmaking, what have been the main changes, the main innovations, from a technological point of view? Let's think of the years since the mid-1960s and let's leave aside the very recent digital developments.[14]

M. Certainly, there have been important technical developments. You remember how, early on, we did some traveling shots from a wheelbarrow or upon a donkey, even while carrying a Cinema-Scope camera? Well, those were experiences of youth, at a time when we had no thoughts for the public because our films rarely reached them. But once you know the film is going to reach the public, the film has to have a certain technical level or the public won't go to see it. I can't imagine myself now with a handheld camera doing traveling shots from a wheelbarrow, and what's more, with the director himself pushing me!

After this early "youthful" phase, there was a second phase that began toward the end of the 1970s and that continued into the early 1990s, as filmmakers changed over to live sound from guide sound recording [Fr. *son temoin*]. With a guide sound track, you'd record the actors using whatever recorder you had, you'd hear camera sound and everything else, but then you'd re-record in the studio, with the original sound being used as a "guide" to situate what the actors said and when. Even up until the early 1990s some directors were still using guide sound. Since the mid-1990s, I think almost everyone has been using live sound.

Also, when you talk today of traveling shots in Moroccan films, these are now real traveling shots, with dollies, tracks, and so on. When you talk of a crane shot there's really a crane being used, and in recent Moroccan films you can see crane shots every-where.[15] I've never used crane shots in any of my films, although I used them when I was the cinematographer and cameraman on Latif Lahlou's film *The Compromise* (1986), when we pulled back from a close-up of a character to bring in all of the people around him who were engaged in a labor strike. The only time I used what you might call sophisticated technology on my own films was when I used a Steadicam in *Looking*. Otherwise, I always try to use the simplest techniques; I'm not trying to complicate things for the spectator.

But, certainly, today you need to have these basic tools to get good live sound and valid traveling shots; you need to have a harness and stabilizer when you're shooting from a vehicle; and so on. That's the minimum. By the way, that's one of the positive effects of all the foreign productions in Morocco: some firms that provide services for the foreign productions have obtained the necessary equipment. This way, instead of the equipment standing unused, Moroccan directors have an opportunity to use it. Of course, sometimes the prices are over the moon but at least cranes and other such equipment are now available.

Still, when I think back, making those first films was really an extraordinary experience, really an adventure. Our main em-phasis then was on the content of the film and not the form. It had to be more or less legible; that was our aim. There were shots where the camera wobbled, where the quality of the image would vary from sequence to sequence, and so on. We had to get our messages out and we didn't care a damn whether we wrote them with a cheap ballpoint pen or whatever.

Now we can really say that things have improved significantly. The film lab here in Rabat is top notch and it obtains absolutely perfect pictures. Sound is improving too—at least we now have acceptable sound and there's an awareness that the technical pos-sibilities are improving day by day. And so much the better.

K. How would you sum up the most important innovations?

M. Live sound, new technical possibilities for shots, the improvement in the quality of the image, and, finally, greater professionalism in some of the technical tasks.[16]

"TRUE PROFESSIONALS . . . ARE SERIOUSLY LACKING"

K. How would you assess the changing competence of Moroccan technicians? And in light of this, how do you go about constituting a crew?

M. If you mean true professionals, they are seriously lacking. Of course, you might also hear that in Morocco you can find any specialty you want. Well, we do have all the specialties in the sense that, if you ask a technician whether he can do such and such, he'll always answer, "Sure, I can do anything." But this doesn't mean he really masters the specialty. I might want to have a Moroccan script girl and I certainly could hire one—people with this title exist—but they just don't have the real skills. As a result I hired a Tunisian. And the same is true for a director's first and second assistants too.

K. What do the first and second assistants do?

M. The first assistant is the director's true lieutenant in working with the actors, with the crew, and so on. The second assistant deals with the actors but also with the extras, with advance preparation, with the set designer, with the shot breakdown [Fr. *le dépouille-ment*], and so on.[17] The shot breakdown is very important: here, starting from the screenplay, you indicate which objects and props are needed for each set, where to get them, when they will arrive, how much each will cost, what characters are present, and so on. Even if you have a diploma in film studies, you have to have considerable experience all the way up the ladder—just like a lawyer in training—before you can perform this task with skill. In all these professions you see the same problems: for example, the fact that you've been an assistant set designer on one film doesn't mean that on the second you're already qualified to become the set designer. But here, with a snap of the fingers, you become a director making your own films.

So, we're lacking those technicians who are the director's immediate collaborators—the script girl, the first and second assistants, the set photographer who knows that it's not a question of taking just any photo. The prop person is very important also, and the head electrician, and the gaffer—all these are functions that have to be developed, that one has to train for.

Take the question of sound. Here again, there are people who have the title of "sound engineer" but who really don't have the skill of a sound engineer. The real problem isn't during the shooting but in postproduction when you have to do the mixing in the studio. That's when you need someone who really has a profound knowledge of his field. We have sound engineers now in Morocco who know how to capture the sound for the film—who know this through their experience on films and their personal quality too. But a true sound engineer has had a real education in the domain, not just practical experience. We have a few of these but, unfortunately, they work with television, they're more in the electronic media.

And we're also missing people qualified in sound effects. This is a key specialty. Even when you're making a film with live sound, you still need to add later a lot of sounds that aren't recorded directly. For example, when you sit down the chair makes a noise, and you've got to have that noise to give the film more veracity. The sound effects person comes to the studio with one or two suitcases with all kinds of objects inside, with which he can make all the necessary sounds. For a car-racing film called *Les 24 heures du Mans,* I saw one guy do all the effects with a piece of paper and a pen, making all the noises of cars taking turns, braking, and so on. These people are immensely talented. We don't have anyone here who can do that and it's an essential function.

K. So what do you do when you need someone like that?

M. Well, for both *Looking* and *Lalla Hobby* I had to do the sound effects abroad.[18]

"CONTINUOUS RETOOLING"

K. How about in your own field, where technology is changing so rapidly—how do you keep up-to-date? Is keeping up-to-date something of a burden or do you do it by inclination?

M. Keeping abreast of new technology and techniques is a part of my life. I don't want to be overtaken by events on the technological level or otherwise. I can't stand taking a camera in my hands and finding an element on it that I don't know how to use, or being in front of a computer with digital editing and having someone else serve as my intermediary. If I'm filming—especially a documentary—I feel a great deal is lost when I have to explain to the cameraman what I want. That goes for editing too—I hate to leave an editor alone with my film for more than ten minutes. I don't like to be in those kinds of situations.

That's why I try to have a kind of continuous retooling, starting with my studies in the United States and continuing up until today with the new technology. In part, this approach may have its source in our training, because at IDHEC we were trained in all fields—I was taught not only how to handle the camera but also to sit and work at an editing console. So I'm always thinking of retraining myself, as I'm now doing, in digital techniques. And God knows there's new technology every day. You can't stay in an ivory tower and say, "I'm a creator and I express myself only with these old noble tools and I reject these new ones." In this profession, you really have to keep awake!

I don't experience this constant retraining as a burden, not at all. In fact it's a pleasure, I'm motivated to do it. It's an enormously rich domain and I learn a lot from many different people. What a pleasure it is to spend a couple of hours with a programmer or with a digital graphic artist who explains to me how things work, the "why" of things. It's all part of our development, part of our mental evolution—to know what means are available to accomplish things in the best way. It's very nostalgic to write with that "Sergeant Major" pen, which was a quill pen with its ink bottle. Well, now we've changed over to the Bic ballpoint.

For example, I'm going to edit my next film, *Abu Moussa's Women Neighbors,* digitally. I can see the gain in time, the increased flexibility. Perhaps there's also less stress—you don't have to think, "I took out two images from that shot—now careful, I'd better not lose them, I'd better stash them over here." Now you can be freed from these problems of detail and concentrate on the editing as a creative act. Of course the sensual side, touching the film, will perhaps disappear, and I can see that that's a problem. But I know that with the digital editing I can focus better on the editing itself.

THE CONSTRUCTION OF TASTE

CHOICE; GOOD TASTE AND BAD

"FANTASTIC . . . TO HAVE SUCH CHOICE"

K. Over the past two decades, we've seen some spectacular changes in Moroccan society and in Morocco's relationship to the rest of the world. These have certainly had repercussions on Moroccan tastes and, in particular, on Moroccan tastes for Moroccan films. In this context, how do you see the changes in Moroccan tastes over the past two decades, roughly since you started directing your own films?

M. First of all, we can see that tastes in filmgoing have changed markedly, starting with the release of Abdelkader Lagtaa's *A Love Affair in Casablanca* in 1992. Since then, although the total number of film spectators has diminished drastically—people don't like to hear these figures but in 1990 we had between twenty-two and

twenty-four million spectators in the cinemas and in 1997 or perhaps 1996, we only had some fourteen million—yet attendance
for Moroccan films since the early 1990s has risen spectacularly.

You can look at this decrease in overall filmgoing in another
way: it's not that spectators are no longer watching films, it's
rather that they've switched from the large to the small screen.
People still see very many films, but now they see most of them
on TV, and this includes very good audience percentages for Moroccan films shown on TV. All this is what I call "the proximity
phenomenon": people now want to see things that are tied to our
society. This is the big change in taste, and it has occurred over a
period of less than ten years.

All this has to be seen in the context of the technological rev-
olution we've been living through. Now, no one can stand outside
of civilization, outside of technology, outside of what is happening
in the world. With all the satellite dishes Moroccans have, we are
no longer handicapped in learning about what's happening in the
world. Now, all you have to do is turn that dish—we just call it
"dish" [Ar. *sahn*]—in the right direction to have a window on the
world. There are more than one and a half million dishes in Morocco, and this means a minimum of ten to fifteen million Moroccans with access to this window.

Although the kinds of images we consume encourage phenomena like emigration because these images mystify the West,
it's still fantastic for the individual to have such choice. There's
diversity and freedom and the power to choose—it's not just THE
NEWS, THE ONE AND ONLY, THE OFFICIAL NEWS, all in capital
letters.

That's already one step toward democracy. At the next level,
you have to learn the difference between a good choice and a bad
one. But you still have to have that first level. I remember, in the
1970s, when the Moroccan authorities would interfere with radio
transmissions from Libya—even faxes were outlawed. Something
like that is unimaginable today—you just can't interfere like that
any longer. For me, that is the greatest advance we've had since
independence.

"REAL *EDUCATION* DOESN'T EXIST"

K. I guess the basic questions are: What do these various images convey? Are they so varied that they really provide a choice? Are
people encouraged to distinguish between a good choice and a

bad one, as you termed it? And what are the effects of all these images on Moroccan taste?

M. How to encourage good taste is a problem that exists at all levels of society. Sometimes when I go into a home—even a professor's or a doctor's, people with a certain intellectual level—the poor taste there is unbelievable. You know: plastic flowers, a wall library because it looks good, objects that suggest some intelligence but without sincerity. It's terrible to see things like that.

When it comes to films, I'm often shocked to see Moroccan films that show the most wretched things. For some filmmakers it becomes their niche in the market, that's how to get noticed and perhaps make some money. On the contrary, each of us in our own way ought to be trying to raise the level of taste, not in order to create one specific kind of taste but to distance ourselves from bad taste. That's the kind of school we ought to be building. But here the structures for that are lacking: neither in school nor on the streets nor with their parents are kids educated in taste— there's a total vacuum. TV has been substituted for everything. The parents do nothing and school just instructs. Real *education* doesn't exist.

"ARTISTIC CREATION . . . LIKE THE PAIN OF CHILDBIRTH"

K. So, how would you define what "good taste" is, how would you determine if something is in good taste?

M. I think that nature itself—nature's harmony—has played an enormous role in our notions of beauty and art. Because that's where much of good taste comes from, from the capacity to adapt to natural things, things that happen of themselves, without cacophony. For me, art isn't about mystifying things but it is about showing things in their true nature, not necessarily in their beauty.

Art also represents, I think, the serene expression of the individual. Even though artistic creation often happens through suffering, its pain is like the pain of childbirth. First of all, in order to create—through a painting, or a piece of music, or a film, or in a literary form—you have to have the desire to do it. It's a great pleasure to be able to give birth to a work of art and then to share it with others. You have to work at it tenaciously, until you're satisfied, and you have to want a kind of communication with the public. It's that tenacity that gives art the capacity to show things in a . . . in a truly *marvelous* manner.

Taste and the Love of Art: "Learning means appreciating"

"In my childhood I was brushing against art every minute of the day"

K. I know that one of the things that gives you great pleasure in life is art—painting, music, and so on. You speak about this often, you're very interested in it, and, obviously, the best evidence for this is in your films. I wonder how your own taste, your aesthetic sensibility, developed.

M. First of all, I think this is a question of culture and education. You've probably noticed that in many of my interviews, again and again I talk about how important it is to educate children's taste for decoration, for dressing well, for marrying colors, for harmony, and so on. When I look at Arab houses in our traditional cities like Fez, Marrakesh, Tétouan—houses constructed without professional architects, mind you, but just according to the owner's concept—you see all the various elements composed in great harmony. So these things exist in our traditional life, you just have to be made sensitive to it.

I'm sure that my own sensitivity to art has its source deep in my past. I think it really started in childhood and adolescence, where in my environment many things were expressed artistically. There was no artwork in the modern sense, but there was art in many other forms. When I saw my mother's embroidery designs or when I saw the mirror my father put in the sitting room and the fine chiseling and other effects it had—these were works of art. When I saw a slate from the Qur²anic school, this too was a work of art. And a decorated page from the Qur²an.

Or, when I crossed the medina of Fez—we lived in one corner of the city and I had to cross through much of the medina to get to school—and saw all its craftsmen: those making turned wood [Ar. *mashrabiya*], for example, and how they worked so nimbly with their feet; or when I watched the men who were fashioning the stencils that were used to make embroidered belts and such things and all the different designs cut in paper; or when I saw the metalworkers [Fr. *dinandiers*] putting designs on copper trays. And, also, the plaster sculpture, or the designs etched on wood, or embellished and embossed leather—all these lead to extraordinary artistic work. Art was absolutely everywhere. It's true that the modern notion of art involves something else, but in my childhood I was brushing against art every minute of the day!

K. When you were growing up, was there anyone in particular who called your attention to artistic things?

M. Yes there was. I had a cousin who spent his time copying the Qur'an with all its illuminations, all its decorations. This took him an incredible amount of time, working with a reed pen and with different colors of ink and gold filigree. I was fascinated by this, I watched him for hours. And he ended up with beautiful manuscripts. Later he became quite successful, and his manuscripts are highly appreciated in Morocco and in the Middle East as well.

"CREATIVE CINEMA [REQUIRES] A VERY
BROAD GENERAL CULTURE"

K. When you began in films your aims were primarily communicative and not aesthetic. When did this aesthetic aspect become important for you in your film work, and when did you actually become conscious of your love for artistic work?

M. When I started in film work, in those first years of independence, with vast numbers of people poor and illiterate, my basic concern was to communicate, largely by means of documentaries. Artistic things weren't my conscious concern at that point.

Once I had moved toward creative cinema and away from the documentary and from the aim of communicating by means of "direct cinema"—not that the need to communicate has disappeared altogether but it has diminished relatively—it became indispensable to have a very broad general culture, in all areas. This means knowing about one's own literature, world literature, music, art, and so on. If you don't know what expressionism is and what neorealism is in cinema, for example, you can't hope to express things well. The same thing is true for literature—the eighteenth-century novel, the "*nouveau roman*" in France, the kind of literature being produced in the United States. If you don't have this general culture to start with, you absolutely must move in this direction.

I did find it difficult at the beginning to appreciate some styles of painting, especially abstract painting. But as I got to know a number of Moroccan painters very well—Farid Belkahia, Qassimi, Fouad Belamin—I began to appreciate this more and more. As with painting, so it was with the other arts. As I frequented composers, musicians—in popular music as well as classical, and in

Andalusian music as well—I learned and appreciated more and more. In filmmaking you come into contact with all different areas of creative activity and this pushes you—or at least it pushed me—to learn more and more. And learning means appreciating and going more deeply into things.

When I really like an artist's work, or a writer's, I always try to find a way to get them to participate in my films. I admired the Moroccan painter Farid Belkahia's work so much that I convinced him to be artistic director on *Badis,* even though at first he said, "But I've never worked on a film—how can I be an artistic director, a set designer and decorator?" I brought him up to the village of Badis and he was totally charmed by the place. It really worked out very well. I never can say this enough: a film is a collective effort, and you have to bring together as many talented people as you can in order to get a successful finished work.

CRITICS AND "REALISM"; CENSORS AND THE "MORAL ENVIRONMENT"

"THE SPECTATOR . . . IS THE REAL CRITIC"

K. Two groups that may have a significant effect on taste are critics and censors.[19] I wonder what role you think these groups have on Moroccan tastes and what influence they might have on you? Let's talk about critics first.

M. Although the observation you frequently hear is probably true—that critics aren't read in this country and that they have no influence on film attendance—they are absolutely necessary just the same, because they reflect what's being done in the creative domain, in film, theater, music, and so on.[20]

That being said, I've reached a point where I'm a very selective reader of critics. There are a few I respect but some of the others are shockingly bad and have no coherent views and no film culture enabling them to form solid judgments, even though they sometimes are in charge of the entire film page in their publication.

M. Have you learned anything from critics?

K. Certainly. I've read some analyses that have shown me subconscious things I might have expressed in a film, things I did automatically, without thinking, but that reflected some other level of my being.

K. In pointing out meaning that is hidden in your work, might a critic influence your orientation, your way of thinking about things?

M. No, not at all! I don't think a critic can change my concerns or my way of looking at things. Even on the psychoanalytic level— if that happened you'd probably not be doing yourself any good and you might actually harm your creative impulse.

I will say that one thing that particularly annoys me is the criticism that parts of a film lack verisimilitude.

K. Can you give me some examples?

M. Sure. In *Lalla Hobby,* Houda hears her case announced on the radio: a legal warning goes out to her husband that if he doesn't present himself within one month his wife will be awarded a divorce. A press critic wrote, and at some length, "This is unrealistic, this kind of thing can't happen, the law doesn't work that way." But you can hear these programs on the radio almost every day and the text was an actual radio text, I didn't change one word.

Then, in *Looking*, Bashir Skiredj, who played the first Hajj Ben Moussa, is from Tangiers so he was supposedly not "realistic" as a Fassi. And the entire clandestine emigration "enterprise" sequence in *Lalla Hobby* was also criticized for being unrealistic. It's as though the critics refuse to see these as "fictions."

K. Perhaps they miss the symbolic aspect too.

M. Yes, as when the lapidation scene in *Badis* was seen as "not realistic." They are so saddled to a certain reality that if you present things differently they see it as absurd. It's one of the reasons that I've been exercising a sort of self-criticism, saying that I should not do too many "magical" things in my films, because if I mix the magical and the realistic too much, people can lose their footing. Now I try to calculate things a little more, thinking of how things might be interpreted. But who should decide what's realistic, what's magical, what makes something a good story? Certainly not the critics.

That's why I've become more sensitive to criticism from the public—it's a more spontaneous and authentic criticism—than from the critics. A lot of studies show that spectators see in a film the things that relate to their own environment, things they are capable of reading. Critics, on the other hand, try to find philosophical, metaphysical aspects that don't concern the public at all, even though it's this public the critic is supposed to be informing or guiding. There's an enormous difference between a professional critic's view and a spectator's, and for me it's the spectator who is the real critic.

"YOU CAN'T SIMPLY BE STUBBORN"

K. Now, turning to censorship and freedom of expression: we've already talked about some of the limitations you impose on yourself because of your own ideas of what's proper and decent, what's appropriate for the screen. And we also briefly discussed how freedom of expression has improved in certain ways. Here in Morocco it's the Supervisory Film Commission that decides if a film is suitable for viewing. What is your attitude toward this?

M. You know, what today we call the Supervisory Film Commission existed well before we had any national film production. Originally, it was instituted by the French to "protect" the Moroccan audience from certain subjects—from violence, sex, some political matters. As it operates today, each representative on the commission has his or her own ideas about what is acceptable, according to his or her function: someone from the ministry of youth and sports would have a different view from someone from the ministry of interior, or from the ministry of communication and information, or from the police. And you'd get a different opinion, too, from the distributor as well as from the exhibitors' representative. I've witnessed some rather wild scenes on the commission, where each person tried to defend a particular pet orientation.

As it turns out, the cases of censorship for Moroccan films are very rare. But this doesn't mean I agree with having such a commission. Concerning freedom of expression, I do not think a film should be censored. But also, I'm not always in agreement with filmmakers who stubbornly stick to a scene that, knowing the society around them, they might have eliminated earlier. There's a kind of red line in certain domains that you shouldn't cross—in religion, morals, and the basic institutions of the state. In the area of politics, on the other hand, almost anything can be discussed and is fully open to interpretation.[21]

K. So, you see freedom of expression as related to its particular sociocultural context rather than as an absolute?

M. Freedom of expression *always* has to be seen in relation to a given context. It's wonderful to laud freedom of expression, but it's not an absolute. It is universal, that's true, but freedom of expression is always, let's say, modulated with respect to the moral system in operation where one makes one's films.

Take an example we've talked about before—all the difficulties Scorsese had making his film on Christ, first at the stage of shooting, then later with its distribution, and so on. I've even seen the theater in Paris, in St. Michel, that had a fire because of this film. Freedom of expression *always* exists within a certain moral environment. Here, in Morocco, I can criticize all sorts of things that I'm not in agreement with—religious fundamentalism, for example. But I should do this within a certain existing morality. On the one hand, you have to find a way to express things without falling into clichés, and here we come back to litote and other techniques; on the other hand, you can always find a way to express things without putting your fist in people's face, so to speak.

So, I agree with the principle of defending and protecting your film and not allowing cuts. But as a filmmaker you also have to ask yourself whether this scene of ten or twenty or even thirty seconds is so important that without it the film doesn't hold together. You can't simply be stubborn on behalf of the principle that there be no cuts. I would have to see what I'm being asked to cut and why, and how important it is to the film. But, fundamentally, I'm against censorship.

K. And who should decide what's appropriate to show and what isn't?

M. It's the person's own choice. I live in a certain system. If I want to communicate with this society, I shouldn't try to shock it.

K. But if a filmmaker wants to shock it, who should decide if this should be permitted?

M. Well, there are institutions for that, that's why the commission exists.[22]

SITUATING TAZI'S FILMMAKING: CHANGING POSITIONS IN A SHIFTING FIELD

FROM DOCUMENTARY TO FICTION

"YOU NECESSARILY INTRODUCE A SUBJECTIVITY, YOUR OWN WAY OF SEEING"

K. Looking over your career and your four feature films, to what extent have you and your orientation toward filmmaking changed over that period?

M. At the outset I wanted to be a communicator by means of image and sound, which meant orienting myself toward documentaries and all sorts of informational and educational films. I did that for about ten years. As time went on I began to see the limits of pedagogy, of being a kind of teacher. I also began to realize that when you make a documentary it's very difficult to argue that it is "objective." Documentaries that perhaps were objective in their conception and that I would have liked to be objective at their completion became, with commentary, with interviews, something quite different. When you see things with your own eyes and film them, you necessarily introduce a subjectivity, your own way of seeing.

Also, the way films were being shown in Morocco was changing during this period. In the beginning our shorts and documentaries were shown in the theaters, in what was called the complementary program for the feature film. But during the 1970s the complementary program was eliminated and people simply went to see the feature film, "basta" [enough, that's all], because that's all there was to see.[23]

As a result of both these factors I began to distance myself from documentary and educational films. But I always loved the cinematographic side—constructing images is very creative work, even when you're doing this for another director. You're the director's very close collaborator and the screenplay becomes something very different when you start to play with the lighting, the sets, the lenses, and so on. But, of course, you couldn't possibly survive as a cinematographer because very few films were being produced during that period and you'd have to wait two years or more between films.

So, for me, going toward fiction and feature films wasn't either accidental or a product of my own ambition. Rather, it was part of the evolution of the sector, in that the professional context of the filmmaker was changing.

TAZI IN THE CINEMATIC FIELD: "STORYTELLER ... [NOT] ONE-MAN BAND"

"NEW PEOPLE ... NEW SOURCES OF ENRICHMENT"

K. Taking your career and approach as a whole, what would you say distinguishes you from other Moroccan filmmakers?

M. That's a somewhat sensitive issue, in that I don't ever want to present myself as a model or appear to be giving advice or teaching anyone anything.

K. I thought one distinction might lie in your having been formed as a cinematographer, another perhaps in your having a certain relationship to writing and reading, or to art. Do you see your films as reflecting differences along those lines?

M. I don't know. Perhaps I have particular concerns in relation to my society and in figuring out how to reflect society in my films. But I find it difficult to answer that question.

K. Well, not every question has an answer.

But let me continue a little more on the same subject. One of the things that seems to me to distinguish your work from that of other Moroccan filmmakers is that your films show great variety. In contrast, the corpus of other filmmakers seems to have greater unity. That's an observation, not criticism or praise. Is that your impression too? And if so, why?

M. Yes, that's definitely true. First of all, many Moroccan filmmakers write their own screenplays, their own dialogue.[24] They are in their own world and it's like a closed vase. For me, the enrichment that a collaborator can bring to the screenplay, to the dialogue, and so on, can change things enormously. Again, I don't want to give lessons, but when you do all those things yourself, you're sometimes too self-satisfied with your own creation, you can get somewhat repetitive and remain imprisoned in your own thinking without confronting it with the ideas of others.

So I do think that is an important difference. And I hope that every time I have the occasion to make a film I have the opportunity to work with new people, so I can have new sources of enrichment. I think it would be a step forward if people understood that when you make a film you can't be a one-man band.

"Not a moralist . . . not a cinema of opposition"

K. One might also say that while your films all address social and societal issues, you don't aim to shake things up, to pierce through taboos. There are some Moroccan filmmakers who, at least in interviews, say, in effect, "I make films to call taboos into question." That doesn't seem to be one of your aims.

M. That's right, and that's because my vision is not of a cinema of opposition but a cinema of storytelling. And a storyteller's raison d'être isn't to revolutionize society but to recount its story, with its blemishes, its deprivations, its humor. In any event, it seems to me that the idea of a political cinema or an oppositional cinema is utopian, because you've never seen people start a demonstration after having seen a film! The only place where a real political cinema has been made is in Cuba, because they had a coherent, militant film policy, with film buses crisscrossing the entire country to politicize the population.

Here the situation is completely different. The cinema has no political orientation in Morocco, we're not trained in any specific approach. To be frank, filmmakers here are more or less completely ignored and left to their own devices. But this neglect has a positive side, because it has allowed us a certain freedom and has permitted the emergence of several different kinds of filmmakers.

I want to remain a storyteller. As storyteller I can approach whatever aspect of society I want to. But I'm not here to say, "You must not do this, this is evil, you must do that." No. I'm not a moralist and I'm not a teacher. I'm a storyteller and I want to tell stories. But obviously, these stories cannot be out of phase with our reality, with our society, with the problems that we're now living through.

TOPICAL CONCERNS, UNIVERSAL APPEAL?

"I DON'T THINK YOU CAN START WITH THE AIM OF REACHING THE UNIVERSAL"

K. Looking over your four films, some of the stories and subjects are more current than others. *The Big Trip* highlights the issue of migration from southern Morocco to the north, a phenomenon related to movement from rural to urban areas and that has a long history here, persisting today. *Badis* sounds a contemporary warning, and *Lalla Hobby* treats the urgent problem of clandestine immigration as well as the power of Europe over the Moroccan imaginary. Perhaps *Looking* is the least current, although its ending raises a very topical issue.

M. Yes, yes. I'd simply add that perhaps you shouldn't look at *The Big Trip* as a reflection of my concerns because we made it from a screenplay conceived, thought through, and written by Noureddin Sail. But, starting with *Badis,* the ideas are *mine*, these are stories I wanted to tell, these are *my* concerns. With Moroccan audiences now watching Moroccan films and no longer so enthralled by films from America, France, Italy, India, and so on, our stories really address the spectators, saying, in effect, "Look, here is your own cinema, mirroring your own society—look at this a little."

K. If *Looking* is your least current film, which one would you say is your most "universal"?

M. First of all, I don't think you can start with the aim of reaching the "universal." But if you deal with subjects that come from your own guts, that you've felt deeply and that you express with real feeling, you have the possibility of reaching a universal public. This is true even if you employ the most specific events in your own history, your own characters, set in your own most remote areas. Taking all this into account, perhaps my most "universal" film is *Badis*—because, even today, there are still many requests for this film.[25]

FOUR FILMS COMPARED

"A GAME . . . A LOVE AFFAIR . . . NOSTALGIA . . .
A CHALLENGE"

K. You've used a number of different words to describe the making of your films but a notion that comes up again and again is that of "challenge." *The Big Trip* was a challenge because it was your first film; *Badis* because, partly in reaction to that first film, you wanted to master the unity of place and direct a number of different characters; *Looking* because, in focusing on the traditional bourgeoisie and using a humorous approach, you were making a very different kind of Moroccan film; *Lalla Hobby* was a challenge in so many different ways that I won't even begin to list them. What kind of challenges do you see in your filmmaking at the moment?

M. First of all, if I had to describe the experience of each film in one word, I would choose a different one for each. I would describe *The Big Trip* as a "game," a game I played with a great friend, we had a very amusing time and it was a real adventure, full of unpredictable moments; *Badis* was "a love affair" because I just fell in love with the setting; *Looking* was "nostalgia," a return home. *Lalla Hobby* is the film I would definitely qualify as "a challenge," for all the reasons we've discussed already.

K. And, just for the record, how would you qualify *Weshma*? Perhaps as "the great disillusion"? [Fr. *la grande désillusion*—I was making an obvious reference here to the well-known film by Jean Renoir *La Grande Illusion* (1937).]

M. Yes, that's very apt. I'd just add, "the great disillusion with collective effort."

THE FIFTH FILM: THE TEST OF AN ADAPTATION

"THE RELATIONSHIP WITH THE AUTHOR IS A CHALLENGE"

M. Of course you're right in saying that all my films constituted challenges in many different ways. But let's face it, if you want to reach higher in your work you always have to confront challenges.

My current project, *Abu Moussa's Women Neighbors*, involves a different kind of test because I'm trying a literary adaptation for the first time. One element in this is the difficulty of the book and the fact that its author isn't used to cinematic expression, visualization, and so on. So the relationship with the author is a challenge—how will he react to visual expression? Will he be shocked? Will he refuse to go forward?

K. Would you say working on this adaptation involves you more creatively than, for example, your work on *The Big Trip*?

M. Yes, definitely. And, while it makes sense to compare the work here with that on *The Big Trip*, because in both I'm starting out from someone else's conception, you also have to consider that I'm twenty years further along in my career and have developed a certain maturity in my approach. *The Big Trip* was my first film and the screenwriter and I weren't asking ourselves all these questions.

"HEADWORK" VERSUS "SPONTANEITY" AND "URGENCY"

K. You've talked about this adaptation as involving a lot of "headwork." What do you mean by that?

M. It means thinking, thinking all the time. When you have an urgent need to express something, this need comes from the heart. But when you're actually working the creation through, you reflect on what your heart wants to express and that reflection comes from the head. This involves a loss of that original momentum, a momentum that comes from youth, or a spirit of adventure, or perhaps even from your own naïveté. When you first start to paint a canvas, at the moment of inspiration you're elated; but then, as things go forward, you start to say, "On this canvas I have to express certain things over here, certain things over there," you begin to dissect everything. I want to express some-

The poster for *Abu Moussa's Women Neighbors*

thing in images, but what exactly do I want to express and how am I going to do it? And how will this be perceived? How will it be analyzed? You can really get fed up going through this kind of analysis.

On my earlier films I did things more or less automatically, there was a spontaneity and often a great deal of pleasure, as well as an urgency to create. With an adaptation the approach has to be different. Rather than starting with something from my own imagination, my own spontaneous, personal expression, I'm working with something that already exists, a text to be read and, in addition, one that had a lot of success and is really an excellent work of literature. For me this is a completely new kind of work, and I think it's new in Moroccan films too. I have to take that document and ruminate it, assimilate it, and then make it come out in the form of image and sound. And, what's more, I have to do this according to my own mold—after all, I want to bring something of my own to this creation and express things that concern me.

CODA: *ABU MOUSSA'S WOMEN NEIGHBORS*

Tazi's *Abu Moussa's Women Neighbors* (*Jaaraat Abi Moussa, Les voisines d'Abou Moussa*) was released in Moroccan theaters at the end of April 2003, too late for an extended discussion of it to be included in this book. Epic in style and thematically a confrontation between good and evil, the film is set in the fourteenth century and is marked by sumptuous ceremonial scenes, luxurious interiors, and impressive street processions with numerous extras, even displays of exotic animals. It recounts the radical transformations in the life of Chama, an angelic young slave girl working in an aristocratic household in Fez who, through events quite beyond her control, first rises to become the valued wife of one of the sultan's ministers; then, upon his death, she comes under the protection of the sultan's wife; then, as the balance of power among the leaders shifts, she is dispossessed and goes to live in an impoverished section of the city of Salé, among prostitutes and other marginal groups, while married to a poor but honest craftsman, a convert to Islam. Through it all, Chama retains her purity, piety, and sweetness and she develops a spiritual empathy with a mute, cave-dwelling Sufi, the eponymous Abu Moussa. The country is suffering through a period of great drought and all official prayers for rain have had no effect. Chama and Abu Moussa join in a supernatural complicity and together they perform the prayer for rain. The film ends with the skies unleashing a storm and blessing the land, relieving the misery of the poverty-stricken multitudes.

The film's shooting was marked by the usual share of "adventures"—for example, while Tazi knew he would have difficulty reconstructing a fourteenth-century urban environment in Salé (a city that neighbors the current capital Rabat), he did not anticipate the disturbance arising, not far away and sometimes directly overhead, when airplanes roared and explosions erupted as Ridley Scott filmed the U.S. blockbuster *Black Hawk Down;* nor did he foresee the freakish incident involving an ostrich he had leased for a procession scene—although he knew ostrich feathers were a prized ingredient of Moroccan witchcraft potions he did not imagine that the extras who shared the set with the bird would pluck so many of its feathers that it would expire even before the shooting ended.

Tragicomedy aside, the itinerary of *Abu Moussa's Women Neighbors* was hindered by more serious incidents. The film's shooting began in early September 2001 and was inevitably disrupted by the events of 11 September; then, less than two years later, shortly after it was released in the theaters in late April 2003, its theater life was drastically curtailed when Morocco experienced its own 11 September—a series of bombings that took place in Casablanca on 16 May and that killed more than forty people in five separate explosions. Following this tragedy, theater attendance plummeted throughout Morocco and *Abu Moussa's Women Neighbors* was taken off the marquee.

Critical response to the film during its brief screening ranged from high praise ("a beautiful historical fable," "a festival of costumes," "a very high quality of technical accomplishment,"[26] "an unleashing of dazzling images," "an abundance of fascinating characters," "a flood of unexpected plot twists"[27]) and suggestions that the film would make good family viewing, that it had "neither vulgarities nor gratuitous erotic scenes,"[28] to negative comments that pointed to its "dialogues . . . marked by slowness,"[29] to scenes "launched coldly, lacking resonance and passion . . . empty of tension . . . without sufficiently stimulating emotions."[30]

The film was doing poorly at the box office when it was withdrawn from the theaters following the events of 16 May. Despite the public's lukewarm response, Tazi stood by his decision to film a story set in the fourteenth century and to take on the onerous historical reconstruction that constituted a new departure both for him and in the Moroccan film corpus. As he said in one interview, "Going back into the historical past allows us to have some freedom in criticizing our contemporary situation. *Abu Moussa's Women Neighbors,* which takes place in the fourteenth century, can also be seen as related to the end of the nineteenth century. And as far as the twenty-first century goes, we can also read this film as commenting on the relationship between citizens and power structures and between the citizen and religion, on the internal wars we are engaged in, and on the problems we now face such as natural catastrophes (drought, flooding . . .)."[31]

One innovation Tazi practiced in *Abu Moussa's Women Neighbors* was shooting and editing the film digitally. This enabled a number of technical operations that would have been impossible otherwise and also affected the film's financing. As Tazi pointed out, shooting digitally allowed him to recreate aspects of fourteenth-century life that could not have been done with conventional filming—he noted, for example, that he was able to erase digitally the TV antennas and satellite dishes that are omnipresent in both Fez and Salé. Also, the film, in Tazi's words, "received no foreign aid. It was made entirely with Moroccan money, and above all with the aid of friends and institutions . . . to produce this film in the classical manner would have required at least double the budget, at the very least."[32] Joking to me in our last discussions, and repeating his point that making Moroccan films was an enterprise radically different from making Hollywood films, Tazi noted that the entire budget of *Abu Moussa's Women Neighbors* would barely have sufficed for ten seconds of *The Matrix Reloaded* (Andy and Larry Wachowski, 2003). At first I thought this an exaggeration but we performed a rough calculation and it proved him right.

Looking Ahead

Having asked Tazi to survey the changes in Moroccan cinema since independence, to assess his own career, and to position his films with regard to the work of other Moroccan filmmakers, I now wanted him to assess the future prospects for both Moroccan filmmaking and his own.

FROM "TESTAMENT"
TO "CONTINUITY"

"YOU END UP WITH FILMS THAT ARE COMPLACENT
AND ACCOMMODATING"

K. How do you feel in general about the prospects for Moroccan film-making?

M. Looking at the past from today's perspective, you see that in the early days making a film in Morocco was quite an adventure, very risky, very chancy. In such conditions, if you got the opportunity to make a film you were going to treat it as though it might be your last and try to put everything into it. Understandably, many filmmakers made this kind of film, the "testament" film, with allusions to their personal situation, the social situation, the political situation, and so on. They paid little or no attention to what might be the future of the film because they knew that, most of the time, it wouldn't even get out of its can! You made the film for yourself and for the pleasure of some friends, and they applauded because you all shared the same views.

But since then things have changed and lucky for that, too. Now when you think of making a film, you're thinking of continuity—completing the film, distributing it, getting the public to see it, and, hopefully, being able to make another film. This creates some movement in the machine and I think we're much closer to this continuity today than we ever were before.

There is a danger, though. People involved in making films may start to think, "Oh, this film was successful so we ought to make a similar film." In fact, this attitude is quite common in Morocco's popular theater where the central motivation is, "The public liked this, so let's please them again in the same way." This takes absolutely no account of the public's intelligence and it's no surprise that mediocrity in these productions is the rule. In the film sector this leads to films made without deep or sincere conviction.

This is one of the reasons I'm somewhat discouraged about our current film production. OK, now we're proud of producing up to nine or ten films a year, but it seems that we're moving toward a pauperization of production, toward films made to satisfy certain expectations, films that are like TV films. You see them and ask yourself, "What is the theme here, what is the reason for making such a film?" Instead of the film adding value to our art and culture it becomes a film made simply to please the public and, what's more, addresses the public in a demeaning manner. As a result, you end up with films that are complacent and accommodating, be they comedies or on social subjects. We're getting a lot of these. There's no sense in naming them but it's very evident that of the ten films we're trying to produce each year, only one or two really reflect a filmmaker's convictions and concerns.[33]

THE NEXT GENERATION

"CONFLICT BETWEEN OUR GENERATIONS . . . HAS BEEN
GREATLY EXAGGERATED"

K. There are now a number of filmmakers in the younger generation, whom many people take to be very promising in their short films and, in a few cases, in their feature films as well. What do you think of their prospects and how might this affect Moroccan filmmaking overall?[34]

M. I'm happy to talk about this younger generation as long as it doesn't involve abstracting from what has already been accomplished. Let's not forget that the people of my generation were the pioneers, we fought battle after battle to win each little advance. Look how many years it took us just to obtain the Support Fund and then the Aid Fund. And how many years since that to reach the situation we have now, where finally our films are sought out by the public.

Also, you have to consider that many of this younger generation have dual citizenship. This allows them to compete for funds both here and in their other country. This way, they have the advantage of being Moroccans when they're here in Morocco, without the disadvantages of being Moroccans when they're abroad. Just the ease with which they can travel, without all the annoying, time-wasting, and often humiliating visa procedures that we have to submit to—that advantage alone is considerable.

K. I sometimes get the feeling that this younger group is the object of some displeasure on the part of its elders, that they're treated as a group that parachutes in here while really being based abroad.

M. I think this question of conflict between our generations of filmmakers has been greatly exaggerated by the newspapers and other publications, which assert that this younger generation is going to give birth to a new Moroccan cinema. But, actually, this younger generation has never made that claim, they are in fact very aware of all the work that preceded them to get us to the point we are today. We of the older generation want nothing more than a group of people to continue our work and take it further; we can't stay around here forever and shouldn't try to protect our place and look at things conservatively. To the contrary: we need a new generation that brings its new blood, new energy. But they have to prove themselves on the screen, not on paper! Some have already shown substantial talent on the level of shorts, but it's a very big leap from shorts into feature films. Then there is someone like Ayouch,[35] who has indeed proven his talent in feature films.

"THIS NEW GENERATION . . . SHOULDN'T BE COMPOSED EXCLUSIVELY OF PEOPLE WHO LIVE ABROAD"

K. Does the fact that they come and compete with filmmakers based here in Morocco for the limited moneys in the Aid Fund pose a problem?

M. Not as far as support for short films goes, because these are part of a filmmaker's training, that's how you learn and money has to be available to encourage this. But you wouldn't want it to become a tradition to give feature film support to those residing abroad. It's great to have this new generation, but it shouldn't be composed exclusively of people who live abroad.

Also, we mustn't have our heads turned by some idea of a "universal cinema." There is such a thing as Moroccan society with its identity, and these people with their feet in two societies have to learn how to handle that.

AUDIENCE ATTITUDES

"WE CAN ACTUALLY REACH OUR PUBLIC . . . [BUT] WE DON'T HAVE TO MAKE FILMS *PRIMARILY* TO PLEASE THE AUDIENCE"

K. And how do you think the currently very positive relationship between Moroccan filmmaker and Moroccan audience might develop?

M. I think we've now reached a point in Moroccan filmmaking where we can actually reach our public with our films. Going to see a

Moroccan film has become something of a habit and, on the aesthetic level, on the narrative level, I think we're showing that we can have a viable cinema. With the support of this public we can start to lay the foundations of an industry—that means, we can start to build on a sense of continuity that we haven't had before. It's only when you have a considerable audience that you can start to deal with the distributors and exhibitors and convince them not to be too greedy.

My aim has never been to make films for a Spanish audience, or French, or English. You have to be reasonable. I make my films—I've said it before and I'll say it again—for a Moroccan audience first of all. It will give me greater pleasure if the film reaches a Maghreb audience but, as far as the Maghreb goes, there are a lot of avatars from the past that have to be corrected. I will have greater pleasure still if the film reaches a wider Arab audience. But here we've seen the kinds of problems that arise in trying to reach an Arab audience—even if these are often false problems that aren't even economic ones but of a so-called language and societal nature.

The most important thing for us now is to make films that bring the public out. But don't misunderstand me: we don't have to make films *primarily* to please the audience—it's perfectly possible to make films that don't please but that still bring the audience out to the theaters.

"THE FREEDOM OF THE PAINTER"

"Ideally . . . no restrictions, prior orientations, or directives to satisfy"

K. And, in the current situation, what do you hope for regarding your own future as a filmmaker?

M. Ideally, what I'd like to do is make films where I can invest myself fully, where the subject grips me, where I'm not out to please either the public or the producer or anyone else. It would be the freedom of the painter in front of the canvas, with no restrictions, prior orientations, or directives to satisfy, and certainly no obligations to make a film according to the requirements of others. Unfortunately, we can't say that the conditions of filmmaking in Morocco at this point allow that kind of freedom.

Refocus: Wider Angle, Smaller Screen
SOCIETY MOVES QUICKLY

Tazi's use of the word "ideally" in the previous thought showed his recognition that such freedom was not a realistic expectation in today's Morocco; nor, perhaps, was it a realistic expectation for the foreseeable future. In any case, Tazi's search for fulfillment in his profession took a radically different course in the summer of 2000 and it is this shift that will occupy us now.

Already in the fall of 1998, when I first met Tazi, he was preparing his next film, *Abu Moussa's Women Neighbors*.[36] First he negotiated with the author for the rights and then, after several false starts, found a screenwriter whose talents suited his needs.[37] In late 1999 Tazi submitted his proposal to the Commission on Aid to Production and learned, after its meeting, that he had received funding to the amount of 3,500,000 DH, the highest award ever given by the commission. He then began to move ahead quickly, hoping to be able to shoot in late spring or early fall 2000 and then, after another two to three months in postproduction, to have the film out in the theaters by the end of that winter, at the latest.[38]

Tazi moves quickly, but the society around him was moving quickly too. With the new coalition government coming into power in 1998 and the new king on the throne since mid-1999, new positions were being created and old positions were being filled with new people. Noureddin Sail, whose name has come up at several points in this book, was one of the new people called upon to fill an old position: in April 2000 King Muhammad VI chose him to run Morocco's second television channel, 2M.[39] In making this appointment, the king was inserting one of the country's most dynamic cultural figures into a key media position and, from one day to the next, the media landscape in Morocco took on a brighter hue. In the year following his appointment, 2M had succeeded not only in winning approximately a 65 percent share of Moroccan stations' audience but had gained between 5 and 7 percent of the satellite television audience. It had also shown an increase in advertising revenue of more than 35 percent, far above its previous annual increases of around 20 percent.[40]

When we recall that Sail, Tazi's junior by about five years, had written and produced Tazi's first film, had been screenwriter on his second and fourth, had frequently called upon Tazi to participate in his television program, and that Tazi referred to Sail as his "great" or "constant friend," it comes as no surprise that, in mid-June 2000, barely two months after his own appointment, Sail called upon Tazi to become part of 2M's new management team and to take up the key post of production director. This position was crucial for implementing Sail's plans to transform the channel from one that simply retransmitted programs produced abroad to one that would begin to produce its own. As production director, Tazi became responsible for creating the channel's production capacity and overseeing all its efforts in producing and commissioning programs.[41]

Tazi's move into television is easily understandable in light of his experience across the audiovisual field and in light of his deep interest in communication. Also, in his role as 2M's director of production, he was not abandoning film production but was, as we will see, playing a different role. For us, Tazi's change of position has the advantage of providing a natural opportunity to explore the relationship between filmmaking and the wider audiovisual field. To begin this exploration, I first asked him to describe the nature of his new position and the kinds of adjustments this required him to make; then I wondered how he saw the relationship between television and filmmaking; and, finally, I asked him how this new position might affect his own filmmaking.

"PRODUCING IN QUANTITY"

"A MORE AMBITIOUS VISION"

K. First of all, could you describe to me exactly what your responsibilities are as program director and how these fit in with the basic orientation of the channel?

M. As director of production, I'm in charge of all the programs the channel produces, whether we produce them ourselves or subcontract to external producers. I supervise building an entire production department from zero and retraining a number of technicians for production functions, so that we can produce one TV film per month, co-produce Moroccan feature films, as well as produce a certain number of subcontracted programs. Producing for TV means producing in quantity. As a whole, we now produce many programs in-house, including variety, news, political programs, a game, a cooking show, and so on. Our one TV film per month is a good beginning and I hope we can eventually reach one per week.

The new emphasis on production fits into a broader plan, a more ambitious vision for the station and for the audiovisual field. We want the station's transmissions to cover the entire Moroccan territory, we want to begin satellite transmission, to transmit in both Arabic and French with a better balance between the two languages, and to develop production in all domains, such as dramas, TV films, news, documentaries. Also, we'll be setting up a radio station and an Internet portal, planned to go into operation during the first trimester of 2001. And since October 2000 we've been transmitting twenty-four hours a day. I also should say that when you talk of a "normal" channel, you also mean boosting advertising revenues and eventually living from advertising alone.[42]

"I DIDN'T HESITATE AT ALL"

K. The move to 2M meant a radical change in your life, both as regards your central activity and your lifestyle. You shifted from a freelance, self-employed filmmaker to holding a managerial position in a large organization with almost six hundred employees. Did you have any hesitation about accepting Noureddin's offer?

M. No, not really. You know that TV communication has always interested me, and I had some important experiences in TV working with Noureddin earlier, as well as in Spain. So, when this opportunity presented itself, I took it without any hesitation, even though I was in the last stages of preparing the shooting of my film. The opportunity was just too interesting to turn down. I'm always rather militant when it's a question of being on the front lines to create something. And for me, this battle to create a TV production capacity, and the other battles in the audiovisual field that would be joined in the context of 2M, are crucial ones. Add to this that Noureddin and I have very similar views regarding the audiovisual field and that after his long absence it was a real pleasure to have him back in the country and to be able to work with him again. So no, I didn't hesitate at all.

TV AND CINEMA

TV FILMS, FEATURE FILMS

K. How would you compare the two contexts of filmmaking—TV and cinema?

M. Generally speaking, producing for TV and for the cinema are two completely different things. I could start by saying that when you're making a feature film in the circumstances we have here in Morocco, it becomes a kind of micro-affair: you have to think it over, prepare it, shoot it, postproduce it, and all that requires a long period. From the moment of conception until the film is out in the theaters can easily take three or four years.

For TV films the means are different. First of all, we work with two, three, or four cameras, sometimes even more, and you gain a lot of time. Also, with the camera's mobility and all the practical possibilities that video offers, shooting is much, much quicker. Third, there are all kinds of possibilities in postproduction: you can do things much more quickly—you don't have to wait for the film to come back from the lab, then get a positive print, then go to the editing table. With TV you just take the cassette out of the camera, go straight to postproduction, and start dressing it as you want.

Also, there are significant differences in budget. The total cost for a TV film lasting one and a half hours is somewhere between 800,000 to 1,000,000 DH, counting the equipment, the human contribution, the industrial contribution and so on. The normal budget for a feature film, on the other hand, is in the neighborhood of 4,000,000 DH. So, for a TV film you're not going to conceive of subjects that are a big burden financially, such as historical films or ones that require reconstituting historical circumstances, although obviously some of the European channels do this. In our situation, we would be choosing subjects that are more "social," that involve situations of proximity, treating subjects that directly concern our audience.

Taking all these considerations together, you can shoot a TV film in three weeks and do editing and postproduction in another two. All in all, once you've got the script, you can get a TV film completed, from start to finish, in under two months.

TV SUPPORT FOR FEATURE FILMS

K. I know that one of 2M's main aims is to encourage the production of Moroccan feature films. How would you assess its role?

M. I think we all recognize that TV is nourished by the cinema. No matter what channel people watch, their viewing is dominated by fiction, that is to say, by the cinema. So it makes perfect sense for TV to support the cinema.

Over the last several years, up to mid-2003, 2M has already co-produced about a dozen Moroccan feature films that also benefited from the Aid Fund, some made by established filmmakers like Farida Benlyazid, Jilali Ferhati, and Abdelkader Lagtaa, some by members of the younger generation—Faouzi Ben Saidi, Narjiss Nejjar, Hassan Legzouli, among others. One of the films 2M supported was *Ali Zaoua* by the young filmmaker Nabil Ayouch, which won the prize for best film at the Sixth National Film Festival in 2001 and also won many international prizes. 2M's contribution is always in the neighborhood of 400,000 DH, which is far from negligible and represents somewhere between one-third and one-fifth of what the film gets from the Aid Fund. This sum really helps the filmmakers get the film off the ground, because we give them three-quarters of the money when the shooting starts. Then, of course, the station also supports the film by programming it one year after its national theater release.

TAZI'S FILMMAKING FUTURE

However interested Tazi may have been in this particular role in production, with regard to his plans to complete his next film, *Abu Moussa's Women Neighbors,* this appointment came at a most inopportune moment. Under the pressure of his work at 2M, he had to delay his film's schedule, and then delay it again. As the summer of 2001 approached, Tazi confronted an immovable deadline— the eighteen-month time limit the Aid Fund imposes from the time of the award until the time shooting begins, beyond which the funds are irrevocably withdrawn. Under this pressure, he decided to begin shooting the film in the summer of 2001, a time of the year most filmmakers like to avoid because of the hot weather.

Over several weeks during my visit to Morocco in January and February 2001, Tazi continued working full-time at 2M, even while preparing his film. This meant that most of his weekends were involved either in scouting locations, lining up personnel for the shooting, preparing the script breakdown, the shot breakdown, or in any of the other tasks necessary for moving the film forward. He felt an urgent need to have more time available for this preparation and was "negotiating" with Sail, at a first stage, to obtain a driver for his daily commute—it took approximately one hour to drive from his home in Rabat to the channel's base in Casablanca—so that he could get another couple of hours work done en route and, at a second stage, to be granted free time when he actually began shooting. Nor did it make things easier when, in January and February, an anthropologist asked for a few hours of his time several evenings a week and once or twice on the weekend. Somehow, Tazi seemed to find the time for all these activities.

"A FILM ROUGHLY EVERY FOUR TO FIVE YEARS"

K. With your time so fully occupied with 2M, what do you think are the prospects for your career as a filmmaker?

M. The rhythm of my film career is already well established—I can make a film roughly every four to five years. Between one film and the next, the time is partly filled by the gestation and prep- aration of a film and partly filled by my other audiovisual activities in the areas of multimedia, institutional films, advertising films, or, in this case, in the field of TV.[43]

Where there's something to build I'm always more or less ready to give it my best effort. Entering TV upstream in the pro- duction process, doing what I call "macro-production," putting into practice some of what I studied years ago in the field of mass communications, is enriching on a general level and it's certainly enriching for me. It's also a wonderful opportunity to utilize all the new techniques and modes of communication other than those involved in the large screen. You learn an enormous amount about the audience, about production, about the people who ac- tually make the TV work. It's very, very stimulating.

"2M . . . OCCUPIES *ALL* MY TIME"

K. Don't you feel a little too dispersed in your activities?

M. No, not dispersed exactly, but it is true that 2M requires an enor- mous amount of time—in fact, it occupies *all* my time and doesn't give me time for anything else. And I absolutely *must* shoot this film before the end of June 2001 or I'll have to forgo all the Aid Fund money. Those are the rules.

K. Given 2M's demands, how will you find the five weeks or so for the shooting and then another couple of months for the intensive work of postproduction?

M. At the level of shooting my presence is absolutely necessary. At the level of postproduction this is less true, because this time we're going to do the editing digitally. With digital editing I can get to see the results at any moment and can question and change things easily. So it will be more a question of supervising and monitoring instead of the continual participation that mechanical editing requires.

K. So what you said to me last year about never leaving an editor alone with your film for more than ten minutes is no longer true?

M. With mechanical editing, it's almost impossible to call into question editing that has already been performed—the little bits of film that have been cut and rejected are often nowhere to be found. But with digital editing, you can call anything into question at any point and, even more important, you can make the changes very quickly. Where digital video editing is concerned you don't have to worry about irremediable changes, because you can always retrieve the "cut" images and because you can easily construct the same scene thirty-six different ways.

"WHAT'S CRUCIAL IS THE FREEDOM WE NOW HAVE TO CONSTRUCT"

K. Without trying too much to predict the future, how do you see things in the near future, say over the next couple of years?

M. Well, I'm someone who works from passion. That means when I'm motivated and love my work, I'm absolutely plunged into it and I can go for fourteen hours straight. But if the work starts to bore me or I see that it's not bringing me anything and that I'm not giving it anything, I drop it pretty quickly. For the moment I'm working from passion and I only hope that this continues as long as possible, and that the policy of our management team continues to be in the direction of greater democracy, opening, freedom of expression. If I start to find too many obstacles in the way I'd have to reconsider my participation.

What's crucial is the freedom we now have to construct a TV that goes in the direction we've traced and the fact that, in Noureddin's appointment, our highest institutions have given their approval to this direction. As long as we have this opening and these possibilities, I think I'll continue to be impassioned by the work. The day that I'm muzzled or my room for maneuver is restricted, I'll probably have to withdraw.

Anyway, I'm a free man and I've expressed this freedom all throughout my career. I've never accepted being a push button nor have I wanted to be an administrator with an ambition to mount the hierarchy. I've always been someone who wanted to express things and I intend to remain that way.

Conclusion

Future Flights of the Bumblebee

Introduction: Closing Questions

Early in our talks, sitting across from me on the sofa in his study, Tazi had encapsulated the central paradox of Moroccan filmmaking by comparing it to the flight of the bumblebee, saying, "according to the laws of aeronautics, it's impossible for that insect to fly. But bumblebees fly just the same! That's just the way it is for our cinema . . . we can't make films but, just the same, we make films!"

Moroccan and other Third World cinemas operate today in very turbulent conditions, marked by significant national events and by far-reaching developments on a world scale in technology, economics, politics, and culture. There is little consensus about the deeper implications of these developments: some will argue that nowadays, across the globe, we all communicate easily and almost instantaneously with one another, that we are increasingly living in one "global village" (a phrase Tazi often uses, but always sardonically); others counter by saying that while these "globalizing" trends may well ease some paths of communication, they hinder or even obstruct others, and that creators in peripheral locations have ever-growing difficulty communicating with publics both within and across national borders, as they face competition from internationally produced and distributed works that have immense financial backing. In these circumstances, what is the likelihood that Tazi, other Moroccan filmmakers, and Third World filmmakers in general will be able to continue to produce films and that these films will "fly" toward their own national and perhaps even international audiences?

To explore these and related questions we need to assess Tazi's work, which means looking more closely at the style and appeal of his films and at his directorial practice, many aspects of which shed light on broader issues of Third World filmmaking and creative activity. Following this, we will turn to examine the prospects for Moroccan cinema and its place within the global film industry. Questions on these three levels—a film career and the films that mark it, the national context within which these are (largely) carried forward, and the global industry that has so great an influence on them—extend those with which we opened this book and that have shaped it from beginning to end.[1]

However, these questions were not set up prior to or even at the outset of this research project but emerged as the project proceeded, in the course of a specific encounter between anthropologist and filmmaker, each carrying with him his own blend of individual, professional, and societal interests. Before we turn to discuss Tazi's work, we should therefore explore the disciplinary context of this project and the way in which the encounter has influenced the outcome.

Anthropology, Filmmaker, Anthropologist

A mere forty years ago, an anthropological study such as this one would not have been possible: not only was the independence of Third World countries in its early days and Moroccan filmmaking not yet born but, on a more modest level, the discipline of anthropology paid little, if any, attention to the creative aspects of film and the audiovisual. However, in the past two decades anthropological concern with these subjects has grown, in part related to a major reorientation in the discipline that involves (but is not limited to) deepening interest in (1) expressive activity (an outgrowth of what used to be called the "anthropology of art"), (2) industrial societies (where the relationship and distinction between "high culture" and "popular culture" are posed), (3) "popular culture" itself (related to the two expanding fields of "cultural studies" and "media studies"), and (4) the notion of culture as a "text" (encouraging anthropologists to look at cultural products, such as films, much as they might look at myth, ritual, or any of the more "traditional" objects of anthropological study). In this context, it is only natural that the study of audiovisual fiction (whether in cinema, television, video, or other), of the worlds it conveys and the worlds from which it issues, would expand too.[2]

In addition, over the past two decades, anthropologists have frequently raised questions of "reflexivity" that call for a questioning of their discipline and their role within it: How is an anthropological text constructed? How does it "represent," give voice to, incorporate the presence of the "other" and the "self"? What is the nature of the "intersubjective reality" that particular encounters between anthropologists and informants lead to and how does that reality come about? Who is the "author" of an anthropological text and how does this text embody, reflect, and/or challenge the cultural and societal interests that lie behind its production?[3] Thinking reflexively leads us to ask a number of similar questions concerning this project: How has this particular encounter between Dwyer and Tazi, each with his own configuration of personal, professional, and cultural dispositions, structured the domain of inquiry? What are the strengths of this construction and what are its weaknesses? What does it enable us to say about Tazi's and Moroccan forms of cultural expression and their place in the global domain? Perhaps just as importantly, what are some of the areas left unexplored?[4]

Comparing this book to two others I have referred to before—John Huston's *An Open Book* and the Welles-Bogdanovich collaboration *This Is Orson Welles*—may help us highlight its particular orientation and the kind of anthropology it embodies, as well as suggest the contribution this anthropological approach may make to our understanding of Moroccan and Third World filmmaking. The three books exemplify a rather densely populated genre, where the focus is on a particular filmmaker's films and career, and all three, in the weight they give to the filmmaker's own words, differ from books in which the critic's voice dominates, where analysis, explanation, and interpretation have pride of place. Yet within this small group of three, each is distinct from the others both in content and in form.

Huston's is the director's monologue, recounting a wealth of very interesting experiences, fascinating to the reader who knows the films and who wishes to learn about the deals and adventures that occurred "in the wings." Bogdanovich—a filmmaker himself—engages Welles in dialogues that span more than a decade, probing from the perspective of his own detailed professional knowledge a man who comes across, not only in his film output but also on almost every page of the book, as a true "original" in the best sense of the word.[5]

Tazi comes to the reader differently from either Huston or Welles: certainly in his own words (translated, however, which raises issues on another level) but discussing his films, his career, and the circumstances within which these were carried forward, in answers to questions posed by an anthropologist with a particular life path—someone whose questions inevitably reflect his own concerns. The focus on the economic, historical, institutional, and cultural context within which Tazi works, and the particular motifs highlighted in our discussions of his films, are just some of the obvious signs of these concerns. Let me now suggest a few specific ways in which my own cultural, professional, and personal inclinations have contributed to constructing this material.

DISCOURSE-TIME, STORY-TIME, RESEARCH-TIME

In studies of narrative and, more particularly, of film, a distinction is often made between "story-time" (the sequence of plot events) and "discourse-time" (how these events are presented in the actual text or film).[6] There is an anthropological counterpart to "discourse-time": the frequently used and consciously invoked fiction of the "ethnographic present" where, in the effort to present the reader with a coherent "story," the anthropologist places the representation in a relatively simultaneous time frame. Reliance on the "ethnographic present" has at least one important shortcoming: it often leads the reader, and sometimes the anthropologist-writer too, to infer that the life portrayed "in the present" was relatively timeless— similar to life in the past and likely to resemble very much life in the future. This is unlikely ever to have been true, but it is certainly false in the domain of Moroccan cinema, changing even as I write this and no doubt continuing to change in the future.[7]

In this book I have neither constructed "discourse-time" as an ethnographic present, nor have I been fully faithful to the "story-time" of Tazi's life by following a strict chronological presentation. The book's structure mixes elements of both. The opening chapter's discussion of *Looking* focuses on a period in the mid-1990s—a watershed in Moroccan film history—when that most popular film was released and when the public first began to show strong support for Moroccan films. Then, as in a flashback, we enter Tazi's youth, follow his own career in mostly chronological order, then bypass *Looking* as we move into the present.

Yet this "discourse-time," while bearing some relation to the "story-time" of Tazi's career, bears little relation to the actual order in which the interviews took place and in which questions were posed, a temporal sequence we might term "research-time" and that would have its counterpart in a film's shooting schedule. Arranged here in a "fictional" sequential order, the interviews have, of course, been fragmented, edited, and recomposed.[8] It is only in the final chapter that "story-time," "discourse-time," and "research-time" come together: this final chapter presents our final formal interviews, held in January and February 2001, after Tazi had taken up a position in television and as he was nearing the shooting of his fifth feature. This particular combination of "fictions" is designed to avoid the worst drawbacks of the "ethnographic present" and to tell a "story" that is both relatively coherent and relatively faithful to the complexity of experience.

CONSTRUCTING THE SUBJECT, CONSTRUCTING THE FIELD

Tazi's words in this book are detailed and self-referential, necessarily so because my questions pushed him in these directions. In our discussions of his films I chose motifs that reflected my own concerns: the position of women; the colonial experience and the relationship between Morocco and "the West"; how the creative effort is shaped by a specific economic, political, and cultural context; and so on.[9] Both these considerations—how the interview material is structured and how context is defined and presented—are evidence of a mixture of Tazi's purposes and mine, sometimes blending as in a cocktail, sometimes bouncing off one another as billiard balls do, sometimes interwoven so finely that it is impossible to distinguish whose hand is responsible. To take one example, the overall pace of this book, which I hope to be leisurely (what Tazi might refer to as an "Oriental rhythm," although I would not use this term), may reflect such a blending, allowing the reader to become immersed in worlds very different from and yet in many ways similar to his or her own, with some of the benefits both of the close-up and the gradual building of familiarity.

Our mixture of purposes no doubt went deeper than form. Just as it is to the filmmaker's advantage to be taken seriously, to become the subject of a book, it is to the anthropologist's advantage to find and represent a subject suitable for a book. As a result, both parties to the encounter are to some extent subject to the encounter's imperatives, constructing themselves both as "useful" and as "sympathetic" to the other, and constructing the other in corresponding ways, too. This may all appear obvious once stated directly; nonetheless, this complicitous dynamic is rarely raised.[10]

However, while some aspects of the encounter no doubt obey our will, many escape it and the encounter proceeds, veers, drifts, or ruptures, according to each actor's complex configuration of partly conscious, partly unconscious, emotions, perceptions, and intentions. It is beyond my purpose here, and perhaps my capacity, to discuss Tazi's views on these deeper aspects of the encounter although there is much that can be read into his lines as well as between them. But I would like now to discuss my own views of our encounter, to the extent that I have become aware of them, in the hope this will help the reader (and myself as well) assess what I have to say about Tazi's personality, films, and career.

A PERSONAL VIEW

Initially purely professional, my relationship with Tazi naturally grew more personal as time went on. Although it occasionally hinted at a level of "intimacy" it never lingered there nor, knowing Tazi (and the anthropologist) as we now do, would we expect it to. Throughout our period together Tazi was always generous with his time, friendly but never presumptuously so, never betraying a hint of false ingratiation. He had given dozens of interviews before, was well practiced in his approach to them, and he was always aware, or almost so, that anything he said might be published. Consequently, he was more or less in full control of the dialectic between "intimacy" and "reserve." These controls eased partially over time: for example, after I made it clear that I was not interested in "gossip" and that I was unlikely to write about it, Tazi began to express himself more freely on that level; also, as this book neared completion, we began to talk more about matters other than film—politics and family life among them. Taken all in all, we may see Tazi as initially rather guarded but more open as time went on (an understandable progression and no doubt not that different from the anthropologist), less than "complete" perhaps (but who could convincingly claim to be otherwise?), but not necessarily less sincere for that. On the whole I came away from these many interviews and from my immersion in Morocco's film world with a deep appreciation for Tazi's historic importance in Moroccan cinema, an abiding admiration for two of his films, a fondness for a third (*The Big Trip*), and a sharper understanding of the difficulties of his disappointing fourth (*Lalla Hobby*). I also greatly valued the relationship we had developed over our time together.[11]

When I asked myself what, in addition to the quality of his work and his contribution to Moroccan cinema, accounted for the sympathy I felt, I could do no better than recall a previous experience I had had in Morocco and that had led to my first book, which was the study of a Moroccan village seen primarily through the eyes of a venerable Moroccan farmer, Faqir Muhammad. That earlier relationship was much more intense—I spent most of two years with Faqir Muhammad and his family, eating with them almost daily, accompanying them to the fields, to the markets, to family gatherings and celebrations, and to many other events. Although my interviews with Tazi took place over a similar stretch of time, we met mostly in well-defined interview settings and we were in actual conversation over periods that, combined, totaled only several months. In the earlier relationship there was a clear contrast between elder and youth—Faqir Muhammad was in his 60s and I then in my late 20s—and clear differences in education, occupation, personal histories . . . the list could go on. Tazi and I, on the other hand, were quite close in age, we each had spent significant periods on the same three continents, and we each had studied in higher educational institutions to learn our respective crafts.

There were certainly very significant differences between Tazi and me in background, interests, orientation, profession, and personality. Yet the structural resemblances of our respective professional activities were striking. Just as the Moroccan filmmaker embarks on a particular project with little or no hope of material gain, with no assurance that the film will be distributed and, even if it is, that it will be viewed by more than a few thousand people, and just as he or she spends several years and a great deal of effort canvassing for funds and preparing and making the film (in some cases, as we have seen, at great risk to health, finances, and human relationships), so does the anthropologist spend years submitting proposals, carrying out research, reading, and writing, with no direct material gain, no assurance that the book will be published or, if it is, that it will reach its desired public.[12]

Faqir Muhammad and Muhammad Abderrahman Tazi, too, for all their differences, had much in common. In their very different domains, each carried a deep personal engagement toward the society around him, each embodied the living history of his profession and each was able to speak of his experiences with seriousness and laughter, as well as with a winning mixture of moral conviction—even self-righteousness—and a definite generosity toward others. Both, too, were the objects of heightened emotions on the part of their contemporaries—complex feelings of admiration, jealousy, and resentment—which is often the lot of people with substantial achievements to their credit.

That I came to concentrate on both Faqir Muhammad and Muhammad Abderrahman Tazi in their two very disparate contexts and to spend a considerable portion of my time with them—without, in fact, having had that as a research objective at the outset in either case—also provides a commentary on my approach to anthropology, as well as on my own personal inclinations: that, in the effort to learn about a vast field of human activity, it can be enormously arresting and stimulating to explore it in close-up, through a focus, intense and prolonged, on the vision of one key person within it. Doing so seems to me to be an extremely fruitful way to pursue what I believe to be one of anthropology's primary aims, that of establishing communication between worlds, making lived experience as it appears in one site accessible to people living in another.

Tazi's Distinctive Features, Tazi in the World

Without diminishing Tazi's uniqueness—on the contrary, this book is largely an exploration of it—I now want to put Tazi's work in perspective, beginning with his upbringing and particular cultural background, then placing his career in the framework of Morocco's film institutions and national history, and of regional, continental and global film structures. From there we will go on to examine the appeal and style of Tazi's films, his directorial practice, and then review, concisely, his "vision."

A CAREER'S IRONIES

Tazi was born into the Fassi bourgeoisie, a relatively wealthy social class with a deep historical tradition of representing "high" Moroccan culture. Today, Tazi's love of "fine" objects is reflected not only in his film's sets, props, and design and the care he lavishes on them but also in his elegant yet functional villa on the outskirts of Rabat, the walls of which display a large number of modern Moroccan paintings, many done by his good friends (juxtaposed with playful paintings by his children and, discreetly placed, posters from his films). In a display cabinet in his dining room is a valuable collection of old cameras, reflecting his training as a cinematographer and his fascination with well-wrought instruments. In the several different rooms he uses as offices are some of the latest tools of his trade, including computers with digital video editing capabilities.

The relative wealth and "high" taste of his milieu of origin served Tazi as springboard—without them he would have been much less likely to earn a baccalaureate in the very early years of independence and less likely too to gain admission to the Institute for Higher Film Studies (IDHEC) in Paris. This milieu also serves as a main pole of attraction, one that he tries, in some sense, both to return to and reconstruct. Had his origins been elsewhere in Morocco, would he have been as likely to develop the love for fine, artistic work that he strives to embody in his films? Would he have been as likely to feel as deeply about "identity" and "heritage" and to formulate and exemplify these themes in the ways he has?[13]

Within its national framework Tazi's career provides, as we have seen, a commentary on the general development of Moroccan national life since independence. A member of the first Moroccan generation to be formally trained in filmmaking, Tazi was an early participant in the process of building national competence. Tazi's work over more than a decade within the state institution of the CCM, first making documentaries and then becoming director of its weekly news review, contributed significantly to the filmed images that were providing Morocco with some of its most formative and integrating impressions. That he afterward turned to freelance audiovisual contracts, to assisting on foreign productions, and then to making his own feature films, testifies to the growing but always unsure strength of the Moroccan film sector and to its changing relationship to the national audience. The financing of his films, too, followed changes and developments in the film sector, with his first two films benefiting from the initial form of state aid (the Support Fund), his next two from the subsequent form (the Aid Fund), and with several of these films also gaining financing from abroad in the form of international co-productions, with some of the tensions that seem inherent in this pattern.

Yet it would be a mistake to see Tazi's career as a one-dimensional reflection of the national film sector's development, for it is a career filled with ironies that provide a deeper and more ambivalent commentary on the situation of many Moroccan and Third World filmmakers. Furthermore, although we might expect these ironies to diminish or resolve themselves as his career progresses and attains its undeniable successes, they appear on the contrary to become sharper, reflecting in a complex way the problematic nature of Moroccan cinema.

There is a first, foundational, irony: that someone trained in a filmmaking specialty at considerable state (and personal) expense has been obliged to spend much (and perhaps most) of his time in ancillary activities such as fund-raising and other production tasks as well as taking on many assignments simply to earn a living. There is the related irony that Tazi makes only five feature films over two and a half decades, which nonetheless ranks him among Morocco's most prolific filmmakers. Then, in each of the four films we have explored here, there is the irony of a filmmaker torn between his desire to captivate the audience with a story and his wish to explore issues of acute social significance, between his wanting to give in to the story's narrative and symbolic power yet also to control the message his film will convey, between his deep need to amuse and transport the audience yet to communicate with and instruct it too.

We then reach the rich ironies embodied in the making of his fifth film, in preparation during the period of our interviews. For this project he receives the highest amount of state funding ever awarded but, consumed by the obligations of a new job, he is unable to devote the time and energy necessary to secure all the additional funds he desired. This fifth film—a historical reconstruction—may promote his notions of patrimony and identity, instilling life into valued objects and practices from Morocco's heritage, yet this film is made digitally, perhaps contributing to the erosion of valued aspects of his own craft's heritage—the "touch of film," say, or the achievement of subtle shadings in lighting. To what extent does his use of these new techniques reinforce his vision or, on the other hand, undermine it?

Finally, there is the crowning irony embodied in this stage of his career: a filmmaker who has struggled to promote the feature film now turns toward television production, which many see as cinema's main competitor, at just the moment when Moroccan cinema seems launched on a period of expansion—in quantity certainly but perhaps in quality too. This irony is an open-ended and inconclusive one: Is filmmaking losing primacy in his life just when it might have had its best opportunities? Is the turn toward television a sign of continuing domination of the large screen by the small (as is the case throughout the Third World, where governments quickly appreciated the capacity of television to directly address the population and for the most part avoided promoting the national cinema's capacity to do so)? Or does it herald, perhaps, a new mutually enhancing relationship between the two screens along the lines of the French model, in which television's support for financing and distribution is essential to the film sector's health?

Ironies subvert the simplicity of categories and are a sign that categories themselves, however necessary they may be to our thinking, are reductive interpretations of realities that are always much more complex. One example: Tazi's career is emblematically "Moroccan," yet to call it "Moroccan" implies neither insularity nor clear boundaries between "inside" and "outside," between "authentic" and "hybrid," between "local" and "global"—indeed, as we have seen, both Tazi's career and the place of Moroccan cinema in the world push us to question the meaning of these paired terms and the meaning of the term "Moroccan" as well.

TAZI'S WORK AND THE THIRD WORLD CONTEXT

In his openness to the world beyond his nation's borders, Tazi follows an imperative of his condition as a Third World citizen: an aspiring filmmaker must go abroad to gain advanced training and to hire some of the specialists needed to finish a film. Yet Tazi's career testifies too, as does that of many Third World filmmakers, to a deep and abiding loyalty and sense of obligation to his own nation and people, in part a product of the painful historical injuries suffered during colonial rule, in part due to the continuing effects of today's gross imbalances in power and resources on the international level. Both of these aspects provide a commentary on the specific nature of globalizing trends when seen from the perspective of a Third World citizen: societies are indeed increasingly integrated into a world system but, as in the past, that system is characterized by systematically unequal flows of resources, opportunities, and benefits, and these imbalances are likely to obtain for a long time into the future. Tazi's work—and this is true for that of most Third World creative artists—participates, by its very existence, in the struggle to redress these inequalities, because it expresses universal human qualities of innovation and productivity and reflects the creator's refusal to be relegated to the relatively passive role of consumer.

Attempts to generalize about creative activity in the Third World are no doubt bound to fail, but it is nonetheless worth pointing out that, while Moroccan cinema possesses some traits common to Third World film sectors, neither it nor Tazi's work within it fits easily into the broad sequence that has been suggested for African cinema as a whole: first, that of a "committed, engaged" cinema prolonging into the 1980s the élan of the early years of independence; then, with the new nation-state's efforts to solve many basic social and societal problems miscarrying—what has often been called the "failure of the development paradigm"—a turn to more "novelistic" approaches; that is, more personal, subjective, and paradoxical representational modes.[14]

It is indeed true that during the first decades of Moroccan independence there was profound and widespread enthusiasm for the nationalist project; filmmakers shared this enthusiasm and, in the documentary and news sectors (the only areas of national film production for more than a decade), directly participated in the project of nation building. However, as feature film production began to take hold in the early 1970s, it did not reflect in any transparent manner the aims of "nation building," either in theme or in style. "Engaged" and "committed" Moroccan filmmakers certainly were during this early period, but with the aim of building a national cinema as a sign *of* nationhood, rather than attempting to mobilize the population *for* nationhood (a function partially fulfilled by the short films of an educational or documentary nature). This latter aim could not in any case have been a realistic one for makers of feature films, given that the private control of distribution and exhibition made it impossible for the emerging Moroccan cinema to meet and have any real purchase on its public. It was a stage similar to what Bourdieu has called the "heroic period" in the construction of an artistic field, when the position of "art for art's sake" is first staked out.[15]

Filmmakers' lack of direct access to their national audience no doubt had a deep stylistic effect on many Third World filmmakers of this period, including Moroccans like Tazi—it necessarily placed them in an "auteur" stance, with films made for the directors themselves and others in the film world rather than for a wider public. This led one African film commentator to suggest that "African films are foreigners in their own countries."[16] If it is indeed accurate to say that during the 1980s a number of African filmmakers adopted more "novelistic" approaches (in the sense referred to previously), such approaches were already being put into practice by Moroccan filmmakers in the 1970s and have been a strong characteristic of productions in subsequent decades.

TAZI'S FILMS: APPEAL AND STYLE; DIRECTORIAL PRACTICE

APPEAL AND STYLE

The Three "V's": Voyeur, Visceral, Vicarious

One writer (himself a documentary filmmaker) has schematized neatly three kinds of appeal a film may possess: "voyeur" appeal, allowing us to see things we cannot ordinarily see—the appeal of the "prying observer"; "visceral" appeal, bringing us close to experiences that are exciting, shocking, terrifying, that arouse our species being, that bring forth "the gut reactions of the lizard brain"; and "vicarious" appeal, enabling us to share in another person's deep emotions, that "puts our heart in the actor's body."[17]

Tazi's cinema is not meant to have voyeur appeal. We may indeed witness events we wouldn't otherwise see, but Tazi is reluctant to "pry," to violate intimacy. Indeed, for Tazi, intimacy has something of the sacred about it: as a relationship between the individual and a privileged realm of being, it is an intensely private experience not to be disrupted by an outsider's intrusion. The camera, and through the camera the audience, has no right to gain access to this domain and Tazi deliberately argues and works against violating it.

No doubt Tazi is here "reflecting" in some way notions of decency as they are articulated and expressed as dominant themes in Moroccan culture. But this is clearly also Tazi's personal preference, and he expresses this at several points in our discussions—he has no desire to confront or challenge these basic values and seems to be fully at home with them. Consequently, in his films Tazi shuns displays that might violate intimacy: illustrations of sexual intimacy are absent, shows of blood and violence are minimal, and scenes of prayer ("private" communion between the individual and God) are avoided.[18]

Consonant with this vision, Tazi has developed the notion of an objective, somewhat distant camera, a camera that is pre-eminently realistic in its effects. As "technique" this approach may be a product of Tazi's earlier training in newsreels, a parallel he himself has drawn. Whatever its origins, the "objective" camera is a striking feature of his style. One of the effects of this approach is that close-ups are rare and extreme close-ups may be completely absent. Comparing Tazi's camera, which sees people in mostly medium shots, with that of a filmmaker such as Bergman, who might be described as addicted to close-ups (I am thinking, in particular, of his *Autumn Sonata*, but this is a feature of other Bergman films as well), we can certainly see the distinct effects wrought by close-ups and what is foregone in eschewing them.[19]

Tazi is less reluctant to appeal to the visceral. While not interested in shock for the "thrill" of it, nor in arousing other heightened sensations in the audience's "lizard brain," Tazi has composed endings in *The Big Trip* and *Looking for My Wife's Husband* that certainly generate great anxiety in the spectator—in both, the central character awaits an uncertain fate in a flimsy boat on the Mediterranean. *Badis*'s ending strikes even more deeply on the visceral level: first we witness the harrowing death of two women by stoning; then, at the film's end, we watch the benumbed schoolteacher mechanically throwing pebbles to the ground while the "vegetative" father sits sullenly outside the village café. We leave the film feeling depressed, despairing (an effect criticized, as we saw in chapter 4, by women who challenged the film's "defeatist" mood). Yet the "visceral" appeal of Tazi's films is necessarily attenuated, even somewhat ambiguous, because it is coupled with the desire to respect intimacy and maintain distance. This is what we would expect of such a "tasteful" filmmaker.

It is surely on the vicarious level that Tazi's films have their greatest appeal, and this fits most closely with the storyteller function Tazi has emphasized again and again. Indeed, his delight in a story's telling, his penchant for lingering over it and slowly tasting its pleasures, may to some degree compensate for the weakened "voyeur" appeal that his distanced, objective camera imposes. What is lost in forgoing the close-up may, to some extent, be regained through a growing familiarity with characters engendered over time. With such familiarity, perhaps a character's stance or movements, seen in medium long shots, can show as much as a face in close-up—returning to *Badis*, perhaps the changes in Moira's gait over the course of the film or, in the closing scene, the schoolteacher's awkward, obsessive, symbolic lapidation, convey as much power as would close-ups of the face.[20]

The "Puzzle" in the Story

There are, of course, other ways of conceiving appeal. For example, Mulvey argues that whereas the appeal of most Hollywood films resides in the attraction of "glamour" (not a relevant aspect of Tazi's films nor of Moroccan films in general, because this is closely related to the "star system," which, as we have seen, is absent from Moroccan cinema), some films enlist the spectator in an attempt to solve a "puzzle" or unravel a secret.[21]

The "puzzle" is a very salient element in the appeal of each of Tazi's films. In *The Big Trip* will Omar, on the relatively straightforward route from Agadir to Tangiers, survive what we quickly understand will become a tortuous series of ordeals? In *Badis*, even while we are denied intimate access to the characters, our concern for them grows as the puzzle is revealed: Will the two oppressed women try to escape their misery? If so, how? And will they succeed? *Looking* sets a conundrum from the moment we learn its title and the entire film is riddled with the structuring puzzle: How can Hajj Ben Moussa find a husband for his wife? In *Lalla Hobby*, will the Hajj surmount all the problems Europe poses and collar his third wife's absconded husband? In none of these films is glamour an element nor is there any hint of exposure of the intimate. Yet in them, and particularly in the two that are for me Tazi's strongest—*Badis* and *Looking*—the "puzzle," the conundrum, the "enigma" serves to captivate the spectator and push the story forward.[22]

The "Wake-Up" Appeal

Tazi is also interested in what we might call the "wake-up" appeal of film. Tazi has invoked this aspect with regard to each of his films, most explicitly in talking about the stoning scene in *Badis*, meant, as he said, to sound an alarm. In each of his other films, the "wake-up" function is an important one: in *The Big Trip* we are made to attend to the phenomenon of south-north migration, to the cruelty of the "road," to the sometimes nasty character of the Moroccan "mosaic," to the desperation of those without property and means of support who seem to have no recourse other than emigration; in *Looking* and

Lalla Hobby the plight of the emigrant, particularly the clandestine emigrant, is treated directly and to great effect.[23]

BEHIND THE CAMERA—"THIRD WORLD" FILMING PRACTICE

Tazi directs his films in circumstances similar to those of most Third World filmmakers who are pushed, from a variable combination of necessity and choice and to a greater or lesser extent, to work under what we might call "neorealist" conditions, characterized by nonprofessional actors and technicians and other collaborators who are not fully specialized; shooting in natural locations; using relatively inexpensive, rudimentary equipment; a lack of dedicated studios and/or film labs—all of which are traits of a sector that is more like a craft than an industry. Sometimes these "neorealist" elements are primarily in front of the camera, as in *Badis,* sometimes behind the camera, as in *Lalla Hobby,* and sometimes in both places, as in *The Big Trip.* In any case, the film is often made in a context where most of the surrounding community is not "professionally" involved in filmmaking.

In such situations the filmmaker has to have great qualities of improvisation and adaptation (as we have seen during each of Tazi's film experiences but perhaps most clearly in *Badis* and *Lalla Hobby*). Early in his career, Tazi no doubt had to be very inventive as a cinematographer, solving intricate problems of lighting, camera angle, and so on. Broadening into the role of film director, Tazi becomes shrewd and sometimes manipulative, as is no doubt necessary when facing hurdles than can put an entire project at risk. In any event, Tazi often refers (with some pride) to the tricks and subterfuges he has come up with to deal with unexpected problems, on occasion describing this flexibility as "Third World" filming practice.[24]

Another implication of "neorealist" filming conditions may be that the filmmaker needs to be immensely strong willed, probably quite self-centered, and certainly unwilling to turn away from challenges (and perhaps even to relish them) to see a film through to completion. He or she also needs great economic discipline, which certainly has a significant effect on the planning and shooting of a film and may reduce flexibility at the editing stage.[25]

Even under such constraints and pressures, Tazi finds room in his films for his private amusements, obsessions, and whims. Not only do we find references in his films to his personal life (sometimes coded and perhaps even unconscious, as in *Badis;* sometimes transparent, as in *Looking*), and not only do we see him insisting on his own endings, often over the opposition of his main collaborators, but we also find playful notes inserted at his pleasure—the series of flashbacks in *The Big Trip*, the many props and accessories in *Looking*, the nods to the sea at his films' beginnings and/or endings.

With his will and abilities so often tested, one would understand Tazi if he were to claim full, even exclusive credit for his successes. Yet he appears very reluctant to do so. He sounded completely sincere in his repeated references to the need for collaboration; he unfailingly cited the names of his collaborators without being prompted, even those whose functions might seem secondary or tertiary to someone like myself with no direct experience of the filmmaking process. One symptom of Tazi's willingness to share credit was his consistently ascribing film's power to the couple "image and sound," when we might expect someone trained as a cinematographer to privilege the visual.

REVIEWING TAZI'S VISION: "CONSTRUCTIVE NOSTALGIA" AND A "CINEMA OF PROXIMITY"

Aware as we must always be of the risks of oversimplification, how might we nonetheless sum up Tazi's general approach and his vision of film, filmmaker, and filmmaking? For Tazi, the filmmaker is not an iconoclast or an experimentalist but, rather, a builder, a constructor, which is a vision consonant with his reaching maturity during the first decades of Moroccan nation building. His sensibility is primarily visual or, better, corporeal, rooted in the body. He loved the physicality of deep-sea diving, enjoyed the constant traveling and rough-and-tumble of early documentary filmmaking, and of organizing and coordinating activities for foreign productions. And, as he says, he just "loves" the feel of the camera in his hands, even as he loves to experiment with the latest in digital technology.

Although he reads widely and, as he said to me, can easily tell a story, he also told me that he could not and would not want to write one. His sensibility is not textual and certainly not scriptural. He is neither a film theoretician nor a film historian nor a film critic, although he is to no small degree conversant with each of these fields. He is more interested in creating a story-world for the spectator—one related to reality in significant ways—than he is in transporting the spectator into a fantasy world or in making a film that comments on prior film history or constitutes an innovation with regard to theory. To be motivated to make a film Tazi has to be moved "viscerally," the project has to strike him in his "guts," not simply in his mind or in his imagination.

Implicit (and sometimes explicit) in the story-world that Tazi creates is a committed, engaged filmmaker. However, Tazi's aims are organically contained in the story rather than simply reflected in a message; they are conveyed by the story rather than themselves conveying the story. In James Agee's terms, Tazi's films are made from the inside out rather than from the outside in. Tazi's aims—let us label them, in shorthand, the fostering of "a cinema of proximity" and encouraging "a constructive nostalgia"—are not purposes behind his films nor exterior to them, but ones that are intrinsic to his lived and filmic worlds.

To some, Tazi's vision may sometimes suggest a "self-Orientalizing" one, as when he discusses "Oriental rhythm" or "Oriental narration," heritage, identity, and similar notions. To take a concrete example: when Tazi alludes to the distinction between the "inside, domestic, private" domain of women and the "outside, societal, public" domain of men, we are encountering one of the staples of the "Orientalist" vision of Arab and/or Islamic society. In this vision, the outside world constitutes a negative force for women, negative both in the sense that woman is an object of (man's) desire rather than a desiring subject, and negative too in that she is dependent on man for her economic well-being and is therefore especially vulnerable.

We see elements of this view reflected in Tazi's films as well as in his discourse. Tazi portrays and speaks of woman as man's prototypical other, of women as besieged by an outside world that men dominate. He also sees women as men's "other" in a number of positive senses— women are full of life, song, dancing, stories, tenderness, strength, and knowledge, and, very importantly, the desire to inculcate and share all this, to engage in a kind of communication that men (as fathers and husbands) do not lend themselves to or encourage.

However, to characterize Tazi's view as "Orientalist" is, I think, to misunderstand the label, the person, and his films. The failing of an "Orientalist" vision is not that it is "untrue to reality" or a simplification (traits that characterize all visions to some extent), or that it is "inauthentic" and created by "outsiders" (however imprecise such terms may be). Rather it lies in the kinds of simplifying abstractions the vision promotes and the aims to which these are put—often dehumanizing reductions that deprive subjects of "agency" or interpret that agency as "irrational" or "culturally determined," and that easily buttress, deliberately or not, larger political projects of domination. As abstractions, "Orientalist" views are radically decontextualized, divorced from the ambiguities and complexities of lived experience and from the larger forces that help shape that experience.[26]

Tazi's vision, as we see it in his richly textured films, in the care he lavishes on the smallest details, in his attention to human ambivalence and the intricacies of human relationships, in his portrayal of human potential (as in Lalla Hobby's adroitness in taking over the jewelry store), is deeply contextualized and clearly counter to such simplifications, just as it is counter to what he sees as the "exotic" focus of foreign productions on camels, tents, the desert, and so on. If we recall, too, his challenge to the simplifying notions of "Moroccan-ness," of a Moroccan "specificity," and his offering in their stead the view of a Moroccan "mosaic" replete with many varieties and blends of Moroccan "particularities," I think we are closer to his view of the relationship between living individuals and cultural abstractions.

In attending to Tazi's "constructive" orientation, to his function as "builder," as well as his enthusiasm for his "productive" role in television, we can better appreciate his adherence to creativity as a central human quality. In essence, Tazi is engaged in implementing a vision for the future in which simplifications of an "Orientalist" nature would give way to increasingly nuanced interpretations of human experience that challenge certain aspects of current imbalances of power—in particular those that enable some parts of the world to be producers of images and put others in the straitjacket of enforced consumption.

Tazi's interest in building a story-world rather than a theoretical or experimental one, a world rooted in the "real" rather than in fantasy but giving ample space to imagination is, as it happens, one that I find particularly congenial. It fits well with my own vision of anthropology and with my aims in this book, which are not primarily those of providing a theoretical or cultural commentary on Tazi's world (although this book may do that a good part of the time) but which involve placing us in the filmmaker's world, exploring how that world may have come about, rendering us sensitive to its most crucial issues, and constructing from this complexity a "story" that can be communicated from place to place. These aims—both Tazi's and mine—embody outlooks that try to encompass and express both past and present, and to do so in ways that promote a future open to human creativity. It is to this aspect—to whether the future appears likely to be open to creative filmmaking in Moroccan and other Third World contexts—that we now turn.

Moroccan and Third World Cinemas in the Global Film Industry: Projections

CURRENT GLOBAL TRENDS

As we saw in the introduction and then in more detail over the course of this book, the Moroccan film sector owes its particular characteristics both to the barriers a worldwide culture industry based in a few metropolitan centers erects to the emergence and continuity of smaller national cinemas and to the specifics of Moroccan society—characteristics we might summarize schematically by recalling that exhibition and distribution in Morocco are in private hands, that distributors prefer, on purely economic grounds, to promote cheaper imports rather than national films costing more to rent, and that, consequently, national films are rarely profitable and funds for production must therefore come from other than commercial capital investment.

Yet, on both the global and Moroccan levels the situation is extremely unstable. Looking first at the global industry, we see it undergoing significant and in some ways radical changes. These include, but are not limited to, major reorganizations that at times create, at times break down giant media conglomerates (such as recent transformations involving AOL Time Warner and Vivendi Universal, to name just two large and problematic reorganizations), "delocalizing" investments by major First World film producers and distributors in filmmaking abroad (such as Sony-Columbia's recent investments in Hong Kong and Brazil), the increasing importance of blockbusters (and sequels) at the expense of smaller films (with advertising growing as a percentage of film budget and becoming an ever-greater driving force in a film's success, and with tie-ins constituting a large portion of revenue), changes in distribution (DVDs, video on demand, Internet distribution, all raising issues of monopoly control and challenging the various existing notions of intellectual property rights), rapidly changing technology (digitalization of production and delivery, moves toward animation), pressures from the World Trade Organization (WTO), and no doubt some other changes as well. In these changeable

circumstances, national governments are taking many varied steps
that affect the film sector, which is being transformed in important
ways. Yet it is very difficult at this point to discern clear trends, as we
will see now, as we first focus on Europe's struggle to encourage its
own cinema in the face of U.S. films' domination and then glance at
some Third World cases.

European cinema appeared to make significant inroads against
U.S. film domination in 2001, when it regained market share on the
continent at the expense of U.S. films. However, many of these gains
were reversed in 2002, when Hollywood had a very good year. At the
same time, in a number of European Union countries (among them
Germany, Italy, the UK) that had adopted measures to support the
film sector, in some ways resembling those of France, results in several
areas were encouraging. Yet in terms of overall financial health, the
European industry in 2002 was not faring well, as there appeared to
have been a "clear decline in the [operating] margins of the 50 most
important European [film] companies," whereas the margins of the
Hollywood majors showed healthy figures.[27]

France, with its extensive and long-standing support for the national cinema, once again provides useful lessons regarding the capacity of a national cinema to continue to produce a significant number of films and to battle for a solid place in its domestic market. As I
write this the outcome of this battle is unclear but I would like to
point out here some of the crucial features that will affect the outcome, to put us in a better position to appreciate the problems facing
Third World cinemas.

Hollywood's domination of France's domestic market is a relatively recent phenomenon—1989 was the first year in decades when
the U.S. films' share of France's domestic market was significantly
greater than 50 percent (the share gained by French films sunk to 34
percent), whereas prior to the mid-1980s French films had consistently outdrawn U.S. films by a good margin.[28] What lay behind the
resurgence of French cinema in 2001 (an eloquent example of the
broader European cinema recovery) and then the setbacks of 2002?[29]

While in a number of areas cinema in France is doing well (for
example, total attendance and numbers of screens have been rising;
the numbers of films produced has remained at the healthy level of
around two hundred) and while the basic state support to the sector
continues to provide an encouraging framework, this support, while
necessary, is not sufficient and there are several aspects that particularly worry members of the French film world. These include: (1) a

growing number of theaters are tied to major distribution-production companies; (2) rapidly increasing amounts are being paid for the promotion of blockbusters; (3) exhibitors increasingly are not honoring commitments that would allow smaller films time to gain a following by word of mouth but are rapidly switching to major films after a period of only two weeks, whereas several years ago this period commonly lasted up to three months; and (4) there is continuing and growing pressure to delocalize production.[30] In addition to the various forms of state support for film financing, distribution, and exhibition, one of the keys to the health of the French film sector is the contribution from television to film financing, and the amount and stability of this support have recently become problematic.[31] All of these developments contribute to the growing marginalization of smaller films and independent producers and consequently sharpen the threats to "cultural diversity." This has led to what is frequently called a "crisis" in French film financing and to a series of governmental proposals and measures to palliate the weaknesses.[32]

With a cinema as strong as France's having such a difficult time, it is not surprising that in most Third World cinemas the situation is much, much worse. However, in several countries with smaller cinemas, such as Brazil, South Korea, and Nigeria, there have been positive developments for a variety of different reasons, including an improved legal situation, the institution of quotas in the theaters, and allowing the development of video distribution circuits.[33]

MOROCCAN CINEMA— PROSPECTS

In these circumstances, what can we say about the future of Moroccan cinema? What are the prospects for continuity in Moroccan filmmaking, for it to keep attracting its national audiences and perhaps to make an international breakthrough as well? Let me suggest some answers to these questions by, first, exploring how some of the changes in global filmmaking—particularly the technological changes involving digitalization—may affect the Moroccan film sector; second, examining some of the continuing structural difficulties in the Moroccan film sector itself; third, looking at the recent production of Moroccan films for some sign of whether official proclamations and declared intentions are indeed reflected in quality of output; and finally, looking at Morocco's current social, cultural, and political climate. I will conclude with some considerations concerning the general situation of filmmaking and creative activity in the Third World, in the context of debate over the "cultural exception" and "cultural diversity."

NEW TECHNOLOGY

In the areas of production and postproduction, digitalization offers very significant advantages in speeding up and reducing the cost of both shooting and postproduction, benefits that are crucial for Third World filmmakers hard pressed for funds. With initial shooting costs so much lower, new financing opportunities become possible: filmmakers may seek funds on the basis of video rushes (or versions further along) and may obtain money stage by stage, as the film moves toward completion. Although a major cost is incurred in transforming video into 35 mm format, there are more than enough areas in which economic savings are gained for the entire cost of the digital video production process to be less onerous than traditional 35 mm production. A number of Moroccan filmmakers have taken advantage of these reduced production costs and have shot and edited their films digitally, and the trend in this direction is clear.[34]

We have already seen how, in some Third World countries, significant video production and distribution networks have formed (with Nigeria a prime example). In Morocco's case, the past decade has seen a growth in commercial video production, primarily among Berber-speaking communities and including narrative fiction among the genres. With perhaps some 30 percent to 40 percent of Morocco's population speaking Berber, predominantly in rural areas where the overall national decrease in the number of theaters is irrelevant since none exist there in any case, and with only an occasional feature film having any Berber dialogue, there is obviously a large potential public for video productions and, apparently, great local initiative in this sector.[35]

The situation is less clear with regard to screening. Whereas the cost of making and delivering a digital copy is significantly less than printing a 35 mm copy from a digital video format, a digital projector is a very expensive item, with a cost approximately ten times that of a traditional projector. This greater cost makes the goal of internationally democratized leveling (where all countries would enjoy more or less the same screening facilities) more difficult to reach and is likely to lead, instead, to a dualization of the distribution and exhibition circuits, where rich countries would produce, distribute, and exhibit digitally and Third World countries would again find themselves dependent on an outdated technology. Clear consequences would include ever more restricted film choice in the Third World and mounting weakness in their film sectors.[36]

FILM SECTOR PROBLEMS

Whatever the nature of these broader developments—some of which Moroccan filmmakers find encouraging, some of which they see as threats—there are a number of fundamental national film sector problems that need to be solved if Moroccan cinema is to have a productive future.

Distribution and exhibition—keys to the health of the film sector—continue to constitute weak points. Today, while Moroccan audiences retain their desire to view Moroccan films, Moroccan distributors and exhibitors have not reached any clear policy or practice that would support such films and help satisfy that desire. During some extended periods the situation has even seemed to be deteriorating.[37] In addition, only some 30 of Morocco's total complement of theaters (today numbering less than 170) provide a level of return that is attractive for a Moroccan film's distributor-producer—that is, it is only in these theaters that a percentage of box-office receipts may lead to significant returns. In almost all other theaters, the flat fees an exhibitor pays are very low (approximately 1,000–1,500 DH per week) and, even worse, the projector and conditions are so bad that the damage done to the film itself is often greater than the fee paid to rent it.[38]

On the production side, in addition to the usual problems of financing little progress has been made toward developing a set of fully specialized producers—people whose function it is to put together the package of elements necessary to make a film (property, writer, director, cast, and so on) and who then oversee the film's completion. Currently, a Moroccan director seeking to enlist a producer's assistance is likely to meet a response along the lines of, "Look, you go and get 70 percent of the funding for this project, and then we'll talk." The time-consuming and exhausting fund-raising tasks thus remain in the hands of the director, and the producer's role will usually be limited to providing some staff and technology once the project appears viable.

Producers and directors continue to have their organizational problems. As we saw in chapter 6 and as Tazi had predicted, the Producers' Guild—long prey to internal conflict—split in mid-2001, with some of its most respected members leaving to form the Group of Writers-Directors-Producers (GARP—Fr. *Groupement des auteurs-réalisateurs-producteurs*). GARP thus added its name to those of other groups (the Producers' Guild, AMPAC, the National Film Federation—see chapter 6) attempting to influence policy affecting the film sector. The very profusion of these groups is not necessarily a sign of more effective promoting of Moroccan filmmaking, and it remains to be seen whether in conjunction or alone any of these groups will make much of a difference to Moroccan film policy in the medium and long term.

In the area of policy there have been a number of positive, although modest, developments. During the year 2000 and into the year 2001, new statutes governing the film sector were elaborated and submitted to Parliament. With a number of filmmakers adopting a position on this similar to Tazi's—that the proposal offered very little in the way of encouraging Moroccan production but focused instead on enumerating offenses and mandating punishments—professionals mounted an extended media campaign against the proposal and, although they were not able to stop its adoption, they did delay its passage and succeed in raising the level of public discussion.

Among the issues professionals in the film sector raise again and again are those relating to the status of the artist and to creators' rights (Fr. *les droits d'auteur*). As we saw in Tazi's discussion, filmmakers and creative artists in general are self-employed and, unlike full-time workers in other sectors, do not enjoy social benefits provided by the state, such as health care, retirement plans, maternity and sick leave, and so on. However, in mid-2003, a ministry of culture initiative began to address these questions, as well as the broad issue of how to structure the creative artistic sector, what rules would govern professional membership, and related aspects.

In Morocco, artists receive no systematic royalties from their work and often complain that even the state organs—television channels, radio stations, theaters, and so on—do not compensate them properly for use of their work. Filmmakers, as we have seen, find pirated videotapes of their films openly available for sale in many of the markets throughout the country, with none of the revenue from these sales reverting to the artist. And no clear remedies for this situation are in sight.[39]

While some film professionals are more concerned with the commercial aspects, many are concerned with promoting quality. The Aid

Fund and the way it has been administered are prime targets in this regard (GARP, very vocal on this matter, argues for greater transparency in the deliberations and more emphasis on quality in the awards). One spur to these arguments was the astonishing performance of the Aid Fund Commission at its session in June 2001 when, for the first time since its founding, it refused to grant any awards at all, rejecting proposals by established filmmakers (Jilali Ferhati, Mustapha Derkaoui) as well as by Nabil Ayouch, despite the remarkable success of his *Ali Zaoua*.[40] Since then, the commission's composition changed and it restored support, with the total awarded annually reaching approximately twenty million DH (two million dollars). If these sums continue to be made available, Moroccan cinema would be in a good position to approach the level of ten productions annually, and the official middle term target of fifteen features per year would still be in sight, both numbers constituting significant advances on the past.[41]

Censorship, although imposed infrequently, is always a threat. In one notable recent incident a film by Nabil Ayouch, *One Minute Less in the Sun*, was ruled unsuitable for screening unless several scenes were shortened or cut. The filmmaker refused and, as of this writing, the film has not yet been allowed in the theaters. This case is particularly striking given that Ayouch's previous film, *Ali Zaoua*, had been a great popular and critical success, won many international awards, and was also awarded the prize for best film at the Sixth National Film Festival in Marrakesh in 2001.[42] Filmmakers are also unhappy with an aspect of the Aid Fund they feel serves a censorship function: the final one-quarter of the award is handed over only if the commission approves the completed film, and the frequent withholding or reduction of this portion has often been experienced by the filmmakers as censorship and placed them in very difficult financial straits.

QUANTITY INTO QUALITY? A REVIEW OF MOROCCAN NATIONAL FILM FESTIVALS

There is perhaps no better way to assess the prospects for Moroccan films, the quality of current output, the excitement they generate, and the symbolic importance of films in national cultural life than by surveying Morocco's various National Film Festivals and speculating on what they are likely to offer in the near future. The National Film Festival was inaugurated in 1982 to show off the results of the then newly instituted state aid to production. It has been held at irregular intervals ever since, each time showing all (or almost all) of the national films produced in the intervening period. Two clear trends appear since the 1982 event: first, the festivals are now being held at more regular and frequent intervals (every two to three years) and the rate of film production has been increasing; second, as the rate of production has increased, so have tensions and the urgency with which the same questions are posed again and again—"Has Moroccan filmmaking finally made the leap from increased quantity to improved quality?" "Have Moroccan films finally learned how to entertain the public?" Or, more angrily, "Are Moroccan films continuing to waste public money?"[43]

Already at the sixth festival in 2001, the Moroccan government had promised a greater commitment to film production than it had evidenced previously, with the ministry announcing that the amount of state aid to production would increase by 25 percent, that the budget for television advertising would jump from 300,000 DH to 500,000 DH per feature, and vowing that the rate of production would continue to increase and that fifteen films per year would be the new production target for the middle term.[44] This festival constituted something of a watershed for Moroccan films because its news was reported beyond national borders: festival officials were no doubt pleased when the widely respected French newspaper *Le Monde* led off a full-page review with the headline "The Sudden Abundance of National Films on Moroccan Screens"; they were probably even more pleased to read further down the page that "Morocco would finally be inscribing the Maghreb in a lasting manner on the world atlas of active cinemas."[45]

However, many of the Moroccan filmmakers, critics, and public who attended the sixth festival were much less sanguine. They spoke of "a falling-off in quality," the Moroccan cinema's "shaky state," one good film being "unable to hide a forest that needs pruning," and a festival that was "radiating a general mediocrity." Some of the films at the festival were characterized as "frankly repulsive." And several filmmakers offered extremely harsh criticism of the quality of a number of the films on offer: one film "shamed the entire profession . . . weakening the credit we have taken years to accumulate . . . I can't find the right words to express my indignation, I was so revolted, disgusted, appalled. . . . We can't continue to waste public money like this." Tazi's own view was certainly more judicious but not enthusiastic, "On the purely cinematic level, I must admit that I'm somewhat disappointed. Quality didn't really put in a strong appearance. I'm not talking here of technical aspects—image, sound, and so on—where we can see that definite progress has been made. I'm talking more of style, of narration . . . and of certain themes, such as the insulting image of women who have here been limited to roles such as night-club dancer, prostitute, or idiot."[46]

The prizes, too, generated controversy, with several critics claiming that some of the top prizes went to the worst films and at least one of the uncrowned filmmakers relaying rumors that "the jury was put under a lot of pressure . . . from outside." One of the filmmakers even claimed that the projection of his work at the festival had been "sabotaged."[47] Yet, at the same time, the award for best film was almost unanimously saluted—*Ali Zaoua* had already won a number of prizes at international festivals (it went on to garner more than twenty such awards) and was the second effort by Nabil Ayouch, a binational Moroccan/French citizen. Also coming in for general praise were the short films of a number of younger Moroccan filmmakers, many of whom had been raised or were residing abroad.

Many of these issues were echoed a little more than two years later, when the Seventh National Film Festival was held in the city of Oujda in June 2003. The Oujda festival maintained the quantitative level of production that had been established in recent festivals and, leading up to it, the entire Moroccan film world had high expectations, with a considerable budget of some three million DH allocated to make it a success.[48] But many of the criticisms had a familiar ring: the composition of the jury was challenged amid claims that some of its members had close ties to filmmakers whose films were competing for prizes, and the prizes themselves were criticized on related grounds of personal favoritism, with claims being made that many awards were undeserved, or that too many prizes were given to too few films, or that important films were completely bypassed in the awards. Accusations of sabotage recalled those made at the previous festival, with some filmmakers wondering privately why there were projection and sound problems for some films and not for others.

There was, in addition, a new criticism, which may indeed be symptomatic of a larger problem (or several of them). This had to do with the choice of venue, Oujda, a large provincial capital in the northeast of the country, near the Algerian border.[49] Oujda is an important regional city but, like most cities outside the handful of major ones, it has few theaters (six), only one of which could be expected to provide projection and viewing conditions at a level appropriate for an event of the festival's importance. As it happened, viewing conditions even at this theater were worse than merely uncomfortable and the projection was so deficient that the festival jury felt duty bound to forgo awarding prizes for sound and cinematography (among others) because they felt unable to judge all films equally.[50]

In addition to the obvious problem of the lack of adequate theaters outside the major urban areas (the previous festivals had been held in the relatively well-equipped cities of Casablanca, Marrakesh, Tangiers, Meknès, and Rabat), one of the further consequences of holding this festival in Oujda was that the event, unlike the previous one in Marrakesh, received little, if any, international coverage—for example, the French newspaper *Le Monde*, which had so favorably reviewed the previous festival, made no mention of this one, a failure noted by many festival participants. Oujda as venue also raised a larger issue: Was the festival being instrumentalized and used to satisfy other aims (regional development, decentralization, shoring up the standing of the king [who had recently visited the area and promised new initiatives]), rather than its primary one of promoting and encouraging Moroccan films? In any event, the venue occasioned much controversy and discussion, and the CCM came in for particular criticism for not having ensured that, at least at the main festival theater, conditions and facilities would be acceptable.[51]

Many of the opinions concerning the quality of the films, the organization of the festival, and the work of the jury may, of course, be merely subjective. At worst, they may reflect self-interest and the desire to benefit any of the various factions, clans, regional groups, political parties, and so on—motives that do indeed cloud the cinematic landscape and that the public, filmmakers, and critics alike are quick to put in the forefront of discussion. But this only reinforces the general contention that the stakes in these disputes are highly valued ones and that the symbolic significance of success and approval in the film sector are, if anything, in ascendance. From this perspective, even the disputes constitute a healthy sign for the future of cinematic creation in Morocco.[52]

However justified the various criticisms of the festival may be, they should not blind us to the fact that there were a number of significant advances in the films themselves. First of all, several of the established filmmakers—Tazi himself and Abdelkader Lagtaa (b. 1948) among them—presented films that were widely, if not unanimously, praised. Another of this generation—Mustapha Derkaoui (b. 1944)—presented the most controversial film of the festival, a controversy fueled by the somewhat paradoxical fact that the film had been an overwhelming box-office success when it was released earlier in the year despite almost unanimous critical condemnation.[53] Also noteworthy was the fact that a number of new themes were introduced at this festival and some well-known themes were presented in new ways: Tazi's historical reconstruction was a first in this genre, showing Morocco as it might have been in the fourteenth century; emigration was a frequent theme, often with a focus on the problems of returning migrants or the return of their children; and some of the most sensitive aspects of the Moroccan political system were highlighted—political imprisonment, corruption, the periods of widespread repression during prior decades.

Most importantly for the future of Moroccan cinema, several first features by members of the younger generation were received very positively, particularly the contributions of Faouzi Ben Saidi (b. 1967), Hakim Belabbes (b. 1961), and Narjiss Nejjar (b. 1971), as were some short films presented by younger filmmakers. Most of the attention went to the two feature films that had been presented a month earlier at the Cannes Film Festival, *A Thousand Months* (*Mille mois,* Faouzi Ben Saidi, 2003) and *Dry Eyes* (*Les yeux secs,* Narjiss Nejjar, 2003). This was the first time in more than thirty years that Moroccan films were selected for the world's most prestigious film festival, and Ben Saidi's film won one of its section's major prizes.[54]

On the negative side, the festival was also marked by the notable absence of Nabil Ayouch (b. 1969), whose *Ali Zaoua* had won the award for best picture at the previous festival but who declined to attend this one, perhaps as a reaction to the censorship problems and adverse public response his recent film had occasioned.[55]

Given the promise shown by several members of the younger generation, it is worth paying a little more attention to their situation. The quality and quantity of their work and the media attention given to it have already generated some controversy (hints of which we have seen in my discussions with Tazi in chapter 6) and their situation highlights some of the ambiguities and tensions in Moroccan cinema as a whole.[56]

These younger filmmakers are well situated to prolong Moroccan filmmaking into the future. Often having roots in several societies, they are able to compete in different national arenas in the difficult task of amassing the resources necessary to make films. Also, by virtue of training abroad, they are on the whole familiar with the latest technology (although, as we have seen in Tazi's case, youth and dual citizenship are not prerequisites in this area).

Nonetheless, these young filmmakers are caught in a wrenching double bind. On the one hand, they and their work are frequently targets of hostile challenges, often raised acerbically by senior Moroccan filmmakers who have constructed their careers within the shaky framework of the Moroccan film world: "Why consider these filmmakers Moroccan, when they may have dual citizenship or, at the very least, may have spent their formative years abroad?" "Why should we call this film 'Moroccan' if, with the exception of the director, almost all technicians and other collaborators behind the camera are non-Moroccans?"[57] Yet, were these younger filmmakers to remain within Morocco's boundaries, they would not only be limiting severely their access to resources but would be truncating radically their own life experiences and sources of inspiration.

The newcomers thus find themselves in a difficult position. Even when able to make their pitch on two or more playing fields, they face intense competition wherever they are and they often feel under undeserved attack from different directions: abroad they are often seen as intruders, as immigrants, and may be resented when they benefit from allowances made for "diversity" or for "southern" origins; in Morocco, many view them as interlopers and, in addition, they face the accusation that they and their work are "inauthentic." These filmmakers are often condemned as foreigners wherever they are.

Still, the work of members of the younger generation augurs well for the future. Perhaps, as their works proliferate, they will contribute to the breakdown of simplistic, dichotomous categories such as Moroccan/non-Moroccan, authentic/inauthentic, and native/immigrant, and their work will be seen as complex expressions of both "Moroccan" and "European" experiences, or even as challenging those categories. A step in this direction is the fact that the tensions between generations that were palpable during the Sixth National Film Festival in Marrakesh in 2001 were much reduced by the time the Oujda festival took place.

There were thus some incontrovertible overall advances in quality and in thematic focus in the period between 2001 and 2003, between the Sixth and Seventh National Film Festivals. For a number of reasons the next festival, likely to be held sometime in 2005 or perhaps early 2006, will probably provide a defining moment: at that time a number of young filmmakers who have made prizewinning shorts will be showing their first feature films; several younger directors whose first features were very promising will probably be presenting a second and Marrakesh prizewinner Nabil Ayouch, the significant absent at the Oujda festival, will likely be presenting another film and hoping to regain some of the critical and popular favor he lost as a result of his disappointing third film; and a number of proven directors with long careers behind them, Muhammad Abderrahman Tazi among them, will be adding to an already estimable corpus and providing critics with further material encouraging an evaluation of an entire oeuvre.[58] But much will depend on developments in Morocco outside the film sector and it is to these that we now turn.

MOROCCAN POLITICS, SOCIETY, AND CULTURE

Ample talent on hand, a younger generation keen to take up the mantle, the government projecting increased financial support—much would seem in place for continued growth and an increasingly dynamic film sector. Yet, as we have seen, the obstacles on the sectoral level are deep and well entrenched.

In addition, uncertainties in Moroccan political, social, and cultural life make the future of Moroccan filmmaking impossible to predict. In the years following the important political changes of the late 1990s (the installation of a government led by parties long in opposition and the accession of a young king to the throne), conflicting and ambiguous signs abounded and the period betrayed no clear pattern. While the new king and government both enjoyed a prolonged public "benefit of the doubt" during the first years of their leadership, social problems persisted, democratization underwent some setbacks, and popular support for the government waned. As the population grew increasingly disappointed with the political parties in power and as the king began to play a more visible public role, Moroccans were reported to be inverting the proverbial phrase and saying, mockingly, that "perhaps it is the king who governs and the prime minister who rules." By mid-2002 neither the government nor the king (whose major public interventions in matters such as poverty alleviation, reducing unemployment, and improving women's status were seen increasingly as largely symbolic) had done much to improve people's lives.[59]

National elections in September 2002 showed a Moroccan political system that was perhaps gaining in routinization (this was the first time since independence in 1956 that national elections had been held exactly when they were legally scheduled, and there were many fewer accusations of irregularities than usual), but where the population displayed little enthusiasm for the government's performance—the rate of voter participation was only 52 percent and the principal party in the outgoing government coalition, the nominally socialist USFP (*l'Union socialiste forces populaires*), barely remained in the lead with just fifty seats, a loss of more than 10 percent. Its leadership was challenged both by a centrist party with a tradition going back to the nationalist struggle (the Istiqlal [Independence] Party, which reached forty-eight seats, a gain of 50 percent), and, even more strikingly, by an Islamically oriented party (the PJD—Fr. *Parti de la Justice et du Développement*), which, although officially formed only in 1999, became the third most important political party by obtaining forty-two seats (a very strong score given that the party entered candidates in only fifty-six of the more than ninety electoral districts).[60]

In December 2002, in an effort to broaden political participation, the king announced that the legal voting age would be reduced to 18. But the new voters had to wait longer to vote than planned, for the pattern of postponed elections reappeared and the communal elections scheduled for June 2003 were put off until September. The delay may have had its source in the officially proclaimed desire to mobilize the electorate more effectively, but it may also have been related to the fear, in government circles and beyond, that the PJD's advances in the national elections might be even more dramatic on the communal level.

However, before these elections could be held, the political situation in Morocco shifted dramatically when, on 16 May 2003, the country was shocked by the bombing of a number of sites in Casablanca (including a hotel and a Jewish and a Spanish cultural center), leading to forty-five deaths, among them the twelve bombers. As we will see, with the widely shared horror at the event placing the Islamically oriented political parties and organizations on the defensive, the communal elections were seriously affected and so too was the response to the king's anxiously awaited proposals for improving women's rights. In addition, the state's increased emphasis on security threatened human rights and public freedoms. Furthermore, with many of the bombers having come from the slums of Casablanca (where the population is estimated to be close to a half million), the conditions of Morocco's very large poverty-stricken and marginalized populations cried out for attention. There was also concern about the negative effects the bombings were likely to have on the national economy and, in particular, on tourism—one of Morocco's main sources of foreign currency—and foreign investment.[61]

In September 2003 the delayed communal elections were held,

but the population's response was again tepid, with voter participation reaching only 54 percent, down from 75 percent for the previous communal elections held in 1997. The parties that came in first and second in the 2002 national elections—the USFP and the Istiqlal—repeated their performance here but in reversed order. The PJD (the only legal Islamically oriented political party) saw its rank fall from third to eleventh (out of twenty-six parties in all), but this figure is misleading since the PJD, accused by much of the political establishment of "moral complicity" in the Casablanca bombings, admitted that it had agreed "voluntarily" to restrict its participation (it presented candidates in only 18 percent of election districts, winning one-seventh of the elections it contested—a good score given the profusion of parties). More significantly, the PJD did very well in a number of major urban areas and in Casablanca came in third overall, with its sixteen council seats ranking it just behind the USFP (seventeen seats) and the Istiqlal (19 seats).

The Casablanca bombings also had a significant effect on the effort to change the Mudawwana, the legal code that directly relates to women's rights. In October 2003, in an address to Parliament opening the legislative year (and during the state visit of French president Chirac), King Muhammad VI finally announced his proposed revisions to the code, based on the recommendations of a royal commission he had appointed more than two years earlier. The proposals, which contained many significant advances in women's rights, met with wide approval across the political spectrum and from many civil society associations, receiving very positive international comment as well. How different this was from the public response three years earlier to a government attempt to change the code. Then, several small popular demonstrations of support were dwarfed by much larger protests mounted by Islamically oriented groups, which brought several hundred thousand people onto the streets of Casablanca and which forced the government to shelve the plan. In contrast, this second effort, now under the king's direction and in a new political climate, gained a quick success, with Parliament adopting unanimously the king's proposals, with minor modifications. Yet, how systematically and fairly the new code will be applied remains to be seen.[62]

The bombing in Casablanca also exacerbated the controversy over human rights and public freedoms. The bombing helped speed adoption of a new anti-terrorism law that broadened the definition of terrorist acts and raised the corresponding penalties. King Muhammad VI articulated the new mood in a speech given within two weeks of the attack in which he stated that "The hour of truth has struck, sig-naling an end to the era of permissiveness toward those who use de-mocracy in order to attack the authority of the state, and those whose ideas provide a crucible for sowing the seeds of ostracism, fanaticism, and unrest."[63] Shortly thereafter the minister of justice announced that judicial proceedings had been instituted against more than a thousand people suspected of direct links to the Casablanca attacks or of being members of groups implicated in or planning other acts of political violence, and trials involving more than seven hundred of these people opened in the summer of 2003. Meanwhile, many in the human rights movement and beyond criticized the new anti-terrorism law as much too loosely defined and as tantamount to "killing liberty" (Fr. *liberticide*).[64]

There was also widespread concern that, in this more security-oriented climate, many of the freedoms Moroccans had come to enjoy over the previous decade would be restricted. One of the specific areas of struggle was freedom of the press. A new law governing the Mo-roccan press (replacing a law dating from 1958) was adopted in May 2002 over the opposition of many journalists, who criticized it for retaining imprisonment as a punishment for defamation of the king or royal family and extending this charge to include defamation of religion or the nation's territorial integrity, as well as for its continuing to allow the seizing and suspending of publications.[65]

Civil society remained a very dynamic domain. One of the more meaningful signs of this was the king's establishing, in late 2003, an "Equity and Reconciliation Commission" charged with shedding light on disappearances, wrongful imprisonment, and other major human rights abuses that had occurred during the more repressive periods of King Hassan II's rule. This gave a formal political structure to inde-pendent initiatives begun several years earlier that had led to a "Mo-roccan Forum for Truth and Justice," a civil society organization that aimed to uncover the truth about human rights violations, obtain compensation for the victims, and assign both individual and institu-tional responsibility for the offenses. The new "Equity and Reconcili-ation Commission" quickly became the focus of a very lively contro-versy—more evidence of the significant advances in the freedom of expression—with many individuals and associations disapproving of the haste with which it was supposed to complete its work (it had a maximum of one year to accomplish its tasks) and criticizing its man-date for depriving plaintiffs of judicial recourse and for emphasizing reconciliation at the expense of truth and justice.

Overall, while the public freedoms to discuss, criticize, and mobilize in defense of objectives that might challenge authority were
sometimes curtailed, and while most Moroccans were consciously and
subconsciously aware of the "red lines" that were dangerous to cross,
the general freedoms that Moroccans have come to enjoy in the public
sphere, and in Moroccan cinema as one of its most important sectors,
have expanded significantly in recent years when compared to previous decades. We have already seen several instances of this greater
freedom in the field of cinema, for example in the strength of the
theme of political repression and political criticism that was in evidence in the Seventh National Film Festival, with this theme also
marking several films that were, at the time of the festival, in prepro-
duction and production stages. There were, as well, a number of positive developments in the broader cultural field, among the most significant being a ministry of education decision taken during 2003 to
begin teaching the Berber language—the mother tongue of an estimated 30 to 40 percent of Moroccans—in the public schools.

The Global Context—"Cultural Exception," "Cultural Diversity"

The wider global context, however, is not encour-
aging and the overall mood in Third World film communities today is
profoundly pessimistic, with the dominant view being that current
global trends foster dependency and homogeneity rather than independence and diversity. One example among many: in a report
adopted at the 18th Session of the Carthage Arab and African Film
Festival held in Tunisia in October 2000, Arab and African filmmakers
"drew attention to the dangers that the acceleration of globalization
will pose to national audiovisual structures in the countries of the
South. . . . There is a real risk that in the 5–10 years to come . . . the
capacity for the countries of the South to regulate and support their
own national audiovisual structures will no longer exist, given that
globalization may soon make such support legally impossible . . . [and
they] run the risk of falling inevitably into a state of growing dependency in the face of the domination by the large image providers coming from elsewhere, leaving them hardly any chance to produce their
own images." In these conditions, will it be possible for cultural creation in the Third World to respond to local, national, and regional

aspirations or will it be submerged by products from the most powerful metropolitan centers?

In the international arena and in the domain of cultural production, this question has often been phrased with reference to the "cultural exception"—the view that cultural products should be excluded
from international free trade agreements and that states should be
permitted to subsidize cultural production and adopt related supportive measures. Within this domain the audiovisual has been a main
target for free trade initiatives, but the field's professionals and supporters have also provided the fiercest arguments in defense of the
cultural exception.[66]

Related to the notion of the "cultural exception" but suggesting a
broader, more constructive approach, is the notion of "cultural diversity." Whereas the former, in excluding cultural products from free
trade provisions, betrays a defensive posture, the latter invokes cultural diversity as of primordial significance to all of humanity and as
requiring active promotion and protection. Much of the work to establish an ethical and legal foundation for cultural diversity has taken
place within the framework of the United Nations Educational, Scientific, and Cultural Organization (UNESCO).

In late 2001 UNESCO adopted unanimously a "Universal Declaration on Cultural Diversity," which argues that "cultural diversity is
as necessary for humankind as biodiversity is for nature" (Article 1)
and proposes to safeguard this diversity both in relations between societies and in activity within them, thus tying cultural diversity to the
fundamental human rights of creative freedom and freedom of expression. More specifically, UNESCO's declaration states that "cultural
goods and services [are] commodities of a unique kind . . . which, as
vectors of identity, values and meaning, must not be treated as mere
commodities or consumer goods" (Article 8). Within UNESCO, a large
group of countries, led by France and Canada, is moving to transform
this declaration into an international convention by 2005, which
would provide enforceable legal provisions as is the case with other
international conventions and enable legal constraints to be imposed
on organizations such as the WTO.[67]

Were some of the basic principles of the WTO's approach to free
trade applied to cinema, the state's capacity to protect and promote its
own film production would be severely crippled. For example, the
principle of treating all foreign-made products equally to domestic
ones would make it impossible for governments to provide aid for
national films. And the "most favored nation" principle—that any fa-

vorable treatment accorded by one nation to another should be extended to all nations—would rule out supportive measures included in bilateral trade agreements (for example, the aid France provides to Third World [and Moroccan] cinemas via its Fonds Sud/ACCT programs would have to be discontinued). Clearly, to subject cultural productions such as film to these kinds of free trade regimes would undermine the support this sector needs from its society's institutions and would undermine, even more fundamentally, the capacity of societies to set their own priorities. Such a regime also transparently skews the system in favor of the large-scale producers and their economies in scale, marketing, distribution, and so forth. Bearing in mind the precarious situation of almost all national cinemas with the exception of the "big five," one can easily imagine the destructive effects on these smaller cinemas of proposals such as the one articulated by the WTO, that state support for film production be limited to 5 percent of costs.[68]

France has long led the defense of the cultural exception and the promotion of cultural diversity.[69] Its successes in this area have not only been national but also regional: within Europe, France succeeded in gaining European Union financial aid for distributing films beyond the producing country's national boundaries—a measure intended to buttress the European film sector in the face of very high penetration of all national markets in Europe by U.S.-produced films.[70]

There is no a priori reason why many of the measures adopted in France and elsewhere to support national film production, distribution, and exhibition could not be adopted by Morocco and other Third World countries where, as we have seen, it is absolutely necessary for financing to come from sectors other than profit-oriented private investment, whether this be from the state, from television, from forms of direct and/or indirect taxation, from levies and obligations imposed on foreign film production in Morocco, from sponsoring and product placement, from international aid, or any combination of these. Financing, legal structures, and institutional arrangements to encourage national production and exhibition, however, aren't the only issues: in the Maghreb and in the wider Arab world, across which there are significant cultural and historical ties, it is also essential to remedy one of the main failings—the almost complete absence (except for Egyptian films) of cross-border distribution. In all these areas, not only state intervention but regional coordination (and, eventually, "South-South" cooperation) are necessary if national cinemas are to survive.[71]

As urgent as these issues are with regard to the capacity of cinema

(and cultural production in general) to respond to the needs and desires of specific populations, culture is not the only domain at stake.
Pressures for "free trade" applied by international organizations and
in bilateral negotiations that would push Third World countries to reduce and eliminate direct and indirect forms of support could negatively affect the provision of other "common goods"—education,
health, scientific research, transportation, environmental protection,
and water and electricity delivery among them—and might make en-
joyment of these goods depend directly on the "consumer's" capacity
to pay for them. All of these sectors are threatened when criteria for
investment and other economic and policy factors are divorced from
the expression of local popular and political will and are determined
in ways that escape local accountability. The negative effects of current
free trade programs—in some cases potential, in others already being
felt—account for much of the widespread hostility throughout the
Third World to rather opaque decision-making centers such as the
International Monetary Fund, the World Bank, and the WTO, where
policies tend to reflect global strategic power rather than the varied
local and national interests and characteristics of the Third World
countries. In this context it is worth recalling, and indeed generalizing,
George Soros's warning that "deregulated financial markets often behave more like wrecking balls than pendulums."[72]

While many supportive measures can be envisaged, these often
involve trade-offs, and one needs to ask where Moroccan cinema will
fit in the priorities of the Moroccan government, the Palace, and Moroccans themselves, and what kinds of policies toward the film sector
and cultural production in general will be elaborated and implemented given the seriousness of the country's social problems. Even
were substantial financial support for film production to continue, will
that support be supplemented by measures in the areas of distribution
and screening, and will it contribute to reinforcing the now well-
consolidated "reconciliation" between Moroccan audiences and Moroccan films? If such complementary measures are not taken there is
every danger that Moroccan cinema, even if it survives, may become
primarily a public relations forum, presenting to audiences a "positive"
view of the country, with the film sector itself empty of creativity. In
front of the camera we would see the cinematic equivalent of picture
postcards designed for international festival audiences; behind it we
would find a tightening of censorship (now relatively permissive),
growing manipulation of the Aid Fund Commission, ongoing fratri-
cidal hostility, personal aggrandizement, clientelism, persisting rigidity

of the administrative bodies that govern the sector, and an over-emphasis on foreign productions.[73] Or, on the other hand, Moroccan cinema may become a purely commercial cinema, leading to a reduced adventurousness on the part of both audiences and filmmakers, a regime where popularity and familiarity would rule. In either case, rather than establishing itself as a permanent and respected contributor to the global film repertoire, producing highly valued films for both national and international audiences, Morocco would find itself to have been merely a temporary fad, as were its North African neighbors Algeria in the 1960s and 1970s, and Tunisia in the 1980s and early 1990s, when each produced a good number of first-class films but neither was able to sustain this quality for an extended period.

There are many reasons to maintain the hope that such outcomes will not occur and that Moroccan cinema will retain the energy, creativity, and diversity that have been such important factors in its growth, its recent success, and its promise. The work of Tazi and of some other senior filmmakers, and the production among the younger generation of challenging short films and features, many of them displaying stylistic, formal, and thematic originality, simultaneously enhance Morocco's artistic achievements, challenge and enrich Moroccan society and culture, and attract Moroccan audiences—all signs that the sector has great flexibility and the potential to produce significant and affecting works.

Whether Moroccan cinema will see a strengthening of its independence, creativity, and audience relationship will certainly depend on filmmakers' own actions and those of other actors in the Moroccan film world—not least on the attitudes of those responsible for financing, distribution, and screening and for creating an encouraging legal and administrative context. But it will also depend on social, cultural, and political developments beyond the film sector, such as whether educational levels will rise, freedom of expression will expand, and disposable income will increase, all of which would contribute to growth in the internal market.

However, while such actions and developments are necessary, they may not be sufficient, for it is an unanswered question whether such strengthening is possible in a country situated as Morocco is with regard to the global marketplace, even if internal factors work in positive directions. But at least we can suggest that currently, with Moroccan cinema benefiting from the groundwork and structures built by Tazi and other pioneers, with Moroccan films' box-office success continuing, and with a political and cultural system rapidly changing in mostly encouraging directions, Morocco is very well positioned to provide an instructive lesson concerning whether this particular national cinema, and Third World cinemas more generally, can grow in their domestic markets and reach international audiences as well.

Trailer: Perpetual Motion and Coming Attractions

The reader who has accompanied us this far will no doubt have foreseen that, as we come to the end of our story, both Tazi and the Moroccan film world continue to be in motion.

At the end of October 2003, Tazi resigned as director of production at the television channel 2M and returned to his own production company in the private sector, devoting himself full-time to filmmaking and other audiovisual activities as he had done before his move to television. Almost immediately, he began work on a project for the Consultative Council on Human Rights (a commission appointed by and advising the king on human rights policy and issues) and started preparing another feature film, which he conceived of as a comedy set in the context of the new Mudawwana and one that would test the capacity of Moroccans to laugh at themselves.

Tazi's resignation followed by less than two months another major personnel shift: in September 2003 King Muhammad VI moved Noureddin Sail from his position as 2M's director and placed him at the head of the Moroccan Film Center (CCM), an appointment that many hoped would have an invigorating effect on Moroccan filmmaking, given Sail's long career of actively promoting Moroccan cinema, from his early days as a leader of the film club movement to the key role he played at 2M in fostering creative activity through increased financial aid to film production and directly commissioning films for television.

The film sector itself remained in a state of flux. During 2003–2004 the Aid Fund—the structure governing the state's pivotal contribution to film financing—underwent significant revisions, many of them in directions filmmakers had advocated. And, as the year 2003 ended, Moroccan cultural figures and organizations had begun to protest against a free trade agreement being negotiated between the United States and Morocco, uniting under a banner proclaiming that "culture is not commodity" and arguing that the accord would make it exceedingly difficult for Morocco to protect and ensure its own cultural production.[74]

What effects will these and subsequent developments have on creative filmmaking in Morocco? Will institutional changes such as Sail's move to the CCM and the new Aid Fund regulations lead to significant advances in the capacity and quality of Moroccan film production or will these amount to distinctions without difference? How will Tazi's own creative activity unfold and to what extent will he prolong, modify, or challenge the creative preferences he has displayed so far? Will an increase in private media ownership lead to a more dynamic and creative communications system or, perhaps, to a profusion of "global" messages designed to satisfy narrowly commercial aims? Will Moroccan television continue to build its own production capacity and to support Moroccan cinema, as it did so effectively during the Sail-Tazi tenure at 2M, or will this orientation disappear without trace, as have so many other promising initiatives? How will Morocco deal with its own societal problems and with the rapidly changing world around it, and how will all this affect the film sector and creative activity in general?

These are just some of the questions that might extend those we have been raising in this book from the beginning—raising them not with the aim of providing definitive answers but to advance our understanding of the complexities of creative activity in a Third World context. Ending our story with such questions in the foreground will, hopefully, sharpen our focus on the deeper forces driving Moroccan and global filmmaking and also help enrich our appreciation of creative attractions yet to come.

Chronology

Date	Tazi's Life and Career	Morocco: Developments in Cinema and Culture	Morocco/Maghreb: Political Developments
Pre-1900		1896: The Lumière brothers shoot some of their earliest film scenes in Morocco 1897: First film projections in Morocco, at the Royal Palace in Fez	1830: French colonization of Algeria begins 1881: France establishes protectorate over Tunisia
1900–1910		1907: Félix Mesguich films French aggression against Morocco	
1910–1920		1912: Public film projections in Fez 1919: First colonial feature, *Mektoub*, shot in Morocco	1912: French Protectorate over Morocco installed. French continue effort to "pacify" Morocco
1920–1930			
1930–1940		1934: There are three film theaters in Morocco 1939: The first film developing laboratory in Morocco is established, in Casablanca	
1940–1950	1942: Tazi born in Rabat 3 July and lives much of this decade in Fez	1941: Morocco's first amateur film club is founded by Muhammad Ousfour, in Casablanca	

(continued)

Date	Tazi's Life and Career	Morocco: Developments in Cinema and Culture	Morocco/Maghreb: Political Developments
		1944: CCM created; film studios and laboratory built in Rabat	
		1945: There are now some eighty film theaters in Morocco	
		1949: Orson Welles begins shooting Othello in Morocco, completing it in 1952 when it shares the Grand Prize at the Cannes Film Festival under Moroccan colors	
1950–1960	1950–1955: Tazi lives in Sidi Slimane until finishing primary school	1956: First Moroccan national film, produced by the CCM, an educational short eleven minutes long	1953: Morocco's ruling Sultan Muhammad ben Youssef (later to become King Muhammad V) is deported by the French to Madagascar as the nationalist movement strengthens
	1955–1961: Family moves with him to Rabat for secondary school	1956: There are now some 150 film theaters in Morocco	1955–1956: Tunisia and Morocco both regain independence from France
		1958: Creation of "Les Actualités Marocaines" (weekly news review on film)	1956: Moroccan population about ten million
		1958: Muhammad Ousfour is the first Moroccan to make a feature film, *Ibn al Aq* (*Le fils maudit*), using his own funds and equipment and shooting in 16 mm black and white	

1960–1970	1961–1964: Tazi studies film in Paris and graduates from the Institute for Higher Film Studies, specializing in cinematography 1962: First marriage (one child; divorced 1972) 1964: Returns to Morocco and begins to work for the CCM 1969–1974: Director of "Les Actualités Marocaines"	1960: Founding of the Moroccan Writers Union 1966: Carthage Film Festival in Tunisia is founded and has its first session 1968: Film laboratory built in Casablanca, replacing the one in Rabat 1968: The first festival of Mediterranean film is held in Tangiers 1968: The first official Moroccan feature film is completed: *Vaincre pour vivre* (*Conquer to Live*) 1968–1969: Second and third Moroccan features are completed	1961: Morocco's King Muhammad V dies and is succeeded by his son, King Hassan II 1962: Algeria achieves independence 1963: Border dispute with Algeria breaks out 1965: Moroccan opposition leader Mehdi Ben Barka is kidnapped in Paris and his body is never found; controversy over Palace and French involvement continues today
1970–1980	1970: Participates in founding of filmmakers' cooperative Sigma 3, which produces *Weshma*, the "first truly Moroccan national film," and on which Tazi is cinematographer 1971: His mother dies 1974–1975: Spends one year studying mass communication in the United States 1975–1985 (approx.): Works often on foreign films being made in Morocco	1970: The first Moroccan film magazine, *Cinéma 3*, starts, directed by Noureddin Sail and produced by the Moroccan Federation of Ciné-Clubs; it is discontinued after four issues are published 1970: The filmmaking cooperative Sigma 3, founded by Tazi, Ahmed Bouanani, and Muhammad Seqqat, produces *Weshma*, directed by Hamid Bennani, which wins the Bronze Prize at the Carthage Film Festival	1971, 1972: Two failed attempts on the life of King Hassan II 1975: The Green March, in which several hundred thousand Moroccans march peacefully into the Spanish colonial territory of the Western Sahara to recover it for Morocco, also serves to mobilize political support for King Hassan II and unite most of Morocco behind him

(continued)

Date	Tazi's Life and Career	Morocco: Developments in Cinema and Culture	Morocco/Maghreb: Political Developments
	1977: Films a documentary in the Philippines 1978: Second marriage (two children; divorced 1990)	1977: The CCM undergoes a reorganization with new laws 1979: Morocco has produced fewer than twenty feature films since independence, whereas over a similar period Tunisia has produced about twenty-five and Algeria more than forty	
1980–1990	1981: Directs *The Big Trip*, his first feature film 1983: His father dies 1986–1990: Moves to Spain with second wife and remains based there until 1990 1989: Directs his second feature, *Badis*, which wins many international prizes	1980: A new color film laboratory in Rabat replaces the laboratory in Casablanca 1980: The Support Fund begins state aid to Moroccan national film production and the number of films made increases rapidly 1982: The first National Film Festival is held, in Rabat 1984: The second National Film Festival, in Casablanca 1984: The first feature film made by a Moroccan woman director, *La Braise* (*The Embers*), by Farida Bourquia	1981: Trade union demonstrations turn into mass protests, with the police and army killing more than six hundred demonstrators 1984: Unrest is widespread across the country following reductions in food subsidies

1985: The number of film theaters reaches 247, its high point, but attendance, after reaching forty-five million in 1980, falls to little more than thirty million in the mid-1980s

1987: The Aid Fund replaces the Support Fund, upgrading state aid to film production

1988: The second feature film made by a Moroccan woman director, *A Door to the Sky* (Farida Benlyazid)

1991: Third National Film Festival, in Meknès

1991: *A Love Affair in Casablanca* (Abdelkader Lagtaa) begins the "reconciliation" of Moroccan audiences with their national films

1995: Tangiers is the scene of the Fourth National Film Festival

1998: The Fifth National Film Festival, Casablanca

1999: Since 1980, Morocco has produced more than eighty features (over fifty in the 1990s,

1998: Elections lead to installation of coalition government led by opposition parties, but the Palace retains most of its power

1999: King Hassan II dies and is succeeded by his eldest son, who becomes King Muhammad VI

2000: Moroccan population numbers more than thirty million

2002: National elections show widespread disaffection with ruling political parties and a new prime minister, close to the Palace, is installed

2003 (Oct.): Resigns from 2M and resumes career as full-time director-producer

(*continued*)

1990–present

1993: Directs *Looking for My Wife's Husband*, which becomes the most popular Moroccan film ever

1996: Third marriage (one child)

1997: Directs *Lalla Hobby*, a sequel to *Looking* and the first Moroccan film to be shot largely in Europe

2000: Named director of production for 2M, the second Moroccan television station

2003: Directs his fifth film, *Abu Moussa's Women Neighbors*, a historical pageant set in fourteenth-century Morocco

Date	Tazi's Life and Career	Morocco: Developments in Cinema and Culture	Morocco/Maghreb: Political Developments
		with ten produced in 1999 alone), whereas Algeria has produced fewer than seventy and Tunisia fewer than fifty	2003 (16 May): Bombings in Casablanca kill more than forty people, including twelve of the bombers
		2001: The Sixth National Film Festival, Marrakesh	2003 (Sept.): Noureddin Sail named CCM director by King Muhammad VI
		2002: There are fewer than 170 theaters in Morocco and attendance for all films has fallen to less than eleven million, although attendance for Moroccan films remains encouraging	2003–2004: King proposes new "Family Code" that significantly advances women's rights and is passed by Parliament
		2003: The Seventh National Film Festival, Oujda	

Detailed Table of Contents

Notes

INTRODUCTION

1. There are good reasons for challenging the broad terms "Third World" and "national cinema," but I think there are better reasons for continuing to use them. I will return to this question in the conclusion. Until then, I hope the reader will accept these terms as convenient shorthand.

2. Thinking only of Africa and the Arab world, Ousmane Sembène in Senegal (*Xala*, 1974, and *Cedda*, 1977), Souleymane Cissé in Mali (*Yeelen*, 1987), Idrissa Ouedraogo in Burkina Faso (*Yaaba*, 1989), Merzak Allouache in Algeria (*Omar Gatlato*, 1976), Férid Boughedir in Tunisia (*Halfaouine, Children of the Terraces*, 1990), Muhammad Malas in Syria (*Dreams of the City*, 1986), and Elia Suleiman in Palestine (*Divine Intervention*, 2001), to name just a few, come immediately to mind. (I am not including Egyptian filmmakers because the Egyptian film sector and South Africa's are the only ones on the continent that deserve the label "industrial" and they have special characteristics.)

3. The Moroccan Film Center (Fr. *Centre cinématographique marocain*, hereafter referred to as the CCM) is the state organization that oversees all film activities. (For more detail, see chapter 2, "Moroccan Cinema from Independence until 1980.")

4. In mid-2003 there were fewer than 170 theaters in Morocco (counting multiplex cinemas according to their number of screens), down by over 30 percent from a high of 247 in 1985. Attendance has dropped continually and even more precipitously, from forty-five million admissions in 1980 to under thirteen million in 1999, then to under twelve million in 2001 and under eleven million in 2002, an overall decrease of more than three-quarters for a population that increased by over 50 percent. The number of imported films has also decreased, from an average of over 300 during the 1980s and 1990s to just over 180 in 2001, although this figure rebounded to almost 250 in 2002. Even at the lower figure this number dwarfs the number of Moroccan films shown in the theaters, although recently this number has been climbing (five in 2000, eight in 2001, ten during the first half of 2003).

In the area of production, foreign features filmed in Morocco during 2001 invested 13 times as much as Moroccan films and employed 4.5 times as many technicians, twice as many actors, and 26 times as many extras; in 2002, foreign features invested 12 times as much as Moroccan features and employed 8 times as many technicians, almost twice as many actors, and 30 times as many extras. If all genres are included (features and short films, advertising spots, video clips, etc.), foreign productions accounted for approximately 90 percent of investment in 2001 and 2002. (All figures in this section are from the CCM.)

5. Morocco has consistently produced between five and ten films per year since the late 1990s and box-office figures show the public's support for these films: in 1998 two Moroccan films were in the top ten films in receipts; in 1999 Moroccan films ranked first, second, and ninth in receipts and occupied three of the top five places in admissions. This trend has continued: in 2001 Moroccan films ranked first and second in both attendance and receipts and in 2002 obtained almost the exact same ranking (Moroccan films ranked first and second in receipts, second and third in attendance, with a third Moroccan film ranking eleventh in receipts). On the whole, for 2002, the average attendance for a Moroccan film far outpaced films of all other nationalities, averaging almost twice as many spectators as the next closest national competitor and, while Moroccan films constituted only 2 percent of all films shown, they drew a significantly larger share of total admissions (7.6 percent; CCM figures).

6. Morocco's National Film Festivals will be discussed in greater detail in the conclusion, when we assess Moroccan cinema's future prospects.

7. Averages over the period 1988–1999 for the "big five" are (with 1995 population in millions in parentheses): India 839 (945), China (plus Hong Kong) 489 (over one billion), United States 385 (216), Philippines 456 (69), Japan 238 (125). Figures in this section on national film production, wealth, and population are taken from *UNESCO: Cinema: A Survey on National Cinematography* (www.unesco.org/culture/industries/cinema/html_eng/survey). (The U.S. population figures in the UNESCO document appear to be inaccurate: the U.S. Census Bureau gives a 1995 population of 262 million, with a 2001 population of 285 million.)

Examples of particularly precipitous decreases among important middle-level producers include Mexico, where annual production went from 124 to 32 and Brazil from 72 to 9, both over the period 1970–1991 (Johnson 1996: 128). Brazilian production has recovered somewhat but Mexican production has fallen further, to only 14 films in 2002, despite increasing overall attendance in the past decade (*Cahiers du Cinéma*, L'Atlas du cinéma, Hors-série, April 2003, p. 82). Egypt, another case of decline, will be discussed in greater detail in the next section; recent trends in global cinema will be discussed in the conclusion.

8. Armes clearly summarizes the economic basis for Hollywood's domination. "It is the peculiarity of film as a commodity that is bought and sold which has defined the structure of the film industry. Just about all the financial outlay in film production goes into the making of the master negative and the first print. . . . it is this mechanical reproducibility of film that is the fundamental source of profit in cinema. The system adopted by Hollywood from the 1920s . . . was firmly based on this principle. Production costs were fixed at a level allowing them to be recouped in the U.S. domestic market. . . . Prints sold in the non-Western world therefore yielded almost pure profit, allowing prices to be adjusted so as to ensure the total control of the market. To take an analogy . . . it was like being able to sell an imported Rolls Royce for less than the cost of the cheapest locally produced car and still make virtually a 100 percent profit" (Armes 1987: 37).

U.S. government policy provided invaluable support in promoting the export of Hollywood's product and continues to do so into the present. As one commentator remarks, "The U.S. government endorses trust-like behavior overseas, whilst prohibiting it domestically. And its local film industry has been aided through decades of tax-credit schemes, film commission assistance, state and Commerce Department representation, the Informational Media Guaranty Program's currency assistance, and oligopolistic domestic buying and overseas selling practices that . . . keep the primary market essentially closed to imports on grounds of popular taste" (Miller 1996: 76).

9. The citation is from Moran 1996: 7–8.

10. Figures on population and national film production come from *UNESCO: Cinema: A Survey on National Cinematography.*

France provides significant support to national production through a series of complex measures that include, on the financing side: (1) imposing a ticket tax that is automatically returned to producers for investing in their next film; (2) a selective award (known as "advance against takings" [Fr. *l'avance sur recettes*]), based on the screenplay, earmarked for films deemed to hold promise of artistic and cultural value, in an effort to ensure that these films will be produced; and (3) obliging television to share in feature film production costs. On the distribution-exhibition side, assistance is provided to theaters that qualify as "*cinémas d'art et d'essai.*" These measures contribute to enabling France's per capita production to surpass both "big five" countries that have comparable wealth: the United States, with approximately five times France's population, produced only twice as many films, and Japan, with twice France's population, produced less than 30 percent more.

In addition to France's supportive policies and relative success, there are other reasons for us to highlight the country here: as the former colonial power throughout the Maghreb and in many African countries its policies serve as a reference for those countries; France is the most important source of foreign funds for film production in many of these countries; and some aspects of the French system of support have recently been adopted in Germany, the UK, Italy, and some Asian countries. Also, as we will see in the conclusion, France has been among the most vocal supporters of the "cultural exception"—the view that cultural products, among them film, should be excluded from free trade agreements.

11. Figures from *UNESCO: Cinema: A Survey on National Cinematography.*

12. Puttnam 1998: 263 (no years are given, but Puttnam is probably referring to figures for the early 1990s; throughout the 1990s the figure for France has fluctuated widely, with the high and low for the decade occurring in two successive years—the high of 11.1 percent in 1998, the low of 2.6 percent in 1999 [Thomas Sotinel, "Millésime d'exception pour les films français," *Le Monde,* 28 December 2001, p. 18]). On the whole, in France, the distribution of non-French and non-American films shrank from 20 percent in 1987 (Carlos Pardo, "Mort programmée du cinéma français," *Le Monde Diplomatique,* July 2001, p. 25) to around 10 percent in the years 2000 and 2001 (Thomas Sotinel, "Millésime d'exception pour les films français," *Le Monde,* 28 December 2001, p. 18).

The general trend of Hollywood eroding other national markets has been termed "indubitable" (Miller et al. 2001: 7), with the authors going on to point out that "in 1985, 41 percent of film tickets bought in Western Europe were for Hollywood fare. In 1995, the proportion was 75 percent" (Miller et al. 2001: 7).

More recent trends will be discussed in the conclusion.

13. As one recent example of the kinds of problems facing film distribution in Africa, FESPACO (acronym from the French *Festival panafricain de cinéma à Ouagadougou*) reports that over the past decade in Burkina Faso (a country known for the support it gives to Third World cinema), of the several thousand films that have been shown in the theaters less than a hundred were of African origin (Pana [AllAfrica Global Media], "Cinéma africain: la distribution en question," *Le Soleil* [Dakar, Senegal], 13 October 2001). The writer makes the argument that the recent success throughout Africa of African films such as *Mobutu, roi du Zaire; Lumumba;* and *Bronx-Barbès* highlights the fact that the problem is not so much audience tastes as it is distributors' practices.

14. Citations from Barlet 2000: 221–230, passim. The internal quotation cites the Tunisian producer Ahmed Attia (no further reference given).

15. Other contributing factors include competition from satellite TV (some 80 percent of households are estimated to have a satellite dish) and videocassettes (many first-run films are available in pirated videocassettes within a month after the film appears internationally; figures in this section come from Jacques Mandelbaum, "Quand l'Algérie rêve de cinéma," *Le Monde,* 17 October 2000, p. 16).

16. There are some signs that suggest but do not prove that perhaps the worst is now in the past. In mid-2000 six feature films were ready to be shot and were waiting only for materials; two others were being financed as coproductions with France. Also, some private investors seem willing to put money into the sector: one was building a mini-multiplex in a suburb of Algiers—four theaters, each containing between 200 and 550 places. In Algiers itself, six theaters have recently been renovated (Jacques Mandelbaum, "Quand l'Algérie rêve de cinéma," *Le Monde,* 17 October 2000, p. 16). However, the situation of Algerian cinema remains very precarious, as discussed at length by Boujemaa Karèche, director of the Algerian cinematheque (Karèche 2003).

17. Among the most notable films of this period are *Sejnane* (Abdellatif Ben Ammar, 1974), *Hyena's Sun* (Ridha Béhi, 1977), *Aziza* (Abdellatif Ben Ammar, 1980), *Crossings* (Mahmoud Ben Mahmoud, 1982), *Man of Ashes* (Nouri Bouzid, 1986), and *Golden Horseshoes* (Nouri Bouzid, 1989). This period also saw first features by two women directors: Selma Baccar's *Fatma 75* (1978), a full-length documentary censored by the authorities, and Nejia Ben Mabrouk's *The Trace* (1988). (As in other domains, women have a stronger professional presence in the Tunisian film sector than in the Moroccan and Algerian. As of the mid-1990s, women constituted five of some thirty-six Tunisian directors, two of forty-four Algerian, and two of forty-four Moroccan [based on data in Armes 1996].)

18. Here is one among many examples of such criticism, referring to Férid Boughedir's 1995 Tunisian film: "very little specialist knowledge about Tunisia or North Africa was necessary to appreciate *Summer in La Goulette*. This was virtually mandated by the economics of the film; *Summer in La Goulette* began with a long list of corporate and governmental agencies that sponsored the film, all of them European. The film was made from the ground up as a production that *had* to be marketed to metropolitan audiences who knew little or nothing about Tunisia" (Armbrust 2000: 298).

19. This pattern continues: in the year 2002–2003 two Egyptian films were each seen by more than five times as many spectators as the most suc-

cessful of the two Tunisian films released during this period (Samira Dami, "La fréquentation des salles dans l'oeil du cyclone," *La Presse de Tunisie,* 29 June 2003). In addition, the number of theaters continues to decrease, with only some thirty left in a country with a population of some ten million, and theater owners' and distributors' revenues are reported to have fallen between 60 and 80 percent over the period 1994–2001 (according to a statement released in June 2002 by the Tunisian *Chambre syndicale des exploitants et distributeurs cinématographiques*).

20. By "industrial" I mean a production system characterized not only by significant production and distribution numbers but also where there exists a full complement of technicians in all film specialties, many of whom are employed full-time.

The reader interested in Egyptian cinema may refer to the mine of information in Wassef 1995 and to the thoughtful study by Armbrust (1996) on the role of Egyptian cinema in Egyptian popular culture and in the construction of modern Egyptian identity. For broad pictures of cinema in the Arab world (including Egypt), the reader may consult Arasoughly 1996, Shafik 1998, and a special issue of *Alif* (15, 1995).

Turkey and Iran, neighboring countries with deep historical relationships to the Arab world and also with Islam as the majority religion, both have what might be termed film "industries," each averaging more than sixty films annually over the past decade. However, neither of these cinemas is present in the normal distribution circuits of Morocco and the rest of the Arab world although, it should be said, Iran offers a model, at times chastening, for Moroccan and other Arab filmmakers who see the recent international success of this national cinema as something of a rebuke to their own. (For a recent assessment of Iranian cinema and a collection of interviews with Iranian filmmakers, see Dabashi 2001.)

21. The quotations in this paragraph are from Malkmus and Armes (1991: 35) and are based on data through the 1980s.

Egyptian production rebounded to thirty-three films in 2001, following the twenty produced in 2000, but then sank to twenty-two in 2002 and to fewer than ten in 2003. (For the 2000 and 2001 figures, see Yasser Mohab, "Le bilan optimiste d'une année agitée," *Al-Ahram Hebdo,* 2–8 January 2002, p. 28; for the 2002 figures, see *Cahiers du Cinéma,* L'Atlas du cinéma, Hors-série, April 2003; for 2003, see Amina Hassan, "L'industrie du cinéma égyptien dans le rouge," *Al-Ahram Hebdo,* 29 October–4 November 2003.) The number of theaters is down too, to somewhat more than two hundred for a population approaching seventy million.

In its overall decline since the 1980s Egyptian film production is just one instance of a more widespread phenomenon, that of decreasing film production in almost all countries other than the "big five." (Figures indicating this trend can be found in the UNESCO report cited earlier.) Bearing this general downward trend in mind, the recent increases in Moroccan production are all the more significant. Some of the other exceptions will be mentioned in the conclusion.

22. The area of Morocco is given as 710,850 sq km in official Moroccan publications (see *Le Maroc en Chiffres 1989* [Rabat: Ministère du Plan, 1989]).

23. The coalition was led by the USFP (*l'Union socialiste des forces populaires*—the Socialist Union of Popular Forces), which had been in existence and opposition since the early 1960s; one of its historic leaders, Abderrahman

Youssoufi, an opposition figure who had spent many years in exile, was named prime minister. What became known more simply as *"l'Alternance"* ("the changeover") was a historic moment in Moroccan political life. One measure of the king's continuing power is the fact that the key ministries of defense, foreign affairs, interior, justice, and religious affairs are all run directly from the Palace, bypassing governmental oversight.

24. The number of civil society associations has gone from approximately eighteen thousand in the mid-1980s to more than thirty thousand today, with the recent emergence of "a new type of organization for protecting [citizens], those concerning human rights, consumer protection, protection of the environment and development" (Dembri Khaled, "Aux racines culturelles des ONG au Maroc," *Libération* [Morocco], 21 July 2001).

Another sign of the growing freedom of expression in the past decade may be seen in the increase in newspaper titles and readership. After remaining roughly constant at between ten and fourteen from the years 1970 through 1994, the number of titles jumped to twenty in 1995 and to twenty-two in 1996. Similarly, the total numbers of copies distributed oscillated near 300,000 from 1970 through 1994, then jumped to 630,000 in 1995 and 704,000 in 1996 (www.unesco.org).

In addition, book publishing has been characterized as "in good health ... having made a noticeable qualitative leap ... publishing some 1,000 books each year in the two languages (30% of them in French ...)" (Adil Hajji, "Malaise dans la culture marocaine," *Le Monde Diplomatique,* September 2000).

25. One indication of the seriousness of the problems: the World Bank estimated in May 2000 that the portion of the Moroccan population living under the poverty line (defined as having an income of less than one dollar per person per day) had risen to 19 percent, from 13 percent in 1991. (These figures are cited in a report to the French Senate—see Charasse 2001.)

Morocco is ranked 126th of 175 countries according to the United Nations Development Program (UNDP) report for the year 2003, finding itself behind its major North African counterparts: Tunisia is at 91, Algeria at 107, and Egypt at 120; also, the trend has been negative in the last few years: Morocco was at 123 in 2002 and at 112 in 2001 (www.hdr.undp.org/reports/global/ 2003, 2002, 2001).

26. Among the most important steps taken toward a new societal transparency was the investigation by a parliamentary committee into the practices and policies of one of the main banking institutions, the Crédit Immobilier de l'Habitat, which led to the uncovering of favoritism and corruption and, perhaps most importantly, the naming of names and the beginning of judicial proceedings in early 2001 against those suspected of crimes. However, there were also some steps in the opposite direction, including the intermittently muscled attacks on demonstrators by the forces of order (such as those occurring in early 2001) and occasional seizing and suspensions of periodicals. These developments led many commentators and observers to be wary and to caution against taking positive trends for granted.

More recent developments are discussed in the conclusion.

27. In boycotting the festival Tazi was protesting, he said, the "flagrant lack of respect on the part of the organizers who decide everything without consulting the filmmakers, where the festival jury has advertisers but no journalists, where the ruling principle is who your friends are, pure and simple"

(Karim Boukhari, "Séisme au cinéma: Mohamed Abderrahmane Tazi dit non au Festival National du Film!" *Al Bayane,* 7 November 1998).

28. Tazi set the time and place and his aim, explicitly, was to position the interviews so they did not unduly disrupt his other work.

29. There is further discussion of this aspect in the conclusion.

30. I have transliterated from Arabic with the general reader rather than the specialist in mind. Common Arabic names have been put in their usual anglicized form: Muhammad, Omar, and so on; I have not distinguished between emphatic and non-emphatic consonants or between short and long vowels, and the Arabic definite article occurs, variously, as al- or el-. In the text, *q* stands for the Arabic letter *qaf,* pronounced as a strong, guttural "k"; *sh,* when occurring together, stands for the letter *sheen,* pronounced as the "sh" in the English "sheep"; *ḥ* is pronounced as a strong, breathy English "h"; *',* the Arabic letter *hamza,* is said as an unvoiced glottal stop; and *ʿ,* the letter *ʿain,* is said as a strong, voiced, guttural consonant.

For exchange rates I have approximated those that were current during the period of research: $1 U.S. = 7 French francs, $1 U.S. = 10 Moroccan dirhams.

All unattributed translations are mine.

1. THE MOST SUCCESSFUL MOROCCAN FILM EVER

1. Many of these quotes come from clippings or fliers provided by Tazi, and dates and/or titles are sometimes missing. The information I am able to provide follows: "The first..." (Tahar Ben Jelloun, *Médi 1*); "without doubt..." (Faten Safieddine, *Téléplus*); "we rediscovered..." (Alain Rimu, *Le Nouvel Observateur*); "this new film..." (Ahmed Araib, *Maghreb Culture*); "M. A. Tazi shows..." (Hamid Nahla, "A la recherche de ma femme," *Al-Bayane,* 13 January 1994).

2. More detail on the first success, *A Love Affair in Casablanca* (Abdelkader Lagtaa, 1991), is given in note 10.

3. The discussion that follows relates to distribution and exhibition; the extent to which these new developments in the early 1990s may have been related to the shifting demographics and tastes of Moroccan audiences and the changing nature of the films themselves will be explored in chapter 6.

4. The process of "Moroccanization," whereby Moroccans came to own formerly foreign-owned enterprises, was a complicated one in the film sector. However the structure of the sector remained the same, with the newly named major distributors (Maghreb International Film, Société Marocaine de Film, Univers Films, and so on) relaying firms that had been named, respectively, Warner Bros, Gaumont, United Artists, and so on. (For more detail on this process, see Jaidi 1991: 45ff.)

5. This would in any case have been difficult. As mentioned in the introduction, when Tunisia tried to impose quotas in the early 1960s on the screening of imported films, the international distribution companies initiated a boycott and the Tunisian government had to rescind the quotas one year later. During the early 1980s, fourteen West and Central African countries tried to create a distribution network (the Inter-African Consortium for Film Distribution) to promote and support African films, but this lasted only four years and then dissolved.

6. The quotation is from Jaidi 2000: 21.

Note 4 in the introduction shows the relationship between the high number of imported films and the low numbers produced by Moroccans, and the decline in overall attendance figures and numbers of theaters. It should be noted that the permit to show an imported film is issued for a period of from three to five years, so that the total number of foreign films available for showing in any one year is somewhere in the neighborhood of fifteen hundred, overwhelming the fewer than ten films that Moroccans might produce annually.

On concentration in this area: "the eight groups that dominate distribution-exhibition control 75% of distribution and 25% of theaters . . . thus accounting for 35% of gross receipts. To this one should add the monopoly control in the exhibition sector alone . . . where the main firms own one-third of the theaters, most of them well-situated, which explains the fact that their numbers of spectators and box-office receipts amount to approximately 50% of the total" (Jaidi 2000: 25).

7. Jaidi draws the following conclusion, which is widely shared in Morocco and for good reason: "The operation and maintenance of [this] mechanism for importing cultural products, traditionally imposed and consumed without any discussion, constitutes a sort of permanent cultural aggression which finds its justification in the logic of the cash register, validating the supremacy of a minority which profits from it and [which] structures demand to satisfy its own interests" (Jaidi 2000: 21).

8. Najib Benkirane, personal interview. The Benkirane family was an important player in the distribution field in the mid-1980s, owning eight distribution companies and importing about 25 percent of all imported films. These companies also owned about a dozen theaters (seven in the large cities), which accounted for 8 percent of the total cinema receipts in all of Morocco (Jaidi 1991: 63).

9. Benkirane cited, in particular, *Between Hammer and Anvil* (1990) of Hakim Noury (b. 1952) and Tazi's *Badis* (1989). Regarding the latter, he added, "I just had the occasion to see this film again last year and I was reminded what a great film it is."

10. *A Love Affair in Casablanca* (1991), the first feature film of Abdelkader Lagtaa (b. 1948), is the story of a young Casablancan woman, still in secondary school, who is having an affair with a much older man. She then begins another affair with someone her own age who, unknown to her, turns out to be her first lover's son. *A Love Affair in Casablanca* attracted big crowds when it was released in 1992, drawing a total of more than two hundred thousand spectators, a number rarely, if ever, attained by a Moroccan film prior to that. For a fuller treatment of this film, see Dwyer 2002a.

11. For more discussion of how the subjects and settings of Moroccan films changed during the 1990s, see chapter 6 (the section "Changing Audience, Changing Tastes, Changing Features") and Dwyer 2002b.

Even with these good attendance figures it is very difficult—almost impossible, in fact—for a Moroccan film to make money. The following very approximate calculation demonstrates how difficult it is for a director-producer to recoup the amount invested in a film or, put differently, how unattractive producing a Moroccan film is for a private investor.

Of total box-office receipts, approximately 30–35 percent goes to the distributor with the remainder going to the theater owner. Of the distributor's share, 70 percent goes to the producer—the producer's share thus amounts to around 20 percent of the total.

With this in mind we can make the following rough calculations for an "average" Moroccan film, with all amounts in Moroccan DH, and assuming all additional investment comes from the producer.

1. Average total budget 4,000,000
2. Aid Fund award (approximate amount of state aid to production) 2,000,000
3. Amount required from producer (1 minus 2) 2,000,000
4. Average ticket price 10
5. Amount of average ticket earned by producer (70 percent of distributor's 30 percent share) 2.1
6. Number of tickets needed to be sold to reimburse producer's investment of 2,000,000 (3 divided by 5) 950,000

No Moroccan film other than Tazi's *Looking* has approached this number of spectators. A Moroccan film reaching a theater audience of two hundred thousand (a very respectable performance) will thus still have a producer's deficit of more than 1.5 million DH, more than one-third of its total budget. This provides yet another indication of how important it is for the producer to obtain funding over and above the Aid Fund award.

12. Souheil Ben Barka was head of the CCM and is an established film director in his own right.

13. Today, making a new print costs approximately 18,000–20,000 DH (approximately $2,000) and subtitling, which must be done anew for each copy, approximately $1,000, or about $3,000 in all for a subtitled print. To this should be added the one-off cost of translating the original Arabic into the foreign language, estimated at about 5,000 DH ($500).

14. This enthusiasm also reached the emigrant community in Paris where *Looking* played for twenty weeks (Et-Tayeb Houdaifa, "Genèse de '*Lalla Hobby*': désamour, discorde et peaux de banane," *Téléplus* 78, August 1996).

15. In Islamic law, this process of *taḥlil* ("making licit"), whereby the divorced wife can only become licit to her ex-husband if she first marries another man, is commonly interpreted as a way to punish a man who has lost self-control and behaved whimsically in a matter as serious as marriage and divorce.

16. Yasmine Belmahi, "Mohamed A. Tazi, Entretien," *Le Journal* (Casablanca), date not available.

17. Muhammad V was Morocco's king until his death in 1961, when he was succeeded by his son Hassan II.

18. A Steadicam is a device that stabilizes handheld camera shots, allowing for camera movement where it is impossible to install tracks and dollies. The cost is approximately 10,000 DH ($1,000) per day, including the cameraman.

19. Both Noureddin Sail and Farida Benlyazid appear frequently in this book; I was able to meet both of them several times in the course of my research. Noureddin Sail has been something of a "Mr. Cinema" in Morocco since the mid-1960s: he was head of the Moroccan Federation of Film Clubs (FCM—*Fédération des ciné-clubs marocains*) for a decade starting in the early 1970s and for a number of years had his own film-oriented program on Moroccan television. He produced Tazi's first film and was a screenwriter on three

of his four films. For several years in the mid-1980s he was program director for the Moroccan public television channel RTM (at that time RTM was the only Moroccan TV station), commissioning films from some well-known Moroccan directors and from a number of then little-known ones who went on to have full careers; in the late 1980s Sail went to Paris, becoming program director for the subscriber-based TV channel Canal Plus Horizons. Even while based in Paris he remained a strong presence in Morocco. In April 2000 he returned to Morocco as the head of its second television station, 2M.

Farida Benlyazid (b. 1948), one of Morocco's few women filmmakers, had started out as a screenwriter and had already performed in that capacity on a number of films, including Tazi's previous film, *Badis*. Prior to writing *Looking* she had directed her own first film, *A Door to the Sky* (*Une porte ouverte sur le ciel*, 1988). Her second film was *Women's Wiles* (*La ruse des femmes*, 1999) and her third was *Casablanca, Casablanca* (2002).

20. The passing of a boy from the woman's to the man's world, from going to the *ḥammam* with one's mother to being refused entry with her, is the theme of one of the most successful Maghreb films in recent decades, Férid Boughedir's *Halfaouine, Children of the Terraces* (Tunisia, 1990).

21. Tazi had used these terms in an interview with this title that he gave in *Téléplus*, July 1994 (no further data available).

22. Prior to *Looking*, Nabil Lahlou made six films between 1978 and 1992, all of a sardonic and/or lampooning nature. They were all made before the public's turn toward Moroccan films and the only one of these films to be distributed nationally was the first (*Al-Qanfoudi*, 1978), perhaps because it was co-produced by the CCM.

23. The Mudawwana—Morocco's personal status code—governs marriage and divorce (among other matters) and follows the teachings of the Maliki school of Islamic law as it is practiced in Morocco. According to the Mudawwana, a man has the right to have up to four wives and to gain a divorce at will. The Mudawwana has been the subject of heated debate for many years and in April 2001, after government initiatives to revise it had stalled, King Muhammad VI took the crucial step of appointing a consultative commission to consider changing it. In his charge to the commission, the king stated that it should take into consideration universal human rights values and approach "its task of interpretation in the spirit of the generous design of Islamic Law which consists in . . . the strict equilibrium between rights and duties, in conformity with the divine words, 'women have as many rights as obligations . . . ' " (statement cited in www.central.ma, 29 April 2001). The commission's report was submitted in September 2003. For subsequent developments see, in the conclusion, "Moroccan Politics, Society, and Culture."

24. Interestingly, an audience survey in the early 1990s indicated that, among the film-going public as a whole, laughter was more valued in a film than action, suspense, or deep emotions; this was especially true among students, workers, merchants, and artisans (Jaidi 1992: 47–48; this survey is discussed in detail in chapter 6).

25. Yasmine Belmahi, "Entretien avec Mohamed Abderrahman Tazi," *Al-Maghrib*, 9–10 September 1990.

26. French teachers sometimes imposed similar punishments during the period of colonial rule. The anthropologist and psychologist Lilia Labidi recounts her experience as a child in Tunisia when it, like Morocco, was a French Protectorate: "One day the French teacher, to punish me, shut me up

in a large armoire. There was a rabbit inside there with me! In the dimness I saw the poor rabbit, staring back at me with its shining eyes; I crouched in a corner, terrified, staring back at it. Did I cry? I don't know, but I do remember this incident as striking me at a time when I was just learning to distinguish between good and evil. This French teacher, merged with the colonizer, with colonial authority, how could he be the promoter of good, of what they then called modernity?" (Labidi 2002: 297).

27. Khouribga, scene of an African Film Festival held every few years, is a small inland city about 100 km southeast of Casablanca.

28. El-Alj is a very well-known Moroccan actor and playwright who has been active in radio, television, theater, and film in a career spanning five decades. In addition to sharing credit for the film's dialogue, he also plays the role of the Hajj's fellow jewelry store owner.

29. A scene exemplifying this kind of cruelty, where children leaving school insult and make fun of the "community idiot," occurs in Moncef Dhouib's Tunisian film *Ya Sultan al-Medina* (1992).

30. Tazi was referring to the white sheet with the blood stain, signifying defloration, that is shown to the assembled guests on the wedding night—the Japanese flag has a red circle against a white background.

31. The problem of clandestine emigration from Morocco to Spain is a very serious one and seems to be worsening (a large majority of those involved are Moroccans but there are also a significant number of sub-Saharan Africans using Morocco as a way station). In the year 2000 the Spanish apprehended fifteen thousand illegal immigrants who had used the passage between Morocco and Spain, four times as many as were apprehended the previous year (Roger Cohen, "Illegal migration rises sharply in the European Union," *New York Times,* 12 December 2000). In 2001 the figure rose to more than eighteen thousand (with almost 80 percent using the Straits of Gibraltar and the rest crossing from Morocco to the Canary Islands). To these numbers should be added the more than twenty-five thousand people seeking to emigrate who were arrested by the Moroccan authorities in the year 2000 (the rate increased to twenty-one thousand for the first eight months of 2001), and also the twenty-one thousand Moroccans rejected at normal Spanish border stations during 2001. The total number of Moroccans estimated to attempt a clandestine crossing of the Straits of Gibraltar each year is between one hundred and one hundred ten thousand ("Par dizaines de milliers," *Le Monde Diplomatique,* June 2002, p. 17, citing official Spanish government figures and those provided by the Association of the Friends and Families of the Victims of Clandestine Immigration [*l'Association des amis et familles des victimes de l'immigration clandestine*—AFVIC], founded in Morocco in 2001).

More recent figures continue to show an increasing trend: in 2002, 29,490 people were apprehended in Morocco attempting to emigrate clandestinely (slightly more than half were Moroccans, the rest were from sub-Saharan Africa) and, during the first quarter of 2003, the rate increased to 9,800 apprehensions (of which one-third were Moroccans; "Immigration clandestine," www.liberation.press.ma, 10 May 2003); in the first eleven months of 2003, the Spanish authorities apprehended more than 18,000 people seeking to reach the Spanish coast from Morocco, while giving aid over the same period to almost 5,500 people who had begun their voyage in Morocco but were stranded at sea ("Le détroit et les 'itinéraires bis,'" *Le Courrier International,* 11–17 December 2003, p. 51).

Among those who try the crossing, many die. According to AFVIC, more than three thousand corpses were fished out of the Straits between 1997 and 2001. Estimates are that for every body found three escape detection, giving a total of more than ten thousand deaths over a five-year period, or an average of more than two thousand per year (Pierre Vermeren, "Les marocains rêvent d'Europe," *Le Monde Diplomatique*, June 2002, pp. 1, 16–17, citation from p. 16).

Ships from five European nations (Spain, France, Italy, Portugal, and the UK) are now patrolling the Mediterranean in an effort to stem this phenomenon (Emma Daly, "Anti-migration patrols start in Mediterranean," *New York Times*, 29 January 2003).

32. Each of Tazi's first four films either begins or ends with the sea or is set on the coast. Why he takes the sea to be so important will be discussed later, in the interlude following chapter 4.

INTERLUDE:
FILM'S POWER AND FUNCTION

1. The expression *"l'Alternance"* (changeover, changing of the guard) referred to the coalition government formed in March 1998. For more detail see the introduction.

2. Ibn al-Muqaffa' (b. about 102/720, d. 138/756), an Arabic author of Persian origin, was one of the first to translate literary works from India and Persia into Arabic. His translation of the celebrated collection of Indian tales *Kalila wa-Dimna* is widely known and he himself is considered one of the creators of Arabic literary prose.

3. Tazi here cited a book, *Us et Coutumes au Maroc*, that Ahmed Tayyeb el-Alj (see note 28 for chapter 1) wrote and that treated the subject of *safih*. *"Sans vergogne"* ("shameless") was Tazi's translation of this into French; other meanings given in Wehr's dictionary include "stupid," "foolish," and "incompetent."

4. A survey carried out in Morocco in 2001 showed that 82 percent of secondary school students wanted to emigrate to Europe, with the figure rising to 94 percent among youth under 30 who have no stable income. Among this latter group, 62 percent said they were ready to emigrate clandestinely (Pierre Vermeren, "Les marocains rêvent d'Europe," *Le Monde Diplomatique*, June 2002, pp. 1, 16–17, citation from p. 16).

5. This problem will be explained in chapter 3.

6. The Gharb (meaning "the West") refers to the very fertile area of land in western Morocco situated between the Atlantic coast near Rabat and the city of Fez.

7. We discuss at length Tazi's ideas about narration in the interlude after chapter 4.

8. One Egyptian example of this is discussed by Armbrust, who writes of the "christmasization" of Ramadan, where among "local Ramadan practices are new habits of consumption and consumerism," particularly the use of television programs to encourage "a 'Christmas-like' association of materialist mass consumption with cultural value . . . increasingly tied to the promotion of the interests of multinational corporations, as well as those of the state" (Armbrust 2002: 335, 336).

2. BUILDING THE NATIONAL CINEMA, BUILDING A CAREER

1. When independence from France was formally obtained, Spain also renounced many of her claims but retained some enclaves on the Mediterranean and Atlantic coasts as well as the large territory of the Western Sahara. By the mid-1970s almost all of these had been ceded to Morocco, with the exception of the Mediterranean towns of Melilla and Ceuta and several small possessions off Morocco's Mediterranean coast (one of these, a small fortress outpost, provides the setting for Tazi's second film, *Badis*).

Since independence France has continued to play an important economic and cultural role in Morocco, with many programs of technical and cultural assistance. Even today her influence, although much attenuated, remains significant and she remains by far Morocco's most important trading partner, accounting for approximately 25 percent of its imports and exports. France provides the overwhelming portion of Morocco's foreign aid (half of Morocco's total aid in 1998, according to a report to the French Senate by Michel Charasse, "Les crédits d'aide publique au développement affectés aux pays du Maghreb," *Rapport d'information* 083 [2000–2001]—Commission Des Finances). France also contributes, through technical and cultural assistance programs, most of the external aid for filmmakers (although it should be noted, according to the same report, that total sums for cultural and technical cooperation given to Morocco by the French ministry of foreign affairs fell by almost half between 1991 and 2001, pushing Morocco from first to fourth in rank in terms of countries receiving French foreign aid).

2. The figures on urban and total population come from Miège 1966: 52, 58.

The situation in the education sector is indicative of the general problem: in 1955 only 11.2 percent of school-aged Muslims were in primary school and only 1.2 percent were in secondary school; during the entire forty-four years of the French Protectorate a total of only 530 Moroccans had passed the baccalaureate examination at the end of secondary school, a prerequisite for attending university (Eickelman 1998: 345). After independence the Moroccan state invested heavily in education and, with the aid of a 1963 decree that declared education obligatory for all children between the ages of 7 and 13, the proportion of those attending primary school rose quickly to 60 percent (Miège 1966: 65).

3. In advancing Morocco's claim to the Western Sahara, Hassan II took what turned out to be his most inspired initiative. In November 1975, while the area was still under Spanish control and while Spain was occupied with the lingering illness and then death of Franco, the king mobilized 350,000 Moroccans to stage a peaceful "Green March" into the territory, gaining him almost unanimous support within Morocco and stalemating the external opposition. Although Moroccan sovereignty over the area is still contested and Morocco has suffered some important diplomatic defeats over the years (as when, for example, the Organization of African Unity [OAU] recognized the Polisario Front's Saharan Arab Democratic Republic as a member state, leading Morocco to suspend its participation in the organization), Moroccan military, political, and economic measures appear to have borne fruit and most of the area has become progressively integrated into Morocco. A referendum under

U.N. auspices to settle the fate of the area was first planned for 1992, but Morocco and the Polisario Front have not been able to agree on a list of eligible voters. In mid-2001 a new U.N. plan envisaged greater autonomy for the area under Moroccan rule while not excluding the possibility of a referendum in the future. Diplomacy continues and new proposals proliferate but, whatever path this takes it is difficult to imagine Morocco agreeing to any conditions that might seriously weaken its hold over the area, beyond according some small measure of autonomy that would not amount to any substantial loss of control.

4. Tazi estimated that in the late 1960s about sixty copies of the news review were sent out every week to theaters all over the country (Moulay Driss Jaidi, "On ne peut pas toujours faire des films avec de petits moyens: un entretien avec Mohamed Abderrahmane Tazi," *L'Opinion*, 16 April 1982). Film buses may be finding new uses today: in 2003, during the month of Ramadan (October–November), a Moroccan portable telephone company sponsored a film bus tour of ten cities, showing two Moroccan feature films— Tazi's *Looking* and Farida Benlyazid's *Women's Wiles*. (For the use of film buses in conjunction with digital projection in some African countries, see note 36 in the conclusion.)

5. The figures on theaters and attendance for 1980 and 1981 were provided by the CCM; the other figures in this paragraph are from Ouchen 1998: table 2a.

By 1999, the numbers of theaters and total attendance had retreated to approximately the levels at independence, despite a tripling of population and continuing urbanization.

Obviously, one of the reasons that numbers of theaters and attendance reached these heights when they did and fell precipitously thereafter can be found in competition from television. In 1962 Morocco officially had only some five thousand television sets, the number growing to more than one million by 1984 or roughly one set for twenty people (Jaidi 2000: 58). By 1997, this had increased to more than three million sets, or one set for less than nine people (www.unesco.org).

The trend toward urbanization continued throughout, so that by 1996 the urban population came to comprise more than one-half of the total population (Ouchen 1998: table 2b). This trend is continuing today.

6. Of the three directors two—Ahmed Belhachmi and Larbi Bennani— were trained at IDHEC (*l'Institut des hautes études cinématographiques*) in Paris— and the third, Larbi Benchekroun, in Rome and the University of Southern California in the United States (El Khodari 2000: 45, 103). A fourth, Ahmed Mesnaoui, was self-taught and had made a number of short films before independence, then received formal training at UNESCO in Egypt (Bouanani 1984: b; the pagination in this manuscript being irregular, I have created my own).

7. One earlier full-length fiction film, *The Accursed Son* (*Le fils maudit*) had been made in 1958 by Muhammad Ousfour. Ousfour, an actor who had performed in many European-produced films made in Morocco during the colonial period, had taught himself a number of basic filming and laboratory techniques and, with little more than spit, polish, and glue and working out of his own garage, completed this film and a number of shorts, as well as another full-length film in 1970, *Diabolic Treasure* (*Le trésor infernal*). Ousfour's films were, understandably, technically amateur and had little direct effect on

later Moroccan filmmaking. However, his indirect effect was substantial since several Moroccan filmmakers, among them Ahmed Bouanani and Muhammad Reggab, were introduced to films in Ousfour's garage (Araib and Hullessen 1999: 26; for more detail on Ousfour, see Bouanani 1984 and Fertat's biography [2000]).

8. These details are from Bouanani 1984: 74–75. This finely wrought, insightful, very readable, very personal but unfortunately unpublished manuscript by a major figure in Moroccan cinema—the poet and filmmaker Ahmed Bouanani—provides the best appreciation of Moroccan filmmaking from independence through the early 1980s.

For this period Carter 1999 also provides much detail, summarized in Carter 2000.

9. These include *A Thousand and One Hands* (Souheil Ben Barka, 1972), *About Some Meaningless Events* (Mustapha Derkaoui, 1974), *Chergui* (*The Wind from the East*, Moumen Smihi, 1975), *Hole in the Wall* (Jilali Ferhati, 1977), *The Days, the Days* (Ahmed Maanouni, 1978), *Al-Qanfoudi* (Nabil Lahlou, 1978), *The Postman* (Hakim Noury, 1979), and *The Mirage* (Ahmed Bouanani, 1980).

These films account for the Tunisian filmmaker Férid Boughedir's 1981 observation that some Moroccan films showed an "intellectualist" orientation "devoted to the search for original forms of artistic expression . . . that distanced themselves from Western film clichés . . . and drew upon the Moroccan collective imaginary." In Boughedir's view, this "intellectualist" current was responsible for Morocco having become, despite its low quantity of production, the most advanced of Maghrebin countries, "as far as creating an original Maghrebin cinematic language is concerned" (Boughedir 1981: 207–209).

10. From twenty-one clubs in 1974, the number advanced to fifty-seven in 1981. In this area, as well as in theater numbers and attendance, the early 1980s marked the apogee. From a high of sixty-two clubs in 1982 (the last year of Sail's leadership), the number decreased to thirty-one in 1984 and to only eighteen in 1994 (these figures are from Ouchen 1998: 65). The generally moribund state of the film clubs has continued into the twenty-first century (see Mohamed Bakrim, "Que sont les ciné-clubs devenus," *Libération*, 29 March 2003).

11. The participants, eight of whom were IDHEC graduates, included Bouanani and Tazi. The 18-page dossier presented in *Souffles* contained a detailed three-page analysis and proposals submitted to King Hassan II (*Souffles*, deuxième trimestre 1966). Another significant publication of this period, founded in the same year as *Souffles* and also giving space to cinema, was *Lamalif*. *Souffles* was outlawed in 1972 (Bouanani 1984: 119–120). *Lamalif* had a much longer life, ceasing publication in the early 1990s, after a period in which it was put in difficulty by the authorities.

12. Cited in Bouanani 1984: 122.

13. Ouchen 1998: 56.

14. More detail on filmmaker organizations is presented in chapter 6.

15. The film was Souheil Ben Barka's *A Thousand and One Hands* (1972; Bouanani 1984: 94 gives the distribution numbers, 1984: 89 the attendance figures).

16. Ahmed Maanouni, director of *The Days, the Days* (1978), cited in Bouanani 1984: 111.

17. Bouanani 1984: 96.

18. Between 1980 and 1984, Morocco produced some thirty films. Over the two decades between 1980 and 2000 Morocco produced more than ninety features, compared to some sixty for Algeria and about forty-five for Tunisia (El Khodari 2000 for Morocco; Armes [1996, 2000, forthcoming] for Algeria and Tunisia).

19. Obviously, these kinds of activities aren't peculiar to Moroccan children. Laure Adler recounts the childhood of Marguerite Duras, growing up in Vietnam: "Marguerite is 14 years old, her brother 17. With him, she kills monkeys, birds. [Marguerite writes] 'It was horrible, we killed everything we found.' Caimans, panthers, snakes" (Adler 1998: 61).

20. One of Morocco's earliest IDHEC graduates (1957).

21. Sensitometry is "the study of the effect of light, under various conditions and with various intensities, on photographic emulsion" (Konigsberg 1997: 352).

22. Welles, speaking of Toland, says, "His whole point was, 'There's no mystery to it.' He said, 'You can be a cameraman, too—in a couple of days I can teach you everything that matters.' So we spent the next weekend together and he showed me the inside of that bag of tricks, and, like all good magic, the secrets are ridiculously simple" (Welles and Bogdanovich 1998: 60).

23. Photometry is "the science of light measurement" (Konigsberg 1997: 293).

24. Jean Mitry (1904–1988) was a French film critic and teacher who also made a number of experimental film shorts aiming to underscore the relationship between editing and music. He is perhaps best known as author of *Esthétique et Psychologie du Cinéma* (1963, selections of which have been translated as Jean Mitry, *The Aesthetics and Psychology of Cinema* [Bloomington: Indiana University Press, 2000]).

Georges Sadoul (1904–1967) was a French film critic and historian whose broad and detailed knowledge of film history made him pre-eminent in this field in France immediately after World War Two. Among his many works of reference the best known is his multivolume *Histoire générale du cinéma,* the first volume of which appeared in 1946.

25. Arthur Honegger (1892–1955) was a Swiss-French composer.

26. Dziga Vertov (1896–1954) was a Soviet filmmaker specializing in newsreels and documentaries, known for his commitment to unstaged reality and dynamic editing, brought together in his notion of *Kino-Pravda,* "film truth."

Chris Marker (b. 1924) is a French filmmaker closely associated with La Nouvelle Vague of the late 1950s and early 1960s and an important cultural figure of the left, who extended Vertov's principles and whose film *Le joli mai* (1963) was a significant signpost of La Nouvelle Vague. He filmed all over the world and also made some short fictions, of which *La Jetée* (1962) is the best known.

Joris Ivens (1898–1989), a Dutch filmmaker also strongly influenced by Vertov's school of filmmaking, is perhaps best known for films that unite poetic feeling and revolutionary hope.

27. Tazi was referring to EIRESH (*l'Equipe interdisciplinaire de recherche en sciences humaines*—the interdisciplinary social science research team), directed by the Moroccan sociologist Paul Pascon. Latif Lahlou headed the audiovisual section, which also had Abdellah Zerouali, both of whom had been earlier

IDHEC graduates and who had left the CCM to work with EIRESH. There were also two French sociologists (François Chevaldonné and Serge Moity) and one Tunisian (Rashid Bouderbela).

28. "Peter Bogdanovich: How do you decide where you're going to put the camera?

Orson Welles: I don't make a conscious decision—I know instantly where it goes. There's never a moment of doubt" (Welles and Bogdanovich 1998: 62).

29. The three films were *Conquer to Live* (*Vaincre pour vivre*, Mohamed B. A. Tazi and Ahmed Mesnaoui, 1968) for which Muhammad was the cinematographer, *When the Dates Ripen* (*Quand mûrissent les dates*, Abdelaziz Ramdani and Larbi Bennani, 1968), and *Spring Sunshine* (*Soleil de printemps*, Latif Lahlou, 1969). There is no kin tie between the two Tazis and the resemblance between the names has led to many errors of attribution.

30. Hennebelle 1981: 213. In this interview Bennani goes into some detail regarding the Islamic, Moroccan, and especially the psychoanalytic symbolism that permeates the film.

31. Ahmed Bouanani also attributes the failure of Sigma 3 to Bennani, at least in part, saying, "The indescribable attitude of the official 'director' of the film put an end to a cooperative effort that would have been without precedent in the film history of the Maghreb" (Bouanani 1984: 133).

Tazi told me that these bad feelings led the other members of Sigma 3 to take away Bennani's rights to show or distribute the film. These rights were given to Tazi. Nonetheless, in the year 2000 Bennani managed to sell rights to show the film to the European-based television station ARTE, for the substantial sum of 300,000 French francs (approximately $40,000), which he kept for himself.

32. Georgakas and Rubenstein (1983a: 155–172).

33. Graduates from IDHEC in Paris constitute some 50 percent of Moroccan directors, followed by graduates from Poland and the former Soviet Union. Only five received their training in the Arab world. Two were trained in the United States (these figures come from El Khodari 2000: 74).

34. These numbers are tallied from Armes 1996: 66–67. The development of state aid to production will be treated in more detail in chapter 4.

35. Ben Barka had not yet been named director of the CCM, which happened in July 1986.

36. Tazi had one daughter with his first wife, a son and daughter with his second, and a daughter with his third and current wife.

37. A coincidence calls for inclusion here: as I was writing this chapter I fortuitously came across an article in *Scientific American* tracing the belief that it has been scientifically "proven" that a bumblebee cannot fly. Characterizing this belief as "an urban legend of science . . . often cited as an inspiring example of persevering in the face of overbearing dogma," the author traced its origins to a 1934 book by a French entomologist whose argument was "presumably based on the fact that the maximum possible lift produced by aircraft wings as small as a bumblebee's wings . . . would be much less than the weight of the bee." The author notes, with considerable understatement, that such considerations are irrelevant to understanding a bee's flight, for "it is apparent to the casual observer that a hovering insect, its wings a blur, does not fly like an aircraft." The author continues, "The reason insects represent such a chal-

lenge is that they flap and rotate their wings from 20 to 600 times a second
. . . creating aerodynamic forces that change continually and confound both
mathematical and experimental analyses" (Dickinson 2001: 36).

Revising Tazi's example in this light, perhaps we should say that it may
not be impossible to understand how a Moroccan filmmaker manages to make
a film, but the phenomenon does come close to confounding analysis.

INTERLUDE: A FIRST FEATURE— *THE BIG TRIP* (1981)

1. Tazi reckons that a normal crew consists of a minimum of thirty people
(Fatiha Layadi and Narjis Rerhaye, "Mohamed Abderrahman Tazi, cinéaste,"
Al Bayane, 16 July 1998).

2. Taking Omar to be a Candide-like character was something of a commonplace in the critical discussion of the film: for example, Bouanani entitles
his chapter on the film "Candide, ou la carte du tendre" (Bouanani 1984) and
Férid Boughedir cites Voltaire's Candide in referring to the film (Férid Boughedir, "De beaux jours pour le cinéma méditerranéen," *Jeune Afrique,* 21 October 1981).

3. Tazi was naming here two religious brotherhoods known for their "ec-
static" behavior.

4. Again, this subject will be taken up in the interlude following chapter 4.

5. I didn't fully agree with Tazi on this, nor did a number of critics, among
them Noor Eddine Ben Mansour, who notes that "the fatalism strikes harshly
and leaves the spectator with no way out" (Noor Eddine Ben Mansour, "Le
Grand Voyage," *L'Opinion,* 18 January 1982). Bouanani, once again, puts it
very well: "The film's moral is clear: there is no longer any hope, there's a
calm but, beyond the calm, there's just a dead end" (Bouanani 1984: 156).

We return to the question of open endings in discussing Tazi's second
film, *Badis,* in chapter 4.

3. HUSTON, WISE, COPPOLA, CAMUS . . . AND PASOLINI, SCORSESE . . . AND SOME OTHERS

1. One of the clips Tazi is talking about—a very amusing one—shows a
peasant couple (played by two very well-known Moroccan actors, Khadija
Assad and Aziz Saadallah, who are also man and wife) going to a rural market,
the husband spending all his time in the market café, chatting with friends,
while the wife works selling their merchandise and buying goods for the
household. On the return home the husband, acting tired from his "exhausting" activities, wants to ride the mule. But the mule throws him off and,
breaking into speech in what has so far been a film without dialogue, says,
"That's really too much! I just have to speak up at the way you've been
treating your wife." The wife looks on with a big smile on her face. (*The
Indignant Mule,* 1991, made for the United Nations University and the World
Institute for Development Economics Research [WIDER].)

2. Over the period of our interviews, Tazi had a number of such contracts,
among them producing CD-ROMs on "Moroccan Marriages" for the Paris-

based *Institut du Monde Arabe* and on "The Fantasia," for the Hannover Expo 2000.

3. For film production during Morocco's colonial period, see Araib and Hullessen 1999 and Jaidi's more detailed study (2001).

4. Berrah et al. 1981: 206.

5. The French military action in Casablanca was ostensibly to retaliate for the killing of a number of workers constructing the port of Casablanca but was also part of France's strategic policy to gain control of all of Morocco.

6. Cited in Araib and Hullessen 1999: 12. (The quotation is originally from Félix Mesguich, *Tours de manivelle* [Paris: Grasset, 1933].)

7. As recounted in Araib and Hullessen 1999: 13.

8. Araib and Hullessen 1999: 13. Four theaters were established in Casablanca in 1915; by 1935 there were only slightly more than twenty-four hundred theater seats in all of the country. The number had grown to more than seventy-three thousand by 1952 (Ouchen 1998: table 3).

9. For some discussion of film activity in the two zones, see Jaidi 1995: 19. The total of eighty comes from the CCM's publication *Regard sur le cinéma au Maroc*.

10. Welles's filming of *Othello* shows, among many things, the continuity in filmmaking problems and how resourcefulness has to be one of a director's salient qualities. Welles speaking: "Two days later [after the crew's arrival in Mogador, now Essaouira], we got a telegram saying the costumes wouldn't come [from Italy] because they hadn't been completed. A day later, a telegram came saying they hadn't been started. And then a telegram came saying that Scalera [the Italian financial backer] had gone bankrupt. So I had a company of fifty people in North Africa and no money—though we had film and we had our cameras—but how can you shoot Othello without costumes?

"That was how I got the idea to shoot two reels in a Turkish bath, because if people are in a Turkish bath they won't be wearing clothes. And we worked in a Turkish bath for about three weeks while a lot of little tailors in the village—with Carpaccio reproductions pinned on their walls—made the clothes; the costumes were all based on his paintings" (Welles and Bogdanovich 1998: 224).

11. Bouanani, using the credits as his source, lists thirty-five films made during the Protectorate period that had Moroccan participation either behind or in front of the camera (Bouanani 1984: 71–74).

12. The first Moroccan graduate from IDHEC was Ahmed Belhachmi in 1951. The only other Moroccan to complete formal training before independence was Larbi Bennani (IDHEC 1954). In 1958–1959, Belhachmi became the first Moroccan director of the CCM (El Khodari 2000: 91).

13. These numbers are taken from the CCM's *Regard sur le cinéma au Maroc*, through 1995; from *CinéMaroc* 8, December 1998 for 1996–1997; from CCM figures for 1998.

14. More than 285 million DH were invested for *Kundun* in 1996, out of a total of just under 570 million for all foreign feature productions; in 2001 (a year in which total investment suffered following 11 September) *Black Hawk Down* invested 230 million out of a total of 350 million (Ouchen 1998: table 19, for *Kundun*; CCM figures for *Black Hawk Down*).

Investments by foreign productions reached 450 million DH in 1986, then fell to little more than 50 million in 1987 and remained near that amount through 1994. Then the total climbs rapidly; 1995, 100 million DH; 885,575,000 DH ($98 million) in 1996–1997; 480 million DH ($51 million) in 1998; down to 350 million DH in 2001 but back up to 415 million DH in 2002 (1986–1995 figures from Ouchen 1998: table 2; 1996–1997 from *CinéMaroc* 8, December 1998; 1998 and later figures provided by the CCM).

The dip in investment toward the end of the 1980s may be explained by new restrictions on importing artificial arms (Ouchen 1998: 105). Investment has increased markedly since 1995, when the ban was lifted. (This import restriction may not have been as foolish as it seems. In mid-1999, a Moroccan plane was hijacked to Spain; the hijacker had done this with the aid of a toy gun. It turned out that the hijacker had often been employed as an extra on foreign productions and Moroccan filmmakers were quick to suggest that this was how he had obtained the gun.)

15. One sign of Morocco's eagerness for the funds foreign productions provide lies in the lack of control and oversight the country exercises over productions such as *Rules for Engagement,* which was widely viewed as a fundamentally anti-Arab film and became the object of protests in a number of countries on these grounds.

The importance of foreign productions and the welcome they are given by Moroccan institutions is summed up by Mustapha Stitou, secretary-general of the CCM: "Every trimester two or three feature films are shot in Morocco. If we add to this the shorts, advertising spots and reportages, we give out some 500 to 600 shooting authorizations each year. We also offer reductions in air fares—from 40 percent to 60 percent on the normal Royal Air Maroc fares—special prices at hotels and for renting vehicles, and customs facilities in each of the country's airports, where specialized agents enable us to solve every problem the same day" (quoted in no author, probably Olivier Schmitt, "Un immense studio pour les Européens et les Américains," *Le Monde,* 10 February 2001). In *Alexander the Great,* director Oliver Stone had the use of two thousand to three thousand Moroccan soldiers as extras over a period of some twenty days (Aziz Daki, "Le Maroc a gagné la bataille d'Alexandre," *Audjourd'hui le Maroc,* 7 November 2003).

16. In 1996 and 1997, Moroccan films invested 21,556,000 DH, amounting to slightly more than 2 percent of the foreign production total; in 1998, 31 million DH, slightly more than 6 percent (1996–1997 figures from *CinéMaroc* 8, December 1998; 1998 figures from the CCM). As mentioned earlier (introduction, note 4) the amount invested for Moroccan feature films continues to be under 10 percent of that invested by foreign features, which also continue to employ many more technicians, actors, and extras. Some categories of technicians are in very short supply. The Moroccan filmmaker and dramatist Nabil Lahlou noted that of the fifteen Moroccan feature film productions at the Fifth National Film Festival held in Casablanca in 1998, only two had Moroccan cinematographers. The remaining thirteen films had their photography, sound, and montage done by foreigners (Nabil Lahlou, "Leurres, mensonges et bluffs," *Maroc-Hebdo International,* 16 January 1999).

17. "Morocco has become, in less than twenty years, an immense studio for European and American companies . . . their investments only allow the training of local technicians and the employment of local actors on the margins. But their presence is massive. Ouarzazate has thus become a truly international film studio . . ." (no author, probably Olivier Schmitt, "Un im-

mense studio pour les Européens et les Américains," *Le Monde,* 10 February 2001).

18. The minimum wage for an extra in Morocco, according to CCM guidelines, is fifteen dollars per day (or sixty dollars per week). The corresponding minimum, according to the 1998 Theatrical Motion Pictures and Television Contract Summary, is ninety dollars per day. *The Spy Game,* a film by Tony Scott shot in Casablanca in early 2001, called for the use of five thousand extras and allotted 2 million DH (about $200,000) to this item in the budget (A. R., "Casablanca et ses drôles de stars," *Le Journal,* 3–9 February 2001). Compared to what these costs would have been in the United States, the amount saved on this item alone is in the neighborhood of one million dollars. It might also be noted that the amount allotted to extras in *The Spy Game* is approximately half of the entire budget for a Moroccan film.

An interesting thirty-minute film short by Ali Essafi (*Ouarzazate Movie*) gives a good picture of what it is like to be one of these extras. In the film, Essafi notes that, on the margins of the immense studio that Ouarzazate has become, both of the town's theaters are now closed and the one film club that exists has no facilities to show 35 mm films.

19. For the dates, I have used those contained in the CCM's *Regards sur le cinéma au Maroc,* except for those films that were not completed and for which Tazi gave me the approximate year during which he worked on it.

20. A *moussem* is a festival, usually held once a year in honor of a local "saint," and is an occasion for celebrating, storytelling, marketing, and general amusement. Some other aspects of *moussem*s are mentioned in the interlude discussion of *The Big Trip* after chapter 2—"A barroom brawl. . . ."

21. Cutaway shots are shots "away from the main action but used to join two shots of the main action" (Konigsberg 1997: 82).

22. Tazi said "Mister" in English, rather disdainfully, the same way he had used the term "Monsieur" when referring to the director of *Weshma.*

23. This is in southeastern Morocco, about 300 km from Marrakesh through the High Atlas Mountains.

24. The term "sheikh" here denotes a local official who represents a particular residential community.

25. Sometimes, movie sets become tourist sites in their own right. In southern Tunisia there is a tourist site at ʿunq Jmel, where George Lucas filmed the second installment of *Star Wars: Episode 1—The Phantom Menace.* Here, a giant screen has been erected where the film itself is sometimes shown for visitors. As a Russian TV journalist remarked after such a showing, "It was an unforgettable moment. Ah, if we could only see other films screened at the very place they were shot . . ." (H. Hanachi, "Un plat savoureux et un délicieux désert," *La Presse de Tunisie,* 15 November 2000).

26. John Huston's perspective on the filming is very different and is worth quoting at length for the vision it gives us of a foreign filmmaker in Morocco, for its similarities and contrasts with Tazi's view, and for Huston's rather idiosyncratic perception of Moroccan society at that time.

After discussing how the "package" was put together—Paul Newman and Robert Redford were originally meant to play the leads but Newman suggested Michael Caine and Sean Connery instead, and the film, set in Afghanistan, was originally destined to be shot in Turkey but political differences between the United States and Turkey made this impossible. Huston continues:

"There was no question but that the picture could be filmed there [in Morocco] in its entirety. Even the market and street scenes could be shot in Marrakesh and made to look sufficiently Indian . . . Marrakesh itself was an experience. The hotel was fine, the food was excellent, but the overall atmosphere was unsettling. It has since become the capital of the haute couture, I suppose partly because little boys are available in abundance. Depravity is looked on with an understanding eye. . . . In fact, there is an understanding between boy prostitutes and the police that, following an encounter with a foreigner, the boy is to report it to the police along with whatever else he may have been able to learn about his consort. . . .

"How much baksheesh was given to corrupt officials by our company, God only knows. There was no avoiding it, for nothing could be done unless sums were forthcoming. . . . This kind of corruption existed on every level.

". . . other scenes were [shot in] actual villages in the Atlas Mountains. The Khyber Pass scenes were shot in a very dramatic pass in Morocco with high, sheer walls that at places were no more than fifty feet apart. . . . After we had set up camp near the Atlas Mountains, the Berbers came down from the hills. They are a bizarre, wonderful, wild people, and we employed large numbers of them, using their actual tents and other paraphernalia in many scenes. . . . [and] the head of the wardrobe department . . . dressed 2,000 extras daily and had the clothes washed and ready the next day.

". . . When it came time to shoot the Khyber Pass scenes, we learned that the tribes in our area would not allow their women to be photographed. Undaunted, Bert [Bert Batt, the assistant director] went to the nearest cities and recruited women from the brothels. We had been warned not to touch any woman in public—even a whore was someone to be protected from foreign infidels, and the tribesmen in this place carried knives or weapons of some sort. . . . at a turnstile which was supposed to mark the border between Afghanistan and India, one of the women froze and refused to move. The camels were piling up behind her. . . . She simply froze and refused to budge. Bert Batt walked up behind her and kicked her right in the ass. . . . The woman only had to make an outcry and Bert would have been cut to ribbons. Instead she hung her head as if to say, 'Yes, Master,' and moved on to join the others. . . ."

Huston ends his account with a very apt characterization of the film and a story that conveys his relationship to the local population. "I could have spent three times as long on *The Man Who Would Be King*, but I'm not sure it would have been a better picture for it. It doesn't strive for perfection. . . . The picture has its faults, I suppose—but who gives a damn? It plunges recklessly ahead. It swims toward the cataract.

"One day I saw an old man. . . . He was bearded. I was the only other person there with a beard. He came forward and pulled it, then muttered some words of approval. . . . It struck me that he might be right for Kafu Selim, the High Priest in the picture . . . we got him two assistant 'priests,' one a patriarch in the local mosque and the other an ancient Berber from the high mountains. They were all very good indeed. You couldn't tell them what to do, you could only try to make them understand what the scene was about and then let them do it. Once they got the drift of it, they acted it out naturally.

"Toward the end of the picture I had these three old men come in and see themselves on film. They had never seen a motion picture. . . . After the lights came up, they talked rapidly and excitedly among themselves . . . I turned to the translator. 'Ask them what they think of what they saw.'

"Kafu Selim answered for them: 'We will never die' " (Huston 1994: 355–360).

27. Written by Muhammad Choukri, a Tangiers writer, who has also been associated with Paul Bowles.

28. Tazi gave the French title, *Les récits de mon quartier.* The Arabic original, *Hikayat Haratina* (1975), has been translated into English under both the literal title given in the text and the title *The Fountain and the Tomb.*

29. Tawfiq Saleh (b. 1926) is an Egyptian filmmaker who has made some of the most powerful political films in Egyptian film history, including *The Rebels* (*al-Mutamarridun,* 1968), and later, after encountering difficulties in Egypt, *The Dupes* (Syria, 1973) and *The Long Days* (Iraq, 1980). *The Long Days* was Saleh's last film. Afterward he returned to Egypt and now teaches at the Film Institute in Cairo. His first feature film, *Street of Fools* (1955), had Naguib Mahfouz as screenwriter.

30. Muhammad Abbazi, a Moroccan filmmaker who often worked with foreign productions during this period, recently published an open letter in a Moroccan newspaper, obliquely confirming Tazi's version of events. Abbazi writes that the CCM director asked him to welcome Scorsese upon his arrival in Morocco to begin filming *The Last Temptation of Christ,* but also told him not to cite others who might be available to assist Scorsese, thus keeping work related to Scorsese's film "in-house," so to speak. Abbazi refused to do the job under these conditions, noting, "I knew that Muhammad Abderrahman Tazi had been preparing this film for four months. Sets, wardrobe, and other preparations were already at an advanced stage. My answer was that I refused to be the stick with which to beat another Moroccan filmmaker who needs to earn his bread, just as I do, so that he can make Moroccan films" (Mohamed Oumouloud Abbazi, "Un cinéaste en colère," *L'Opinion,* 26 January 2001).

Controversy over *The Last Temptation of Christ* was not limited to the United States. Tazi refers later to an incident in France (in chapter 6, see "Critics and 'realism' ") and, in the UK, the film topped a list of the most complained-about television shows since 1991 (Jason Deans, "Scorsese movie tops TV complaints list," *Guardian,* 17 December 2003).

31. Ibn Rushd (1126–1198, known in the West under the Latinized name Averroes) is a major figure in Islamic and world philosophy, famous not only for his commentaries on Aristotle but also for his arguments in favor of philosophical as opposed to theological reason. He lived much of his life in Andalusia and died in Marrakesh. A number of his followers were condemned in Europe for following his doctrines.

32. Tazi was probably referring to Chahine's *Golden Sands* (1968), filmed in Morocco and starring Omar Sharif and Faten Hamama. Araib and Hullessen point out that the Egyptian filmmaker Hussein Kamal made a film in Morocco in the mid-1970s (Araib and Hullessen 1999: 52). There may be some others as well.

33. The question of inter-Arab and regional co-productions will come up again in chapter 5.

34. Here Tazi was referring to two other Moroccan filmmakers who also frequently worked on foreign productions during that period.

35. Tazi was referring to Scorsese's film *Kundun.*

36. The quantity of damaged film amounted to between 10 and 15 percent of what Tazi normally shoots for an entire film. Had Tazi not had insurance, the most popular film in Moroccan history might never have been finished. The history of Moroccan cinema and of filmmaking in Morocco have been shaped in significant ways by such fortunate and unfortunate decisions, circumstances, and twists of fate. This history is also formed, similarly, by the many projects Tazi and other filmmakers have been involved in that never were brought to completion or were completed in severely altered form. We have already seen several examples of these—Tazi's truncated work with Scorsese, Camus's failed effort to adapt Mahfouz, Chahine's disappointed intention to film in Morocco; several more will be mentioned further on.

4. *BADIS* (1989)

1. These experiences are discussed in chapter 5, when we explore what happens when Tazi goes abroad in his film work.

2. The sums offered varied between 150,000 DH and 500,000 DH for films that usually cost well over a million DH. As we have seen, the funding Tazi was awarded for his first film, *The Big Trip*, was given under these conditions.

3. In 1977, as part of a broad reform of the CCM and the film sector, Moroccan film directors became legally required to form production companies in order to make films and thus became director-producers.

4. Of the approximately 120 feature film proposals submitted to the Aid Fund between 1988 and 1999, about 50 were accepted (Royaume du Maroc, Ministère de la Communication, CCM, *Soutien financier à la production cinématographique nationale: Fonds d'aide 1980–1999* [Rabat: CCM, 2000]). The sums offered were between one million and three and a half million DH, usually amounting to less than half the film's budget.

5. The portions are awarded (1) four weeks before the start of filming, assuming that shooting authorization has been obtained, (2) halfway through shooting, (3) during the first week of postproduction, and (4) after the standard copy has been seen by the full committee on aid.

6. To fill out this schematic presentation: for the Aid Fund's operations between 1988 and 1999, seven feature films that received awards were never made, either because the director-producer withdrew or because the sums were withheld because deadlines were not met; eight films were made despite being denied an award; and sixteen films had either all or part of the final one-quarter of their award withheld. (For all this information, see Royaume du Maroc, Ministère de la Communication, CCM, *Soutien financier à la production cinématographique nationale: Fonds d'aide 1980–1999* [Rabat: CCM, 2000].)

As mentioned in the next section, the ministry of culture and communication recently decided to ensure a certain amount of money would be available for Aid Fund awards, regardless of the level of movie attendance. This will be discussed further in the conclusion.

7. We saw in chapter 2 how the Sigma 3 cooperative structure managed to produce one film, *Weshma*, before disbanding. Another attempt was made later in the 1970s, involving a number of Casablanca filmmakers hoping to benefit from some economies of scale and more efficient use of technicians and equipment. This attempt also only managed to produce one film (*Cinders of the Vineyard*, 1979). It was weakened by technical problems, interruptions

in shooting, and lack of clear definition in roles, among other problems. The Casablanca group contained filmmakers who were to become among Morocco's best-known including Hassan Ben Jelloun, Saad Chraibi, Mustapha Derkaoui, Abdelkader Lagtaa, Hakim Noury, and Muhammad Reggab. A number of these were involved in a further cooperative effort in the late 1980s, which, after facilitating the production of several films, also dissolved. (For some detail on this later effort, see Carter 1999: 430–431.)

8. The Fonds Sud is an umbrella organization that offers film production assistance to countries of the "South" and coordinates the French ministries of cooperation, culture, and foreign affairs; ACCT (*l'Agence de la coopération culturelle et technique*), now known as the *Agence de la francophonie,* promotes the use of French overseas and within this framework also offers financial support for Third World film production.

9. A particularly striking case occurred with regard to the Moroccan filmmaker Abdelkader Lagtaa's film *al-Bab al-Mesdud* (*The Closed Door,* 1998), a film co-produced with Algeria and France. The French co-producer went bankrupt and finding the money to make the first print of the film took several years.

10. We will see several concrete instances of this in chapter 5 when we examine, among other subjects, Tazi's experience with foreign distributors and co-producers.

11. Seventeen films were made in the first half of the 1990s; the pace quickened thereafter, with some thirty films produced in the second half of the decade, a rate that continued into the new century.

The Aid Fund provides more money per film than the Support Fund did and also has awarded much more money yearly, greater than five times more on average. (The total funds awarded by the Support Fund for feature films over its eight-year period was just over 11 million DH, or 1.375 million per year; the Aid Fund over a twelve-year period awarded just under 86 million DH, or over 7 million DH per year [see Royaume du Maroc, Ministère de la Communication, CCM, *Soutien financier à la production cinématographique nationale: Fonds d'aide 1980–1999* (Rabat: CCM, 2000)].) By 2002 the amount awarded exceeded 23 million DH.

12. The role of TV financing of feature films will be addressed in more detail in chapter 6.

13. This subject will be discussed again in chapter 5.

14. Al-Murabitun (Almoravids) and al-Muwahhidun (Almohades) were dynasties of Moroccan Berber origin that ruled over Morocco and Muslim Spain consecutively from the mid-eleventh century well into the thirteenth. *Al-mudejar* refers to the experience of Islamic communities in Spain after Christian reconquest of Spain in 1492.

15. Maribel Verdu has had a full career as a Spanish actress. For some further discussion of her career, see the relevant note later in this chapter (note 28), during the discussion of the film's seventh motif.

16. ETA is the acronym of a movement struggling for Basque independence from Spain.

The other islands in Spain's possession on Morocco's Mediterranean coast are those just east of the Spanish enclave of Melilla (the Jafarin Islands, Sp. *Islas Chafarinas*) and, farther west, those off the coast at al-Hoceima. In the summer of 2002, a dispute broke out between Morocco and Spain over a Spanish-controlled uninhabited island (Ar. *Leila,* Sp. *Isla del Perejil*) at the Straits of Gibraltar east of another Spanish enclave, Ceuta, which the Spanish recovered militarily, without casualties, after it had been occupied by a hand-ful of Moroccan soldiers. The dispute was settled by diplomatic means but points to a much more significant bone of contention: the continued Spanish occupation and control over the Mediterranean coastal enclaves of Melilla (population sixty thousand) and Ceuta (population seventy-three thousand), both of which have significant Muslim populations, operate as important sources of goods smuggled into Morocco, and have been under Spanish con-trol for more than four centuries.

17. In addition to being used during the Roman period, Badis was used by "the Almoravids, the Almohads and the Marinids . . . as a naval base. . . . Less than 100 meters out to sea there were two small rocky islands . . . in 1508 [the Spanish], in order to put an end to the activities of the pirates, occupied it and fortified it." The Spanish then lost control of it and, under Turkish control, it was used as a base for corsairs. In 1564 the Moroccan Sultan, "fear[ing] that the Turks might use Badis as a base from which to undertake the conquest of Morocco . . . handed [the town and the islands] over to the Spanish" (Encyclopedia of Islam, CD-ROM Edition v.1.0, article "Badis").

The saint Tazi was referring to was probably Abu Ya'coub Yusuf al-Zuhayli al-Badisi, "saint and savant of the 8th/14th century, who is buried outside the town . . . Ibn Khaldun regarded him as the last of the great Moroccan saints . . . Leo Africanus speaks of his shrine which is still venerated . . ." (Encyclo-pedia of Islam, CD-ROM Edition v.1.0, article "al-Badisi").

18. Approximately 400 km, over roads that were not of the best.

19. For example, Ahmed Bouanani, referring to The Big Trip, says, "the profound error—desired or not—inherent in the screenplay itself, is to present us with an idealized world, a reality reduced to a simplistic manicheanism" (Bouanani 1984: 155).

20. This was said in a tone of voice indicating it was meant as a simpli-fication. For discussion of the role of autobiography in Arabic literature see Reynolds 2001 (which contains many historical examples) and Alif 2002 (fo-cusing on contemporary autobiography and personal testimony).

21. Tazi had heard Badis villagers use this expression, which alluded to using kittens as bait for fish, and had taken the expression from them. Meta-phorically, this meant "You don't tell soldiers they will be used as cannon fodder." Tazi said he had never actually seen kittens used in this way.

22. On the tenth day of the month of the Pilgrimage (Dhu al-Hijj), the pilgrims, to ward off the devil, throw seven small stones at a construction called Djamrat al-'aqaba.

23. I was joking here, but also thinking of several films with scenes of stoning, such as Zorba the Greek (Michel Cacoyannis, 1964) and al-Gu' (Hunger, Ali Badrakhan, Egypt, 1986).

24. Sembène: "European filmmakers often use music which is gratuitous. It's true that it is pleasant to hear but, culturally, does it leave us with any-thing? I think the best film would be one after which you have to ask yourself, 'Was there any music in that film?' " (Georgakas and Rubenstein 1983a: 47).

25. Farida Benlyazid was also quoted as saying that Tazi had stereotyped women as victims in Badis and that "Women have more strength than he shows them as having" (Lynn Teo Simarski, "Through North African Eyes," Aramco World, January–February 1992, p. 35).

26. Naima Bouanani (wife of the filmmaker and poet Ahmed Bouanani)

was associate producer on *Badis* (she also often works on foreign productions). She sometimes has a brief role in Tazi's films and her strong-featured face makes her appearance very noticeable. In *Badis* her appearance was even more noticeable than usual—she plays the woman who throws the first stone.

Regarding her work as associate producer, Tazi told me that "the one indispensable person for me on my films is Naima Bouanani."

27. This same judgment was voiced by John Huston in chapter 3.

28. I do not know enough about Maribel Verdu's very full career—she has acted in more than forty films—to speak about it in detail, but the little I do know suggests that nudity continues to be a leitmotif (at the very least) in her roles. I have seen her only in *Goya en Burdeos* (Carlos Saura, Spain, 1999), in the role of Duchess of Alba who poses as a nude model, and *Y tu mamá también* (Alfonso Cuarón, Mexico, 2001), the highest-grossing Mexican film in history, in which she has a lusty role involving several nude scenes.

29. The idea here is similar to that expressed by T. E. Lawrence in the film *Lawrence of Arabia* (David Lean, 1962) when he says, "My name is for my friends." Once given out, your name can be used against you. For a richly textured discussion of this film, see Caton 1999.

30. Let me simply recall that *Badis* was released before Moroccan films were given systematic distribution in Morocco and that it was screened in Morocco in only one theater, it played in that theater for only one week, and over that week it drew only some three hundred spectators. However, after this "release" it had a significant subsequent life in Morocco, being shown frequently at festivals and at meetings of civil society associations, film clubs, labor unions, and so on.

INTERLUDE: TELLING A STORY—NARRATIVE AND SYMBOLS

1. For example, one article in the Moroccan press had for a headline, "Finally, a Moroccan Film That Tells a Story!" (A. N. Refaif, "Enfin un film marocain qui raconte une histoire!" *al-Maghrib,* 17–18 December 1989).

2. Tazi was referring to a biographical romance of the eponymous hero, composed in Mamluk Egypt, in the fifteenth and sixteenth centuries, set in "the mythical primordial universe, where men and *djinns* associate together on familiar terms, where sorcerers, wizards and enchanters engage in dogged combat, competing for power or for the mastery of natural forces. This universe is steeped in impiety and the worship of false gods . . ." (for more detail, see the article by J.-P. Guillaume, "Sayf Ibn Dhi Yazan, Sirat," in Encyclopedia of Islam, CD-ROM Edition v.1.0).

3. He had expressed this viewpoint in several interviews in the following ways. "I don't think 'western.' The narrative form in my films is oriental. The western and oriental rhythms differ just as does the perception of narration" (Yasmine Belmahi, "Je refuse l'étiquette de cinéaste marocain sous influence occidentale" [interview], *al-Maghrib,* 9–10 September 1990). Also: "in Arab tales, *slowness* is the main element in the fascination, even the hypnotism, experienced by the listener/spectator. So, our notion of the value of time is very different" (A. Berrigan, "Pour un 7ème art qualitatif" [interview], *el-Moudjahid* [Algiers], 4 October 1990).

4. This rhyming prelude is sometimes prolonged with an additional phrase that extends the rhyme: ". . . *nabit fi kull al-makan.*" A literal translation

of the full expression might be, "There once was, among the things that were, in ancient times, basil and lilies planted everywhere." After this the "story" proper begins.

5. The question was, "Some have noted a slow (painful?) [sic] rhythm in the cinematic narration in the two films [*The Big Trip* and *Badis*]. How do you assess this evaluation?" To which Tazi answered, "Truthfully, I would have preferred an even slower rhythm to the one noted by the spectators" (A. Berrigan, "Pour un 7ème art qualitatif" [interview], *el-Moudjahid* [Algiers], 4 October 1990).

6. "[A]t a certain point if I become too much of a voyeur it can hurt the narration" (Khalil Samlali, "D'un espace éclaté à un espace clos: sur l'oeuvre de A. Tazi" [interview], *L'Opinion*, 30 March 1990).

7. This term was apparently applied to the North Atlantic in part because of the sea's "bad weather and dangerous character" (Encyclopedia of Islam, CD-ROM Edition v.1.08, article "Al-Bahr al-Muhit").

8. "OW: . . . I hate symbolism.

PB: Fritz Lang said he dropped the use of symbols when he came to America because somebody at M-G-M said to him, 'Americans don't like symbols.'

OW: I'm one of those Americans. I never use it. If anybody finds it, it's for them to find. I never sit down and say how we're going to have a symbol for some character. They happen automatically, because life is full of symbols. So is art. You can't avoid them; but if you *use* them, you get into Stanley Kramer Town" (Welles and Bogdanovich 1998: 82).

9. See Mohamed Jibril, "Le grand voyage ou la solitude des symboles," *Lamalif* no. 136, May–June 1982.

10. For detail on the Mudawwana, see note 23 in chapter 1; for recent developments, see, in the conclusion, "Moroccan Politics, Society, and Culture."

5. THE OTHER SIDE OF THE WIND, ALMOST

1. Because of the lack of trained technicians in Morocco in a number of areas, certain tasks must be carried out abroad. In *Lalla Hobby*, for example, whereas the color and light matching (Fr. *étalonnage*) were done in Morocco, sound mixing had to be done in Italy because there was no fully qualified Moroccan sound technician able to work with the film's digital sound.

2. Et-Tayeb Houdaifa, "Abderrahmane Tazi: il n'y aura pas de suite à mon film" (interview), *TéléPlus*, July 1994, pp. 14–19.

3. The budget for this most successful of films was approximately 5.6 million DH. 1.75 was provided by the Aid Fund and another 2.2 came from various other sources, leaving 1.65 needing to be recovered. Receipts from screenings in Morocco totaled 3.5 million, of which approximately 20 percent goes to the producer, thus roughly 700,000 DH. The shortfall is almost a million DH.

4. Tazi had paid two of the actresses in *Looking* 100,000 DH for an estimated ten days shooting, calculating their fee to be 10,000 DH/day; for the sequel one of these requested, through her agent, 150,000 DH for one week. Also, one well-known supporting actor asked for 100,000 DH for one day's shooting. Tazi added that he unfailingly pays the fee at the end of the shooting, which is an earlier stage than many other directors. He cited the case of one

of his actresses whose contract for the entire shooting of a film made for another director in 1991 called for her to be paid 10,000 DH; almost ten years later she had still not received that money.

5. The question of financing through international co-production was dealt with in some detail in chapter 4; here we will focus on the other stages in the filmmaking process although, inevitably, co-production will come up at several points.

6. Ramdani had directed one of the very first Moroccan feature films, *When the Dates Ripen* (1968). For some discussion of the context in which that film was made, see chapter 2.

7. Tazi cited the original French title, *Une enquête au pays*. I have put a literal translation in the text. The novel has been published in English as *Flutes of Death*. The Moroccan filmmaker Nabil Lahlou later received Aid Fund support to film Chraibi's novel and it was completed in 2003 under the title *The Years of Exile* (*Les années d'exile*). Lahlou too had problems with the fees the publisher Le Seuil required.

8. Tazi said the price for a new copy of a film was approximately 8,000 French francs, with subtitling, which must be done anew for each copy, costing another 7,000 French francs. A new subtitled copy thus costs in the neighborhood of 15,000 French francs, or somewhere between $2,000 and $2,500.

9. When I spoke to Farida Benlyazid she confirmed this story but added that the distribution company in question had improved its procedures and was now paying her regularly.

10. Tazi was probably referring here to the Argentinian film *La Isla* (Alejandro Doria, 1979).

11. About $3,500.

12. Morocco, where Egyptian films have a very small market share, constitutes something of an exception to this pattern. The reasons for this, having to do with a Moroccan boycott of Egyptian films starting in the early 1960s, were mentioned in chapter 2.

13. The other Moroccan filmmakers included Saad Chraibi, Ahmed Boulane, and Abdelkader Lagtaa.

14. Among the countries and regional organizations with which Morocco has formal co-production and film exchange accords are Argentina, Belgium, Canada, Egypt, Spain, France, Italy, Mali, Senegal, Tunisia, and the Arab Maghreb Union. One of the questions Tazi raises implicitly in this section is the extent to which these formal accords are, in fact, implemented with concrete results. (For the texts of the accords, see CCM, *Accords de Coproduction et d'échanges cinématographiques* [Rabat: CCM, 2000].)

15. For the sake of comparison, let us recall that France—not a typical case but nonetheless a point of reference in each Maghreb country—produces close to two hundred films a year for a population of about sixty million but still has great difficulty penetrating export markets.

16. The film shot partly in Libya (and Tunisia) was *Le feu vert* (Abdellah Mesbahi, 1974); it had Libyan and Tunisian co-producers (El Khodari 2000: 265). Souheil Ben Barka's film is also known under the name of *Knights of Glory*.

The filming of *Woman of Cairo* (*La dame du Caire*) in Egypt does not appear to have been successful and Egyptians involved in this film told me it had left a very bitter aftertaste.

17. It might be pointed out here that the difficulties Third World film-

makers have in filming abroad has made such filming almost nonexistent, thus depriving many Third World cinemas of one of film's great attractions, that of giving the spectator visual access to exotic locations elsewhere in the world.

18. Fr. *l'Agence de la coopération culturelle et technique,* known by the acronym ACCT (see also the more detailed note 8 in chapter 4 during the discussion of co-production).

19. The entire budget for *Lalla Hobby* was almost 8 million DH. This compares with slightly more that 5.5 million for *Looking* and, five years before that, just under 3 million for *Badis* (Ouchen 1998: table 11).

20. Tazi was referring to the killing in 1995 of a young Moroccan, Brahim Bouraam, who had been attacked by four youths participating in a National Front march and then thrown into the Seine.

21. For a lengthier exploration of FESPACO in Ouagadougou that echoes Tazi's view, see Turan 2002: 65–80.

INTERLUDE: *LALLA HOBBY —* THE FILM

1. For figures concerning clandestine emigration, see the relevant note in chapter 1 in the discussion of *Looking's* seventh motif (note 31).

2. Since *Lalla Hobby,* Akkariou has had important roles in several films and a starring role in Farida Benlyazid's second film, *Women's Wiles* (1999). The school in Rabat that trained her, *l'Institut des arts dramatiques et de l'animation culturelle,* is commonly known as ISADAC.

3. The Moroccan Arabic term *Makhzen* (literally, "storehouse") is synonymous with "government, ruling authorities," and is usually used to connote the authoritarian, patrimonial, paternalistic relations that are seen as marking Moroccan society and Moroccan history, and marking too the corresponding psychology of both ruler and ruled.

4. *The Gulf War . . . and After?* (1992), produced by CinéTéléfilms, Tunisia.

6. REFLECTIONS AND PROJECTIONS

1. Focusing state attention on television may have been a wise policy during the first decades after television's introduction in the early 1960s, given the fact that state television reached so many more people than cinema. However, had greater early investment been made in film production, both the film and TV sectors might be reaping some rewards today from the needs satellite channels and other programming sources have for fiction fare.

2. In addition to having Tazi as its president, other officers included Abdelkader Lagtaa as vice president and Hakim Noury as a member of the advisory committee; younger filmmakers in the group include Nabil Ayouch, Faouzi Ben Saidi, Narjiss Nejjar, and Noureddin Lekhmari—names that will come up again in the conclusion.

3. GARP Charter, 15 July 2001.

4. GARP, undated statement.

5. The French committed 70 million DH in bilateral aid to help establish

this institute but, at the time of writing, this had not yet worked its way through the Moroccan administration.

This and related issues are discussed in the conclusion under "Film Sector Problems."

6. Anecdotal evidence indicates that King Muhammad VI has helped in a number of cases (one was that of Muhammad al-Keghat, a well-known Moroccan theater figure—and one of the principal actors in *Weshma*—who was operated on in Paris at the king's expense but who unfortunately died shortly thereafter) but that this aid has not been as consistently offered as King Hassan's.

7. The ancillary activities Tazi lists here all referred to jobs he had taken on recently.

8. In more detail: almost 85 percent of Moroccan film spectators were aged between 15 and 34, with those between 15 and 24 representing 53 percent of spectators; 27 percent of spectators were women, with a high proportion (74 percent) aged between 15 and 24 and 80 percent unmarried. Thirty-eight percent of filmgoers were students (secondary and higher); 28.5 percent workers, merchants, or artisans; 21.5 percent white-collar workers or from the liberal professions; and 12.5 percent unemployed. Seventy-six percent of all filmgoers had completed secondary school at least.

The figures in this section, except where indicated otherwise, are all from Jaidi 1992 and the categories are his: the first socio-professional class groups students in secondary school and higher; the second, workers, merchants, artisans; the third, white-collar workers and members of the liberal professions; the fourth, the unemployed.

9. Over the years 1980–1995, the percentage of films exhibited across Morocco according to nationality of origin showed the United States first (32 percent), followed by India (18 percent), France (14 percent), and China (12 percent), with Egypt (2 percent) and Morocco (1 percent) trailing. However, when audience preferences are polled, although films from the United States continue to rank first, preferences do not correlate with films exhibited in either the case of Egypt, which comes in second (at 24 percent), or Morocco, which comes in third (at 18 percent). The relative importance of Moroccan (and Egyptian) films in viewer preferences is borne out when television viewing is taken into account: here, viewers surveyed prefer, in descending order, news programs (60 percent), American films (54 percent), documentaries (48 percent), Egyptian fictions (43 percent), Moroccan films (32 percent), with French films ranking much lower (15 percent) (Jaidi 2000: 217–218).

Preferences for Chinese karate (9 percent) and Indian films (8 percent) is significantly lower than percentages of films exhibited (Jaidi 2000: 173). The rather high level of Indian imports is explained by their serving as a substitute for Egyptian films and their relatively low cost to the distributor-exhibitor (Jaidi 2000: 176). It also seems that Chinese karate films have gone into a steep decline recently (Jaidi 2000: 177).

Recently these percentages have changed significantly: of the 253 films approved in 2002 for distribution, slightly over half (131 films) were of U.S. origin, 25 percent (63 films) were Indian, 12 percent (30) French, under 4 percent (9) were Egyptian, just over 3 percent (8) were Moroccan, and all other countries totaled less than 5 percent (12; CCM figures).

10. Against the general downward trend in the number of theaters, sev-

eral new upmarket venues have been established in the past ten years, including a fourteen-theater multiplex in Casablanca in 2002, seating a total of more than thirty-six hundred spectators. A number of the new theaters seem to be doing relatively well financially.

11. Women were the central characters in so many films of the 1990s that some filmmakers and critics began to speak of a "saturation" point being reached. However, there is little sign that the public shares this view and women continue to be the main protagonists in several of the most popular recent Moroccan films, including *Jugement d'une femme* (Hassan Benjelloun, 2001), ranked second; *Histoire d'amour* (Hakim Noury, 2002), ranked first; and *Casablanca by Night* (Mustapha Derkaoui, 2003), ranked first over the first half of the year. (It is perhaps worth pointing out that filmmakers and critics are overwhelmingly male, whereas the public, as we have seen previously, is growing increasingly female.)

12. Films of this sort are too numerous to mention but, already in 1981, the Tunisian filmmaker and critic Férid Boughedir had referred to a "sociological . . . neo-realist" strand in Moroccan films (Boughedir 1981: 209). The most recent, among the most effective, and certainly the most honored example of this strand is Nabil Ayouch's *Ali Zaoua* (2000).

13. For humor, see Tazi's *Looking*, Saad Chraibi's *Women and Women* (1998) and Hakim Noury's *She's Diabetic, Has Hypertension, but Refuses to Kick the Bucket* (2000); for the daring and provocative, see Abdelkader Lagtaa's *The Closed Door* (1998) and *The Casablancans* (1998); for narrative thrust see Nabil Ayouch's *Mektoub* (1997); for televisual style, see the previously mentioned *Women and Women* as well as many of the films of Hakim Noury. For more discussion of the styles of recent Moroccan films and some examples, see Dwyer 2002b.

14. There will be some discussion of video and digital later in this chapter, as well as in the conclusion.

15. Tazi here referred to recent films of Hakim Noury and Mustapha Derkaoui.

16. Here Tazi cited, as two examples of improvement, the directing of actors and elaborating the script breakdown ("the breakdown of a film script into groups of individual scenes and shots that are to be photographed together at the same locations and the same times, whether in narrative sequence or not" (Konigsberg 1997: 348; Fr. *découpage*, which Tazi himself translated as "detailed script").

17. The "shot breakdown" is defined as "a list of all the shots to be used in a film presented in proper order and including the location for each shot as well as the performers, personnel, and equipment necessary" (Konigsberg 1997: 360).

18. Tazi also went abroad to have the sound effects done for his subsequent film, *Abu Moussa's Women Neighbors*.

19. Censorship may affect filmmakers' expression directly, when a film is denied a license to be shown, or indirectly, by influencing filmmakers' assessments of what they believe is permissible—what we commonly call "self-censorship." In Morocco the institution charged with issuing licenses is the Supervisory Film Commission (Fr. *Commission de contrôle des films cinématographiques*), established under the French Protectorate in 1940 with enabling legislation that, significantly, continues to be in effect today. The commission, with members representing various ministries as well as various professional

guilds, views the film and then may either issue the so-called *"visa d'exploitation,"* a license that allows the film to go forward as is, or may impose cuts, or may simply judge the film unsuitable and refuse to issue a license for it.

20. Support for the view that critics are relatively unimportant for film-goers is given by Jaidi, whose study shows that only 18 percent of the audience pays attention to critics in choosing to view a film (36 percent pay attention to their friends' opinions, 30 percent to the stars, 27 percent to the genre, 22 percent to the story, and so on; Jaidi 2000: 179).

21. The notion that "red lines" define the limits of free expression is a commonplace in Moroccan discourse, and they usually come in trinitarian form. One example, taken more or less at random: "the red lines . . . [that is to say] the royalty, territorial integrity, and religion" (A. D. A., "Les points de discorde," *Maroc Hebdo International,* 8–14 June 2001).

22. See Dwyer 2002a for discussion of a Moroccan filmmaker, Abdelkader Lagtaa, who does seek to shock. Censorship will be discussed again in the conclusion under "Film Sector Problems."

23. When vertical integration in the film sector began to occur internationally, international distribution companies demanded higher prices for individual films. Consequently, theater owners were pushed to increase admissions by showing the feature as many times per day as possible, leading to a reduction in double features and elimination of the lead-in, complementary program.

24. I had cited Hakim Noury, Jilali Ferhati, and Abdelkader Lagtaa as examples. Tazi agreed, adding that this was true for Mustapha Derkaoui and Nabil Lahlou as well.

25. For a contrast between Tazi's views here and those of Hakim Noury, a Moroccan filmmaker who argues for deliberately seeking the universal, see Dwyer 2004.

26. Salah Sbyea, "Le plaisir du conte et de la fable," *Libération* (Morocco), 2 May 2003.

27. Ouafaa Bennani, "Une 'première' en ouverture du club du 7e art à Salé," *Le Matin,* 25 April 2003.

28. Abdelouahad Zaari, "L'avant première du film: 'les voisines d'Abou Moussa,' " *Libération* (Morocco), 1 May 2003.

29. Salah Sbyea, "Le plaisir du conte et de la fable," *Libération* (Morocco), 2 May 2003.

30. M'barek Housni, "De l'autre côté du roman," *l'Opinion,* 6 June 2003.

31. M'hamed Hamrouch, "Reculer dans le passé pour critiquer le présent" [interview], *Libération* (Morocco), 30 April 2003. Had this interview taken place several weeks later, Tazi would undoubtedly have added earthquakes to his list of natural catastrophes, since a murderous one struck Algeria in May 2003. Less than a year later Morocco was struck by a quake that killed more than 500 people around al-Hoceima, recalling for many a particularly destructive one that killed some ten thousand people in Agadir in 1960.

32. Ilham Khalifi, "Tazi, à la recherche de la pureté" [interview], *La Nouvelle Tribune,* 8 May 2003.

33. Noureddin Sail has pointed out that such a rate is only normal, "When you take French cinema which produces 130 films per year, there are 20 films which are interesting. As far as Morocco goes, it's producing 10 films a year? Well, one of those will be interesting. So the proportion is kept"

(Amale Nazih, "Les ambitions d'une chaîne de télévision: entretien avec Nou-reddine Sail, directeur général de 2M," *Le Temps du Maroc,* 6 April 2001. Web-site).

34. I discuss the younger generation of filmmakers again in the conclu-sion.

35. Nabil Ayouch, director of *Ali Zaoua* (2000), the prizewinning film at the National Film Festival held in Marrakesh in early 2001, had also directed an earlier feature, *Mektoub* (1997).

36. From the novel of the same name by the historian Ahmed Taoufiq.

37. The screenwriter was Amina Mouline, born in 1961, with a univer-sity degree from Paris III in English and Arabic literature (Abla Ababou, "Une scénariste de talent," *Le Journal,* 13–19 May 2000). Amina Mouline had never worked in films before but Tazi had read some of her short stories and had been very impressed by the quality of writing, the sensibility they conveyed, and—especially relevant in adapting this particular novel—their visual rich-ness.

38. Tazi figured approximately four months in all from the end of shoot-ing until the final copy was ready for distribution.

39. For a summary of Sail's career, see chapter 1, note 19.
Morocco's first television channel, the very "official" TVM, had been founded in 1962 and it took almost three decades, until 1989, for Morocco to obtain its second channel, the privately owned, pay-TV station 2M, founded by ONA, Morocco's largest industrial conglomerate (ONA—Omnium Nord Af-ricain—has, among its major stockholders, foreign banking and financial in-stitutions [BNP PARIBAS], as well as the Moroccan royal family, which con-trols some 14 percent. It is the largest enterprise in Africa if South Africa is excluded and, with its subsidiaries, constitutes approximately half of the stock value of all publicly traded stocks in Casablanca).

2M was designed to appeal to Morocco's middle class, retransmitting pro-grams made abroad, primarily in French, and its funds were meant to come from advertising revenue and customer subscription fees. However, with a growing number of people "pirating" 2M's signal and with increasing com-petition coming from satellite channels, 2M began to lose money. (In the early 1990s satellite dishes were available in Morocco for little more than $100 and the number of television sets per capita had increased by more than 50 percent between 1990 and 1996–1998; somewhat ironically, Noureddin Sail was a key figure in one of the main competing satellite channels, Canal Plus Horizons.)

In 1996, the state bought a majority share in 2M (ONA retained signifi-cant holdings) and the transmissions became available freely to the general public, rather than by subscription, with approximately two-thirds of its bud-get provided by the state and the rest by advertising revenue. (For the infor-mation on ONA see Jaidi 2000: 79–80 and Tuquoi 2001: 187–188; for the numbers of television sets see Sakr 2001: 112, citing UNDP figures.)

40. The first figure was given to me by Tazi; the next two were offered by Sail in an interview (Mohamed Belhaj, "Noureddin Sail, directeur général de la deuxième chaine," *Libération,* 24 April 2001). These figures were largely confirmed in the company's year 2000 annual report (see Mohammed Bou-darham, "Les millions de la pub sauvent 2M," *Libération,* 5 July 2001).

41. Sail's views regarding the importance of the channel becoming a pro-ducer are very strong. Elaborating on an interviewer's point that "Your plans for 2M focus on the theme: television isn't simply diffusing, it's especially

production," Sail answered, "I'm extremely determined on this issue. The watch-word is: produce, produce, produce. Because producing means creating capital. What you yourself produce belongs to you. It's crucial, given what the future has in store, that everyone be the owner of what defines them. . . . It's a necessity in order to exist at the national level (more proximity, more identity, more direct contact with the people) but also at the international level. . . . What I'm trying to introduce here . . . is that the act of producing not be an exceptional occurrence happening during Ramadan, but a routine act—normal, daily, weekly, monthly" (Mohamed Belhaj, "Noureddin Sail, directeur général de la deuxième chaine," *Libération,* 24 April 2001).

42. All the objectives in this paragraph except the last were implemented in the months after Tazi and I spoke about them in early 2001. Also, by mid-2003 2M was producing two TV films and two TV plays per month.

43. When we last spoke in person and at length, in mid-2003, shortly after his fifth film had been released, Tazi indicated that he was already at work preparing what he thought would very likely become his sixth feature film—a film he conceived of as a small, "intimate" one, very different from the epic scale of *Abu Moussa's Women Neighbors.*

CONCLUSION

1. A number of writers have questioned the appropriateness of the terms "Third World" and "national cinema," but I continue to find them useful. As promised in the introduction, here are some of the arguments against these terms and my reasons for keeping them.

The usefulness of the category "Third World" in the domain of cinema has been challenged on the grounds that film production in almost all countries outside the "big five"—whether Third World or First World—is in a similar predicament. Armes argues this on the ideological level, saying that "in many ways the struggles of film production in Australia and Canada—which can hardly be considered as belonging to the Third World, however wide we cast the net—offer some of the clearest examples of certain ideological aspects of cultural neocolonialism" (Armes 1987: 3). These similarities include the structure of the film sector, and the following description of the situation in the UK could be applied almost word for word (with some figures reduced) to Morocco: "The diminishing profitability of film production . . . encouraged major British companies to abandon production in favour of distribution and exhibition and other non-film interest . . . [leading] to an almost complete divorce within the industry between producers on the one hand and distributors and exhibitors (primarily devoted to showing Hollywood films) on the other. This meant that the increasingly risky business of production was left in the hands of independent production companies who put together projects on an irregular or one-off basis (often involving quite labyrinthine funding arrangements as a result of the absence of any one major source of finance). As a result, no less than 342 production companies were involved in film production during the 1980s and, of these, 250 participated in only one film" (Hill 1996: 108).

Despite these and similar arguments, "Third World" as a category is useful in the domain of cinema (and other forms of cultural production) because Third World countries have many common traits affecting the film sector that distinguish them from First World countries (which have, for example, richer internal markets, vastly greater investment capabilities, more urbanized and educated populations, etc.). Although the symptoms of film sector weakness may appear to be much the same—scant national production and foreign imports inundating national distribution networks—the remedies would necessarily be somewhat different given the distinct kinds of problems.

Another challenge to the term "Third World" would replace it with the term "postcolonial." Here the argument focuses on the confluence of two phenomena, one from the political realm—"the tendency of the African state and of African nationalism towards disintegration . . ."—and another from the realm of theory—"a tendency in the Western academy towards the abandonment of grand narratives, including those involving the state and nationalism . . ." (Haynes 1999: 21, adopting from Aijaz Ahmad the idea that " 'Third World literature' gets rechristened as 'postcolonial literature' when the governing theoretical framework shifts from third world nationalism to postmodernism" [Ahmad 1992: 1]. But Haynes cautions, "Africans have reason to be distrustful of post-modern post-colonialism as another foreign regime that tends to compromise crucial projects" [Haynes 1999: 21].)

This challenge rejoins the criticism sometimes made of the term "national cinema" (as in Malkmus and Armes 1991)—that cinema is a global culture industry and that focusing on the nation as a unit draws attention away from the global.

I hope this book bears out my view that, while any national film sector is certainly subject to international forces and may itself cross national borders, the nation-state is the primary unit within which the film sector operates—particularly in the case of Third World and other smaller cinemas—with the consequent national legal, financial, and administrative structures. In addition, the simple fact that "national cinema" is a concept with which most Third World (and Moroccan) filmmakers work is perhaps on its own sufficient reason for retaining the term and keeping it as a main focus of analysis, even while remaining aware of its limitations.

2. Some examples of this recent interest among anthropologists working on the Middle East can be seen in the writings of Armbrust (1996, 2000) and Abu-Lughod (1995a, 1995b, 1997).

Certainly, anthropology has had a longstanding interest in film, but this has meant mainly documentary filmmaking and film as a technique for communicating anthropological knowledge. In a subdiscipline that has come to be called "visual anthropology"—characterized by one of its most active practitioners as "dominated primarily by an interest in pictorial media as a means of communicating anthropological knowledge, that is, ethnographic films and photographs and, secondarily, the study of pictorial manifestations of culture" (Ruby 1996: 1345)—visual anthropologists tended to concentrate on the former and, where they did engage in the latter, paid little attention to mass visual productions, such as feature films. Ruby goes on, "The anthropological establishment has yet to acknowledge the centrality of the mass media in the formation of cultural identity in the second half of the twentieth century. Consequently, visual anthropologists sometimes find themselves involved with the research and thinking of professional image makers and scholars from other disciplines—visual sociology, cultural studies, film theory, photo history, dance and performance studies, and architectural theory—rather than with the work of other cultural anthropologists" (Ruby 1996: 1345; it should be noted that Ruby himself in this very article fails to treat the mass media in any but the most cursory manner, and then only insofar as they provide support for narrowly "ethnographic" film activity—see Ruby 1996: 1350).

This vision of the subdiscipline is a controversial one—readers interested in exploring some of the disputed issues may consult a recent review of Ruby's work by Fadwa El-Guindi (2001) and will find a well-developed alternate view expressed in MacDougall 1998, especially the final chapter.

3. Several ethnographies written in the late 1970s and early 1980s were among the first to make these themes central, among them Rabinow 1977, Dumont 1978, Crapanzano 1980, and Dwyer 1982. All but Dumont's concern Morocco and these Moroccan works were then critically assessed by Geertz (1988). More recently, Trencher (2000) examines the four ethnographies and sees them as marking a turning point in U.S. anthropology and as signs of broader changes in U.S. culture as a whole.

4. In an earlier book (Dwyer 1982) I examined in some detail the relationship between anthropologist and informant, an issue I have not made central to this book, although I have tried to write it in a form that would allow readers so disposed to explore the relationship in some depth.

With regard to "unexplored" areas, let me mention three: (1) Tazi's personal life as an adult—his marriages, relations with his children, his close friendships and sworn enmities; (2) Tazi's relationships with his colleagues; and (3) what might be called Tazi's "psychology" or "inner life."

The first area did not seem to me directly relevant to Tazi's professional career. Also, it is not an area that interests me deeply nor do I expect it to be one that Tazi would talk about openly. I think the absence of such discussion reflects both Tazi's and my respect for "intimacy."

The second area: while collegial relationships within Morocco's film world span most human emotions—from conflict, gossip, shifting loyalties, mutual accusations of bad faith, and envy to friendship, respect, admiration, and so on—it often appears that negative, ad hominem, and uncharitable remarks dominate discourse. As our perspective shifts from the reflexive, through the local, to the global, we may ask a series of questions, such as: To what extent is this the researcher's subjective impression? Is this a "cultural style" of Moroccan discourse going well beyond the film world? To what extent may this style be a feature of Morocco and/or other Third World countries where the sectors and cohort are relatively small, where everyone knows everyone else, where the competition for scarce goods is acute? To what extent does such behavior characterize similarly situated groups in First World contexts, say academic departments in U.S. universities? Even more generally, to what extent may these traits be characteristic of intellectual and creative activity, whether in Morocco or elsewhere, where individuals are pushed to clearly demarcate themselves from their colleagues, to establish their particular "positions" within a given cultural "field" (to use terms made current by Pierre Bourdieu)? To treat these very interesting questions would require another, quite different book.

On the third: my main concern throughout this book has been to explore the worlds within which Tazi creates and the worlds that he creates, rather than try to enter into the psychological world within which he dwells. Keeping my distance from that world was a conscious decision—not only is the psychological not my area of professional competence but it is also, for me, something of a Kantian "thing-in-itself" which we cannot know directly but which we can, if we are so disposed, speculate about through its products.

My own preference is to examine, explore, criticize, and appreciate the products—those elements of personal lives that exist in the public sphere.

These explanations should not be taken as criticisms of research that moves in directions different from mine but simply as part of the effort to help us all (reader, writer, and filmmaker alike) better understand why the material in this book takes the shape it does and why certain aspects do not appear. All these considerations contribute to this particular (and partial, in the sense outlined in the introduction) construction of the domain.

5. The Bogdanovich-Welles collaboration is referred to by V. F. Perkins as "one of the few really indispensable books on the movies" (Perkins 1999: 12). I fully share this assessment.

6. See, for example, Chatman 1992: 404–405.

7. The assumptions underlying the convention of the "ethnographic present" and its effects have been criticized sharply by Johannes Fabian (1983), among others. See also Dwyer (1982).

8. For a discussion of similarities between film editing and anthropological writing, see Marcus 1990; for a discussion of some of the implications of this kind of dialogic reconstruction and of the benefits of attempting, in particular texts, to preserve "research time," see Dwyer (1982: 275–285); for a fine example of how raw interview material may be transformed into a final text, see Narayan (1997: 223–225).

9. Of course, often the concerns I had—such as the depiction of women—are not uniquely mine but have been raised again and again in Moroccan discussion and publications, as should be clear from the presentation of *Badis* in chapter 4.

10. One book that does make this a central theme is Malcolm 1990.

11. I am not the only researcher who has found Tazi to be remarkably open and candid. Ouchen (1998) makes the same point at several places in his study and Carter (1999) notes that Tazi is one of the few Moroccan filmmakers who has been communicative about his films' budgets.

12. It is therefore not purely coincidental that I began this research project when Tazi was in the earliest stages of securing rights to the book he would adapt for his next film and that I completed it just as this film reached the screen, almost five years later.

Another resemblance between us is that our careers took a roughly similar path: "institutionalized" right after completing our studies (he at the CCM, I as a university professor), then two decades or more mostly in somewhat unorthodox extensions of our training (he as a filmmaker engaged in the many varied activities we have seen, I as department head in an international human rights organization and later as a freelance researcher and consultant), and then, most recently and within a year of one another, "re-institutionalized" (he as director of production in Moroccan television, I as professor of anthropology at the American University in Cairo).

13. Tazi is an exception to what Roy Armes sees as the predominantly petty bourgeois origin of Third World filmmakers (Armes 1987: 15). Of course, other Moroccan filmmakers do fit Armes's pattern—for example, Majid Rechiche, one of Tazi's contemporaries at IDHEC, was the son of a postal worker.

14. See Barlet (2000: 14–20) for discussion of such a scheme, although several specific cases in Africa—Nigeria and South African cinemas, for example—come immediately to mind as exceptions to this pattern.

This sequential scheme extends Franz Fanon's discussion of the relationship between artist and society in the Third World into the independence period, a natural extension in that Fanon died in 1961, before the newly decolonized states had much experience, if any, of independence. In Fanon's first stage the artist is concerned primarily with the colonizer's culture; in the second, "we find the native disturbed; he decides to remember what he is . . . [but] since he has only external relations with his people, he is content to recall their life only. . . . Past happenings of the bygone days of his childhood will be brought up out of the depths of his memory . . . legends will be reinterpreted in the light of a borrowed aestheticism and of a concept of the world which was discovered under other skies." In the third phase, "the fighting phase," the artist becomes "an awakener of the people" (this summary is based on Armes 1987: 25–26, with the quotations taken by Armes from Fanon's essay "On National Culture"). Armes goes on to say that "What Fanon's formulation perhaps underplays is the indivisibility of the three stages, that is, the necessity of both an interaction with Europe and a concern with local tradition" (1987: 26). With specific reference to Moroccan cinema, and perhaps other African cinemas as well, Fanon's scheme also underplays the degree to which the artist's separation from the national public was, in effect, a forced estrangement. Certainly by the 1990s and the turn by the audience toward Moroccan films, this division no longer holds.

15. This "heroic period" occurs, in Bourdieu's view, when the artist begins to free his or her work from the demands of the economic and political domains, when the artist "[does] not recogniz[e] any jurisdiction other than the norms specific to one's art" (Bourdieu 1996: 76–77, 113). In the cinematic field, because of the significant financial investment required and other economic and political considerations, it would be a mistake to see this "heroic period" as leading to one where the field becomes to a large extent autonomous, as Bourdieu sees the development of the literary field in France. As we have seen here, with regard to Moroccan cinema, the dialectic between autonomy and dependence is a very complex one.

16. Sama 1996: 148.

17. Boorstin 1995 (the quotations are from pp. 12, 110, and 67, respectively).

18. Of course, this does not mean that Moroccan culture and society, seen in their complexity, have little or no place for the ribald, the indecent, the transgressive (the reader may refer here to Dwyer 1982: 195–203, for one such example, and there are many others available). However, decency and reserve are valued elements in "proper" behavior and are particularly important in the public sphere although, even here, there are exceptions as, for example, in the films of Nabil Lahlou and Abdelkader Lagtaa, to name just two Moroccan filmmakers who transgress dominant norms. In any event, Moroccan culture (and the same can be said for almost any analytic abstraction of this sort) needs to be seen as a complex interweaving of sometimes mutually reinforcing, sometimes neutral, sometimes contradictory strands. Many have made this and similar points; here I will simply cite Moroccan sociologist Muhammad Guessous who, when interpreting proverbs, argues that they "are not univocal: they have many meanings . . . to give this corpus some measure of its real complexity, you have to see it as having three structures at least: an actual structure—the meanings that are clear, manifest, dom-

inant, most frequent; a potential structure—the range of possible variations in meanings; and a counter-structure—the meanings that challenge and contradict the dominant meanings . . ." (cited in Dwyer 1992: 121).

19. Bergman has said, "Our work begins with the human face. . . . The possibility of drawing near to the human face is the primary originality and the distinctive quality of the cinema." (This is a citation at three removes: I found it in MacDougall 1998: 51, who found it in Deleuze 1986: 99, who is citing Bergman from *Cahiers du Cinéma* 1959, with no further bibliographical information given in Deleuze.) Welles takes a different view, "Most of my close-ups are made because I'm forced to. It's always better to avoid them when you can. . . . A long-playing full shot is what always separates the men from the boys" (Welles and Bogdanovich 1998: 201).

The extent to which a reluctance to use close-ups may be characteristic of African cinema in general is discussed by Barlet: "When they film conversations, African filmmakers prefer to use long shots or mid-shots taking in elements of the backdrop, rather than the traditional shot/reverse-shot approach. . . . But how could shot/reverse-shot—the alternation between close-ups of each protagonist as they speak—be used when the very culture is opposed to it?" To support his contention Barlet cites the Burkinabe director Maurice Kaboré: "In the Mossi region it is not proper for a woman to look a man in the eye. When a young couple converse, the woman will be attentive, but her head will be lowered." Barlet comments, "If such a scene is filmed in the shot/reverse-shot style, the woman will almost seem blind and the scene will assume another meaning" (Barlet 2000: 159–161, citing his 1995 interview with Kaboré). A similar argument, that "In general, African cinema is not very fond of intimate scenes," is taken a step further in referring to the reluctance of African films to show intimate views of the human body or of bodies in intimate contact (Tcheuyap 2003: 39).

I am not qualified to evaluate these broad assessments of African cinema. In Barlet's case, he may be adducing this one instance to confirm a general contention rather than making what would be an unwarranted extrapolation from the Mossi region to all of Africa. Weakening his argument, however, is a counterinstance occurring in his own book—his discussion of close-ups used in Gaston Kaboré's *Wend Kuuni* (Barlet 2000: 172).

(Barlet's book, originally published in France and winner of France's National Film Center's Book of the Year award in 1997, is full of suggestive and fertile remarks. One of its faults, however, may lie in generalizations used somewhat too freely. I offer Barlet's and other generalizations about African cinemas with some diffidence. Not myself being a long-time, close observer of African cinema, I would echo the following thoughts of someone who is: "If I have learned anything in nearly 15 years of research on filmmaking by Africans, it is that not enough is known about filmmaking in every Sub-Saharan African country to make generalizations about the subcontinent. . . . The result has been many inaccurate generalizations about filmmaking in Africa . . ." [Schmidt 1999: 277]. Nonetheless, to go forward some generalizations are necessary, hopefully ones that are not too tendentious.)

20. Barlet argues that slowness of pace is a characteristic of African films, adducing for support the Senegalese filmmakers Ababakar Samb Makharam and Moussa Sene Absa, the Burkinabe director Idrissa Ouédraogo, and the Tunisian director and critic Férid Boughedir, all of whom argue for the uses of slowness. As many spectators know, if imagination and attention are

heightened, supposedly "slow" games like chess and cricket can be experienced as gripping. Even where slowness engenders "boredom," this response can lead to questioning and then, "as Raoul Ruiz suggests, be the secret weapon of a different cinema . . ." (Barlet 2000: 171–172, paraphrasing Raoul Ruiz, *Poétique du cinéma* [Paris: Editions Dis Voir, 1995]).

21. In making this argument Mulvey refers specifically to Orson Welles's films. "One of the ways in which *Citizen Kane* seems strikingly anti-Hollywood is the absence of the glamour effect generated by a female star" (Mulvey 1992: 17). She then goes on to see "puzzles" in both *Citizen Kane* and *The Lady from Shanghai,* in which "the [latter] film's central enigma gradually crystalises around Elsa, [whereas] in *Citizen Kane* the film firmly displaces its enigma away from a simple equation with the feminine. . . . Liberated from its erotic obsession with the female figure, cinematic voyeurism is displaced and replaced by a different currency of exchange between screen and spectator" (1992: 17).

22. The "puzzle" mood is often established at the outset. With reference to *Citizen Kane,* Mulvey suggests that "The film's opening sequence sets up the relationship between camera and spectator and establishes it as one of curiosity and investigation" (1992: 24). The same might be said of the opening sequences in *The Big Trip,* where Omar is presented without commentary and we gradually piece together the purpose of his adventure; and most relevantly of the opening of *Badis* where we watch a bus winding its way through the mountains and then depositing a married couple in a remote village where they are obviously newcomers—how will these transplanted urbanites fit into surroundings that are completely alien, "other," to them?

23. There is an obvious parallel here with Fanon's third phase.
Each element on Boorstin's list begins with "v"—voyeur, visceral, vicarious—giving his scheme great mnemonic merit (or should I say virtue?). The "puzzle" fails to fit the mnemonic but the "wake-up" appeal can be made to fit if we resort to French (as we have done in much of this research), in which "w" is termed "*double v.*"

24. Such problems are not exclusive to Third World filmmaking, of course. Peter Bogdanovich recalls: "John Ford said that the best things in pictures happen by accident. And Orson Welles on another level said that a director is a man who presides over accidents" (Sherman 1976: 153). One could no doubt make the further argument that certain kinds of accidents are more likely to occur under "neorealist" Third World filming conditions than elsewhere.

25. Tazi reports that his shooting ratio—the quantity of film shot to the quantity of film in the final copy—is often as low as three to one. In normal feature filmmaking a more common ratio is between five and ten to one, with documentary filmmaking having even higher ratios (Konigsberg 1997: 357).

26. For an examination of the way in which simplifying abstractions of an "Orientalist" sort structure Western notions of Middle Eastern attitudes toward human rights, see Dwyer 1997.

27. In 2002, both Hollywood and Europe produced roughly the same number of films as in the previous year but in other areas Hollywood outperformed Europe, not only showing its greatest year-on-year increase in box-office receipts in two decades (13.2 percent) but regaining some of the market share in Europe that it had lost in 2001. European attendance, on the other hand, was stagnant after the 10 percent increase it had shown in 2001. Of

particular significance was the fact that European films did poorly outside their own national markets: in 2001 European attendance at European films in other than their national markets reached 102 million, but in 2002 this fell back to approximately sixty million. Still, it should be noted that the market share in 2002 of European films in the European market (27.6 percent) constituted a significant advance over the share two years earlier, when it reached only 22.9 percent.

(This information as well as the quote in the text is taken from www.cannesmarket.com, Focus 2003, where "operating margins" are defined as "the ratio of operating profit to operating revenues.")

Here are more detailed figures for the major European cinemas (collated from www.cannesmarket.com, Focus 2003; *Cahiers du Cinéma,* L'Atlas du cinéma, Hors-série, April 2003; Rogemont 2002: 52–55).

(1) Germany: attendance declined in 2002 by almost 10 percent, reversing a positive trend; the number of films produced over 2001–2002 remained constant (in the low 80s), showing a slow but steady increase over previous years; the national films' market share declined in 2002 to 11.9 percent, after having increased from 12.5 percent in 2000 to 18.4 percent in 2001 (with the market share for U.S. films remaining around 80 percent).

(2) Spain: admissions fell by 4 percent in 2002, reversing a decade-long positive trend; films produced in 2002 increased, up to 137 films from 107 in 2001 and continuing the positive trend that started in 1999; however, their share of the national market went down to 13.5 percent in 2002, after having risen from 10 percent in 2000 to 18.2 percent in 2001.

(3) Italy: admissions remained stable while production advanced, with 130 films produced in 2002 compared to 103 in 2001, reversing a long period of decline and stagnation; the national films' market share continued on an upward trend, going from 17.5 percent to 19.4 percent in 2001 (with the U.S. share down from 69.5 percent to 59.7 percent), then up to 22 percent in 2002.

(4) UK: admissions in 2002 jumped by 13 percent, continuing a decade-long trend; production remained relatively constant and the market share for national films was relatively healthy (24 percent) in 2002.

28. For this point, see d'Hugues 2002: 183.

29. In France in 2001: attendance overall was up 12 percent on the previous year and French films gained a 41 percent share, a vast improvement over the very poor performance in the previous year, when French films gained only 28.5 percent of the internal market (the improvement in 2001 came entirely at the expense of American imports, the market share of which fell from 63 percent to 49 percent). As far as production is concerned, amounts invested in French films reached an all-time high in 2000, and this was reflected in the number of films produced during 2001, reaching 200, a marked increase over the 171 films produced in 2000; the year 2001's success was built on a significant number of high-grossing films (both blockbusters and *films d'auteur*) and an audience profile that showed an increased portion of the youthful audience attending French films; also, a number of the successful French films had significant box-office receipts abroad. Yet, success in 2001 did not reflect the beginning of a positive trend. While again involved in producing 200 films in 2002, France's role as the sole or main producer obtained in only 163 of these, a retreat from the 172 in 2001, and the national films' share in the domestic market fell to 34.3 percent in 2002 from 41.6

percent in 2001. (Figures here are taken from CNC, "La production cinématographique en 2002," conférence de presse du mardi, 11 mars 2003, and
Cahiers du Cinéma, L'Atlas du cinéma, Hors-série, April 2003.)

30. The number of screens in France increased from 4,272 in 1993 to
5,236 in 2002 and amounts spent on film advertising went up from thirty-
three million euros in 1992 to 218 million in 2002 (C. Pardo, "Le cinéma
indépendant marginalisé," *Le Monde Diplomatique,* May 2003). For the other
points in this paragraph see N. Vulser, "Le blues s'installe chez les producteurs
indépendants," *Le Monde,* 23 October 2002.

31. This particularly concerns the support provided by the pay-TV channel Canal Plus, which is the largest single contributor to production financing:
its contribution has often been higher than 20 percent of total investment in
French cinema, 45 percent of its contribution must go to smaller films, and
on the whole it supported 70 percent of French films made in 2000. But Canal
Plus's own financial difficulties have weakened this support.

Canal Plus's difficulties arise not only from increasing competition from
other satellite channels and from what appears to be a slow decrease in audience preference for fiction films on television (although this remains the
preferred genre overall), but also from complications following the takeover
of Canal Plus by the Vivendi conglomerate. Canal Plus's contribution to films
of French initiative fell from 147 million Euros in 2001 to 117 in 2002, and
its investment in 2002 amounted to only 18 percent of total investment in
French films, having fallen consistently from 25 percent in 1999. Canal Plus's
agreement to support film production was due for renegotiation in 2004. (For
the preceding figures, see CNC, "La production cinématographique en 2002,"
conférence de presse du mardi, 11 mars 2003. For further discussion of these
and other related issues, see Carlos Pardo, "Le cinéma français, otage de la
télévision," *Le Monde Diplomatique,* May 1999, p. 29; J-M. Frodon, "Le bilan
du CNC affiche les chiffres paradoxaux du cinéma en France," *Le Monde,* 14
May 2000; Carlos Pardo, "Mort programmée du cinéma français," *Le Monde
Diplomatique,* July 2001, p. 25; Thomas Sotinel, "Millésime d'exception pour
les films français," *Le Monde,* 28 December 2001, p. 18; Samuel Blumenfeld,
"Canal Plus, investisseur forcé," *Le Monde,* 28 December 2001, pp. 18–19; Guy
Dutheil, "Les fictions ont été les programmes préférés des téléspectateurs en
2002," *Le Monde,* 28 March 2003.)

32. Measures under consideration or recently adopted include increasing
taxes on DVD and video sales, providing financial incentives for regions to
promote film production, assisting film exports, giving tax shelters to production companies, and broadening the financial contribution of pay-TV channels. (For more detail, see J.-M. Frodon and N. Vulser, "Le gouvernement
réforme le financement du cinéma," *Le Monde,* 2 May 2003.)

33. Brazilian production, after a long period of decline, has now recovered somewhat, producing some twenty-five films per year and gaining approximately 10 percent of the domestic market (as reported in Walter Salles,
"Mort et renaissance d'un cinéma national," *Le Monde,* 20 May 2000, pp. xii–
xiii). In 2002, thirty films were produced with an 8 percent market share
(*Cahiers du Cinéma,* L'Atlas du cinema, Hors-série, April 2003, p. 82), an upturn
that one Brazilian filmmaker commented upon, saying, "we have now come
out of the great crisis in Brazilian cinema and, with a new audiovisual law
encouraging investment, we're back to 30 films a year, although this is far

from the 120 films shot each year between 1960 and 1970" (Thomas Sotinel, "Rencontre: Andrucha Waddington, de Rio au sertao," *Le Monde,* 26 December 2001, p. 15).

South Korea provides a good example of how important ensuring the access of national films to the theaters can be. Since the systematic application of screen quotas in the mid-1990s, national films have consistently won 30–40 percent market share, with Hollywood, Japanese, and other imported films all retreating (Yong-Kwan Lee, "Le cinéma coréen: miracle ou stratégie gagnante," in *CinémAction, Hors-série. 2002. Quelle diversité face à Hollywood,* edited by Thomas Paris [Paris: CinémAction-Corlet, 2002], pp. 160–167). With each film theater obligated to show Korean films for a minimum of 146 days per year, market share reached almost 50 percent in 2002, compared with only 16 percent in 1993. While the quota system has clearly had a positive effect on South Korean cinema, its role has been repeatedly challenged during negotiations designed to lead to a bilateral investment agreement with the United States, challenges coming both from the U.S. negotiators and from South Korean politicians opposing the government's protective policies (Samuel Blumenfeld, "La menace qui pèse sur le cinéma coréen pollue le Festival du film français de Séoul," *Le Monde,* 25 June 2003).

In Nigeria, video accounted for the total production of 650 legally approved films in 2000 (with more than half of these in Nigerian languages other than English), and the well-developed distribution circuits reach into the neighboring states of Cameroun, Benin, and Togo, as well as the Nigerian diaspora in the United States and UK (Montfort 2002: 47). In this, Nigeria may be pointing one way to the future and among African countries Ghana and Gabon appear to be following Nigeria's example (Wendl 2003; Ivanga 2003).

34. Among the areas in which digital savings are substantial are camera costs, short-circuiting laboratory costs and thus reducing shooting time (digital video rushes can be viewed immediately and editing can begin at the same time), and smaller crews—for example, much less artificial lighting and fewer lighting technicians are needed.

Moroccan filmmakers who have recently shot and edited digitally include Tazi (*Abu Moussa's Women Neighbors,* 2003), Abdelkader Lagtaa (*Face to Face,* 2003), and Nabil Ayouch (*One Minute Less in the Sun,* 2002).

35. In both the Moroccan and Nigerian cases it is difficult to know how much of video production is digital, but no doubt digital will play a growing role in this sector. For a very interesting discussion of Berber videos, see Carter 1999: 569–581 (and, for a partial list, Carter 1999: 709). Carter reports that there are at least five companies producing videos in Tachelhit (one of the three main Berber dialects), in genres such as "drama, melodrama, filmed theater, autobiography, and comedy" (1999: 570).

36. Recent figures support this contention: in late 2003 there were some 80 cinemas in the United States with digital projectors, with no more than 120 in the rest of the world, most of which were in Europe and Japan (Eric Taub, "Digital projection of films is coming. Now, who pays?" *New York Times,* 13 October 2003). In what may amount to a challenge to this pattern, in late 2003 Brazil, building on recent success in its film production, was the scene of initiatives to install a cheaper digital production system in up to a hundred art-house and independent cinemas (Alex Bellos, "The main attraction," *Guardian,* 4 December 2003).

Other forms of distribution and screening that make use of digital technology are being put into practice in some areas—film buses, perhaps similar to those used in the early decades after independence, are being used in a number of countries (among them Nigeria), and DVD projects are making inroads in African villages (with the support of European donors, particularly the French). (For the film buses in Nigeria, see Montfort 2002: 51; for DVD distribution, see Thomas Sotinel, "En Afrique, le cinéma revient au village sur DVD," *Le Monde Supplément Cannes,* 16 May 2002, p. 8.)

37. For most of the year 2001 one of the major exhibitors systematically refused to show Moroccan films out of what may have been personal pique, a settling of accounts, financial motivation, or some combination of these.

38. The high-return theaters are those in the new multiplex in Casablanca (with its fourteen screens), a similar number of Dawliz cinemas (owned by a former CCM director), and several others in Morocco's major cities.

39. It is very simple to go to almost any major marketplace in urban Morocco and find DVDs of recent international films for sale at 15 to 20 DH, that is, $1.50–$2.00. Video/DVD sales can constitute a significant portion of the income from a film: in the United States, for example, income from video/DVD made up almost 60 percent of the domestic film revenue for the year 2002 (Eric Taub, "Movie DVD's that are meant for buying but not for keeping," *New York Times,* 21 July 2003).

40. Interestingly, this so-called "Zero Commission" followed by just one year the example of the Tunisian funding committee, which in June 2000, also for the first time ever, gave no awards.

41. In early 2001 the ministry of communication announced that it was establishing a minimum of 20 million DH per year of Aid Fund support, however much below that amount the standard sources for this fund produced. The Aid Fund Commission meets twice a year and in its July 2003 meeting (the most recent at the time of writing), awards were made to eight feature-length films and four shorts, for a total of 14 million DH, an increase over the usual amount by some 4 million DH, an increase that the ministry of communication decided on, "in view of the number and significance of the projects presented" (www.2M.tv, 4 July 2003).

42. Ayouch's censored film, co-produced for the French-German television station ARTE, was shown during 2003 on ARTE and was widely seen in Morocco by those who had access to satellite television. On the whole, viewers were greatly disappointed by the film's overall quality and were shocked as well by some scenes that suggested unorthodox sexual activities. In my own view, on quality alone this film does not measure up to the high standards established by Ayouch's previous films and must be counted a failure.

43. The Rabat festival in 1982—the first—showed thirteen feature films and ten shorts; the second, in Casablanca in 1984, showed eleven features and eight shorts. The third was not held until seven years later, in Meknès in 1991, and showed twelve feature films and five shorts. Tangiers, in 1995, was the scene of the fourth (ten feature films and twenty-two shorts); Casablanca, in 1998, the fifth (twelve features and eighteen shorts); Marrakesh, a little more than two years later in early 2001, the sixth (fifteen features and seventeen shorts); and Oujda, the seventh, in June 2003 (sixteen features and seventeen shorts).

Since 2001 Morocco has regularly held an annual International Film Festival, in Marrakesh, in the fall. These have been moderately successful (despite the first having been held in the shadow of the events of 11 September). This festival is a showcase for international films rather than national ones and is therefore not directly relevant to our subject, other than as a sign of Morocco's efforts to attract foreign film productions to the country. (One of GARP's aims is to have this festival reorganized so that it provides greater support for Moroccan films, and the group has suggested measures such as ensuring that a minimum number of Moroccan films be selected for the competition.)

44. MAP [Maghreb Arabe Presse], "Une édition pas comme les autres," *Le Matin du Sahara*, 29 January 2001.

45. Olivier Schmitt, "La soudaine profusion des films nationaux sur les écrans du Maroc," *Le Monde*, 10 February 2001.

46. "a falling-off . . ." (Muhammad Bakrim, "Marrakech et après," *Libération*, 3 February 2001); "shaky state" (S. I., "Des prix et des larmes," *Al Bayane*, 5 February 2001); "unable to hide . . ." (K. R., "Zaoua oui-oui," *L'Opinion*, 6 February 2001); "radiating . . ." (Noureddine Kachti, "Que veut le film marocain?" *Le Reporter*, 15 February 2001); "frankly . . ." (Khalil Rais, "Soif du cinéma," *L'Opinion*, 2 February 2001); "shamed . . ." ("Les cinéastes font le point," *La Vie Economique*, 9 February 2001; the words quoted were uttered by the filmmaker Hakim Noury). The quotation from Tazi appeared in Mohammed Bakrim, "Entretien avec Mohamed Abderrahmane Tazi: produire notre propre image," *Libération*, 26 February 2001.

47. On giving prizes to the worst films: "they've just given four prizes to one of the worst films . . ." ("Les amoureux des 'amours de Hadj Mokhtar Soldi,' " *L'Opinion*, 10 February 2001); "the jury . . ." (Amine Rahmouni, "Une 'Soif' inextinguible" [interview with Saad Chraibi], *Le Journal*, 16 February 2001); "sabotaged" (MAP, "L'équipe du film 'Amour sans visa' crie au 'sabotage,' " *Al Bayane*, 8 February 2001; the word is quoted from the filmmaker Najib Sefrioui).

48. This sum and the 2.5 million DH awarded for the sixth festival in Marrakesh, constituted an increase of some 50 percent over the budget for the fifth festival, held in 1998 in Casablanca.

49. The border has been closed since 1994 because of tensions between the two countries following Moroccan claims that authors of a hotel bombing had crossed into the country from Algeria.

50. One of the younger filmmakers based in Europe walked out early on a showing of a Moroccan film featured at the 2003 Cannes festival and likely to be distributed in France, saying, "The conditions are intolerable, I'd prefer to wait and see it in Paris." Of course, this option is not open to everyone.

51. GARP was very vocal in its criticisms of the festival, arguing that it should not be held hostage to priorities other than the one of supporting the national film sector. GARP also claimed that the decisions of the jury were deeply flawed, both by conflicts of interest and general standards of judgment. GARP made these criticisms despite the fact that its secretary-general/treasurer was the jury's chair.

52. The contrast between the great cultural significance accorded to Moroccan cinema today and the situation in the late 1980s couldn't be clearer. As Susan Othman noted in 1990, "In spite of several promising films, such as Farida Belyazid's *A Door to the Sky* and M. A. Tazi's *Badis*, cinema is spoken of less and less in Morocco. . . . The intelligentsia is more interested in television and in public opinion polls than in film club discussions" (Othman 1990: 187).

53. Derkaoui's film is the story of a 14-year-old girl, enamored of belly

dancing, who, to help defray the cost of surgery her young brother requires, takes her dancing talents into Casablancan night life and its questionable morality. Derkaoui's film won no awards (although his previous film, also widely condemned by critics, had won several at the sixth festival, including that of best director).

Lagtaa's film, although not winning any of the official festival prizes, was given both the critic's prize and the press award for best feature film. Tazi's film did not win any awards at the festival, although its being bypassed occasioned much negative comment, with critics feeling it could easily have won the award for best director or, perhaps, for cinematography, or, at the very least, for costume and design. Tazi, while defending the film, himself recognized that it needed cutting—at the time of the festival he told me that he had decided to cut some twenty minutes from the two-hour version and that he already knew where those cuts would be made. He also admitted that the demands of his work at 2M had made it difficult for him to devote as much time and energy to this film as he would have liked and that the film no doubt suffered somewhat from this.

54. At Oujda Nejjar's film gained three prizes and Ben Saidi's none, an imbalance many felt was undeserved. Almost a year passed before these films appeared on Morocco's commercial screens.

55. Ayouch's *Ali Zaoua*, the films of Ben Saidi and Nejjar, and Belabbes's *The Threads of Life* all expose the complexity and "mosaic" nature of Moroccan society in their representation, respectively, of street children, political repression, prostitution, and a family's hold over its children.

56. The Moroccan diaspora is not the only filmmaking diaspora in this situation. For a discussion of the dynamism among Nigerian and other African diaspora filmmakers in Europe, see Barlet 2002.

57. This last question was posed frequently with regard to the winners of the best film award at the two festivals preceding Oujda—Nabil Ayouch's *Ali Zaoua* (winner in 2001) and Fatima Jebaili Ouezzani's *La maison de mon père,* winner at the 1998 festival in Casablanca.

58. Those presenting a first feature are likely to include Aziz Salmi, Noureddin Lekhmari, Leila Marrakchi, Hicham Fellah, and Muhammad Cherif Tribek (all but the first of whom won major prizes for shorts at the sixth or seventh festivals); those presenting their second will probably include Faouzi Ben Saidi, Narjiss Nejjar, and Ahmed Boulane; among the proven directors with long careers behind them likely to be presenting films, are, in addition to Tazi, Farida Benlyazid (Morocco's only established woman director), Abdelkader Lagtaa, Nabil Lahlou, Hakim Noury, and Mustapha Derkaoui, among others.

59. Some figures to indicate the gravity of the social situation: 7.5 million people (of Morocco's population of some 30 million) live on one dollar a day or less, illiteracy affects some 50 percent of the population and unemployment reaches 20 percent in urban areas. These figures and the paragraph's quotation come from Florence Beaugé, "Le gouvernement d'alternance a déçu les espoirs populaires," *Le Monde,* 25 January 2002, p. 4. On the delay in efforts to reform the Personal Status Code (Mudawwana) and improve women's rights, see Florence Beaugé, "La réforme du statut de la femme au point mort," *Le Monde,* 25 January 2002, p. 4. Recent developments in this area are treated later in this section.

60. Following the national elections, King Muhammad VI named a cen-

trist prime minister, Driss Jettou—a man with no political party affiliation but who had significant experience in Morocco's economic world, having exercised, among other functions, that of directing the National Phospate Company and, not incidentally, managing the royal family's wealth. The legislature elected in 2002 had thirty-five women members, a dramatic increase over the 1997 legislature in which there had been only two. Among the thirty-eight members of the government led by Prime Minister Jettou, three were women, also a significant increase.

61. The Casablanca attack also led a number of European countries (including France, Italy, Spain, and Britain) to form a permanent committee to examine questions of terrorism and illegal immigration (Reuters, "Cinq pays européens créent un groupe permanent d'experts sur le terrorisme et l'immigration clandestine," *Le Monde,* 20 May 2003).

62. In the king's proposals the family is placed under the joint responsibility of the couple (previously the husband had primary responsibility) and the provision requiring the wife to owe obedience to her husband is eliminated; a woman no longer needs to have a male guardian (Ar. *wali*) oversee her marriage and the marriageable age for women is raised from 15 to 18 years of age, equal to that for men; severe restrictions are imposed on a man's legal right to have up to four wives—a woman can now include in her marriage contract a provision precluding her husband's taking a second wife and, even without such a provision, both her approval and a judge's are required before an additional marriage can take place; a husband is no longer able to divorce his wife by repudiation, all requests for divorce must be approved by a judge, and the wife gains easier access to a judicial divorce and greater custody rights in the case of a divorce. Other provisions give the wife greater inheritance rights and more say in the disposition of the couple's wealth, and provide for recognition of paternity if a child is born out of wedlock.

63. Speech given by King Muhammad VI on 29 May 2003, cited in www.liberation.press.ma of 2 June 2003. The king's relatively short reign has twice been marked by tragic events that seriously dampened what would have been moments of national celebration: in early 2002, in response to events in Palestine, he postponed for three months his long-awaited wedding (it finally took place in July 2002, in a subdued manner), and the Casablanca bombings curtailed celebrations related to the birth, one week earlier, of the royal couple's first child, a boy destined to become Morocco's next king.

64. In early July 2003, in the first of the trials following the attacks, the repressive mood was made more concrete when ten death sentences were given to members of a group (Salafiyya Jihadiyya) deemed responsible for several attacks over the previous years. There were also eight sentences of life imprisonment, among thirty-one accused. Several more death sentences and many more convictions were handed down in subsequent months.

Some sense of the ideological stance of the more radical Islamic movements in Morocco (as distinguished from the PJD and the Justice and Charity group [Fr. *Justice et Bienfaisance,* Ar. *al Adl wa al-Iḥsan*]) may be gleaned from the following commentary: "at the exits of Casablanca mosques [one may receive] . . . a pamphlet coming from this movement that lashes out at Moroccan society 'which has lost its bearings' and at its leaders—first among them being the 'heretic sultan'—termed 'renegades' and 'apostates.' 'Jihad is needed to change the situation and to replace heretic law by God's law.' In the coming struggle, the pamphlet continues, 'it is legitimate to kill all those who protect a miscreant. . . . No protection is due to women and children because the children of miscreants are part of that group' " (Ali El Sarafi, "Tour de vis sécuritaire au Maroc," *Le Monde Diplomatique,* July 2003).

The PJD itself was among the many opponents to the proposed anti-terrorism law while it was being drawn up prior to the bombings of 16 May, but the party withdrew its objections after the bombings and the law was voted almost unanimously by Parliament (one legislator abstained; Ali El Sarafi, "Tour de vis sécuritaire au Maroc," *Le Monde Diplomatique,* July 2003).

65. Concerning freedom of the press, the international NGO Reporters without Borders noted that, in the first five months of 2002, the director of one weekly was under prosecution and three publications had been censored for offenses against the new press law (Léa Girault, "Une réforme mantient les peines de prison pour les délits de presse au Maroc," *Le Monde,* 23 May 2002, p. 22).

The new anti-terrorism law may also be used to muzzle the press; in early June 2003, the publisher of an Arabic language weekly, *Al-Ousbu'*, was held for questioning, on points resembling the new law's wording, for having published a letter that took responsibility for the 16 May attacks (K. B. Mustapha Alaoui, "Première cible de la loi anti-terroriste," *Le Journal,* 7–13 June 2003).

The most highly publicized case prosecuted under the new press law was that of the journalist Ali Lmrabet, who had the two publications he directed suspended and who, in mid-2003, was sentenced to four years imprisonment (eventually reduced to three on appeal) for, among other accusations, "insults to the king." The wide publicity this case received was due, in part, to the journalist's binationality (Moroccan and French), to the nature of the offense (which involved several cartoons deemed insulting to the king, as well as publication of the Palace budget), and to the journalist's embarking on several hunger strikes, one that lasted almost two months and that he abandoned only after a visit from Moulay Hicham, the king's cousin known for his "progressive" views and often referred to as *"le prince rouge."*

Yet, the latitude that journalists enjoy in Morocco is still substantial and allows much freedom of expression. A decade or more ago, it would have been much more risky than it is today to publish the following: "Four years ago King Muhammad wanted to free himself from his father's image. Today he is trying to emulate him, or even go him one better. In the meantime the menu has changed. Instead of Basri, a corrupt elite, and an arbitrariness which might erupt at any moment, our very new era gives us a cocktail of the security-obsessed, an elite of the salons, laws that are arbitrary in themselves, and courts which carry forward the injustices of the police stations" (Driss Ksikes, "Les 'nouvelles ères,' " *Telquel,* 14–20 June 2003).

In January 2004 King Muhammad VI pardoned all journalists who were still in prison—they then numbered seven—including Ali Mrabet, who was in the fifth week of a hunger strike.

66. The central role played by the audiovisual in this controversy has several different sources: (1) audiovisual productions in general, and feature films in particular, are among the forms most vulnerable to the removal of supports, because such productions require massive investment at the point of creation, whereas in poetry and literature considerable (if much lower) amounts are needed only at the later stages of mass production and distribution; (2) audiovisual productions have shown themselves to be readily amenable to international marketing and therefore have the potential of gener-

ating significant profits; and (3) the role audiovisual products play in leisure activities makes them, unlike books, readily assimilable to other "entertainment" activities and to their being seen as simply one commodity among others, as mere objects for consumption, without the specific cultural value that attaches to products of "high culture."

67. The UNESCO document is available at http://unesdoc.unesco.org/images/0012/001271/127160m.pdf. With the United States having rejoined UNESCO in late 2003 (after an absence of almost twenty years) and having consistently promoted the view that cultural goods and services should be treated like other commodities, the effort to elaborate an international convention on cultural diversity is unlikely to go smoothly.

68. The question of whether systematic application of free trade principles would promote "development" in poorer countries is too complicated for us to examine here. However, I share the central argument of many writers on the subject who argue that free trade, in itself, is not necessarily conducive to development but may be made so only if it is designed and implemented in ways that make the needs of poorer countries central—measures that would include reducing or eliminating First World trade barriers, subsidies, and other supports that are prejudicial to Third World products (such as textiles and various agricultural goods), devising fairer schemes of commodity pricing, loosening intellectual property rights stipulations that make it difficult for poorer countries to gain access to medicines and other technological advances, and so forth. The World Trade Organization negotiations that took place in Doha (Qatar) in November 2001 saw an attempt by Third World countries to give such concerns higher priority and this led to a number of commitments on the part of the wealthier nations to ease the lot of the poorer, particularly with regard to agriculture and medicines. However, the meeting two years later in Cancun, Mexico, that was meant to advance this agenda ended in failure and recriminations, and the outlook for systematic progress on these issues within the framework of the WTO is not promising. There is also the danger that stalemate in the WTO will lead to a renewed emphasis on bilateral negotiations, where the bargaining power of Third World countries is very weak. Morocco itself was engaged in such negotiations with the United States and an agreement was expected to be reached during 2004.

Furthermore, a convincing historical argument has been made that the development of First World countries was aided by protective barriers and other state supports for certain essential and/or expanding productive sectors, and by loose interpretations of intellectual property rights. To deprive Third World countries of the possibility of implementing similar policies is tantamount to perpetuating their dependency and to making their development all but impossible. (For a comprehensive treatment of how trade might be made more equitable, see Oxfam 2002; for the historical argument just outlined, see Chang 2002.)

69. Canada has also been an articulate proponent of the cultural exception and was able to have the audiovisual domain "excluded" from the ALENA accords reached with the United States in 1988 (Regourd 2002: 83). The controversial French position that the audiovisual be excluded from free trade discussions was articulated forcefully during the 1994 negotiations in the framework of the General Agreement on Tariffs and Trade (GATT) that led to the formation of the World Trade Organization (WTO) as its successor organization. No agreement on the French position was reached so that, techni-

cally, this is neither an "exclusion" nor an "exception" but the status of the issue is left undecided. In principle, the question may be raised anew at any subsequent meeting of the WTO (see Regourd 2002: 85–86). It is impossible to resist pointing out the coincidence of these 1994 negotiations having taken place in Morocco (in the city of Marrakesh).

70. Understandably, many Moroccans and other North Africans, still smarting from the colonial legacy almost a half-century after the end of French rule, find France's plight as it fights to preserve its cultural independence from the hegemonic tendencies of U.S. and other international media conglomerates, worth an ironic smile accompanied by some well-earned Schadenfreude.

France should not be seen as a selfless hero in this tale. France's policy of providing aid to Third World cinemas has had the effect of perpetuating the latters' dependence on the metropole for technical assistance (see, for example, Diawara 1992: 21–34, and Andrade-Watkins 1996). As one writer remarks, "France's protective stance on 'cultural heritage' is likely to be of most benefit to large capitalist interests in Western Europe and of little assistance to film producers in countries such as those in Africa" (Moran 1996: 14).

Even within Europe, many of the measures France proposes are tailored to its own situation as a country with high production levels but low exports, rather than to promoting "cultural diversity" across the board. In the European Union distribution aid mentioned previously, France lobbied successfully for measures to help a national cinema (like its own) that has assured its own production but faces international distribution problems, but lobbied (again successfully) against measures that would encourage increased production for those countries where production itself was the problem.

71. Effective regional coordination does not appear imminent. We have already seen, in chapter 5, how difficult it has been for filmmakers within the Arab world to collaborate across national boundaries, for a number of complex reasons. With regard to the more limited geographical area of the Maghreb, attempts at regional political and economic integration have advanced at a snail's pace. Late 2003 saw yet another failed attempt to hold a summit meeting of the leaders of member states of the Arab Maghreb Union (Morocco, Algeria, Tunisia, Libya, and Mauritania), meaning that no such summit has taken place since 1994.

On a national level, there are no limits to the kinds of financing schemes that might be devised, including direct state support, indirect public support through lotteries, and so on. Among the measures that might be adopted, we find "financing credits; low interest loans; state backed co-productions; various kinds of subsidies and subventions, distribution advances; co-productions between the state and private producers or between the state, private producers and foreign concerns; box-office taxes; taxes on profits, remittances by foreign distributors; and taxes on the production sector" (Moran 1996: 8).

From a more systemic perspective, one might distinguish between "restrictive, supportive and comprehensive protectionist policies. A restrictive policy, which includes such measures as screen and import quotas as well as import tariffs and customs duties, is designed to give the local industry some breathing room by impeding a complete takeover of the local market by foreign concerns. A supportive policy includes direct state support of the industry in the form of bank loans and credit, prizes, production subsidies and other forms of film financing, assistance in reaching foreign markets, and training of film industry technicians. Restrictive policies provide indirect support of the industry while supportive policies lend direct financial support. A comprehensive state policy would include both restrictive and supportive measures" (Johnson 1996: 135, referring to work by Jorge Schnitman).

72. Paraphrased by and cited in John Gray, "Does globalization bring liberty," *Times Literary Supplement*, 17 November 2000, p. 18.

The glaring inequities and lack of balance contained in some of these policies—for example, in the pressure toward opening Third World markets to First World industrial products while at the same time maintaining the "agricultural exclusion" that allows subsidies for the production and export of Western farm products—make this hostility all the easier to understand. Even while the head of the World Trade Organization voices these concerns, the policies themselves continue: "on 7 February [2002], in Kenya, Mike Moore [then head of the World Trade Organization] explained that, if the West rescinded the subsidies it gave to its farmers, Africa would gain in its export income 'three to five times all the development aid it receives and nine times the debt reductions that it is accorded' " (Stephen Smith, "Paris accueille un sommet africain pour organiser la relance du développement du continent," *Le Monde,* 9 February 2002, p. 4).

For a sharp critique of the ways in which one major international economic institution, the International Monetary Fund, neglects the particularities of local situations in its pursuit of a "one size fits all" liberalization and therefore works against Third World development, see Stiglitz 2002.

73. It appears that Australian cinema found itself in just such a situation when, during the 1970s, " 'As a result of all that talk and declamation ["the rhetoric of lobbyists and journalists, the speeches and statements of politicians, the annual reports of government bodies, the pamphlets and documents of contending interest groups within the industry, and, finally, in the films themselves"], "the industry" was already an over-determined and even fetishized object *before* it had any claim to material existence' " (Dorland 1996: 119, with the citation in single quotation marks taken by Dorland from a 1987 study of Australian cinema by Dermody and Jacka).

74. The head of the Producers' Guild was quoted as saying that, under such an agreement, "American filmmakers will have the same rights as Moroccans to financial aid from the CCM [and] they will be able to demand that this aid be eliminated if they don't benefit equally from it (cited in Aziz Daki, "L'accord qui menace la culture marocaine," *Aujourd'hui le Maroc,* 29 December 2003). The text of the final agreement had not been made public at the time of this writing, but reports suggested that Morocco would indeed be able to maintain the Aid Fund in its current form; however, the agreement would allow the theaters and distribution circuits to turn fully toward foreign productions and to become foreign-owned entities, and there would be no limits on concentration in the sector. One effect of this agreement was that a new audiovisual law that would reorganize Moroccan public broadcasting and encourage private investment in radio and television stalled in parliament, because some of the provisions in it that protected Moroccan audiovisual production conflicted with the agreement.

GARP (the organization Tazi headed) was a member of the coalition protesting the free-trade agreement and was also among the groups in the Moroccan film world that had argued for revision of the Aid Fund. Among the changes in the Aid Fund were the following: the Aid Fund Commission would henceforth meet three times a year instead of twice and 10 million DH would continue to be made available at each meeting, meaning a 50 percent increase in annual funding; special awards were instituted to reward quality; it would no longer be possible to withhold the final installment of an award (a practice that filmmakers had frequently criticized as amounting to censorship); and the award would now be in the form of an "advance against takings" (resembling the French model) where, rather than being treated as non-recoverable, the award would consist of an advance to be repaid, at least in part, through a levy on a film's box-office receipts. Amounts recovered in this way would be added to the sum available for future awards. In April 2004 both the new CCM director and the minister of culture and communication promised that, in the near future, the amount the Aid Fund would devote to film production would climb steeply to 100 million dirhams a year—a measure that, if carried out, would dramatically improve Moroccan filmmakers' prospects. However, without corresponding reforms in distribution and exhibition, greater Moroccan film production would not necessarily mean more Moroccan films on the screens.

Bibliography

Abu-Lughod, Lila. 1995a. "Movie Stars and Islamic Moralism in Egypt." *Social Text* 42: 53–67.

———. 1995b. "The Objects of Soap Opera: Egyptian Television and the Cultural Politics of Modernity." In Daniel Miller, ed., *Worlds Apart: Modernity through the Prism of the Local,* pp. 190–210. London: Routledge.

———. 1997. "The Interpretation of Cultures After Television." *Representations* 59: 109–133.

———. 2002. "Egyptian Melodrama: Technology of the Modern Subject." In Faye D. Ginsburg, Lila Abu-Lughod, and Brian Larkin, eds., *Media Worlds,* pp. 115–133. Berkeley: University of California Press.

Adler, Laure. 1998. *Marguerite Duras.* Paris: Gallimard.

Ahmad, Aijaz. 1992. *In Theory: Classes, Nations, Literatures.* London and New York: Verso.

Alif. 1995. *Arab Cinematics: Toward the New and the Alternative.* Vol. 15. Cairo: American University in Cairo Press.

———. 2002. *The Language of the Self: Autobiographies and Testimonies.* Vol. 22. Edited by Ferial Ghazoul. Cairo: American University in Cairo Press.

Andrade-Watkins, Claire. 1996. "France's Bureau of Cinema: Financial and Technical Assistance 1961–1977—Operations and Implications for African Cinema." In Imruh Bakari and Mbye B. Cham, eds., *African Experiences of Cinema,* pp. 112–127. London: British Film Institute.

Araib, Ahmed, and Eric de Hullessen. 1999. *Il était une fois . . . le cinéma au Maroc!* Rabat: EDH.

Arasoughly, Alia, ed. 1996. *Screens of Life: Critical Film Writing from the Arab World.* Quebec: World Heritage Press.

Armbrust, Walter. 1996. *Mass Culture and Modernism in Egypt.* Cambridge: Cambridge University Press.

———. 2000. "The Golden Age before the Golden Age: Commercial Egyptian Cinema before the 1960s." In Walter Armbrust, ed., *Mass Mediations: New Approaches to Popular Culture in the Middle East and Beyond,* pp. 292–327. Berkeley: University of California Press.

———. 2002. "The Riddle of Ramadan: Media, Consumer Culture, and the 'Christmasization' of a Muslim Holiday." In Donna Lee Bowen and E. A. Early, eds., *Everyday Life in the Muslim Middle East,* pp. 335–348. Bloomington: Indiana University Press.

Armes, Roy. 1987. *Third World Film Making and the West.* Berkeley: University of California Press.

————. 1996. *Dictionary of North African Film Makers/Dictionnaire des Cinéastes du Maghreb*. Paris: Editions ATM.

————. 2000. "Reinterpreting the Tunisian Past: *Les Silences du Palais*." In R. Kevin Lacy et al., eds., *The Arab-African and Islamic Worlds: Interdisciplinary Studies*, pp. 203–214. New York: Peter Lang.

————. Forthcoming. *Post-colonial Images: Studies in North African Film* (provisional title). London: Flick Books.

Bakari, Imruh, and Mbye B. Cham, eds. 1996. *African Experiences of Cinema*. London: British Film Institute.

Barlet, Olivier. 2000. *African Cinemas: Decolonizing the Gaze*. London: Zed Press. (First published as *Les cinémas d'Afrique noire*. Paris: Harmattan. 1996.)

————. 2002. "L'exception africaine." *Africultures* 45 (February 2002): 5–8.

Berrah, Mouny, Victor Bachy, Mohand Ben Salama, and Hamdy Kandil, eds. 1981. "Cinémas du Maghreb." *CinémAction* 14 (Spring).

Boorstin, Jon. 1995. *Making Movies Work*. Los Angeles: Silman-James Press.

Bouanani, Ahmed. 1984. "La Septième Porte: histoire du cinéma marocain." Unpublished manuscript.

Boughedir, Férid. 1981. "Les quatre voies du cinéma marocain." *CinémAction* 14 (Spring): 207–212.

Bourdieu, Pierre. 1996. *The Rules of Art*. Stanford, Calif.: Stanford University Press.

Carter, Sandra G. 1999. "Moroccan Cinema: What Moroccan Cinema?" Ph.D. dissertation, University of Texas at Austin.

————. 2000. "Moroccan Cinema: What Moroccan Cinema?" *Maghreb Review* 25, no. 1–2: 65–97.

Caton, Steven C. 1999. *Lawrence of Arabia: A Film's Anthropology*. Berkeley: University of California Press.

CCM. [1996.] *Regard sur le cinéma au Maroc*. Rabat: Morocco.

Chang, Ha-Joon. 2002. *Kicking Away the Ladder: Development Strategy in Historical Perspective*. London: Anthem Press.

Charasse, Michel. 2001. *Les crédits d'aide publique au développement affectés aux pays du Maghreb*. Rapport d'information 083 (2000–2001)—Commission Des Finances. Paris: Sénat de France.

Chatman, Seymour. 1992. "What Novels Can Do That Films Can't (and Vice Versa)." In Gerald Mast, Marshall Cohen, and Leo Braudy, eds., *Film Theory and Criticism*, pp. 403–419. Oxford: Oxford University Press.

CinéMaroc 6 (October 1998).

Crapanzano, Vincent. 1980. *Tuhami: Portrait of a Moroccan*. Chicago: University of Chicago Press.

Dabashi, Hamid. 2001. *Close Up: Iranian Cinema—Past, Present and Future*. London: Verso.

Deleuze, Gilles. 1986. *Cinema I: The Movement-Image*. Minneapolis: University of Minnesota Press.

Dermody, Susan, and Elizabeth Jacka. 1987. *The Screening of Australia: Anatomy of a Film Industry*. Sydney: Currency Press.

d'Hugues, Philippe. 2002. "Une Amélie ne fait pas le printemps." In Thomas Paris, ed., "Quelle diversité face à Hollywood." *CinémAction*, Hors-série: 182–187.

Diawara, Manthia. 1992. *African Cinema: Politics and Culture*. Bloomington: Indiana University Press.

Dickinson, Michael. 2001. "Solving the Mystery of Insect Flight." *Scientific American* (June): 34–41.

Dorland, Michael. 1996. "Policy Rhetorics of an Imaginary Cinema: The Discursive Economy of the Emergence of the Australian and Canadian Feature Film." In Albert Moran, ed., *Film Policy: International, National and Regional Perspectives,* pp. 114–127. London and New York: Routledge.

Dumont, Jean-Paul. 1978. *The Headman and I.* Austin: University of Texas Press.

Dwyer, Kevin. 1982. *Moroccan Dialogues.* Baltimore: Johns Hopkins University Press.

———. 1992. *Arab Voices: The Human Rights Debate in the Middle East.* Berkeley: University of California Press.

———. 1997. "Beyond a Boundary? 'Universal Human Rights' and the Middle East." *Anthropology Today* (UK) 13, no. 6: 13–18.

———. 2002a. " 'Hidden, Unsaid, Taboo' in Moroccan Cinema: Abdelkader Lagtaa's Challenge to Authority." In Dorit Nauman, ed., *Middle Eastern Film and Media Arts,* Special issue of *Framework* 43, no. 2 (Fall 2002): 117–133.

———. 2002b. "Moroccan Film-making: A Long Voyage through the Straits of Paradox." In Donna Lee Bowen and E. A. Early, eds., *Everyday Life in the Muslim Middle East,* pp. 349–359. Bloomington: Indiana University Press.

———. 2004. "Un pays, une décennie, deux comédies." *CinémAction* 111: 86–91.

Eickelman, Dale F. 1998. *The Middle East and Central Asia: An Anthropological Approach.* 3rd ed. Upper Saddle River, N.J.: Prentice-Hall.

El Khodari, Khalid. 2000. *Guide des réalisateurs marocains.* Rabat: Imprimerie El Maarif Al Jadida.

El-Guindi, Fadwa. 2001. "Beyond Picturing Culture: A Critique of a Critique." *American Anthropologist* 103, no. 2 (June 2001): 523–527.

Fabian, Johannes. 1983. *Time and the Other: How Anthropology Makes Its Object.* New York: Columbia University Press.

Fertat, Ahmed. 2000. *Une passion nommée cinéma: vie et oeuvre de Mohamed Osfour, premier cinéaste marocain.* Tangiers: Altopress.

Geertz, Clifford. 1988. *Works and Lives.* Cambridge: Polity.

Georgakas, Dan, and Lenny Rubenstein. 1983a. "Ousmane Sembène: Filmmakers Have a Great Responsibility to Our People." In Dan Georgakas and Lenny Rubenstein, eds., *The Cineaste Interviews,* pp. 41–52. Chicago: Lake View Press.

———. 1983b. "Tomàs Gutierrez Alea: Individual Fulfillment and Collective Achievement." In Dan Georgakas and Lenny Rubenstein, eds., *The Cineaste Interviews,* pp. 155–172. Chicago: Lake View Press.

Harrow, Kenneth W., ed. 1999. *African Cinema: Postcolonial and Feminist Readings.* Trenton, N.J.: Africa World Press.

Haynes, Jonathan. 1999. "African Filmmaking and the Postcolonial Predicament." In Kenneth W. Harrow, ed., *African Cinema: Postcolonial and Feminist Readings,* pp. 21–43. Trenton, N.J.: Africa World Press.

Hennebelle, Guy. 1981. "Wechma. Hamid Bénani: 'Décrire un malaise intérieur.' " *CinémAction* 14 (Spring): 213–217.

Hill, John. 1996. "British Film Policy." In Albert Moran, ed., *Film Policy: International, National and Regional Perspectives,* pp. 101–113. London and New York: Routledge.

Huston, John. 1994. *An Open Book.* New York: Da Capo Press.

Ivanga, Imunga. 2003. "Le renouveau du cinéma gabonais." *CinémAction* 106 (first quarter): 226–229.

Jaidi, Moulay Driss. 1991. *Le cinéma au Maroc*. Rabat: Almajal.

———. 1992. *Public(s) & Cinéma*. Rabat: Almajal.

———. 1995. "Flash-back: le Maroc, terre d'élection des cinéastes." *Téléplus* 70 (December): 18–19.

———. 2000. *Diffusion et audience des médias audiovisuels*. Rabat: Almajal.

———. 2001. *Histoire du cinéma au Maroc: le cinéma colonial*. Rabat: Almajal.

Johnson, Randal. 1996. "Film Policy in Latin America." In Albert Moran, ed., *Film Policy: International, National and Regional Perspectives*, pp. 128–147. London and New York: Routledge.

Karèche, Boujemaa. 2003. "Le cinéma algérien en 2000, c'était: zéro production, zéro salle, zéro distributeur, zéro billet vendu." In "Où va le cinéma algérien?" *Cahiers du cinéma*, Hors-série (February–March): 36–41.

Konigsberg, Ira. 1997. *The Complete Film Dictionary*. New York: Penguin.

Labidi, Lilia. 2002. "Thinking of Violence." In Elizabeth Warnock Fernea, ed., *Remembering Childhood in the Middle East: Memoirs from a Century of Change*, pp. 295–301. Austin: University of Texas Press.

MacDougall, David. 1998. *Transcultural Cinema*. Princeton, N.J.: Princeton University Press.

Malcolm, Janet. 1990. *The Journalist and the Murderer*. New York: Vintage Books.

Malkmus, Lizbeth, and Roy Armes. 1991. *Arab and African Film Making*. London: Zed Books.

Marcus, George. 1990. "The Modernist Sensibility in Recent Ethnographic Writing and the Cinematic Metaphor of Montage." *Society for Visual Anthropology Review* 6, no. 1: 2–12, 21, 44.

Miège, Jean-Louis. 1966. *Le Maroc*. Paris: Presses Universitaires de France.

Miller, Toby. 1996. "The Crime of Monsieur Lang: GATT, the Screen, and the New International Division of Cultural Labour." In Albert Moran, ed., *Film Policy: International, National and Regional Perspectives*, pp. 72–84. London and New York: Routledge.

Miller, Toby, Nitin Govil, John McMurria, and Richard Maxwell. 2001. *Global Hollywood*. London: British Film Institute.

Montfort, Patrice. 2002. "Nigeria: le raz-de-marée de la *home video*." *Africultures* 45 (February): 47–48.

Moran, Albert. 1996. "Terms for a Reader: Film, Hollywood, National Cinema, Cultural Identity and Film Policy." In Albert Moran, ed., *Film Policy: International, National and Regional Perspectives*, pp. 1–19. London and New York: Routledge.

Moran, Albert, ed. 1996. *Film Policy: International, National and Regional Perspectives*. London and New York: Routledge.

Mulvey, Laura. 1992. *Citizen Kane*. London: British Film Institute.

Narayan, Kirin, in collaboration with Urmila Devi Sood. 1997. *Mondays on the Dark Night of the Moon: Himalayan Foothill Folktales*. New York: Oxford University Press.

Othman, Susan. 1990. "Le cinéma marocain et l'authenticité: discours et image." *Les Cahiers de l'Orient* 18 (3rd trimester): 175–188.

Ouchen, Tarik. 1998. "Le marché du cinéma au Maroc. Thème du mémoire." Mémoire en Economie de l'entreprise, Faculté des sciences juridiques, économiques et sociales, Université Cadi Ayyad, Marrakesh.

Oxfam. 2002. *Rigged Rules and Double Standards: Trade, Globalization and the Fight against Poverty*. Oxford: Oxfam.

Perkins, V. F. 1999. *The Magnificent Ambersons.* London: British Film Institute.

Puttnam, David. 1998. *Movies and Money.* New York: Vintage.

Rabinow, Paul. 1977. *Reflections on Fieldwork in Morocco.* Berkeley: University of California Press.

Regourd, Serge. 2002. *L'exception culturelle.* Paris: Presses Universitaires de France.

Reynolds, Dwight F., ed. 2001. *Interpreting the Self: Autobiography in the Arabic Literary Tradition.* Berkeley: University of California Press.

Rogemont, Marcel. 2002. *Le cinéma.* Rapport d'information No. 3642—Commission des affaires culturelles, familiales et sociales. Paris: Assemblée Nationale.

Ruby, Jay. 1996. "Visual Anthropology." In David Levinson and Melvin Ember, eds., *Encyclopedia of Cultural Anthropology,* vol. 4, pp. 1345–1351. New York: Henry Holt and Company.

Sakr, Naomi. 2001. *Satellite Realms: Transnational Television, Globalization and the Middle East.* London: I. B. Taurus.

Sama, Emmanuel. 1996. "African Films Are Foreigners in Their Own Countries." In Imruh Bakari and Mbye B. Cham, eds., *African Experiences of Cinema,* pp. 148–156. London: British Film Institute.

Schmidt, Nancy J. 1999. "Sub-Saharan African Women Filmmakers: Agendas for Research." In Kenneth W. Harrow, ed., *African Cinema: Postcolonial and Feminist Readings,* pp. 277–304. Trenton, N.J.: Africa World Press.

Schnitman, Jorge. 1984. *Film Industries in Latin America: Dependency and Development.* Norwood, N.J.: Ablex Publishing Corporation.

Shafik, Viola. 1998. *Arab Cinema: History and Cultural Identity.* Cairo: American University in Cairo Press.

Sherman, Eric. 1976. *Directing the Film: Film Directors on Their Art.* Venice, Calif.: Acrobat Books.

Stiglitz, Joseph E. 2002. *Globalization and Its Discontents.* New York: Norton.

Tcheuyap, Alexie. 2003. "Le sexe hors cadre." *CinémAction* 106 (first trimester): 37–40.

Trencher, Susan R. 2000. *Mirrored Images: American Anthropology and American Culture, 1960–1980.* Westport, Conn.: Bergin and Garvey.

Tuquoi, Jean-Pierre. 2001. *Le dernier Roi: crépuscule d'une dynastie.* Paris: Grasset.

Turan, Kenneth. 2002. *Sundance to Sarajevo: Film Festivals and the World They Made.* Berkeley: University of California Press.

Wassef, Magda, ed. 1995. *Egypte: 100 ans de cinéma.* Paris: Institut du Monde Arabe.

Welles, Orson, and Peter Bogdanovich. 1998. *This Is Orson Welles.* New York: Da Capo Press.

Wendl, Tobias. 2003. "Le miracle vidéo du Ghana." *CinémAction* 106 (first quarter): 182–191.

Index

Italicized page numbers indicate illustrations.

Abu Moussa's Women Neighbors (Moroccan feature film, directed by M. A. Tazi): as adaptation, 286, 288; audience and critical response to, 289; budget of, 290; difficulty completing, 299–301; digital technology used in, 273, 290, 300–301; as historical reconstruction, 289–290; ironies in making of, 311; poster, *287;* pre-production and post-production of, 295, 396n38; shooting of, 289; sound effects done abroad, 394n18; summary, 288–289; affected by world events, 289

African cinema (*see also* Barlet, Olivier): assessments in general of, 402n19; close-ups in, 402n19; diaspora of African filmmakers, 409n56; digital technology in, 407n36; distribution problems in, 366n13; filmmakers' difficulties in, 8–9; pace of films in, 402–403n20; stylistic changes over time in, 313–314, 400–401n14; video production and distribution in, 406n33

Aid Fund and/or Support Fund. *See* Moroccan cinema, state's role

Alea, Tomàs Gutierrez (Cuban filmmaker), 95

Algeria: war for independence, 82–83

Algerian cinema: history of, 9, 341; situation today in, 366nn15,16; women filmmakers in, 366n17

Ali Zaoua (Moroccan feature film). *See* Ayouch, Nabil

Ambiguity (*see also under The Big Trip*): vs. caricature, 178–180

Anthropology (*see also under Badis; Beyond Casablanca,* the making of): anthropological writing and film editing compared, 400n8; anthropologist-informant encounter in, 304, 399n4; author's approach to, 309, 320; au-

thor's career in, 2–3, 12; *Badis's* anthropological themes, 164–165, 192–197; and dialogue, 400n8; and film studies, 19, 303–307, 398–399n2; and narrative, 305–306; partiality and mixed purposes in, 16–17; recent developments in, 303–304; reflexivity in, 304, 399n3

Arab cinema. *See* Algerian cinema; Egyptian cinema; Moroccan cinema; Tunisian cinema

Armbrust, Walter, 366n18, 374n8

Armes, Roy, 366n17, 379n4: Franz Fanon discussed by, 401n14; "national cinema" and "Third World cinema" criticized by, 397–398n1; on Third World filmmakers' class origins, 400n13; on U.S. domination of world cinema, 364n8

Atemporality (*see also under Looking for My Wife's Husband,* issues raised by): and social criticism, 60–61, 210

Autobiography (*see also under specific film titles*): in Morocco and Arab world, 180–181, 388n20

Ayouch, Nabil (Moroccan filmmaker), 392n2 (ch. 6); achievements of, 293, 396n35; *Ali Zaoua* as "sociological" film, 394n12; and censorship, 327, 407n42; and National Film Festival, 331, 409nn55,57; TV support for, 299

Badis (Moroccan village), *160, 166, 186;* history of, 167, 388n17

Badis (Moroccan feature film, directed by M. A. Tazi): audience response, 30–31, 154, 195, 197, 389n30; abroad, 2–3, 222–224, 226–228; author's response, 14–15; distributor's response, 370n9; Verdu's response, 194;

Kevin Dwyer is Professor of Anthropology at the American University in Cairo. He is author of *Moroccan Dialogues: Anthropology in Question* and *Arab Voices: The Human Rights Debate in the Middle East.*